Shepherds
of the Sea

ROBERT F. CROSS

Shepherds
of the Sea

DESTROYER ESCORTS
IN WORLD WAR II

NAVAL INSTITUTE PRESS
Annapolis, Maryland

This book has been brought to publication with the generous assistance of Marguerite and Gerry Lenfest.

Naval Institute Press
291 Wood Road
Annapolis, MD 21402

Library of Congress Cataloging-in-Publication Data
Cross, Robert F., 1950-
  Shepherds of the sea : destroyer escorts in World War II / Robert F. Cross.
    p. cm.
  Includes bibliographical references and index.
  ISBN 978-1-59114-144-0 (alk. paper)
  1. Destroyer escorts—United States—History—20th century. 2. World War, 1939-1945—Naval operations, American. 3. World War, 1939-1945—Campaigns—Atlantic Ocean. 4. United States. Navy—History—World War, 1939-1945. 5. Sailors—United States—Biography. 6. United States. Navy—Biography. I. Title.
  D773.C76 2010
  940.54'5973—dc22

                                                        2009052943

Printed in the United States of America on acid-free paper

15 14 13 12 11 10   9 8 7 6 5 4 3 2
First printing

For Sheila, again
With love and appreciation

All I knew was that the pointed end of the boat went first.

—*William Riemer, gunner's mate, USS* Frederick C. Davis

CONTENTS

ILLUSTRATIONS

FOREWORD

Christopher du P. Roosevelt

I was born just fourteen days after Pearl Harbor. My father, Franklin Delano Roosevelt Jr., had already enlisted in the U.S. Navy and was training to become an officer. He eventually served as executive officer on board a destroyer and as the "skipper" of one of these destroyer escorts. (He loved that word "skipper" because when it was used by his crew, it was an acknowledgment of their acceptance of him as just another man and of their loyalty to him as their leader.) His father, FDR, gave the famous "Day in Infamy" speech about the Japanese attack on Pearl Harbor. My mother drove a Red Cross ambulance during the war, transferring incoming wounded (primarily from the European front) to hospitals in the New York City and Long Island (New York) area. I still have her Red Cross driver's license in my desk. Each of my uncles served in some capacity in World War II, and my brother served on a U.S. minesweeper in Japan in the 1960s. One would think I would have a very strong impression, indelibly imprinted on my psyche, about service and sacrifice in time of national and worldwide need. If I do, it clearly is not enough, judging from my sense of unbridled awe and respect for the individuals Robert F. Cross writes about—and through whom he tells his history of destroyer escorts in this remarkable book.

Near my home town in southeastern Connecticut, there recently was a small air show featuring Boeing B-17 and B-24 bombers and a North American P-51 Mustang. At the show a former pilot who fought in World War II was quoted in the local paper as saying, "In my squadron, out of 160 men, only 18 guys survived. The losses over Europe were terrible." That's a survival rate of 11 percent. Devastating odds. And to a parent, a family, and a community, just devastating, period. The same could be said for the survival rate during the war in the North Atlantic (and, later, the Pacific), where literally tens of thousands of American sailors lost their lives and American warships and merchant marine ships were lost to torpedoes, bombing, strafing, and kamikaze attacks. Some 2,800 merchant marine ships were sunk by German U-boats in just the six months between December 7, 1941 (Pearl Harbor), and June 1, 1942.

That was before a new and very effective weapon could be developed, one that was sought by Churchill and my grandfather as early as 1940, was initially opposed by the U.S. Navy's top brass, and finally made it to sea in January 1943. That weapon was the "mighty little ship that could"—the new class of destroyer escort designed and developed to help save shipping on the high seas. These agile, indomitable, and dangerous (to the enemy) little ships were almost anthropomorphized, the human characteristics of courage, durability, steadfastness, and survivability attributed to them. While the destroyer escorts were smaller and slower than World War II destroyers, they had almost the same firepower, they possessed greater maneuverability, and, above all, they cost significantly less and could be mass-produced quickly. Overall, some 563 destroyer escorts were produced for the war effort. And more than 1,300 men lost their lives serving on board these ships. Thousands more returned home with serious injuries, both physical and psychological, that they would carry with them for the rest of their lives.

Cross tells us they are "heroes." That is certainly true (and an understatement). But as is the case with most real heroes, they do not strut and boast; they are modest, and they speak in terms of teamwork and being part of crews that accomplished incredible feats. Their human stories, as told to and superbly related by Cross, are vivid and challenging—and sometimes excruciatingly bloody and violent. But their stories are really about human beings, Americans, rising to challenges never before faced by Americans, with ramifications far beyond our own shores at a time when isolationism was a significant political force in the United States. Their human stories still challenge us today in the sense that we are more than a generation away from their experiences and that distance has never felt greater.

Cross's *Shepherds of the Sea* comes at a critical time in U.S. history: We need to be reminded of the commitment, valor, personal sacrifice, and patriotism of our recent forebears. And Cross does so with a grace and sensitivity to the personal lives of countless young men and their families in a time of great national and world need. He has told their stories with eloquence and, sometimes, in graphic detail, portraying the pain, the injury, and, yes, the blood and gore that are a necessary part of war.

While this may appear to be a story of limited scope—the destroyer escorts of the U.S. Navy—in reality it is a story of the heart and soul of our country and we as its people. And it is critical for our time if only because so little has been passed along—from just the last generation—of the impact of the war on countless individuals and families, and of the personal sacrifice, courage, and determination that made Americans some of the toughest soldiers in the world, fighting for a just cause.

Much has been written about the slaughter in the trenches of World War I, the devastating loss of lives, the impossible, inhumane conditions on the various war fronts, and the first real documentation of what was then called "shell shock" (now called posttraumatic stress disorder). Much has been written of the world politics that led up to World War II and the manipulations, machinations, and strategies that brought the Axis powers together and their opponents, the Allies, together. But little has been written, especially from a naval warfare perspective, about the human beings who contributed so greatly to wining World War II in the Atlantic and Pacific—about the decision that a new class of warship was needed, the designing and building of that new class, and those who manned the instruments of war so critical to ultimate victory.

Despite what one might expect—the "dryness" of the history of a very specialized class of warship—Cross has brought about nothing less than a moving and thrilling story consistently focused on the people involved and almost miraculously evoking the special character of the destroyer escorts, the ships that proved their usefulness in a wide variety of demands placed upon them by a nation struggling to rebound from both an economic crisis and a potentially unstoppable enemy. This history is told through the lives and experiences of individuals, most of whom actually served on board these ships. They are ordinary Americans, and as we discover, these ordinary Americans became heroes, large and small, whose personal sacrifices and complete commitment became the backbone of the American war effort.

Possibly because of the "excesses" we all have read about and lived through over the past few decades, of greed beyond belief, of serving self-interest beyond normalcy, of putting the interests of others, especially "community," out of mind, I fear that we have become a self-focused and soft society incapable of rising courageously to serve and sacrifice for needs great than our own.

But then, as I think about our service men and women on constant vigil around the world and fighting in Iraq and Afghanistan, I know I am wrong.

Clearly the seeds of this country's greatness are still here, the courage and values still present and strong in the hearts and minds of our service men and women (and their families). Yet I still worry that there is too much detachment and distance between most of us here at home and those who serve, too much "insulation" between the hardships and sacrifice many experience and the relatively cushy lives we live, not threatened with a loss of freedom, with economic hardship, or even with inadequate food on our table.

In his inaugural address on January 20, 1961, President John F. Kennedy said, "Ask not what your country can do for you—ask what you can do for your country." He was one of the last presidents of "that generation," the generation who lived through World War II and experienced the saving graces of values, commitment, and sacrifice. It has been almost a desert in between, with admired presidents espousing both self-interest and self-service, encouraging greed and ignoring those less fortunate, and, perhaps most important, not leading the country to a greater sense of (and respect for) our fellow human beings. I hope that today we are beginning a new and different era, both with our national leadership and with a book that tells of the lives of the leaders, ship designers, builders, and ordinary sailors who had the gift of understanding what was needed of them in service to their world, their country, and their communities.

PREFACE

This is a story about American heroes. They came from farms, small towns, and large cities all across this nation. Many still too young to shave, they brought along their own brand of unbridled energy and a strong sense of duty and love of country as they courageously went to sea to help fight the greatest war this world had ever seen.

Teenagers with little or no experience on the water, these boys were determined to fight for their country. They dropped out of school, ran away from home, and lied about their age so they could put on the uniform and defend their homeland. As Nazi U-boats were sinking Allied ships at a rate faster than they could be replaced, Winston Churchill warned that the sea soon would become America's cage. Churchill argued that something had to be done, and done quickly, to stop Adolph Hitler before he ruled the Atlantic Ocean, cutting off all commerce between the United States, England, and Europe. Fortunately, President Franklin D. Roosevelt was listening.

To carry out this mission, America turned to an unseasoned crop of teenagers, sending them out to fight the Nazis in a new type of warship—the destroyer escort (DE)—a novel and untested vessel that some U.S. Navy officials viewed as a waste of money. But Roosevelt and Churchill believed it offered the Allies the best hope to turn the tide in the Battle of the Atlantic.

The United States was pinning its very future on these newly minted bluejackets and their officers—Ivy League college boys more accustomed to being on board yachts than warships. Out to sea they went in the new vessels, designed by a man who had no formal training in ship design and who used whatever available parts he could find to build the new ships. Before long they became the most valuable and successful antisubmarine vessels in the U.S. fleet.

With their teenage crews and young skippers, destroyer escorts plowed through the stormy and dangerous North Atlantic, shepherding merchant ships and Allied convoys carrying needed supplies, equipment, and troops for the war. Using the most sophisticated sonar and radar equipment available, they searched for enemy submarines along the way and used the latest antisubmarine weapons to sink them. Finally it appeared the U-boats had met their match.

President Roosevelt, one of the earliest proponents for the construction of destroyer escorts, believed they would be best equipped to battle Hitler's skillful U-boat commanders because they were smaller and more maneuverable than larger ships. He first ordered them built in 1940, but the Navy brass did not agree with their president and convinced him to use the nation's limited resources to build more American destroyers instead. That mistake would carry a heavy price.

U-boats slaughtered Allied vessels and their sailors on the Atlantic Ocean with great effectiveness—some twenty-eight hundred ships were sunk in only the first six months following the Japanese attack at Pearl Harbor. As Germany increased its stranglehold on the Atlantic and the outlook for the United States and England appeared grim, the Navy decided to take another look at FDR's idea to build the smaller vessels. And not a moment too soon. Hitler's men were courageous and brazen, using the lights from America's cities to target and sink Allied ships with Americans watching in horror from shore as ships burned in the distance. There was little time left to end the carnage and turn the tide of the war.

The new ships were built by untrained men and women at a fevered pitch in seventeen shipyards all around the country, 563 DEs in all, 17 rolling off the production lines in a single month. Shipyards stayed open around the clock turning out the new vessels, which, although tardy in their arrival, would quickly be taking their place along the front lines on the dangerous seas.

Navy officials accelerated the mass production of these new ships, with large sections fabricated in factories many miles from the shipyards and welded, rather than riveted, to save additional time. The first DE, outfitted with the latest sonar, radar, and antisubmarine weapons, went to sea in January 1943. The sturdy little ships waged war against German submarines and torpedo bombers in the Atlantic and Mediterranean and then went on to fight in every major battle in the Pacific, where they went toe-to-toe against the largest battleship in the world.

But this is not a story about ships. Ships did not win the war against Germany and Japan—courageous young American sailors, soldiers, and airmen did that job. Away from home for the first time in their young lives, many—more than 1,300 DE sailors, in fact—would never see their families again. Others would return with serious injuries, physical and psychological, they would carry with them for the rest of their lives. Today they speak, many for the first time, about their harrowing days at sea.

This chapter in American history has been largely overlooked in the annals of World War II. Since 2003, when I first considered writing a book about the men who sailed on these trim but deadly little ships, I have interviewed scores of DE veterans, most in their eighties and nineties, humble and reserved, and every one with a story to tell. Finally, in their twilight years, these aging heroes have decided to speak, and I am honored to be the one to hear their tales and write them down for the ages.

I conducted ninety-one personal interviews with World War II naval officers and enlisted men who served on board fifty-six different destroyer escorts; reviewed dozens of oral histories and letters; and poured over secretly kept war diaries, ship logs, and countless other documents and photographs that help to illuminate the remarkable contributions made by these men. Until today many of these diaries and other documents rested in dusty attics, basements, and storage closets far removed from our view. Now a new window has been opened, allowing all Americans to see in crystal clarity the sacrifices made by these young sailors and their families so many years ago—sacrifices, in fact, that allow us to live today as a free nation rather than, as President Roosevelt once said, at the point of a gun.

But the story about destroyer escort sailors is not just a story about battles. It is a story about growing up in the Great Depression, American genius and ingenuity, hard work, honor, and fear, and it includes a small but historic first step toward ending racial discrimination in the United States' armed forces. All of this and more are part of the remarkable tale these men have told about themselves and their service to the nation. These are their words, these are their stories—I am simply the messenger privileged to share them with my readers.

All too frequently authors will tag their books as "the untold story of . . ." I have resisted doing that here. But it should be very clear that this, indeed, is a story about World War II that has remained virtually hidden in

A sailor spends a quiet moment alone on the deck of the USS *Liddle* as the sun sets over a calm North Atlantic. Life on board the ships could be very lonely as the ships "mothered" slow-moving convoys across the vast, U-boat–infested waters of the North Atlantic. DEs started rolling out of shipyards in record numbers beginning in 1943 and quickly became the most important antisubmarine vessel in both the U.S. and British fleets, credited with sinking nearly seventy U-boats. *Photo taken by Harold S. Deal; courtesy Jeff Deal*

the minds and hearts of the destroyer escort veterans. Although they are aging and, unfortunately, we are losing them too rapidly, their recollections are clear, the memories are focused, and their stories offer a vital lesson for the United States today. It is a lesson of service, honor, responsibility, and tolerance. These men came forward to serve their country during one of the most dangerous and fearful periods in American history. Today their numbers may be diminishing, but their contributions to this nation will forever live in our collective memories. Heroes, you know, never really die.

ACKNOWLEDGMENTS

Back in 2003, while my wife Sheila and I were enjoying a pleasant dinner one evening as guests in Albany, New York's venerable old Fort Orange Club, Frank Lasch, president of the Destroyer Escort Historical Museum, asked if I might consider writing a book about the stories of those sailors who served on board destroyer escorts in World War II. He knew my first book, *Sailor in the White House: The Seafaring Life of FDR*, was finished and I was looking for a new project.

Although the idea sounded interesting, I first wanted to do a little research to see if there really was a story to tell. Well, it did not take long for me to determine that not only was there a remarkable story to tell, but it was one that was little more than a footnote in American history—except, of course, among destroyer escort veterans. While they knew what they had done for their country, most Americans had never heard of this remarkable group of teenage sailors.

So I set out to tell their stories and ensure that their contributions to our nation were recorded in the historical record. First, I want to offer my deep appreciation to the ninety-one DE veterans who took the time to speak with me at great length about their days at sea, along with the scores of others who shared their diaries, letters, photographs, and personal memories of their days—and nights—battling Hitler's U-boats and Japan's kamikazes. Without their help, this book simply would have relied upon dry archival records detailing various battles. Instead, using their own words, the stories of these brave and daring young Americans come alive in these pages.

Many others generously gave of their time and efforts so I could better convey the story of these American heroes. Tim Rizzuto, executive director of the Destroyer Escort Historical Museum, provided invaluable assistance by putting me in touch with sailors all around the country and offering expert advice and counsel throughout the course of this project. Tim is assisted by individuals, both in Albany and beyond, who provide him with essential advice in restoring and operating Albany's world-class museum ship, the USS *Slater*. Several of those individuals provided gracious assistance to me, including Sam Saylor, Marty Davis, Pat Perrella, Anne McCarthy, Pat Stephens, Victor Buck, Don Montrym, Rosehn Gipe, Eric Rivet, Katie Kuhl, and my friend and cousin, Diane Lobb Boyce. I also appreciate the strong support of Frank Lasch and the rest of the museum's board of trustees, who do a spectacular job overseeing the *Slater*'s miraculous restoration.

A number of others have been very helpful in locating various documents so I could better tell this story, including Robert Clark, supervisory archivist at the Franklin D. Roosevelt Presidential Library in Hyde Park, New York; Robert B. Hitchings and William Troy Valos of the Kirn Library in Norfolk, Virginia; Lester Weber of the Mariner's Museum in Norfolk, Virginia; Therese Gonzalez of the Great Lakes Naval Museum in Illinois; and Donald Cavanaugh, formerly of Gibbs and Cox. I am certain someone has been left off this list, and I hope you will forgive me, knowing that I appreciate all you have done to help me along the way.

While I conducted ninety-one interviews and reviewed dozens of documents, letters, war diaries, and photographs, I could not include every story from every sailor in this book. Because of space limitations many fine stories and eyewitness accounts had to be left out. Although your specific stories may not show up in these pages, rest assured they were essential to my understanding of destroyer escorts and the courageous contributions you made to this nation's security.

Now for a note on photographs. As I have said previously, this is not a story about ships. It is a story about an unseasoned crop of teenagers and their young skippers who went to sea to defend their homeland. Unfortunately most archives are filled with photographs of ships and hold very few lifestyle photographs showing the sailors on board these tiny warships, sometimes at sea for months at a time. Thankfully I stumbled upon a collection of remarkable photographs taken by a small-town pharmacist from New Berlin, New York, who, at the age of thirty-one, left his family and one-year-old child to join the Navy. He went on board the USS *Liddle* as a pharmacist's mate.

Although cameras generally were not allowed on board ships during wartime, the pharmacist's mate was asked by his captain to photographically document life on board their ship.

Harold S. Deal, the small-town pharmacist from upstate New York, was happy to oblige because photography was his hobby. He quickly sent a letter to his wife asking her to mail his camera equipment to the ship. His superb work has provided us with a rare behind-the-scenes look inside the little warship. It was not until after his death in 1991 that Deal's family discovered the photographs. Although he never spoke about the war years, today his photos give us a glimpse into everyday life on board a destroyer escort. I am indebted to his grandson, Jeffrey Deal, and his family for allowing me to use these wonderful photographs.

The hardest part of being an author, I have found, is balancing the personal responsibilities of everyday life and work with the all-consuming effort needed to research and write a history book. Fortunately I am blessed with supportive friends and family who, although they may not like it, understand that my absences from family and other functions are part of the all-engrossing job of writing a book. I could not ask for more caring and loving sisters than Janet Dobbs of Port Jervis, New York, and Linda DiPanni of New Canaan, Connecticut. My parents, Francis and Rita Cross, gave me the opportunity to study and learn, for which I always will be grateful.

Over the course of this project, my dear wife, Sheila, has taken on many responsibilities, freeing up my time to conduct interviews, pore over war diaries and ship logs, and try to put it all down on paper in what I hope is a coherent and compelling narrative. But Sheila has given me more than just the gift of time. She is my most important critic, and her careful and precise editing of the manuscript made *Shepherds of the Sea* a much better and more readable book. That is why, once again, I have dedicated this work to her.

1

Like Lambs to the Slaughter

Sixteen-year-old James Graham and a handful of his tenth-grade class-mates decided it was time to fight for their country. Six months had passed since the Japanese attacked Pearl Harbor and these teenagers were determined to do something about it. Climbing into a bus in Lake City, South Carolina, passengers cast wary glances at the kids, and although there were plenty of unoccupied seats up front, the driver waited until they walked to the back of the bus to be seated before continuing on his route. It was 1942, after all, and the African American students knew where they had to sit if they ever hoped to get to the Army recruiter in Charleston.

A rude surprise was waiting for these patriotic boys—all of whom wanted to be pilots—once they arrived. "We don't take colored boys in the Army Air Corps," the recruiter told Graham and his classmates. Heads bowed in despair, the dejected students started to leave but were stopped by a Navy recruiter, who called them over and invited them to join up. Graham was hesitant be-cause he knew that the Navy only allowed African Americans to work as mess attendants or shore laborers loading and unloading ships. "I won't cook or clean up behind anyone," Graham told the recruiter. "My sister does that for me." But things had changed in the Navy, the recruiter said, and now they were accepting African Americans in the seaman branch, "same as the white guys." With that assurance Graham lied about his age and signed the papers on the spot enlisting in the U.S. Navy, where he and his fellow African Americans would be destined to make history in spite of the antiblack sentiment among many of their fellow sailors and officers, a sentiment that reached all the way to Washington, D.C. Eventually Graham would join a complement of other African American sailors to step on board the USS *Mason*, a destroyer escort and the first warship in American history to be manned by a black crew.

1

During World War II, James Graham's story was repeated in cities, towns, and villages all across America. Young men of all races—many of whom had not even started to shave—heeded the call to serve their country, running away from home, fibbing about their ages, and devising all sorts of schemes to enlist in the military. These young men were determined to fight for their country and would do whatever it took to put on a uniform. Many would never return home.

Walter Roberge, a spindly sixteen year old, boarded a bus leaving his small hometown of Lansing, Illinois, bound for the big city. He was slight for his age and height—129 pounds fully clothed on a skinny five-foot, eleven-inch frame. As the bus slowly inched away from the curb on that spring day in 1943, Roberge's eyes widened with excitement as he anticipated his big plans once he arrived in Chicago. But those plans were quickly dashed when the government recruiter got a look at him.

"You could count my ribs at five yards," Roberge said. The recruiter told him, "Come back in six months when you put on some weight." Roberge had hoped to join the Navy. "I wanted to enlist when I was fourteen," he said, but that was a little young in the eyes of his parents, especially his mother, who wanted him to finish high school. Now that he was sixteen years old, he considered himself a man and was determined to go to war.

Not about to wait six months, he started formulating plans for his next visit as he rode the bus back home. Young Roberge had heard that if you ate a lot of bananas and drank plenty of water, you could put on weight very quickly. And that's just what he did for the next six weeks. He then headed back to Chicago for a second try. As extra insurance he took along his birth certificate, which had been "doctored" to show that he was born in 1926, making his age seventeen, old enough to enlist without parental consent. "My mother marked up the birth certificate," he said. In those days birth certificates were filled out in ink, and Roberge's mother didn't have the right color ink to match the original ink on the document. "It was a miserable job, the ink didn't even come close to matching," he recalled.

At the Chicago recruiting office, Roberge handed the document to an official, who peered suspiciously at it through a heavy paperweight-type magnifier. After studying it for what seemed an eternity to the teenager, the recruiter barked, "I don't like this birth certificate. Get a new one." But Roberge knew that if he asked for a new document it might be typed, making it impossible for his mother to alter it since the family did not own a typewriter. So he asked the recruiter if it would suffice for his father to testify that he really was seventeen years old. The recruiter said it would.

So on 5 July he and his father, a veteran of World War I, stood before a notary public and swore that the teenager was seventeen. Even though the banana and water diet had not resulted in much, if any, weight gain, that no longer seemed to matter to the recruiter, and the sixteen year old was sworn into the U.S. Navy. By this time the government was in desperate need of troops and "they would take you as long as you were upright and warm," Roberge said.

"I just felt it was the right thing to do," he recalled. "I could have avoided the war completely if I had just stayed in school. But I wanted to go. I was the adventuresome type. I started fighting for my independence when I was three years old."

When the war broke out his father, who was an ironworker, wanted to join, but a couple of his false teeth were missing. "They told him he would have to get a new set, but he couldn't afford it," Roberge said. "So I went instead." Even though his mother had forged his birth certificate to allow entry into the military, Roberge recalled, she really would have preferred that he stay in school. "But I threatened to run away from home if she didn't do it," he said.

After nine weeks in boot camp at the Great Lakes Naval Training Center along the banks of Lake Michigan in Illinois and five weeks of specialized training in Key West, Florida, Roberge was assigned to the destroyer escort USS *Swearer*, a new type of warship designed to protect convoys from the U-boat menace in the North Atlantic. So in November 1943, a little more than four months after that July day back in Chicago when he and his father swore he was old enough to enlist, the skinny teenager from Lansing was earning seventy-eight dollars a month as Petty Officer Third Class Roberge—and he was at sea.[1]

Like so many others, Roberge was too young to enlist in the armed forces. But during the height of World War II, many young men—fourteen, fifteen, and sixteen years old, caught up in the patriotic wave sweeping the nation—volunteered for service in the Navy in spite of their age and complete lack of experience with anything to do with the sea. In fact, the majority of crew members on board destroyer escorts in World War II were teenagers or just barely out of their teens, most of whose experience on the water, if any, consisted of little more than fishing in a rowboat or paddling a canoe.

The majority of DE sailors were teenagers or just barely out of their teens. The United States pinned its very future on this unseasoned crop of kids who, along with their young skippers, fought Nazi U-boats in the North Atlantic and then fought in every major battle in the Pacific. Radioman William Bryant Graddy of St. Olaf, Iowa, who enlisted in the Navy on his seventeenth birthday, is pictured after receiving orders to board the USS *Liddle*. Graddy was killed a year later when a kamikaze crashed into the ship during the Leyte Gulf operation. *Photo provided to Jeff Deal by Inda Hoover, Graddy's sister*

Sixteen-year-old Terry Thomas and his family had just walked the two miles home from St. Brigid's Church after mass on a cold and blustery Sunday, 7 December 1941. Terry and his father were reading the Sunday newspapers while his mother and sisters, Vera and Rita, were listening to music on the radio in the living room of their tiny house in Detroit, Michigan. "All of a sudden the music stopped," Thomas said. "Special bulletin—our naval base at Pearl Harbor in Hawaii has been attacked by Japanese aircraft." Thomas' father, a tool and die maker who had immigrated from Wales, said, "This means war." The next day Thomas and his classmates started talking about joining the military, although they all were too young to enlist.

Two years later, Thomas decided to join the U.S. Coast Guard after listening to the uncle of a friend who said he should ask for beach patrol on the Great Lakes. That sounded appealing to him and his buddy, so they decided to quit school and sign up. But Thomas will always remember the day he climbed on board an old steam train at the Michigan Railroad Station on his way to boot camp. "As I left with the other enlistees, I heard my mother crying and saying, 'They're so young, like lambs being led to the slaughter,'" Thomas, who stood only five feet, four inches tall, said. "I'll never forget that moment." The old train chugged out of the station carrying Thomas and a motley collection of teenage recruits on their way to Manhattan Beach, the Coast Guard boot camp in Brooklyn, New York. Loneliness and homesickness soon would overtake these kids, most away from their homes and families for the first time in their young lives. But there was no turning back.[2]

Offers to join the military poured into Washington from patriotic citizens in every part of the nation, observed President Franklin D. Roosevelt when he signed the Selective Training and Service Act of 1940. Finally approved after one of the most tumultuous and bitterly divided sessions in the history of Congress, the law required all male citizens between twenty-one and thirty-six years old to visit one of the nearly 6,500 new registration boards set up throughout the nation. But America's first peacetime military conscription did not come about without a great deal of angry debate by antidraft activists, who declared that "American conscription is American fascism."[3]

Women wearing widows' veils took up vigil in the U.S. Senate gallery. Florida senator Claude Pepper, who supported the Selective Service legislation, was hanged in effigy on the Capitol grounds, and fistfights among members of Congress developed before the legislation, commonly referred to as "the draft," could be approved and sent to President Roosevelt, who signed the measure without delay.[4]

William Riemer, who grew up in the small town of Janesville, Wisconsin, was just starting his senior year in high school when the seventeen year old dropped out to join the Navy. He had wanted to join the Marine Corps as soon as the Japanese attacked Pearl Harbor but was only sixteen years old. His uncle, a World War I veteran, assured him that the war would last long enough

Pharmacist's Mate Harold S. Deal, who at age thirty-one was older than most DE sailors. After Pearl Harbor, Deal, who was working as a pharmacist, enlisted in the Navy, leaving behind his wife and one-year-old child. He survived action in both the Atlantic and Pacific theaters and returned home to his family. *Courtesy Jeff Deal*

so he could enlist once he was of age. Several of his friends in the close-knit community of eight hundred were joining the Navy, so when the time came to enlist, Riemer chose the Navy instead of the Marines.[5]

"All I knew was that the pointed end of the boat went first," Riemer recalled, noting that, like so many Navy recruits, his experience with boats and the sea was limited to what he read in books. Although he knew how to swim, that was just about his only experience with water. Like Walter Roberge, he went to the Great Lakes Naval Training Center. Later he was assigned to the USS *Frederick C. Davis*, one of only a handful of the 563 destroyer escorts sunk by enemy action and the last American combat ship torpedoed and sunk by a U-boat during World War II. By the time the war was over, Riemer had learned a lot more than simply which end of a boat went first.

Another novice to the sea who wanted to do his part for the nation, John "Bo" Keally, enlisted in the Navy in 1944 after quitting high school. "It seemed like the patriotic thing to do at the time," Keally said. After his father died, he and his mother moved around the Pittsburgh area frequently, with young Bo attending four different grade schools and four different high schools before finally finding stability in the Navy. Because he was underage, his mother had to sign so he could join.[6] Following a brief stint at boot camp at Great Lakes and specialized training for a gunner's mate, he was assigned to the USS *Johnnie Huchins*.

Keally, like many of the DE recruits, had no experience on the water but felt that joining the Navy would be a good way to see the world. Excited at the prospect of the adventures that lay ahead, he never could have imagined that, within a short time, he would be struggling to survive a major hurricane, which sunk an American destroyer off North Carolina, clinging to a life raft after being thrown overboard off the coast of New Guinea, or engaging in a fierce fight with Japanese suicide midget submarines near the Philippines in what would be the last major surface battle of World War II.

A year after the attack on Pearl Harbor, the Navy continued to recruit rather than draw inductees from the Selective Service system. Trying to lure the "cream of the crop" with slogans such as "Choose while you can," the Navy was able to induct 35,000 men who already had received their Army draft notices. As the war progressed Army officers became alarmed that their service seemed to be getting those the Navy did not want.[7]

To skim off the best potential inductees, the Navy would sign them up early, before they legally could join. Some 120,000 young men were signed up in the Navy's V-12 program, and many of them were sent to college, rendering them "draft proof" under the rules of the Selective Service system: They already were in the service, although not officially on the sea or in the air. Trained at government expense, they would be ready when the Navy called.[8]

Navy service was more attractive to many young men who felt life on board a warship would be superior to fighting the enemy in muddy trenches. The "Choose while you can" campaign resonated with many potential recruits, such as Donald Kruse, who signed up within a few months of graduation from LaSalle School in Troy, New York. His quick action deprived the Army of a GI—the very day he was packing to leave for the naval training facility in Sampson, New York, Kruse received his draft notice. Standing at the door with his bags packed, Kruse told the mailman to return the draft notice and marked the envelope "U.S. Navy."

"I knew they would give me a free meal and a clean sack," Kruse said. Born in Saugerties, New York, Kruse later moved to Catskill, New York, before eventually settling in Troy. His cousins all were drafted into the Army, and wallowing in muddy trenches was not the life he wanted.[9] Sent to the naval training facility in Sampson, along Seneca Lake in upstate New York, Kruse and more than 411,000 sailors would receive their basic training there over the course of the war. One of seven naval training centers in the nation, Sampson, along with facilities in Bainbridge, Maryland, and Farragut, Idaho, was opened within a year of the Pearl Harbor attack.

Four other Navy training facilities were operating at the start of the war, including facilities in Norfolk, Virginia; Newport, Rhode Island; San Diego, California; and the biggest of them all, the Great Lakes Naval Training Center along the shores of Lake Michigan. That is where many of the recruits who eventually would find themselves on board destroyer escorts learned how to swim, tie knots, march, and identify the parts of a ship.[10]

Stepping off the train and taking a bewildered look at their new home, the recruits' eyes widened as they gazed at a compound that certainly was much larger than many of the communities where they had grown up. Great Lakes, the sprawling 1,440-acre facility forty miles north of Chicago boasted a population of more than 100,000 and had all the features of a large city, including a hospital, barber shop, tailor, post office, and laundries. It was about as self-sufficient as a military facility could be and even included recreational and reception centers where recruits could relax and unwind after a week of training and classes.[11]

Construction of what was also the largest naval training facility in World War I was first approved by President Theodore Roosevelt in 1904, despite some concerns about locating a naval facility one thousand miles from the nearest saltwater.[12] By Armistice Day in November 1918, the base had been substantially enlarged from the prewar days to include 775 buildings on 1,200 acres with a peak naval population of more than 47,000 men. More than 125,000 men passed through the facility by the end of the war, a mere fraction of the number that would be trained there for World War II.[13]

Fast forward to 7 December 1941. Within two hours of the Japanese attack on Pearl Harbor, plans hurriedly were put in place to expand the Great

Lakes facility in preparation for America's entry into a new war. With American ships still smouldering in ruins at Pearl Harbor, Capt. Ralph D. Spalding, public works officer at the Great Lakes facility, met with the base's commandant and described his plans to expand the compound. Neither man had the authority to authorize the expansion; however, with chaos rampant in Washington there was no time to seek proper authorization from Navy brass. Work began the very next day, even though formal approval for the project would not come for two weeks.[14]

A herculean effort, construction continued seven days a week, twenty-four hours a day, and involved some twenty-six architectural firms, fourteen general contractors, and 13,000 workers. The final cost for the two-year project exceeded $120 million. As it had in World War I, Great Lakes would again serve as the largest naval training facility in World War II, training more than a million sailors or about a third of all Navy men fighting in the war. But Washington could not wait for the work to be finished before sending recruits, who arrived daily, to the facility, cramming barracks with young men and forcing others to sleep on cots in drill halls. There was no time to delay—the United States needed trained sailors and it needed them now.[15]

Moving ahead without authorization was a bold but wise move because plans for other naval training bases were still on the drawing board. "The speed of construction at Great Lakes was doubly fortunate because delays at Bainbridge, Farragut, and Sampson (new stations authorized in March 1942) made it necessary for Great Lakes to take many recruits who should have gone to the new stations in September and October 1942," observed Lt. T. A. Larson in his official history of the Great Lakes center.[16]

As thousands of so-called boots streamed into the naval training facilities, now commonly referred to as "boot camps," they would soon learn a new way of life—regimented, structured, and strenuous—as they were schooled in the classroom and field training necessary to become a seaman on one of America's warships.[17] "The first day at boot camp was a shock," Robert Holman said. "First off, we took off all of our clothes and stood there buck naked while a corpsman painted a number across our naked chests with methiolate, which is an orange liquid, a mild iodine." The skinny seventeen-year-old kid from Calhoun County, South Carolina, recalled his time at the Bainbridge, Maryland, facility as a "degrading experience," as the naked recruits were poked, prodded, examined, and questioned by Navy doctors.

Over time Holman, who eventually would be assigned to the USS *Frost*, said the recruits became accustomed to the routine of boot camp: "We spent many hours in boot camp tying knots, reading the *Bluejackets' Manual*, learning the Navy language, learning the semaphore, washing clothes, preparing for inspection, keeping our bunks neat. The sheets had to be so tight that a half dollar would bounce on them. We were not allowed to sit on our bunks until after supper. There were benches in the middle of the barracks for sitting."

Young boots also had to learn an entirely new vocabulary, Holman recalled: Floors became decks, walls became bulkheads, ceilings became overheads, halls became passageways, doors became hatches, ropes became lines, ahead was forward and behind was aft, toilets were heads, canteen was the ship's store, the deck force were called swab jockeys, the electricians were sparks, signalmen were flags, afternoon and evening ashore was liberty, and days ashore were leave.[18]

"The officers were a little rough," said Manuel Maroukis, who boasted of being born "with a silver spoon in my mouth" until his father, who owned restaurants and car dealerships, lost everything in the Great Depression and had to go to work as a stripper in a leather factory. Maroukis joined the Navy after talking to both Army and Navy men and realizing that "if you want to be clean, you go in the Navy. If you want to wind up kind of muddy, you go to the Army." Maroukis added, "I decided to stay clean. If I was going to die, I'd die clean anyway."[19]

"My reason for joining the Navy was I wanted to eat three square meals a day, and I didn't want to live in dirt. So I didn't want to go into the Army," said Jersey City native Leonard Bulwicz, who joined right out of high school and served as quartermaster on board the destroyer escort USS *Moore*. Bulwicz also recalled that he felt a sense of patriotism. "I had a duty," he said, especially after Pearl Harbor.[20]

But in the wake of the Pearl Harbor attack, the Great Lakes facility was filled to the brim with recruits who would have gone to other facilities had they been ready. As a result early recruits at the station suffered through a great many discomforts while construction was under way, including very long chow lines, no heat in their barracks, no hot water, and, sometimes, insufficient clothing to provide a full issue to each recruit.[21]

The lack of basic needs such as drinking water and waste disposal continued to plague the station well into 1944. In both cases demand overloaded available facilities, resulting in restrictions on water use in the barracks.

Round-the-clock guards were posted in barracks to ensure that each recruit used no more than ten gallons of water per day. Water was pumped from Lake Michigan and in 1942 was cut off completely when the intake valve froze. A diver had to go down into the frigid waters to remove ice from the intake.[22]

Following 7 December 1941 and through 19 March 1944, the number of recruits showing up at the station varied from 10,000 to 40,000 per month, requiring an adjustment in the length of time recruits would be at the base. A six-week training period was in effect at the start of the war; however, this was shortened to four weeks and then to three weeks in order to accommodate the influx of recruits. All told, a boot's stay at Great Lakes changed twenty-eight times over the course of the war.[23] Because the surprise attack on Pearl Harbor left much of the United States' military unprepared, early training materials at some of the service schools had not even arrived. One instructor at the electrician's mate school was given nothing but scratch pads, pencils, a box of chalk, and two erasers and told to teach the recruits all they would need to know about being an electrician's mate on board a ship—without the benefit of any written training manual.[24]

The *Bluejackets' Manual* was one training manual in good supply. Given to each recruit upon arrival, the 1,145-page 1943 edition contained everything a recruit would need to know about the Navy and would be his "Bible" for his entire tour of duty. First produced in 1902, the manual has seen many revisions and is considered a "Navy primer" to this day. An important chapter for Navy men was titled "Learning to Swim," which began, "If you can perform the physical training exercises used in the Navy you can learn to swim. All human beings other than the most decrepit, the crippled or the deformed possess all of the qualities needed to permit them to stay on the surface."[25]

In theory it seems like every sailor should be able to swim, but only about half of the recruits arriving at boot camps knew how. By 1944 there were twelve swimming pools at the Great Lakes facility, one said to be the largest indoor swimming pool in the world, holding 587,000 gallons of water and stretching 165 feet long and 75 feet wide. "We had to throw away all of the books when we started to give lessons to thousands," said Chief M. J. Howlett, who was in charge of the Great Lakes swimming program. "We had to develop a system of mass instruction which would teach nonswimmers to swim in the shortest possible time." Nearly a million sailors were taught to swim at the facility, with 98 percent of them graduating as competent swimmers.[26]

For Jarvis Baillargeon of Keeseville, a tiny village in upstate New York about fifty miles from the Canadian border, being on water was second nature. Although he never had experienced the ocean, he had paddled a number of rowboats and canoes growing up in the Adirondack Mountains. Baillargeon, whose grandfather was a Civil War veteran and whose father operated a small grocery store in Keeseville, graduated from high school at sixteen and enrolled in Plattsburgh State Teachers College until he decided to join the Navy in November 1943.

"I decided to be a sailor rather than a soldier," Baillargeon said, explaining that he would have been eligible for the draft when he turned eighteen in two months so decided he'd better sign up for the Navy before his Army "Greetings" letter arrived. "I raised my hand and swore allegiance to the United States Naval Reserve in Albany, New York, on November 17, 1943," Baillargeon said. Within a few days he was shipped off on a steam train to the Navy's training facility in Sampson, New York. Having experienced the snow and cold of Adirondack winters, he had hoped to be assigned to a warmer training facility in Florida. But the Navy had other ideas.

Sampson was a "flimsy operation," obviously constructed with great haste following Pearl Harbor, Baillargeon said. "The barracks were just shells with a coal stove for heat," he recalled. "Getting uniforms, shots and lots of lectures plus physical training filled our days, with occasional guard duty at night." After boot camp and sonar school, Baillargeon was assigned to the USS *Rudderow*.[27]

Arriving at Sampson at about three in the morning, Brooklyn, New York, native John Acer and his fellow recruits were given the traditional "first meal" consisting of a bologna sandwich and an apple and then told to get a little sleep before reveille at 5:30 AM. Upon awakening, the recruits again were sworn into the U.S. Navy and then they began the hurried pace of abandoning all aspects of civilian life for their new life in the military.

"The first thing they did to you is they gave you a big pillowcase, a big sheet. You had to put all your clothes in it," nineteen-year-old John Acer said. "They kept throwing all these things at you—underwear, pants, suits, jackets, sweaters, hats. They all kept coming at you." Acer, who had just graduated from Erasmus Hall High School, grew up in a big family in the Parkville section of Brooklyn, but as he gazed at the camp, he realized he would be living with a much larger "family" now.

The young Brooklynite recalled that those early days in Sampson were "go, go, go, go from the time you get up until the time you go to bed. It never stopped." After receiving his first military haircut, a battery of examinations, and tests, Acer and his fellow recruits started training for the day when they would be assigned to their first warship. "Everything was done by running, or walking very, very fast," he said. "You do basic things. They would have knot classes, have classes where they take you out in a whaleboat and show you how to use oars and how to use the engine. They take you out to the rifle range and show you how to shoot, how to shoot a rifle and how to use a submachine gun."

Cleaning the barracks and washing your own clothes came as a rude awakening for some recruits who grew up with their mother and others handling those everyday chores. "The chief boatswain's mate would come down in a nice clean, brand-new white uniform and get down on the floor and roll over a couple of times," Acer said, "and if he picked up any dirt or any mess on the floor on the clean whites, you'd be down there scrubbing it up again until you got it cleaned up."

"I never had to do any of this work because my mother and father had maids," one recruit said to the chief in charge of the barracks. "From now on," the chief barked, "you will be my maid."[28]

The young age of the recruits did cause some concern among officers, most of whom were relatively young themselves. Eleanor Roosevelt recalled her twenty-nine-year-old son, FDR Jr., visiting her after being installed as the skipper of the *Ulvert M. Moore*, a destroyer escort commissioned in July 1944: "I remember so well when that little ship of his was getting into commission in Brooklyn and he came over one day, looking rather weary, and announced that it was quite a problem having a crew whose average age was seventeen and a half, most of whom came from country areas or small towns and were seeing New York City for the first time in their lives."[29]

Jerry Hammon was one of those teenage country boys who had never seen the big city. The nineteen-year-old son of a clothing store merchant in the small town of Logan, Ohio, was in his first year at Ohio State University when he decided he had better join the Navy before he received his Army draft notice. Hammon recalled that he had two ambitions in life: to be a naval officer and to become a physician. In those days, Hammon said, it was not common to become a naval officer and a physician unless you were fortunate enough to be chosen for the United States Naval Academy. Being from a relatively poor family with no political connections, Hammon instead applied and was admitted into the V-12 program. He was sent to Miami University at Oxford, Ohio, before assignment to midshipmen school at Notre Dame. Commissioned an ensign in the fall of 1944, one of America's "90-day wonders," he was sent to sub-chaser school in Miami, Florida, where he learned to handle small ships. Hammon was assigned to the USS *Otter*.

Unfortunately it would take an unusually long time—full of false starts, frustration, and disappointments—before this newly minted ensign would actually step on board his ship. In fact, at times it seemed to Hammon like he was never going to go to sea as days stretched into weeks and then into almost two months—a full fifty-four days—until he finally boarded the destroyer escort. His saga begins following graduation from sub-chaser school, when Hammon was flown by a Navy air transport plane to New York City to pick up his ship. When he arrived the *Otter* already had set sail.

So the Navy put up the young ensign in a fancy Manhattan hotel for the next ten days in what turned out to be an exciting time for a poor country boy from Logan, Ohio. While staying in New York City, Hammon said, he painted the town and dated a girl who came from a wealthy family. One evening the girl's father arranged for the young couple to have dinner in the Persian Room at the Plaza, where they were seated at a table alongside Irving Berlin, who was celebrating his fiftieth birthday, a remarkable eye-opener for a small-town country boy.

By this time the *Otter* had returned from sea and was docked in Boston. So the Navy told Hammon to pack his seabag and head to Boston to pick up his ship. But because of bad weather his airplane trip was delayed a couple of days and by the time he arrived in Bean Town, the *Otter* again had left. So the Navy put Hammon up at the Copely Plaza in Boston, where once again he sampled the city's high life—again at government expense—until the Navy notified him that the *Otter* had returned to port and this time was waiting for him in Portland, Maine.

Climbing on board another Navy transport plane, Hammon made the relatively brief flight to Portland, where, again, he discovered his ship had sailed. But he wouldn't be as lucky in Portland as he was in New York City and Boston. "It's time you did something for the Navy," an officer told Hammon, who was assigned to radio school on an island in Casco Bay, where he learned Morse code for about two weeks. Hammon was flown to an air base in Argentia Bay, Newfoundland, where he was to pick up the *Otter*. But when he arrived, just like the other three times, his ship was gone.

In Newfoundland without a ship, Hammon was assigned to the staff of an admiral of the North Atlantic Fleet, but there was simply no work for the young ensign. "Do you like to fish?" the admiral asked Hammon. He assigned the sailor a car and driver and outfitted him with fishing equipment and foul-weather gear and sent him up in the mountains to go trout fishing. "I went trout fishing one day in the mountains and slipped on a log and fell in because there was still ice along the edges," Hammon said. "I darned near got pneumonia and died, but I had a great time, caught all kinds of wonderful trout, and brought them back and the mess boys fixed them for chow." Hammon also recalled the mess boys having lobster pots in the bay, and every Wednesday they had all the fresh lobsters they wanted for lunch.

But Hammon's two-month odyssey lounging in fancy hotels, rubbing elbows with celebrities in five-star restaurants, trout fishing in the icy mountain waters of Newfoundland, and dining on all the lobster he could eat was about to come to an end. The USS *Otter* finally arrived in Argentia Bay and young Ens. Jerry Hammon was there to meet it and go on board as the ship's sole ensign. Out to sea they went, and before long they encountered one of the worst storms Hammon had ever experienced, a storm so severe it cracked the hull of the destroyer escort and the tiny ship started to take on water. "I was on the flying bridge, tied on and looking up at the next wave coming right at me—and the flying bridge was forty-two feet above the sea level," said Hammon, who had the midnight watch that day. "We cracked our hull like the old Liberty ships, which would go down when they cracked like that. But we didn't, and took the ship into dry dock for repairs."[30]

Despite their young age and inexperience these men were determined to serve, and many, such as young Martin Davis, who grew up in Elizabeth, New Jersey, went to great lengths in order to enlist. Growing up during the Great Depression, Davis remembers when "a penny would buy something, and three pennies would buy a lot." Young Martin would watch workmen trudge past his house each morning, black lunch pails in hand, on their way to their jobs at the Singer Sewing Machine Company. They were lucky to have work. Many of the workmen smoked, but they could not afford a whole pack of cigarettes. "They would buy two or three or four cigarettes at a time," Davis said.

Life was about to change for everyone, including Davis, on 7 December 1941. The fourteen-year-old boy was skating at the roller rink in Newark, listening to the organ music and enjoying a carefree Sunday afternoon, when suddenly, the Pearl Harbor announcement came over the public address system. Although most his friends did not know where Pearl Harbor was located, bright young Davis did, and he figured that if the Japanese were attacking there, it would not be long before they would be attacking other parts of the United States.

"I wanted to enlist," Davis said, but of course he was too young. "I couldn't wait to enlist. I dreamt of it every day." Davis, whose brother was a Navy seaman captured and imprisoned by the Japanese, would have to wait a while longer before he would be at sea. But the New Jersey kid had more than his age to overcome before he would be able to enlist in any branch of the service. Davis had bad eyes.

Under the regulations in effect at the time for the Navy, Coast Guard, and Marines, a recruit had to have 20/20 uncorrected vision. Davis' vision was 20/70, unacceptable to all three branches. But bad eyesight was not going to keep Davis from joining, so the enterprising young man went to the recruiting offices and watched how recruits were examined. "I saw that they examined your eyes and they asked you to read the chart," something he would not be able to do. An avid reader, Davis recalled an article in *Popular Science* about "invisible eyeglasses," which turned out to be an early version of contact lenses. "I arranged to get a set of primitive contact lenses as part of an experimental patient," Davis said. One day he took the train into New York City and asked to be included in the program. Plaster casts of his eyes were made, from which they crafted the lenses. "It brought my vision to 20/20, even though I ended up looking goggle-eyed, like Peter Lory."

Davis chose to enlist in the Coast Guard because he believed he could better fool the recruiter after observing the method they were using to check recruits' eyes. First they examined the eyes in one line, and then they told the prospective recruit to go into another line and read the eye chart. That gave Davis just enough time to slip in his contact lenses, which could be kept in the eyes for no more than three hours, without being noticed.

"Read the bottom line," the recruiter barked. "How far down?" Davis asked. "As far down as you can go," the recruiter said. "P-A-T," Davis read, to which the recruiter exclaimed, "What are you reading?" Davis told him he was reading the bottom line. "You're reading patent pending. You have a vision of 20/10, like a hawk."

So young Martin Davis, who a few months earlier had been listening to the Shadow and Jack Benny on the radio with his family and had never been away from home, now suddenly was grown up. Seaman Second Class Davis was on board the USS *Pettit*, one of thirty DEs manned by the Coast Guard, and was on watch for prowling U-boats as the ship escorted convoys through the very dangerous waters between New York City and Londonderry, Ireland.[31]

Fellow Coast Guardsman Terry Thomas, the seventeen-year-old Detroit boy who had left his mother crying at the train station the day he left for boot camp, finished his training in Manhattan Beach, and on Christmas Eve 1943 he and his buddy Joe Smith boarded a cold, dirty train bound for the Norfolk Naval Base. "All of us were very quiet," Thomas said. "We didn't know at that time where we were going or why." He added, "We heard that we were going to landing barge training. None of us wanted this," noting that landing barges were being steered by Coast Guardsmen with little protection. "This was a heavy fatality job."

That night on the train, Thomas sadly recalled, while the old steam train chugged through the lonely darkness, he thought of his family "and remembered all the wonderful Christmas Eves I had spent at home. They played Christmas music on the radio for us. I had never been, and have never been since, so lonely and homesick." Three days later he and his pal Joe Smith would board a brand-new American warship, the destroyer escort USS *Rhodes*. As his ship pulled away from the dock and headed out into the vast open ocean, Thomas could not help but remember the words of his crying mother only a few weeks earlier as he climbed on board that old steam train and headed to boot camp "like lambs being led to the slaughter."[32]

2

Good Luck . . . and Good Hunting

The black armor-plated Lincoln convertible slowly rolled down a ramp and into the Washington Navy Yard. A contingent of Secret Service agents stood on the car's running boards with a sharp eye on the Sunshine Special's passenger, President Franklin D. Roosevelt, who was not feeling well that Saturday afternoon, plagued with a constant headache and still recovering from a recent surgical procedure to remove a sebaceous cyst from the back of his neck. Eleanor Roosevelt and Anne, his son John's wife, were in the back-seat with the president.

Concerned about the president's health, Margaret "Daisy" Suckley, the president's cousin and one of his closest confidants, urged Roosevelt not to put the convertible's top down, as he usually liked to do, especially following his recent neck surgery. "I'll wear a scarf," the president told his worried cousin in a telephone conversation the night before his trip. "Will that cover it [the surgical site]?" Suckley inquired, to which Roosevelt replied that it would not. Suckley urged him to wear an ear muff. "Yes, & have the other ear muff over my forehead," Roosevelt joked.[1]

Roosevelt ventured to the navy yard on that cold February day in 1944, Lincoln's birthday, to commemorate "the ancient friendship between France and the United States" and to transfer to the Free French a new warship, the destroyer escort *Senegalais*. Roosevelt began speaking via a radio hookup in the back of his open car parked next to the new ship as the Stars and Stripes and French Tricolor whipped from the shiny vessel's main masthead in the brisk winter wind. "On behalf of the American people, I transfer to the Navy of France this warship—built by American hands in an American navy yard." Roosevelt continued: "She is a new class—a destroyer escort—speedy and dangerous. I want to tell you something else about her—that there are more where she came from. Under our Lend-Lease agreement, she is not the only ship that you will receive from us—we are building others for your sailors to man." Roosevelt concluded by saying, "Good luck, *Senegalais*—and good hunting" as a full crew of American-trained French sailors stood on the deck in full salute to the American president.

In remarks broadcast by shortwave radio to France and North Africa, Roosevelt said the transfer might better be described as a "reverse Lend-Lease" because in his nation's early days the situation was reversed. "At that time," the president noted, "instead of France receiving an American-made ship, the young nation of the United States was glad to receive, happy to receive, a ship made in France by Frenchmen—the *Bon Homme Richard*—a ship made illustrious under the command of John Paul Jones, in the days of our Navy's infancy." Roosevelt, a student of naval history since childhood, went on to remind listeners that the ship was named in honor of America's minister to France, Benjamin Franklin, "that wise old philosopher who was the father of the close friendship between France and the United States."[2]

Named in honor of the French West African natives who assisted in the American invasion of North Africa, the *Senegalais* was originally commissioned as the USS *Corbesier* in January 1943 and would become one of six destroyer escorts transferred to the Free French, fighting under British control. Other DEs sent to France included the USS *Cronin*, USS *Crosley*, and three other ships (DE-109, -110, and -111) not named before transfer to the French.[3]

This new class of warship, the destroyer escort, was smaller than the traditional destroyer. The ships were more agile and maneuverable with a smaller turning circle than their larger cousins, allowing them to better track, attack, and evade German submarines. They also carried the latest antisubmarine equipment, including sonar echoing used to find German U-boats using supersonic sound transmission. Built in six different designs using available power plants, the warships ranged from 1,140 to 1,450 tons unloaded, were 290 to 308 feet long, and carried a complement of men ranging from 180 to 220, including officers. They were mass-produced and could be built faster and more cheaply than destroyers, costing about $5 to $6 million each compared to a price tag of $10 million for a traditional destroyer.[4]

The USS *Liddle*'s captain, R. M. Hinckley Jr., peers from the bridge as the DE makes its way through the stormy North Atlantic. Commissioned in December 1943, the *Liddle* safely escorted three convoys to Wales, Gibraltar, and Tunisia. Later it was converted to a high-speed transport ship and assigned to the Pacific, where it successfully shot down five Japanese kamikazes. *Photo taken by Harold S. Deal; courtesy Jeff Deal*

Sailing at speeds ranging from twenty to twenty-four knots (destroyers could sail at forty knots or more), the ships also carried an ample amount of fire power. Ships had two depth-charge racks on the stern, which housed twenty-four drumlike units often called "ash cans," each packed with two hundred to six hundred pounds of trinitrotoluene or TNT. These rather crude implements were the original antisubmarine weapons used in World War I, when submarines did not operate at great depths. They would be dropped from the stern of the vessel and set to explode at a preset depth based on water pressure, destroying U-boats prowling below.

DEs also carried another weapon that would prove deadly for Hitler's U-boat fleet: hedgehogs—twenty-four individual bombs, each packed with thirty pounds of TNT—that could be launched simultaneously in an elliptical pattern 270 yards ahead of the ship and would explode on contact with any solid object, such as a submarine. The weapons, developed by the British,

Sailors on board the USS *Liddle* watch depth charges explode off the stern of the ship. DEs had two depth-charge racks on the stern, which housed twenty-four drumlike units, often called "ash cans." Packed with two hundred to six hundred pounds of TNT, the ash cans were dropped over the stern and set to explode at a preset depth based on water pressure, destroying any U-boats prowling below. *Photo taken by Harold S. Deal; courtesy Jeff Deal*

earned their odd name because, when unloaded, the rows of empty spigots where the bombs fit were said to resemble the spine of the small mammal. A hedgehog would not require the ship to be directly over a submarine to launch, as depth charges did, but could be fired ahead of the ship to clear its path. The ships also had antiaircraft guns and three torpedo tubes.

Hedgehogs explode off the bow of the USS *Liddle* in the North Atlantic in 1944. These British antisubmarine weapons consisted of twenty-four individual bombs—each packed with thirty pounds of TNT—launched simultaneously in an elliptical pattern 270 yards ahead of the ship. They would explode on contact with a solid object, such as a submarine. The photo also captures two of the still-unexploded bombs in the air. *Photo taken by Harold S. Deal; courtesy Jeff Deal*

Life for the sailors on board these tiny ships was not always a comfortable one. More than two hundred sailors cramped into a vessel about 300 feet long and 35 feet wide made for interesting but necessary sleeping arrangements. Some sailors had assigned bunks or hammocks, while others slept in the mess, where their bunks were turned up to make room for sailors to dine. Often there were more sailors on board then there were lockers, forcing some to live out of their seabags. They slept with their uniforms placed carefully under their two-inch-thick mattresses so that they would be pressed and ready when the ships were in port and sailors were given a few hours liberty. In the Pacific liberty often consisted of a few hours on a sandy beach with each sailor given two or three cans of warm beer to quench his thirst.

In order to pass the time, many sailors kept a diary of their days afloat. Although strictly forbidden by the Navy, sailors such as Jim Larner of the USS *Day* made daily entries into his journal beginning the first day he stepped on board the destroyer escort in June 1944. "I recorded a lot of information I saw, heard and experienced," Larner recalled, describing how he would lie in his

DE sailors had plenty of chores to do while on board ship, including swabbing the deck, chipping paint, repairing guns, and cleaning the engine rooms. All living spaces were swept down three times a day. Here two sailors are scrubbing their hammocks on deck. Because of limited space, many new arrivals slept in hanging hammocks instead of bunks. *Photo taken by Harold S. Deal; courtesy Jeff Deal*

bunk backward while he wrote in his diary. "No officer ever tried to look to see what I was doing and I never told any of my shipmates, who were always playing poker down below me."

Larner's bunk was number 206 up on top, between a steam pipe and the port side hull, with the deck just above his head. "In the North Atlantic Ocean, I slept beside that steam pipe and it was nice and warm," Warner said. "But as winter was coming on, the deck above my head and the port side wall was getting cold."

Sometimes at sea for months at a time, sailors had to rely on their shipmates for many basic grooming and personal care services. Eugene Squires of Aynor, South Carolina, uses his barber skills to give a trim to Yeoman Clarence W. LaFollette of Hazelpark, Michigan, while the USS *Liddle* escorts a convoy through the North Atlantic. *Photo taken by Harold S. Deal; courtesy Jeff Deal*

Despite their smaller size, these new warships were built to be taken seriously, as German U-boat captains were about to discover. Although they were tardy in arriving to the war, DEs would end up being the Allies' most efficient and effective vessel to detect and destroy submarines and would be credited with playing a key role in halting the massive slaughter of Allied and merchant vessels at the hands of German submarine commanders.

But these novel new vessels would not carry out their mission without some casualties, as the youthful sailors on board the Coast Guard–manned USS *Leopold* discovered when, on one cold moonlit night in March 1944, the four-month-old *Leopold* and five other DEs were escorting a fifteen-ship con-

Of the 563 DEs built in World War II, only sixteen were lost to enemy action over the course of the entire war in both the Atlantic and Pacific theaters, a remarkable record since these little vessels were sent out in harm's way. Only five of the sixteen were sunk by U-boats, including the USS *Fiske*, pictured above, disappearing beneath the waters of the North Atlantic. The DE was sunk by *U-804* east of Newfoundland, killing thirty-three American sailors and badly wounding fifty others. *U.S. Navy Photograph, courtesy the Destroyer Escort Historical Museum*

voy across the North Atlantic from New York to Ireland. Sounds of the Mills Brothers' popular new hit, "Paper Doll," emanated from the midship compartment. A five-piece ragtag band of DE sailors was playing the song that catapulted the African American entertainers to stardom in 1943, while sailors dreamed about their upcoming liberty in Ireland. The weather was rough, said Signalman J. Armond Burgun, and it took tremendous effort just to keep the convoy of ships from drifting apart as they sailed through the turbulent and dangerous waters about 540 miles southwest of Iceland.

Son of a traveling eyeglass salesman, Burgun left school to enlist in the Coast Guard when he was only sixteen years old after lying about his age. After boot camp at Manhattan Beach, Brooklyn, where former heavyweight boxing champion Jack Dempsey taught him physical education, Burgun went to signal school before being assigned to the *Leopold*, under construction in Orange, Texas.[5] Making its first convoy from Norfolk to Casablanca in January, the ship was escorting vessels loaded with ammunition, food, and troops. The crossing took about a month and was uneventful except for one sailor falling overboard and disappearing beneath the turbulent ocean waters. They never even picked up any sonar contacts in the waters that were believed to be rife with prowling German U-boats.

On their next convoy in March 1944, things would change. Fifteen tankers carrying high-octane aircraft fuel for use in shuttle bombing by England were being escorted by the *Leopold* and USS *Joyce*—both running along the convoy's flank—and four other DEs, all manned by Coast Guard crews under the command of Lt. Cdr. Kenneth Phillips. The waters were rough and the weather stormy. "Just keeping the ships together was murder," Burgun said, adding that it was fortunate tankers ride low in the water and were fast. The *Leopold* also was equipped with a high-frequency direction finder, nicknamed Huff Duff, for use in monitoring German radio traffic in order to triangulate a position of the U-boats.

"I was reading some letters from home at 7:20 that night," Seaman Lucas Bobbitt said. "I had just washed and pressed my tailor-mades. We were all getting excited about liberty. We hadn't made any liberties in Ireland. The guys were wondering if you could get some beer and what the girls were like," Bobbitt said. "In the midship compartment a jam session was going on. We had a five-piece band, trumpet, clarinet, guitar—couple of other instruments. It was just a pickup band, but they were good."[6]

That night, as the happy musicians played "Paper Doll," the alarm sounded and everyone rushed to battle stations, preparing for a yet-unseen enemy. Sailors first thought it was just another drill, but they soon realized that this was the real thing. The *Leopold* quickly reversed course racing to investigate the radar contact about five miles south of the convoy, and it wouldn't take long to find what their radar had detected. Dead ahead, about two thousand yards, was the German submarine *U-255*, sitting on the surface in the stark winter moonlight and brightly illuminated by star shells fired from the *Leopold*. The DE skipper gave the order to commence firing and to stand by to ram the submarine at flank speed. "We fired everything we had," Burgun said.[7]

Captain Erich Harms, commander of *U-255*, had been tracking the convoy, but he and his crew were startled that they had been discovered while presumably surfaced to recharge their batteries. Scrambling off the deck of the submarine, the Germans quickly plunged down the conning tower hatch and prepared to dive—but not before firing an acoustic torpedo at the *Leopold*. It was a direct hit, with a violent explosion nearly splitting the destroyer escort in half. Lights and communication on board the ship instantly were knocked out and the dreadful sound of groaning metal could be heard as the mortally wounded ship started to break in two. The *Leopold*, which had been built in a near-record ninety days and commissioned only four months earlier, would earn the dubious distinction of being the first destroyer escort sunk in the Battle of the Atlantic. It would not be the last.

"The main lamp exploded in my gut," said Burgun, who was on the signal bridge getting ready to illuminate the submarine. The torpedo tore through the ship, lifting it right out of the water. Burgun said, "I was thrown about twenty yards," whacking his head and fracturing his leg. The captain ordered the injured sailor to get a damage report. Hobbling as best he could on one leg, he went down the ladder to the engine room to find out the condition of the ship. "The keel is broken," the damage-control officer told Burgun. Rushing back with his report to the skipper, Burgun heard the order to abandon ship. "That's the worst thing you can hear in the North Atlantic," with its forty-foot waves and 22-degree temperatures, Burgun said.[8]

"The explosion threw me against the breech of the gun. I had a shell in my hand," Seaman Bobbitt said. "The grating from the deck was ripped loose and hit me on the side of my right leg. I got up. The second loader had the whole side of his face blown off. He was begging for a pharmacist's mate." Seaman Troy Gowers also was at the gun station when the torpedo hit. "I was blown right out of my shoes and into a life net a dozen feet away," he recalled. "I crawled back to my station, and without power, tried to work the gun manually, but it was jammed."[9]

Seaman Richard Novotny, a quartermaster trainee, or "striker" as it is known, had just hit the sack because he had the midnight watch. Jumping out of bed, he raced to his battle station on the 20-mm starboard-side gun. Turning, Novotny saw the submarine's conning tower off the port bow, now brightly illuminated by the star shells. "It appeared we were running at flank speed, approaching the sub bow on, and about to smash into the conning tower," he said. Suddenly, disaster struck the DE as the torpedo ripped through its hull. "I was in and out of a conscious state," Novotny recalled. When he awoke he found himself struggling to stay afloat in the frigid water, clad only in shredded dungarees, swimming with one arm to a life raft some fifteen yards away. He was not able to use his left arm or his legs to propel himself since the explosion had severely damaged three of his spinal vertebrae.

Gazing up at his wounded ship, Novotny saw the chief quartermaster, William Graham, hanging by his foot on the starboard anchor's fluke as dozens of his shipmates struggled just to stay alive in the freezing waters. A delirious Novotny lapsed in and out of consciousness.[10]

Scrambling across the deck awash with blood and dodging the body parts of shipmates, Burgun, the signalman with the broken leg, leaped into the icy water filled with burning debris and corpses bobbing up and down near the buckling ship. Fortunately for Burgun he had been on watch and was dressed in foul-weather gear, which acted as a sort of wet suit, helping him to survive in the freezing waters. Grabbing hold of a float, Burgun and twenty-seven of his shipmates gripped the raft in the freezing water and would wait more than ten hours before help arrived. When the USS *Joyce* finally came to rescue the sailors the next morning, only six of the original twenty-seven were still alive.

"We had to stay awake. We sang, we yelled at each other, we slapped each other to try to not go to sleep," Burgun said, noting that once sailors fell asleep they often lapsed into unconsciousness and died. Hope among the shivering sailors was raised as the *Joyce*'s silhouette appeared in the moonlight around midnight. But those hopes were dashed when Capt. Robert Wilcox of the *Joyce* came out on the bridge and, using a bullhorn, said, "We're dodging torpedoes. God bless you. We'll be back," and the destroyer escort sped away into the darkness as the freezing sailors watched in despair. Burgun held one of his shipmates in his arms all night, hoping to keep him awake and warm so he would live. He did not survive, and Burgun handed the lifeless body to sailors on board the *Joyce* the next morning. Only twenty-eight sailors of the crew of two hundred on board the *Leopold* survived. All thirteen officers went down with the ship. And *U-255* escaped and returned to France unharmed.[11]

With one DE under their belt, it was not long before Adolph Hitler's men took aim at more of America's newest U-boat fighters since, after all, the little destroyer escorts were starting to rack up a respectable number of "kills" sinking nearly a dozen U-boats in only five months following the torpedoing of the *Leopold*. During that same period two additional destroyer escorts—the USS *Fechteler* and USS *Fiske*—were sunk by U-boats and four others badly damaged by German torpedoes, sending more than 130 young American sailors to watery graves.

But destroyer escorts had more to worry about than just Hitler's U-boats. There was danger in the skies as well, as Germany's highly trained Luftwaffe targeted the little ships sailing on the dark and lonely oceans of the world. Terry Thomas, the seventeen-year-old son of immigrant parents living in Detroit, was on board the Coast Guard–manned USS *Rhodes* when he was jarred awake in the wee hours of the morning of April Fool's Day 1944. His ship, along with several other DEs, was escorting a convoy of ninety-eight ships carrying vital war supplies through the Mediterranean Sea en route to Bizerte, Tunisia. Thomas soon discovered this was no April Fool's joke.

The DE picked up a voice radio signal that enemy bombers were overhead. Sailors topside peered into the eerie darkness but could not see any planes, although they could hear the telltale sounds of aircraft engines nearby. Immediately opening fire at the unseen enemy, they hoped it would keep the Germans from attacking the convoy. It didn't work. Nazi bombers and torpedo planes dove out of the night sky, dropping flares to illuminate the convoy and firing at the destroyer escorts and their charges. When the call to battle stations rang out, Thomas could tell from the urgency in his captain's voice that this was no drill. He jumped from his bunk and ran up to the 20-mm guns where he served as a loader.

The night sky was illuminated by tracer bullets, and the young sailor was struck by how beautiful they looked—just like fireworks he remembered at home. But he knew this was no Fourth of July show and that mortal danger lurked in that darkness. The planes were flying very fast and so low that he saw the face of one of the German pilots and the swastika emblazoned on the plane's fuselage as it dived about fifty feet above the Mediterranean waters. They continued to fire on the convoy as the little DEs peppered them with antiaircraft fire. The mast of his ship was nearly hit twice by the low-flying planes, Thomas recalled, but the bombers were turned away by the incessant antiaircraft firing. "We got one German plane," he said, "and everybody claimed it." Five German aircraft were shot down during the battle.

Sailors on board the USS *Savage,* another Coast Guard–manned DE in the convoy, also pounded the night sky with gunfire. Radioman Daniel Farley, who grew up in Methuen, Massachusetts, as the son of a textile mill worker, was asleep when the call came to man battle stations. "Boy, you wake up quick and run up the ladder to your post," Farley said. During the attack one of Farley's shipmates was injured when he was struck in the ankle by shell fragments.

A Liberty ship, the SS *Jarard Ingersoll* was heavily damaged by the German aircraft and started to sink. The USS *Mills*, another destroyer escort, rushed to rescue survivors, then came alongside the blazing ship in order to put a fire-control party on board to extinguish the flames. The battle with the Luftwaffe lasted only about a quarter of an hour, but for the sailors on those DEs firing at unseen targets in the darkness, it seemed a lot longer. The destroyer escorts USS *Tomich, Sloat,* and *Sellstrom* also participated in repelling the German air attack.

John W. Avener was a nineteen-year-old torpedoman on board the USS *Ramsden,* a six-month-old DE built in Houston, Texas, and manned by the Coast Guard. Once the German bombers retreated, Avener said, an incident every bit as chilling and unsettling as the attack itself occurred: "After the firing was over we saw a flare go up from a life raft off the port beam." It was still dark out and they could not use their powerful searchlights to find the location of the raft for fear they would be seen by the enemy. "Hang on old fellow, we're coming to get you," the captain broadcast over the loudspeaker, as the *Ramsden* headed in the direction of the flare.

"As we approached the raft, someone threw a line toward his voice. It must have missed as he yelled, 'No good, no good.'" Then the unthinkable happened: "In trying to maneuver the ship closer, the engines suddenly reversed and he [the man on the raft] was sucked into the screws. Come daylight we searched the area but found nothing."[12]

Ten days later destroyer escorts would again encounter the German Luftwaffe, but this time the Americans would not fare as well. The USS *Holder* was leading a convoy of sixty ships carrying vital supplies through the dangerous waters off the coast of Algeria in the Mediterranean. As a near-full moon reflected off the dark ocean, the *Holder* had taken the place of the flagship USS *Stanton* as head of the convoy, about a day away from reaching its port.

Holder signalman Edmond J. Anuszczyk had watch on the bridge around midnight on 11 April when suddenly a red flare, the color of grinding cast iron, dropped dead ahead of the ship, followed by four bright yellow flares off the three-month-old vessel's starboard side. Anuszczyk watched the flares descend slowly from the dark skies, as though attached to parachutes. The

.sounds of airplane engines pierced the darkness as alarms were sounded. The *Holder* fired into the darkness and smoke machines were activated to help hide the ships, but by then it was too late.

Suddenly thirty-five German bombers and torpedo planes struck in a coordinated attack as they dived down, skimmed the water, and launched a torpedo, which ripped right through the *Holder* amidship on the port side below the water line. Joseph Carinci, gun captain on board the sister ship USS *Hissem*, fired more than 150 rounds from his 3-inch guns but the planes quickly veered off into the dark skies, out of the range of fire.

The *Holder* went dark as all power and communication were knocked out and the vessel began to list to starboard. Fires erupted with flames reaching into the night and the ship, which now lay motionless, began to take on water. The brave young sailors remained at their battle stations as their ship, engulfed in flames, pounded the night sky with gunfire to keep the bombers from returning and harming any other ships in the convoy. Damage-control sailors were able to keep the ship seaworthy and the destroyer escort USS *Forester* came alongside to assist with the dead and injured.

Seaman Charles Grunewald said the *Holder* was a sitting duck for the Germans, "a perfect silhouette" in the bright moonlight, as the flares helped even more to pinpoint the vessel for the German bombers. The explosion "blew me higher than the stack because when I started down, I could see inside of it." Signalman Anuszczyk also was blown into the air, and he lapsed into unconsciousness for a period of time, waking up in a half-sitting position against the bulkhead, his face and forehead streaming in blood. Sixteen sailors, including the ship's chief engineer, died, and thirteen others were wounded in the attack.

Still afloat, the crippled ship was towed to Algiers for temporary repairs before joining a convoy of ships back to the United States. Damage was extensive—the *Holder*'s first battle with the enemy would be its last. But the destroyer escorts had done their job—not a single merchant ship was damaged, and their essential supplies were protected during the barrage, which lasted for more than an hour and a half, according to a report prepared by the yeoman on the *Hissem*, on its first combat mission during the *Holder* assault.[13]

Within three weeks of the *Holder*'s demise, two more destroyer escorts—the USS *Menges* and USS *Donnell*—would suffer extensive damage and another would be sunk at the hands of German submarines. The *Menges*, a

Coast Guard–manned ship only seven months old, was part of an eighty-ship convoy traveling along the African coast when the entire collection of ships nearly ran right into a German submarine, surfaced near Bougie to recharge its batteries. On its maiden convoy, the destroyer escort already had distinguished itself by splashing a German aircraft after thirty torpedo bombers—on their way to the East Coast of the United States—attacked and sunk an American destroyer, the USS *Lansdale*. The *Menges* rescued more than two hundred survivors. But the young ship's luck was about to run out.

Realizing he had been detected, Captain Horst-Arno Fenski, commander of *U-371*, quickly dived his boat in the early morning hours of 3 May 1944, but not before firing an acoustic torpedo at the destroyer escort, closing in for what he hoped would be a U-boat kill. The *Menges* deployed its foxer gear after seventeen-year-old sonarman Robert McMichael detected the boat. "I had just picked up the sub, made one complete sweep and started back when we were hit," McMichael recalled.

The submarine's torpedo ripped through the ship's aft section, destroying the vessel's propellers and rudder. The blast carried every one of the ship's depth charges into the sea and was so violent that it hurled a washing machine, bolted to a lower deck, 150 feet forward and upward until it smashed against an antiaircraft gun on the upper deck. Apparently the foxer gear, which consisted of metals rods towed behind the ship that would hit each other theoretically to create a sound louder than the ship's propeller, failed to attract the acoustic torpedo, which wrecked one-third of the ship's stern. Thirty-one American sailors died and twenty-five others were wounded.

As the young destroyer escort continued its death throes, the U-boat went deep and crept silently along the coast with two other destroyer escorts and other Allied vessels in hot pursuit, bombarding the waters with depth charges, which caused damage and flooding on board the submarine. But Fenski went deeper—more than 750 feet below the water—where he lay silently for the rest of the day. Without a full charge in his batteries, however, the air inside *U-371* was starting to foul and flooding was said to be "knee deep." The commander needed to surface.[14]

Waiting on the surface were six Allied warships, including the destroyer escorts *Joseph E. Campbell*, *Pride*, another Coast Guard–manned ship, and the *Senegalais*, the DE given to the French by President Roosevelt only three months earlier. As the submarine surfaced the Allied vessels closed in, firing their guns at the fleeing boat. Fenski fired an acoustic torpedo, which hit the *Senegalais*, killing 49 of the 179 men on board. Realizing he could not escape, the submarine captain ordered his men to abandon ship and scuttle the boat. Prisoners, including the captain, were taken on board the *Campbell* and *Senegalais*, the latter towed to Bougie and repaired.[15]

That very same day, the USS *Donnell* was steaming east on its fifth crossing, screening a convoy of tankers to assist in the buildup for the cross-Channel European invasion. Sailors on board the destroyer escort were conducting an antisubmarine drill that, unknown to them, was about to turn into the real thing. Lurking nearby was one of Hitler's U-boats, *U-473*, commanded by twenty-seven-year-old Captain Heinz Sternberg, traveling silently at periscope depth. Sternberg had sailed from Lorient with several electronic specialists on board who were testing radar and radar detectors. The Nazi captain peered through the periscope as the convoy steamed about 280 miles east of Ireland. Suddenly battle stations sounded as the *Donnell*'s sonar picked up an echo, and within minutes Sternberg's periscope was sighted piercing the water's surface. The *Donnell* left the convoy and took off after the submarine.

Twenty-four-year-old seaman Daniel Sileo rushed to his battle station behind the torpedo tubes as sailors readied weapons. But it was too late. Sternberg already had fired an acoustic torpedo at the DE, which blew off the stern of the American ship. It all happened so fast that there was little time to fire weapons or deploy the foxer gear.

Although the ship remained afloat, twenty-nine American sailors lost their lives from the explosion, which left another twenty-five battered and bleeding. Sileo, who left his job as a color grinder at the Atlas Powder Company in Stamford, Connecticut, after being drafted into the Navy in 1943, recalled one of his shipmates was found alive floating on a mattress some two hundred yards from the ship. In addition to the explosion from the German torpedo, some of the *Donnell*'s own depth charges exploded, causing additional damage to the vessel. "I can still see her, dead in the water," recalled Radioman A. J. Petty, "her after-end curled up like a scorpion's tail, up and toward the 1.1 gun." Some speculated that the curled-up tail very well may have saved the ship from sinking.

Daniel Sileo had no desire to go to war. After quitting high school at seventeen, he went to work at Atlas, married, and had a seven-month-old daughter. He was just starting out, had a good job and a young family, and his whole life ahead of him. But the war changed all that, just as it did for so many young Americans, and when the Navy called him to serve, he knew it was his duty. Because of the desperate need for manpower, Sileo spent just two weeks at boot camp in Sampson before being shipped to Pier 92 in New York City, where he went on board the *Donnell*. His ship made four successful transatlantic crossings prior to the fateful one in May 1944, safely escorting convoys through U-boat-infested waters between the United States and Londonderry.

Sileo said the legendary heavy North Atlantic weather battered the ship on some of those convoys. In fact, one crossing was so rough that he could still see the shores of Ireland after being at sea for a full two days. He also remembered another instance when an airplane flew over the convoy and shined a powerful searchlight right on his ship. "I thought it was the last day I would see," Sileo said, noting that the aircraft turned out to be a friendly British plane.

After the 3 May attack, a gravely injured *Donnell* was towed by the destroyer escorts USS *Reeves*, USS *Hopping*, and HMS *Samsonia* to Dunnstaffnage Bay, Scotland. Repairs would have involved extensive reconstruction, so the ship was sent to Northern Ireland as an accommodation ship. Later it became the first destroyer escort to supply electric power from its turboelectric engines to shoreline installations at Cherbourg, France, providing power from August to December 1944.[16]

The slaughter continued. Twenty-four hours later another destroyer escort would meet its match. Little more than one year after commissioning, the USS *Fechteler* was on the Mediterranean returning from Bizerte in the early morning hours as part of a sixty-four-ship convoy bound for the United States, including a hospital ship carrying wounded Americans. Proceeding westward near Elberon Island, radar contact was made by the destroyer escort USS *Laning* indicating a possible submarine about thirteen miles ahead.

The *Fechteler* rapidly maneuvered between the convoy and the possible U-boat contact when suddenly a tremendous explosion lit up the dark skies as a torpedo from *U-967*, commanded by Captain Albrecht Brandi, who had achieved celebrity status in Germany for sinking so many Allied ships, ripped through the DE, wrecking three of the four engineering spaces as seawater poured into the cracked hull. The ship started to break in two.

"The force of the explosion drove me back against the depth-charge racks," recalled Seaman Howard R. Bender, who was at his battle station on the number two, 3-inch, 50-mm gun. "Debris was flying everywhere. I was hit by small particles of metal." Once all depth charges were set to "safe," the order was given to abandon ship. "So we cut the life rafts loose, blew up our life belts, jumped into the water, and swam toward the life rafts, which were drifting away from the ship," Bender said. "Then I heard screaming and yelling, 'Help me!'" Bender swam in the direction of the voice, where he found a badly injured shipmate who had been blown overboard by the explosion. Bender tried to keep him afloat and hold his head out of the water. "I don't know how long we were in the water, trying to stay alive; it seemed like forever to me. The water was very cold and we were getting very tired."

Lt. Burton T. Kyle, the ship's engineering officer, was a Naval Reserve officer and former instructor at both the merchant marine training academy in New Orleans as well as at the Subchaser Training Center in Miami, Florida. But even for an experienced sailor like Kyle, the shock of a torpedo ripping through your ship can be, at a minimum, disconcerting. "A violent explosion filled the passage way with a thick fog of steam and smoke preceded by a heavy shock or jolt strong enough to create a blank space in my mind as to what happened," Kyle said. "When I recovered I was still a little foggy as to what happened."

He soon realized that his ship had been struck by a torpedo, as he observed that the middle part of the ship had settled into the ocean. "Looking aft it was clear that her keel was fractured," Kyle said. Sliding into the water atop a piece of damage-control wood, Kyle gripped the wood throughout the night until the *Laning* and an unidentified rescue tug arrived. "But when the ship threw me a line I could not tie a knot. My fingers would not work. So I wrapped it around me and squeezed it so they could haul me up the fifteen feet or so."[17]

"Everything went pitch black and I knew it was all over for us down there," William Quackenbush, a water tender in the fire room said. The seven men scrambled in a desperate attempt to open the hatches but they could not budge it. After what seemed like an eternity for the sailors trying to pry their way to safety, the engineering officer opened the starboard hatch so the seven men in the forward fireroom managed to get out safely. All men in the forward engineering room and aft fire room died in the blast. Quackenbush and his shipmates dove over the side.

Twenty-nine American sailors were killed and 26 were wounded in the attack. The *Laning* and other ships in the convoy rescued 186 survivors, who watched in horror as their ship, broken in half, buckled and groaned as the bow and stern rose up together 125 feet out of the water. A violent explosion followed as the *Fechterler*, the second destroyer escort sunk in the war, disappeared beneath the waves about an hour and a half after the torpedo struck.[18]

But the United States' new destroyer escorts had much more fighting to do. The next day in what only can be described as one of the oddest confrontations between the U.S. Navy and the Germans during the entire war, crews from the USS *Buckley* and the Nazi submarine *U-66* engaged in hand-to-hand combat using coffee mugs, bare knuckles, and empty shell casings in an encounter the Navy later called the closest naval combat action in modern warfare. The destroyer escort, part of a hunter-killer group looking for U-boats about five hundred miles west of the Cape Verde Islands, was prowling under moonlit seas as Grumman Avengers, so-called Night Owls, streaked through the dark skies on the hunt for enemy submarines. The Tenth Fleet, America's intelligence gathering unit, had picked up a Huff Duff radio transmission from a U-boat and dispatched the hunter-killer group to find it.

Captain Gerhard Seehausen, the twenty-six-year-old commander of *U-66*, already had sunk five Allied ships when he decided to surface his boat to recharge its batteries and allow his crew to get some fresh air. The U-boat had been under way for one hundred days and by now the crew of sixty-two was described as "pallid, haggard, and filthy." They had no fresh water and had long ago run out of lemons, stocked to counter vitamin deficiency. Seehausen hoped a supply boat, *U-188*, a so-called milk cow, would arrive to restore their provisions and fuel, but that submarine was nowhere on the horizon. The captain was growing more and more frustrated and radioed to Admiral Karl Döenitz, Germany's U-boat commander, that refueling was very difficult with the constant stalking by the Allies, most notably the destroyer escorts. So in what would turn out to be a fatal mistake, Seehausen decided to surface.[19]

Armed with radio transmission information, the hunter-killer group had been tracking him for several days by the time he surfaced. In the early morning hours of 6 May, Lt. Jimmie J. Sellars spotted the submarine sitting atop the water as he piloted his Night Owl, which had been stripped of its bombs and machine guns and fitted with extra fuel tanks so it could fly for longer periods in search of U-boats. He radioed the *Buckley*, which rushed at flank speed to the sub's location, seven miles away.

Whether the sub commander mistook the destroyer escort for his long-awaited milk cow is not known, but Seehausen fired three red flares to signal his position, barely missing Sellars' airplane. Capt. Brent Maxwell Abel, a twenty-eight-year-old Harvard-educated lawyer assigned to command the newly commissioned *Buckley* in the spring of 1943, opened fire on the surfaced submarine. "Boy, I have never before seen such concentration," Sellars radioed to the *Block Island*, the group's escort carrier. "Buckley is cutting hell out of the conning tower!"[20]

With guns blazing the two vessels zigzagged, running neck and neck, at times only twenty yards apart. In fact, airplanes launched from the carrier to assist in the attack were not able to bomb or even fire their guns at the U-boat for fear of hitting the nearby *Buckley*. After avoiding a possible torpedo fired directly at his vessel, Captain Abel finally had enough and prepared to ram the submarine. Abel ordered a hard right rudder, and the destroyer escort's bow smashed right into *U-66*'s foredeck, laying atop the submarine like a ship aground, as a startled German captain issued the command to abandon ship.

While most of the Nazis started jumping into the water, about a dozen leaped on board the *Buckley*, startling the American sailors. It had been more than a century since the order "stand by to repel boarders" had been issued on board any American warship, and it is unclear whether it was issued in the dark morning hours of 6 May. Captain Abel only recalled saying something like, "My God, they're coming aboard."

A wild and furious brawl ensued, as American and German sailors fought hand-to-hand, bare-knuckles combat. As the Nazis stormed the ship, one sailor picked up a hammer and threatened a German into surrendering. Another sailor knocked a German overboard by hitting him in the head with an empty ammunition shell. And still another hit a German with a medical kit, as his shipmates kicked him over the side. Clobbered with a coffee mug, *U-66*'s helmsman Werner Frolich later said the mug "didn't injure my head, but the coffee cup was bent thereby. Heads were hard in those days."[21]

Abel reversed engines and separated the two vessels from their deadly embrace. To the surprise of the Americans, the U-boat still had enough crew on board to man the battered boat, which quickly sped away after being freed from the *Buckley*'s grasp. The *Buckley* took off in pursuit, peppering the boat with a hail of bullets. Abel prepared to ram *U-66* a second time, but this time the tables were turned. The U-boat swung around and rammed the *Buckley*, opening a gaping hole on its starboard side and locking the two ships together once again. One sailor leaned over and dropped a hand grenade down the U-boat's open hatch. The submarine, now in flames, veered away out of control, as the remaining Germans on board leaped over the side. The ocean swallowed up the boat, and a few minutes later a muffled underwater explosion signaled its end.

In spite of the *Buckley*'s damage and the real danger that more U-boats might show up, Captain Abel combed the waters for three hours looking for German survivors. Thirty-six survivors from *U-66* were picked up, including four officers. They were allowed to wash up and were given clean clothing, cigarettes, food, and drink before being transferred by breeches buoy to the *Block Island*. Captain Abel noted in his log that the prisoners stated they "were glad we were Americans as the English always beat the hell out of them." The entire battle lasted a mere sixteen minutes. The *Buckley*, with a sheared-off starboard propeller shaft and damaged engine and laundry rooms, went under its own power to New York for repairs.[22]

The next German threat came from the skies as Harold Peterson, chief yeoman on board the destroyer escort USS *Decker* was about to come face to face with the German Luftwaffe as his year-old ship, originally built for Great Britain before the United States decided to keep the vessel herself, was escorting a convoy of seventy ships from Gibraltar to Bizerte. During the evening hours of 11 May 1944, about twelve miles off the north shore of Africa in the Mediterranean Sea, Peterson would witness firepower from the sky.

Alarms sounded as *Decker*'s crew rushed to their battle stations. The skies were thick with Nazi fighter planes flying directly toward the American ships in what was said to be one of the largest German aerial attacks on a convoy in the war. Although the young sailors hurried to their battle stations, eyewitnesses report that heads also were bowed in prayer all over the ship as the Nazi torpedo bombers swarmed through the dark skies honing in on the American vessels. "The planes came in at about three hundred miles per hour and very low, probably thirty feet above the water," Peterson recalled. "The first wave, about fifteen or twenty planes, came directly for us as we were in the goat position, screening the convoy from the front. We opened fire immediately," forcing the planes to break formation.

Thanks to the smoke screen laid out by the escorts, the German bombers had difficulty locating the merchant ships, the main targets of their attack. The

Decker and the other escorts pounded the planes with antiaircraft fire as the little escorts maneuvered at full speed of twenty-one miles per hour, dodging torpedoes launched from the German planes.

Frustrated that the destroyer escorts were able to hide the merchant ships in the heavy smoke, the planes started to open fire on the DEs, Peterson said, sneaking up on the ships and firing their torpedoes. The moonless night made it difficult to spot the planes, which continued their attack, sometimes flying so low they nearly missed hitting sailors standing on the deck of the ship. "He was just over my head and just high enough to clear the ship," Peterson said. Two torpedoes were fired at close range and passed safely directly beneath the ship. Several other planes burst into flames from the antiaircraft fire before crashing into the dark waters.

No ships were sunk nor American lives lost during the attack, but sixteen German planes were shot down during the furious thirty-five-minute battle. Peterson credited Capt. A. B. Adams' deft ship handling with saving the ship from being torpedoed. At least seven torpedoes were said to have been launched directly at the *Decker*, all of which missed their mark. Just in case, the cautious yeoman added, "I had my hand on my life belt and was ready to jump over the side any time."[23]

Three months later another destroyer escort would come face-to-face with a German U-boat, but unfortunately for the Americans, the tale would not end as well for them as it did for the crew of the *Buckley* or *Decker*. The USS *Fiske*, like its sister ship the *Leopold* built at the Consolidated Shipyard in Orange, Texas, was part of a hunter-killer group looking for U-boats that were gathering weather data in the central Atlantic and transmitting it back to Germany.

Eighteen-year-old Robert White joined the Navy while still in high school, went on board as a fireman, and worked in the ship's diesel engine room. He had just finished lunch on 2 August 1944 when the USS *Howard*, another escort in the hunter-killer group, reported a brief sighting of a U-boat conning tower and puff of diesel smoke. Dashing to investigate, the *Fiske* was ordered to accompany it and the pair raced at flank speed to the location of the possible sighting, about 750 miles east of Newfoundland. Upon arriving, they commenced a sonar search, while the accompanying carrier, the USS *Wake Island*, launched a bomber to assist the DEs in the search. Depth charges were ordered and the hedgehogs were manned. Suddenly a strong sonar contact was made less than two thousand yards away. Both ships quickly changed course to intercept, but for the *Fiske* there would be no return.

The hunter-killer group had been dispatched to find the submarine after Allied intelligence intercepted weather report radio transmissions between *U-804* and Germany. White, who was in the forward engine room when *U-804* fired its torpedo at the *Fiske*, first thought the auxiliary boiler, used to make steam for cooking on the ship, had blown up. Every once in a while the finicky boiler would backfire when it was lit and the sailors expected one day it might blow. Some thought this was that day.

But White knew differently, especially as water started pouring into the ship's ruptured hull. Lights went out as the ship lost electricity and one of its engine stalled. Sailors in the engine room clawed their way through the dark compartment to find the hatch. Finally, someone opened a hatch, which provided enough light for the sailors to make their way up the ladder. Climbing up on deck, they were shocked to see their ship had been cut in half by the torpedo. The ship's hedgehog magazine detonated with a blinding flash, filling forward living compartments with a dense, suffocating smoke. White had a buddy who worked in the fourth engineering space in the rear of the ship, and he hurried aft to make sure his friend made it to safety. "I ran back and jumped across the break and opened their scuttle so they could get out," White said, and the sailors scurried out. They quickly donned their life jackets and prepared for a swim in the 39-degree water.[24]

Sixteen-year-old Leo F. Stinson, said to be the youngest sailor on board ship, was eating lunch when the alarm sounded. He rushed to his battle station on the 3-inch gun. The German torpedo struck the *Fiske* on the starboard side amidship. The force of the explosion threw Stinson against the forward gun shield. Debris was flying all over the ship including potato bins, swabs, brooms, as well as one of Stinson's shipmates—a man named "Rocco," a former boxer from Brooklyn who had been catapulted into the air by the explosion.

Stinson knew the ship, now breaking in two, was sinking so he rushed to the starboard side and prepared to jump overboard. That was more easily said than done, though, since the ship was listing heavily to the port side and, in order to avoid hitting the side of the ship, he had to jump outward, far away from the ship to avoid crashing into the hull. With nothing to lose, the young sailor jumped and managed to hit the water and swim to a life raft, where his fellow shipmates were struggling to hang on in the frigid ocean.[25]

Harold Newman raced to his battle station in the sound shack on the flying bridge once the general quarters alarm rang. Anticipation built as the sailors heard the relentless "ping, ping, ping," its frequency increasing, an indication that they were closing in on the submarine. Suddenly, he said, the sonar operator shouted, "Captain, I have a contact . . . down Doppler." Adrenalin was flowing in that sound shack as the operator shouted, "Bearing 010, range 1300"—a German submarine was dead ahead, and the *Fiske* was going in for the kill. But Captain Herbert Meyer, the thirty-three-year-old commander of *U-804*, fired first.

"It felt like an erupting volcano when the torpedo hit us midship on the starboard side," Newman said. "The torpedo had broken the keel of the ship. The bow and stern sections were still connected but only by the deck plates. I found myself with a Thompson machine gun, standing at the port wing of the flying bridge, shouting obscenities at the ocean. I must have sounded a bit crazed because the captain came over to remind me to keep the safety on."

It wouldn't be long before the dreaded order to abandon ship was given by the *Fiske*'s twenty-seven-year-old captain, John A. Comly. "There were about ten of us on the bridge as we started our slow trip to the main deck. I remember tightening my May West [life vest] and noting that the captain was still on the bridge as I started down the ladder," Newman said. The bow had a 15-degree list to port, making the descent a little tricky, and by the time Newman and his shipmates made it to the main deck, the list had increased to 25 degrees. He slid down the side of the ship before sufficiently clearing the vessel so he could jump into the water.

Newman was swimming away from the ship as fast as he could, heading to the life raft. "I looked back at the ship and you could see the deck plates had snapped. It was now in two sections with the bow rolling more and more to the port. At that moment Captain Comly appeared on deck. In true naval tradition, he was the last man alive to leave his ship," Newman said. It took barely ten minutes from the time the torpedo broke the ship's back for the vessel to sink.

In order to stay focused and keep their minds off their injuries, the survivors sang choruses of "Roll Out the Barrel" as they clung to the raft, which pitched in the frigid, white-capped waters. "The water was cold and as the hours passed and the adrenalin wore off, there came the realization that I was in pain. . . . My left ankle was broken. The simple task of holding on to the raft became more and more difficult. I don't remember much after that but some of my shipmates must have recognized my problem because I ended up on the raft, not knowing how I got there."[26]

The ship's skipper, John Comly, was a Philadelphia, Pennsylvania, native who rose from the rank of ordinary seaman to commander in only four years. Comly previously served as ensign on board the USS *Downes*, a destroyer sunk in the Japanese attack on Pearl Harbor, before being promoted to lieutenant in 1942. Now, as the young commander looked out over his buckling and burning escort vessel, he soon realized that, like the *Downes*, his ship was going to sink. Once he reasoned the ship could not be saved, he ordered life rafts and nets be put overboard, with swimmers pulling them clear of the area.

"Wounded men were treated as quickly as they could be—many could not be treated at all," Comly recalled. "As soon as that had been accomplished they were ordered put in the water either taken to rafts or had to get there under their own power." About five or ten minutes after the initial explosion, Comly said, a second explosion occurred in the forward section of the ship in the vicinity of the paint locker or projector magazine, resulting in large quantities of smoke that prevented the men from investigating the area. In spite of his crew being young and inexperienced, the skipper said he was pleasantly surprised "by the absolute lack of any confusion, the absolute lack of any panic on the part of any individual. Each man knew exactly what was expected of him and performed accordingly. All the wounded were diligently looked after. All of them were put on rafts."[27]

George W. Brodie, chief hospital corpsman, had his hands full once the torpedo broke the ship's back. Brodie, in the mess hall at the time of the explosion, made his way to the hatch and climbed the ladder to the main deck, where he found a "certain death-like quietness," as men, some injured and bleeding, walked around in a trance-like stunned state. He quickly set up an emergency dressing station on the forward deck and started to treat the wounded. But he would not have much time to help the injured sailors. Once the order to abandon ship came, Brodie and his shipmates went overboard into the icy water, as the vessel continued its violent death throes.

"The men's teeth were chattering and their color was almost blue from the cold," Brodie wrote. He watched sailors, frozen to the core, shivering uncontrollably. "At the raft I was hanging on to there were about twenty men. One man with a possible fracture of the leg was helped onto the raft, the rest of us hung on via the hand lines." Eventually the destroyer escort USS *Far-quhar* arrived to rescue the freezing men in a rescue operation that lasted about two and a half hours. Thirty-three American sailors died and fifty were badly wounded as a result of the sinking, which became the third DE sunk and the 175th American ship lost since the beginning of the war.

For a young ensign named William Geiermann, the sinking of his ship brought into stark relief for the first time the terror and the real human cost of warfare. The North Dakota native enlisted in the Navy's V-12 program while attending Columbia University and became a commissioned ensign in April 1944, assigned to the *Fiske*. When the order was given to abandon ship on that August day, only three months after he had stepped on board, Geiermann knew his new ship was doomed and he quickly slid down the starboard side of the crippled vessel, swimming a short way to a rope net floating on the turbulent and icy waters.

Later, as the young officer was helped on board the *Farquhar*, he was startled to see the six lifeless bodies of his fellow shipmates laid out on deck. "This was the first time I was fully aware of what had happened," Geiermann said. "As I was taken through the officers' wardroom, I observed two crewmen who were being worked on by the doctor and medic. I learned later that they died." The next day his shipmates were buried at sea and the *Farquhar* made its way to Argentina so the wounded could be treated in a hospital.[28]

Although the loss of the USS *Leopold*, *Fiske*, and *Fechteler* so early after the arrival of destroyer escorts to the battle was disheartening to the Allies, these tough little ships and their courageous young crews were demonstrating their mettle and were credited with helping to turn the tide in the Battle of the Atlantic, the longest and most costly battle of World War II. DEs sunk fifteen U-boats in the first six months of 1944. Before their arrival German submarines had been exacting a heavy toll on Allied merchant ships in the North Atlantic, where the Allies were simply not prepared for a submarine battle.

In 1939 Allied losses exceeded a quarter of a million tons. The following year, as German activity picked up in the North Atlantic, this number jumped to 7.8 million tons. It soon became clear to many, especially President Roosevelt, that something had to be done to curtail the U-boats, otherwise Germany would have a stranglehold over Atlantic Ocean shipping lanes, threatening not only England's survival but also the survival of the United States. The few vessels that were available—a handful of destroyers, wooden submarine chasers, patrol craft, corvettes, and even luxury yachts pressed into government service—were overtaxed and unable to keep up with the increasing number of U-boats prowling through American waters, often right along the coastline.

In the summer of 1940, eighteen months before the United States officially entered the war, President Roosevelt initiated the destroyer escort program. World War II naval historian Samuel Eliot Morison said the president proposed to Frank Knox, a Republican just appointed by Democrat Roosevelt to serve as secretary of the navy, that two experimental DEs be built. Following Roosevelt's direction, the Bureau of Ships produced its first plan for a DE two months later, with additional plans drafted in the fall. But further progress toward DE construction was halted when the General Board of the Navy decided it would be better to use the nation's limited money and steel resources to build destroyers rather than these new type of ships. In what later would be regarded as a serious and costly mistake, Roosevelt acquiesced and agreed to shelve plans to construct DEs.[29]

The president did move ahead on another plan he considered critical "for continental defense in the face of grave danger." Fifty old "four piper" World War I destroyers and ten Coast Guard cutters would be traded to England in exchange for rights to construct naval and air bases on Crown colonies in the Western Hemisphere, including Bermuda, the Bahamas, Jamaica, St. Lucia, Trinidad, Antigua, British Guiana, and Newfoundland. This "destroyers for bases" deal was essential, FDR said, for the United States' "peace and security."

Fortunately for the nation, Roosevelt, who loved the Navy and all things nautical, had taken significant steps to rebuild the Navy after his arrival at the White House in 1933. He had allocated some $281 million from the National Industrial Recovery Act to start rebuilding the Navy. "This was one of the finest and most statesmanlike things Roosevelt ever did," remarked Adm. Harold G. Bowen, who served as chief of the Navy's Engineering Bureau and, later, as chief of the Office of Naval Research. Roosevelt knew if this allocation became public, especially with the increasingly isolationist and pacifist sentiment in the country, he would be roundly criticized. "Claude, we got away with murder this time," FDR reportedly told Claude A. Swanson, his secretary of the navy. But Roosevelt's project did put plenty of people to work building ships, something that few could object to as the Great Depression gripped the country and unemployment continued to soar.[30]

Meanwhile Germany stepped up its assault on the Atlantic shipping lanes, sinking twenty vessels in October 1940 during a raid called "the night of the long knives," and six months later German U-boats sunk forty-five ships in the North Atlantic in a single month alone. Some German U-boat attacks brazenly took place right along the East Coast of the United States both during the day and at night, with Coney Island's Ferris wheel and the lights of New York City glowing in the nearby distance.

"Been fired on by U-boat and sinking slowly. Require assistance," was the SOS message picked up by a radio receiver in Long Island, New York, in the early morning hours of 3 January 1940. The Swedish freighter *Kiruna*, heading with a cargo of iron ore to Baltimore, Maryland, had been torpedoed about 2,200 miles east of New York, and the neutral vessel, along with its captain and crew of thirty-nine sailors, was sinking in the stormy waters of the North Atlantic. Meanwhile, another Swedish freighter, the *Svarton*, was torpedoed by *U-58* off the coast of Scotland, sinking in about a minute and a half, sending twenty of its crew members to their death. Eleven survivors were clinging to a life raft when they were rescued by a fishing trawler.

A few days later, the British freighter *Langleeford* was torpedoed and sunk without warning in the North Atlantic. Fifteen survivors, who managed to make it to two lifeboats as their vessel sunk below the raging waves, were in for a bit of a surprise as *U-26*, the submarine that had just torpedoed them, approached. "The commander (Heinz Scheringer) asked the name of our ship and also the names of some of us," one of the survivors said. "When told that we had only provisions of biscuits and water he supplemented these with two bottles of rum, tobacco, cigarettes, matches and a package of bandages. He was pretty decent to us, even though he sank our ship without warning." Remarkably the survivors were able to reach the western coast of Ireland after being at sea for fifty-six hours, using a sail as well as their oars to make it to safety.

Hostilities between England and Germany also had a chilling effect on plans to build the world's biggest luxury ocean liner designed to carry passengers between Britain and New York. Although fighting was under way, work continued on the new *Queen Elizabeth*, a 1,000-foot, 84,000-ton floating palace, with the ship ready for its maiden voyage just after the waters of the North Atlantic became alive with German U-boats, sinking virtually every vessel they encountered. Quietly and without the usual fanfare accompanying the maiden voyage of an ocean liner, the vessel slipped out of Clydeside and began its passage across the U-boat-infested North Atlantic on 26 February. British minister Winston Churchill wanted to shield the new vessel from becoming a target of German bombers, so he ordered it into exile in America.

In what the *New York Times* described as the "most spectacular and dangerous maiden voyage in maritime history," the ocean liner zigzagged in a mad dash across the Atlantic, arriving off Nantucket Island the evening of 6 March. The next day the vessel, camouflaged in battleship gray, with a still-unfinished luxurious interior, docked safely at Pier 90 in New York City, alongside three of the world's other great ocean liners, the *Queen Mary, Normandie*, and *Mauritania*—all far from the reach of any German submarines or bombers.[31]

Winston Churchill, who had become prime minister in May, was becoming increasingly alarmed as Adolph Hitler's U-boats continued to send more and more merchant ships to the bottom of the ocean. On 7 December 1940 Churchill wrote President Roosevelt a four-thousand-word letter, which he termed "one of the most important I ever wrote," pleading for help to curb "the present destructive losses at sea." In addition to munitions, the prime minister asked for financial help for his cash-strapped country, noting that England had only $2 billion in cash to pay for $5 billion in orders from U.S. factories.[32]

When Churchill's letter arrived Roosevelt was where he most loved to be—on the water. The sea-loving president, just elected to an unprecedented third term, had decided to escape the cold Washington weather, boarding the heavy cruiser USS *Tuscaloosa* for a vacation cruise to southern waters, including Florida and the Caribbean. While the cruiser was at anchor, a Navy seaplane delivered Churchill's correspondence, a letter that profoundly affected the president. Roosevelt sat in his wheelchair on deck alone, reading and re-reading Churchill's letter. It was there, while FDR was enjoying the refreshing salt air and blue waters of the Caribbean, that he hatched an idea that would allow him to provide England with critical financial and other support for the war effort, while still abiding by the law.

The Lend-Lease program thus was conceived, a brilliant and creative means devised by Roosevelt himself to circumvent a 1934 law that forbade the United States from trading with any warring nation, except on a cash basis. The overall goal of Roosevelt's program was to provide material aid to countries whose defenses were vital to the defense of the United States.[33]

Roosevelt returned from his southern cruise with a healthy tan and some big ideas on how the United States could help England fight the Nazis. During a White House press conference on 17 December 1940, the president spoke publicly for the first time about his Lend-Lease concept, which he said would not only help England but also increase productivity here at home, thereby boosting America's national security as well:

> Suppose my neighbor's home catches fire, and I have got a length of garden hose four or five hundred feet away; but, my Heaven, if he can take my garden hose and connect it up with his hydrant, I may help him to put out his fire. Now, what do I do? I don't say to him before the operation, "neighbor, my garden hose cost me $15; you have got to pay me $15 for it."
>
> What is the transaction that goes on? I don't want $15—I want my garden hose back after the fire is over. All right. If it goes through the fire all right, intact, without any damage to it, he gives it back to me and thanks me very much for the use of it. Suppose it gets smashed up—holes in it—during the fire; we don't have to have too much formality about it, but I say to him, "I was glad to lend you that hose; I see I can't use it any more, it's all smashed up." He says, "How many feet of it were there?" I tell him, "there were 150 feet of it." He said, "all right, I will replace it." Now if you get a nice garden hose back, I am in pretty good shape.

As he often did in his fireside chats, Roosevelt used this homespun simile to explain his plan to help Great Britain, adding, "If you lend certain munitions and get the munitions back at the end of the war, if they are intact—haven't been hurt—you are all right; if they have been damaged or deteriorated or lost completely, it seems to me you come out pretty well if you have them replaced by the fellow that you have lent them to."[34]

Four days after his traditional family Christmas celebration at the White House, Roosevelt stepped up his efforts to garner public support for his Lend-Lease proposal, and explain to the American people the great peril the nation would face unless action was taken now. On the evening of 29 December, London was burning as the Nazis bombed the city in one of their heaviest attacks to date. Meanwhile, Roosevelt, who had not walked since polio paralyzed his legs in 1921, was wheeled into the diplomatic reception room in the White House to deliver his sixteenth fireside chat to millions of Americans gathered around their radios in homes all across the country. In the White House the president had his own audience seated before him, including his devoted mother, Sara, movie actor Clark Gable and his wife, and Carole Lombard, along with a host of presidential staff members.[35]

"We must be the great arsenal of democracy," the president declared. "For this is an emergency as serious as war itself." Roosevelt warned that "if Great Britain goes down, the Axis powers will control the continents of Europe, Asia, Africa, Australia, and the high seas—and they will be in a position to bring enormous military and naval resources against this hemisphere. It is no exaggeration to say that all of us, in all the Americas, would be living at the point of a gun—a gun loaded with explosive bullets, economic as well as military," arguing that the width of the oceans no longer protects America as it did in the days of the clipper ship.[36]

The campaign worked, and despite grumbling that the Lend-Lease program was giving Roosevelt a blank check, Congress approved the proposal two months after it was submitted and appropriated the $7 billion requested by Roosevelt. The president signed it into law on 11 March 1941, two days after U-boats sunk five Allied ships in the Atlantic Ocean and four days before thirteen other Allied ships were sent to the bottom of the sea by German submarines. The next month U-boats sank forty-five Allied merchant ships, and in May another fifty-eight Allied ships were destroyed by the Germans. Thousands of merchant seamen were being sent to their deaths as U-boat attacks were reaching a fevered pitch.

Roosevelt gave Prime Minister Churchill the good news about the legislation in a personal note within hours of passage of the Lend-Lease program, and within minutes of the president signing the legislation into law, Army and Navy war materials were speeding their way to Great Britain and Greece. Churchill responded: "Our blessings from the whole British Empire go out to you and the American nation for this very present help in time of trouble."[37]

Now the stage was being set to begin a monumental shipbuilding program, with many of those ships being sent to England, France, and other Allied countries at war with Germany. So in what was nothing short of remarkable, the U.S. government joined with private industrialists to undertake the largest shipbuilding project in American and, perhaps, world history. From 1939 to 1945, 5,777 ships were constructed in more than seventy shipyards, which sprung up, some seemingly overnight, throughout the nation.

More than 640,000 Americans, most of whom had little or no experience in the shipbuilding business, were put to work to start building ships at a faster pace than the Axis powers could sink them. More than 50 million tons of cargo carriers and tankers were built, with 18 million tons built in 1943 alone. This monumental undertaking, helping to create a "bridge of ships" across the ocean, would start to reverse or at least slow down Germany's extraordinary success in the North Atlantic.[38]

But what about those destroyer escorts that FDR wanted the Navy to build back in 1940? As more and more merchant vessels, some of which were flying the Stars and Stripes, continued to be sunk by German U-boats, the Navy brass decided that maybe Roosevelt was right in wanting to build what he later called "speedy and dangerous" warships—the destroyer escorts—to protect convoys of vital supplies, and also search out and destroy those prowling U-boats. But there were still doubters among Roosevelt's top naval advisors, further delaying DE construction so desperately needed by England. Winston Churchill would not be pleased.

On a beautiful June day in 1942, the prime minister delivered his plea directly to the president, in his second wartime visit to the United States. As the small plane carrying Winston Churchill banked over the majestic Hudson River, President Roosevelt waited patiently below in the driver's seat of his blue, hand-controlled Ford. The plane bumped as it landed on the Hackensack airfield near Hyde Park, in what Churchill described as the "roughest bump landing" he had ever experienced. After greeting his English friend, FDR drove Churchill around his Dutchess County estate, talking business and giving the prime minister more than a few scares as the president "poised and backed on the grass verges of the precipices over the Hudson," and drove his car through fields and woods, successfully playing hide-and-seek with his Secret Service guards, who were trying to follow the president. Not to worry, however, as Churchill would soon learn that FDR was quite skilled at navigating his car around back roads using the hand controls that had been installed to allow the paralyzed president to drive. Although the primary purpose of Churchill's visit was to settle on military plans for 1942–43 and discuss with Roosevelt the development of the atomic bomb, he took the opportunity to describe the U-boat attacks on shipping as "our greatest and most immediate danger," raising the need for escort vessels once again.[39]

When Roosevelt and Churchill met in Washington later that week, the subject of DE construction was raised by Adm. Ernest J. King. Opening the conference just before lunchtime, King began by declaring that one ship saved was worth two ships lost, his way of saying that the escort program should be given high priority. Adm. Emory S. Land, head of the War Shipping Administration disagreed, noting that the DE program would use up valuable steel and diesel engines and prevent the building of 100 to 150 merchant cargo ships.[40] Lewis W. Douglas, Land's deputy, agreed with his boss, adding that merchant ships should be top priority because they were in short supply. Churchill, who had voiced strong support for King's stand that DEs should be built, said, "One ship saved may be better than two ships sunk, but it is also far better that one ship deliver munitions to the fighting front than no ships at all."[41] The conference ended, and Churchill would return to England on 25 June without any firm timetable as to when the first DE would roll off the production line.

Franklin Roosevelt could not have been satisfied with this outcome. As assistant secretary of the Navy under President Woodrow Wilson, FDR had been a strong proponent of small vessels—much smaller than DEs—to combat the German submarine menace in World War I and helped influence the development of sub chasers, 110-foot wooden vessels, nicknamed the "splinter fleet." Manned mostly by amateur yachtsmen from the Naval Reserve, these spunky little warships had two officers and about twenty-five enlisted men on board. They were equipped with underwater hydrophones for detecting submarines and two machine guns and two 3-inch, 23-mm guns for battle. By the end of World War I, some 440 sub chasers had been commissioned, thanks in large part to the support of Assistant Navy Secretary Roosevelt.

FDR's interest in antisubmarine warfare can be traced all the way back to the 1920s, during his stint as assistant secretary of the navy. In an article he wrote while vacationing in Warm Springs, Georgia, Roosevelt told of a trip he took to Brunswick, Georgia, and Biloxi, Mississippi, to hear petitions from residents anxious to have the federal government establish naval stations in their harbors. "The harbor entrance in both cases proved too shallow," Roosevelt wrote, "but I remember chiefly for the possum banquet they gave me—every known variety of possum cooked in every know variety of style I ate them all." But dining on possum, one of FDR's favorite dishes, was not the only thing he remembered from his visit.

"It was on this trip, however," FDR stated, "that I first formed the idea of the need in modern naval warfare for a complete chain of anti-submarine and anti-aircraft stations the whole length of our coast. It was obvious that in time of peace the Navy Department could not possibly have enough money each year to maintain such stations, yet it was obvious to me we should need them in time of war."

Roosevelt tried to encourage the General Board of the Navy to prepare a plan of coast patrol for use in the event of war; however, the board rebuffed Roosevelt because they did not think "it worthwhile to bother its head about such little matters." Roosevelt later said, "It is amusing to note that a couple of months before we actually got into the World War, in 1917, the higher naval officers did a lot of running around and planning for the Naval patrol stations which we maintained throughout the war."[42]

During World War II, some of the delay in the construction of escort vessels may also be traced to internal bickering between the Navy and the Army. Battling Nazi U-boats, Navy officials believed, was the responsibility of that agency. The Army had a different view, according to Secretary of War Henry L. Stimson, who fought to change the operational arrangement that put all antisubmarine forces, air and sea, Army and Navy, under control of the Navy.

Stimson argued—and even went so far as to lecture the president and Knox—that the newly developed tool called radar should be installed on Army bombers for antisubmarine duty. Stimson said the ship sinkings were having a devastating effect on the Army with the loss of supplies and equipment necessary to fight the war in Europe. "Though submarine success might hurt naval pride," Stimson wrote in his autobiography, "it was the Army which more seriously felt the pinch."[43] Admiral King believed that "escort is not just *one* way to handling the submarine menace; it is the *only* way that gives any promise of success."

Although King agreed that planes should be equipped with radar to fight submarines, they should remain under the control of the Navy and provide supplemental assistance to his ships. Neither he nor Secretary Knox honestly believed airplanes were effective submarine killers. He argued strongly, and eventually successfully, for construction of more ships to ensure that "every ship that sails the seas [is] under constant close protection." This certainly proved no insignificant task, with more than seven thousand miles of Atlantic coastal sea-lanes, not including the ocean convoy system to Great Britain and Iceland, as well as traffic to the east coast of South America.

King was not alone in his views on the need for escort vessels. The *New York Times*, in a strongly worded editorial in December 1942, urged construction of large numbers of escort vessels, especially what they described as the "rugged, fast, long-ranging destroyer escorts," to protect merchant ships in the North Atlantic. "We cannot built too many ships," the editorial stated, "but there is not much use building great numbers of merchant ships unless we protect them adequately. Today, not enough escort vessels of various types are being built." The *Times*, seeming to echo King's viewpoint, stated: "More escort vessels can materially reduce such losses—particularly so if enough are built not only to provide adequate defensive screens for all convoys but to create so-called 'hunting groups.'"[44]

Finally, in March 1943, the internal disputes and reticence to build escorts started to be overshadowed as Nazi submarines, using wolf-pack tactics, pounded away at shipping in the North Atlantic, sinking an average of three ships every day. More than 500,000 tons of much-needed supplies were lost in the month of March alone. Admiral Karl Döenitz, a former U-boat commander in World War I chosen by Adolph Hitler to head U-boat forces in World War II, would send his submarines out in a fan pattern, with an advance or reconnaissance submarine looking for slow-moving convoys. Once located, Döenitz would coordinate the wolf pack's attack from his central command at Lorient, a French base on the Bay of Biscay, radioing each "wolf" within the area to participate in the convoy attack. This was a highly successful military strategy, one that threatened to defeat Allied forces in the North Atlantic.[45]

Taking a page from Döenitz's playbook, it appeared that the time had come to more efficiently coordinate antisubmarine activity, placing it—at least in the United States—under the umbrella of a central Navy command. Thus the so-called Tenth Fleet was born. A fleet without any ships or guns, and with only a handful of men, it would do its battle huddled over desks in the Navy Department. The men would use brains rather than brawn devising plans to battle the U-boats, for the first time unifying all intelligence and operations under a single command. This type of operation had never been attempted in the history of the Navy.

As Germany's March U-boat blitz continued to send merchant vessels to the bottom of the sea, a conference was called to address the U-boat menace.

American, British, and Canadian officials met for twelve days in Washington in sessions aimed at curbing the success of Admiral Döenitz's wolf packs. The stage finally appeared set for entrance of the previously authorized but long delayed destroyer escort into the thick of battle in the stormy North Atlantic.

But before destroyer escorts would start rolling off the shipyard launching ways, President Roosevelt's predilection for using small vessels to battle U-boats already had taken another interesting twist. Vincent Astor, a close friend and Hudson River valley neighbor of FDR, would propose in spring of 1942 a scheme to equip fishing boats with two-way voice radios so recreational boaters could alert the Navy when they spotted a U-boat or other suspicious object.

Astor, related to FDR by marriage, was founder and owner of *Newsweek* magazine and owned the 263-foot luxury yacht, the *Nourmahal*, that took FDR on three lengthy vacation cruises, two after he became president. Like FDR, Astor loved to sail, and beginning in 1933 and stretching to the early war years, he performed clandestine spy duties for Roosevelt under the guise of "scientific" or fishing trips. As storm clouds gathered around an increasingly unstable world Astor, a commander in the U.S. Naval Reserves would monitor activities in the Caribbean, the Panama Canal Zone, Latin America, the Galápagos, and the Marshall Islands, reporting directly to President Roosevelt.[46]

So when Astor, a former submariner in World War I, proposed equipping fishing boats with radios, President Roosevelt jumped at the idea. "My Navy has been definitely slack in preparing for this submarine war off our coast," Roosevelt wrote to Prime Minister Churchill in March 1942. "As I need not tell you, most naval officers have declined in the past to think in terms of any vessel of less than two thousand tons." Roosevelt told Churchill that England learned that lesson two years earlier. "We still have to learn it," FDR said, stating that he had "begged, borrowed and stolen every vessel of every description over eighty feet in length."[47]

Franklin Roosevelt also was intrigued when fellow white-flanneled yachtsman Alfred Stanford of New York, commodore of the Cruising Club of America, proposed that yachtsmen volunteer their time and yachts to patrol offshore looking for U-boats. Roosevelt loved the idea; however, the Navy did not. Even though U-boats continued to have their own way with Allied vessels in the North Atlantic, the Navy brass did not feel the amateur yachtsmen were up to the job.[48]

After a spat of bad publicity, fanned by the Navy saying they had plenty of small vessels and did not need the private yachts, Admiral King reversed the Navy decision and in May 1942 ordered the formation of the coastal picket patrol, composed of luxury sailing yachts, fishing vessels, and motor boats. They were equipped with ship-to-shore radios, machines guns and some with depth charges, and a grid chart showing which sector they would patrol. The pickets patrolled from the Gulf of Maine to the Gulf of Mexico.

Arthur D. Camp, a volunteer who signed up for a thirty-day stint with the picket patrol, was assigned to guard the Atlantic Ocean between Fire Island, New York, and Nantucket Island, Massachusetts. He was on board a 78-foot sailing schooner, which was equipped with an 80-horsepower engine, hot and cold shower, and an eleven-member crew, including an engineer and a cook. Camp said it took twenty-four hours to sail out to their assigned grid using dead reckoning and the sun to find the way. Once at the site, they shortened the sails and tried to stay in their designated areas watching for U-boats. But with a stiff wind, the schooner would drift off grid in five or six hours.[49]

"When our skipper found that we had drifted off the edge of the grid, he would order us to hoist more sail and we would then tack back to the weather boundary of the station. These maneuvers were repeated endlessly," Camp said, explaining that the sailing tactics employed on picket duty were entirely different than those of a normal yachtsman, who would get the most speed out of the vessel as he raced to his destination. The yachtsmen would stand watches, six hours on and six hours off, from noon to midnight, and four hours on and off from midnight until the next noon. Lookouts were doubled at night. They got very little sleep, and sometimes, when something unidentified was spotted, a yachtsman had to climb up the ratline to the masthead to get a better look. "That is a real sensation when the ship is pitching and rolling, as the top of the mast lashes out like a buggy whip and will pitch a man off if he doesn't have a leech-like grip," Camp stated.[50]

The coastal picket patrol had some successes despite its limitations. During an unannounced Navy test in August 1942, a squadron of ten planes swung across Cape Cod before heading south and west for Philadelphia. Although no naval vessel or shore station reported contact with the planes, four of the coastal picket patrol did report the planes "promptly and accurately." Another picket patrolling south of Long Island in a light fog spotted a U-boat just one hundred yards away. Although the yacht did not have a depth charge, it did man its machine guns and started firing at the submarine, which vanished under the water. In January 1943 Admiral King ordered the picket force cut 35 percent for economy reasons and because smaller Coast Guard cutters were starting to come online.[51]

Another idea strongly supported by President Roosevelt and Secretary Knox, was the construction of small, 1,968-ton cargo freighters propelled by sixteen 110-horsepower gasoline engines. The 270-foot ship *Sea Otter II* could be mass-produced at a low cost and would be able to escape damage by submarines because its shallow draft would allow torpedoes to pass harmlessly beneath the vessel. Designed by an automobile engineer and retired Navy commander, the vessel was to have a ten-foot draft (although the actual draft was nearly double this amount) and gasoline engines without mufflers, which could alert an enemy submarine within a fifty-mile radius. The ship had a lot of problems.

After the *Sea Otter's* maiden voyage in October 1941, Secretary Knox advised Roosevelt that he had already organized a corporation and that money had been provided for the initial forty-eight ships. Knox said that once the sea trials, under way off Charleston, were finished they would be ready for a "quick start." President Roosevelt, who frequently tinkered with ship designs, was "delighted" with Knox's report but said that he did not believe these small vessels should be used on the North Atlantic, except in the summer time, but that they could replace larger ships in the Gulf of Mexico, the West Indies, and the East and West Coasts of South America, as well as in other areas where heavy seas do not often occur.

Although Roosevelt had a lot of faith in the ship's potential, the Maritime Commission and Bureau of Ships were reluctant to divert scarce resources to its construction. Roosevelt, however, remained adamant in his belief that the vessel could serve a purpose. During a news conference on 10 March 1942, the president said the *Sea Otter* was the right size when it was designed but "like so many things it got bigger—grew—the tonnage grew." He said the original idea, which he still believed in, was to use the small ship in coastal trade in the West Indies and along the coast of South America, and in smaller harbors. Although Roosevelt contended that there was a "great deal of merit in the basic idea" and felt that more tests were necessary, the *Sea Otter* idea was not to be. No further design work was done and no more sea trials or tests were conducted.[52]

Vincent Astor's fishing boat idea also was tried but with less success than the picket fleet. By September 1942 some 625 fishing vessels had been equipped with radios, and a year later that number had increased to 845 boats, watching for U-boats as they fished the waters from Maine to Florida. Despite good intentions, however, few valid reports of U-boats were actually made by the fishermen. Furthermore several fishing boats were sunk and crews killed by German submarines prowling along the eastern seaboard. Some fishing boat captains became reluctant to radio sightings for fear of retaliation by U-boats, instead adhering to the age-old adage that "our main business is to catch fish."

This program, like the picket patrol, would not be the ultimate answer to elimination of the U-boat menace, which continued at an alarming pace. Yet if some of these measures had been tried earlier in the war, there might have been a better outcome earlier and the lives of some merchant seamen might have been spared. However, by now it was too late for them to significantly reverse the German slaughter escalating in the North Atlantic. Clearly a stronger deterrent was needed and needed without delay. It appeared the stage finally had been set for the arrival of the destroyer escort—and not a moment too soon.[53]

3

Reversing the Tide

Richard Warner was sipping a cold beer in the officer's club at the Brooklyn Navy Yard when the telephone rang. The twenty-nine-year-old Navy lieutenant, just appointed executive officer on the destroyer escort *Kendall C. Campbell*, reached over and picked up the receiver.

"This is President Roosevelt," the caller on the other end announced to a startled Warner. "Is Frank there?" Warner replied, "No, sir, he went to the head." The president told Warner to give FDR Jr. the message that he had found an ice cream machine at the submarine base in New London, Connecticut, for his son's DE, the *Ulvert M. Moore*. The president promised to have the machine flown to Norfolk, Virginia, FDR Jr.'s next stop.

Warner, who had just finished a tour of duty as commander of a 110-foot sub chaser, had been rushed up to the Brooklyn Navy Yard in August 1944 to become executive officer of the *Campbell* after the ship's captain gave the previous incumbent an unsatisfactory fitness rating. Upon arriving in Brooklyn he met Capt. Robert W. Johnson, who told Warner that the top priority for his new executive officer was to find an ice cream machine for his ship. "I don't give a damn what you do with the ship," Johnson told a surprised Warner, "but I want an ice cream machine."

Thinking this an odd but relatively simple assignment, Warner immediately went ashore and checked the supply depot. He was told that ice cream machines were not part of the standard equipment installed on DEs. So Warner checked the yellow pages and also visited a couple of wholesale companies. No luck. It looked like he was about to fail the first assignment given him by his new skipper and probably would end up getting an unsatisfactory fitness report just like his predecessor.

That evening, Warner was at the officer's club bar enjoying some liquid refreshments when a tall young officer sat down beside him. The officer was captain of the DE *Ulvert M. Moore* and his name was Franklin Delano Roosevelt Jr. Roosevelt had just finished his shakedown cruise in Bermuda and was in the Brooklyn yard for some R&R before heading to the Pacific.

"How are you getting along with your new skipper?" Roosevelt asked Warner, adding, "I understand the *Campbell* is having a few problems." Warner said he really did not have a chance to talk with the skipper, except for a brief meeting that morning. "The skipper told me that he didn't give a damn what I did about the ship, but he wanted an ice cream machine on board."

FDR Jr. turned to one of his junior officers, also propped up at the bar, and asked, "Have we got one?" The officer went down to the ship and returned a few minutes later reporting no ice cream machine on board. "I'll call my dad and see what he can do," Roosevelt said, dialing the White House on the officer's club phone. Warner said FDR Jr. chatted with his father about his ship and his upcoming assignments before he asked the president about the ice cream machine. "Right here in the office," President Roosevelt told his son, "there are three or four guys with lots of gold braid on them, but none of them knows anything about ice cream machines." The president promised to check and get back to his son.

Captain Roosevelt hung up the phone and went to the head. A few minutes later the president called back. Warner recalled President Roosevelt saying, "Just tell him that I've got an ice cream machine for him, and it will be in Norfolk when you arrive in a couple of days." Mustering his courage, Warner spoke up: "Wait a minute, Mr. President, I'm the exec on the 443 and I'm the guy that instigated this thing. We are running buddies and my skipper told me all he wants is an ice cream machine." Roosevelt interrupted, "Oh, you want one too?" Warner said he did, and when the two ships arrived at Norfolk after escorting the carrier *Shamrock Bay* from New York, there were two ice cream machines waiting.

"You can't imagine the service we got," Warner said, not quite prepared for the VIP treatment they received. The massive ice cream machines were floating on barges with cranes and tow boats. "They came in and cut off half the after-deck house, and cranes hoisted these stainless steel ice cream machines into the back of the two destroyer escorts." His first mission accomplished, Warner never got so much as a "thank you" from his new skipper, who, he recalled, stayed to himself, ate ice cream nonstop, and had a fondness for New Orleans–style chicory coffee.

Later Warner would discover why the ice cream machine was so important to his new skipper. During the ship's shakedown cruise in Bermuda, the *Campbell* had a vintage wooden bucket–type ice cream machine with a hand crank. "The captain had the six mess attendants cranking the machine all the time right by his companionway," Warner said, noting once in a while some ice cream would make it into officer's country, but most of it went to the private stash of Captain Johnson. Certainly none ever made its way to the crew's mess. On the way back from the shakedown cruise, the old ice cream machine mysteriously disappeared. The vessel was searched, the crew was interrogated, and twelve hours of general quarters was enforced. Threats were made of no liberty for crew members once they arrived in New York unless the machine was returned.

The ice cream machine was never found, and most agree it likely was resting at the bottom of the sea. Sticking to his word, Captain Johnson restricted the crew to the ship while in the navy yard, although a good number of them went AWOL. No one ever admitted to tossing the old ice cream machine overboard, but with the modern automatic one now on board, everyone—captain, officers, and crew—would enjoy ice cream just like crews of the larger warships, where such machines were standard equipment. Ice cream machines installed, both ships departed Hampton Roads, Virginia, on 5 October, escorting two oilers to Aruba in the Dutch West Indies and then to Balboa, Canal Zone, passing through the Panama Canal on their way to San Diego, California.

Warner, who grew up in California and enjoyed sailing small boats most of his life, recalled FDR Jr. as a "great guy" who also was a very competent commander and good ship handler; he also remembered morale on Roosevelt's ship as being "very good." Of course, Warner said some of that good morale might have been attributed to the amount of special attention given to the *Moore*, due in no small part to its captain with the famous name. Warner recalled that when they were passing through the Panama Canal, Roosevelt "spent a lot of time loading up the ship with liquor," which certainly must have pleased FDR Jr.'s officers but made Warner "more than a bit envious."[1]

The role played by destroyer escorts in both the Atlantic and Pacific theaters was key to the success of the Allies in World War II. Because of bureaucratic bickering, a shortage of materials, and other reasons, they arrived very late to the war, but they were instrumental in protecting convoys and seeking out and destroying both German and Japanese vessels. In fact, Robert E. Sherwood, biographer of one of President Roosevelt's top aides, Harry Hopkins, said the single outstanding American failure, the avoidance of which might have shortened the war, was the lack of destroyer escorts. Of this, Sherwood said, the postwar opinion was unanimous among those involved in the Roosevelt administration.[2]

Captain Herbert A. Werner, a German U-boat commander, lends support to that theory. In March 1943 Werner noted that "the U-boat Force sank over 650,000 tons of Allied shipping—and suffered a sharp and puzzling increase in losses." He attributes the sudden reversal of fortunes for the Germans to the arrival of destroyer escorts, small aircraft carriers, and much-improved radar that had come on the scene, resulting in the destruction of fully 40 percent of the U-boat force within a few weeks, according to Werner. "The Allied counteroffensive permanently reversed the tide of the battle. Almost overnight, the hunters had become the hunted, and through the rest of the war our boats were slaughtered at a fearful rate," Werner noted.[3] Over the course of the war, of the 859 U-boats sent on patrol to the front lines of the war, some 88 percent were sunk, sending more than 30,000 German sailors to their graves at the bottom of the sea.[4]

Prime Minister Winston Churchill was one of the staunchest proponents for the construction of escort vessels. In a letter penned to FDR on Halloween 1942, Churchill called the U-boat menace "our worst danger," adding that "the spectacle of all these splendid ships being built, sent to sea crammed with priceless food and munitions and being sunk—three or four every day—torments me day and night." He continued, "Not only does this attack cripple our war energies and threaten our life, but it arbitrarily limits the might of the United States coming into the struggle." To be blunt, Churchill warned Roosevelt, the "oceans, which were your shield, threaten to become your cage."

"I presume," Roosevelt replied, "that we shall never satisfy ourselves as to the relative need of merchant ships versus escort vessels. In this case I believe we should try to have our cake and eat it too." The president went on to assure Churchill, "We have increased our escort program recently by 70 for 1943, so that we should turn out 336 escort vessels during the next calendar year. I am asking Admiral King to confer with your representative here and make arrangements about the distribution of these ships."[5]

Enter William Francis Gibbs, a self-taught naval architect whose buttoned-down, business-like style would help to change the equation in the Battle of the Atlantic, giving the U.S. Navy the new class of warships, the DEs, which would quickly prove their worth on the high seas. It appeared that the ferocious and highly successful U-boats were finally about to meet their match. Gibbs' influence over American shipbuilding was monumental throughout the course of the war. In fact, one naval officer said the enormous expansion of American sea power during the war was due to three factors: "the Navy, American industry, and Gibbs."[6]

Sporting steel-rimmed spectacles and often wearing shiny clothes with patches to cover holes, Gibbs—known to his friends as William Francis or simply W. F.—was the United States' foremost naval architect and head of the firm Gibbs and Cox, the largest private ship–designing firm in the world. His firm turned out designs for thousands of wartime vessels, nearly three-quarters of all naval vessels built during the war, including Liberty ships, landing ships, destroyers, cruisers, destroyer escorts, picket ships, mine sweepers, cutters, icebreakers, aircraft carriers, tenders, repair ships, and tankers—some $12 billion worth of ships. At its peak, Gibbs and Cox issued 10,000 blueprints a month and 6,700 purchase orders each day, according to a company history. During the war years the firm designed more than 63 percent of all oceangoing merchant vessels as well. Gibbs centralized purchasing and revolutionized the mass production of ships, designing them to travel faster and farther, and he was hailed by the Navy's chief engineer as the "greatest influence on naval design since John Ericsson," who in 1862 designed the *Monitor*, which stopped the Confederate's *Merrimac* during the historic Civil War battle at Hampton Roads.[7]

All of this came from a man who never took a single lesson on ship design in his life and had no formal training in architecture or engineering. In 1906 Gibbs, born to a wealthy Philadelphia family, attended Harvard University, where he refused to follow the formal curriculum and instead studied economics and science, graduating without a degree. His father, a prominent and successful financier, did not think highly of engineers, regarding them as impractical and unstable. He wanted his son to study law.

In 1911 William Francis enrolled in Columbia Law School, where he did graduate with a law degree, the same year he also took a master's degree in economics. But Gibbs always had an interest in ships and the sea. Like his older contemporary and later boss, Franklin Delano Roosevelt, Gibbs often tinkered with ship designs and sketched his first drawing of a boat at the age of three (FDR sketched his first sailboat in a letter to his mother at the age of five, and FDR also attended Harvard and Columbia Law School, as did William Francis.) Designing ships evolved from a hobby to a passion for this self-taught naval engineer and eventually consumed Gibbs for the rest of his life.

During his college days Gibbs devoured books on marine engineering and naval architecture, which had little to do with his actual class work. His dormitory room was filled with blueprints and engineering drawings of ships. Gibbs daydreamed about ship design.[8] After working briefly as a lawyer—and hating every minute of it—William Francis and his brother, Frederic H. Gibbs, joined the International Mercantile Marine Company in 1915 and, with the backing of J. P. Morgan and President Woodrow Wilson's secretary of the navy, Josephus Daniels, started to work on the design for a 1,000-foot ocean liner capable of crossing the Atlantic Ocean in four days. Sadly for the Gibbs brothers, World War I intervened and their plans to design the world's largest and fastest ocean liner were shelved.[9]

William Francis quickly rose through the ranks and became chief of construction for the company in 1919. Following the war he and his brother organized Gibbs Brothers in New York City in 1922 (succeeded by Gibbs and Cox in 1929, when Daniel H. Cox, a prominent yacht designer, joined the firm) and, at the request of the Federal Shipping Board, Gibbs undertook a project to convert the mammoth German ship, the *Vaterland*, into a luxury American ocean liner. After being taken as a war prize by the United States at the start of the conflict, the 950-foot vessel did duty as a troopship, shepherding more than 110,000 U.S. troops to France and Germany, the largest ocean liner ever to fly the Stars and Stripes. Renamed the *Leviathan* at the urging of Mrs. Woodrow Wilson, there was widespread public support for converting the ship into an American passenger liner at war's end.

Gibbs undertook the assignment with great gusto. He traveled to Germany to secure a copy of the ship's original plans only to find that its builders, Blohm and Voss, wanted $1 million for a copy of the plans. "I think," remarked Mr. Gibbs quite cooly, "that we will make our own set of working plans from the *Leviathan* itself."[10] Gibbs returned to New York and hired one hundred naval draftsmen, who inspected and measured every square foot of the ship, whose overall area totaled 7.5 acres. They even were required to take meticulous measurements of the ship below its waterline, since there was no dry dock in New York capable of handling a ship the size of the *Leviathan*. After twelve months of extraordinary work, a complete set of drawings of the ship was produced. Down to Newport News the ship went, and one year and $8 million later, a shining new ocean liner was christened, with William Francis Gibbs supervising every detail of its reconversion. The giant ship sailed from Virginia to Boston on its maiden voyage. An exasperated tug captain, obviously overwhelmed by the vessel's size, was overheard saying, "Where do you tie up a line on this goddamned hotel?"[11]

In fact, when William Francis once was asked to provide a definition of a super liner, the nation's foremost naval architect replied, "A super liner is the equivalent of a large cantilever bridge covered with steel plates, containing a power plant that could light any of our larger cities, with a first-class hotel on top." And who would know better than William Francis? He had just created the largest ship in the world.[12]

But William Francis was not yet done designing passenger ships of gargantuan proportions. In 1924 he and his firm designed and supervised construction of the largest and fastest passenger liner built in the United States, the SS *Malolo*, Hawaiian for "flying fish," the first American liner constructed exclusively from his plans. It was here that Gibbs would earn high marks for designing a ship with extensive safety features, including an arrangement of watertight bulkheads, connected by hydraulically operated sliding doors controlled from the bridge, as well as a strengthened hull that was designed not buckle if hit by another ship. As a boy Gibbs was said to be deeply impacted by the *Titanic* disaster and insisted on designing a ship that would not sink.[13]

Although his design of these passenger ships was of herculean proportions, everything else about the complex and secretive William Francis was understated. As head of Gibbs and Cox, he was boss to 2,500 employees yet did not have a private office, desk, leather chair, telephone, or any other executive perks typical for someone in his position. Instead, he worked at a simple drafting table while perched on a wooden stool. Gibbs was nicknamed the "Undertaker" because he often wore a nondescript black suit and tie. It was said he chose this simplified dress because, dressing all in black, he never had to waste time or thought deciding which color tie to wear with which color suit. He was too busy for such foolishness.

Thus his attire was standardized and interchangeable, following the same principle he championed when designing ships: standardize the parts and make them all interchangeable. On the rare occasion that William Francis took time away from his work to relax, engineering was always on his mind. When listening to certain symphonies, especially Bach, the designer said it was like looking through glass at a ship's machinery in action. He also enjoyed watching jugglers because he valued balance and symmetry, and once said that "designing a ship is like keeping nine balls in the air all at one time."[14]

Although regarded as the most important naval architect of the twentieth century, Gibbs shunned ceremony and publicity even though he was married to Vera Cravath, whose father was a prominent New York City attorney and chairman of the Metropolitan Opera for many years. She and William Francis met at a dinner party and married within a month. "She goes her way and I go mine," Gibbs once told a reporter in describing their relationship, perhaps due in no small part to his intense devotion to his work. He went to the office seven days a week, arrived early, and stayed late working on his ship designs. Every day he ate a simple lunch of dry toast and coffee.[15]

Conscientious and goal-driven, Gibbs was exactly the type of individual the United States needed to design and coordinate the largest shipbuilding program in the nation's history. Recognizing the tremendous abilities of William Francis, the Roosevelt administration tapped the naval designer as its new controller of shipbuilding in December 1942. Gibbs agreed to work for no compensation—a so-called dollar-a-year man—and would be directing general policies and coordinating shipbuilding efforts between the War Production Board, the Navy, the Army, and the Maritime Commission. The appointment allowed him to continue supervising Gibbs and Cox by freeing him of any administrative duties in his governmental post.[16]

Gibbs continued directing its day-to-day activities and supervising all details of ship design—as he had since 1929, and as only he could do. He argued that designing ships is a "distinctly personal" undertaking that depends upon the designer's skill and experience and cannot be delegated to others, especially with the tremendous number of designs under way. The Roosevelt administration agreed, and the War Production Board issued a press release on 18 December announcing his appointment.[17]

When Franklin Roosevelt assured Prime Minister Churchill that he would accelerate the production of destroyer escorts in 1943, he may have been confident that the job would be done because he knew William Francis Gibbs would be the man directing it. In what Gibbs and Cox described as the "most complicated and difficult multiple shipbuilding program" the company handled during the entire war, Gibbs, who was said to be able to construct a complete ship in his imagination, and his team went right to work designing the new warship, producing design plans in record time. Although the firm had designed some DEs in 1942 for the British navy, designing an American version in such large numbers and in such a short time frame was, indeed, an undertaking of monumental proportions—but one William Francis relished. Dealing with a shortage of various parts as well as propulsion equipment made the task even more difficult, as designs for four different ships had to be developed in order to meet President Roosevelt's deadline. He had to use whatever parts were available and design the ships accordingly.

Gibbs designed the ships so they could be mass-produced at a rapid pace. The machinery plans for three of the types of diesel-driven DEs were produced simultaneously and completed in seventy-three, eighty-five, and ninety-eight days, according to a company history. "The procurement problem was enormously complicated due to the five designs of ships and numerous changes in the assignment to yards and numbers at yards," Gibbs and Cox stated. But it has been argued that this new technique, along with diesel engines, contributed significantly to the superiority of American naval vessels.[18]

The Navy scheduled 270 DEs for 1943, and a full month ahead of schedule that goal was achieved, due in no small part to the conscientious dedication of William Francis and his staff. In a priority telegram to "The Men and Women of Gibbs & Cox," Rear Adm. Edward L. Cochrane, chief of the Bureau of Ships and one of the earliest proponents for the construction of DEs, praised the firm and its staff, saying, "You who participated in the design of these ships and the procurement of the necessary components must be commended for the part you have played in helping to make possible a record which emphasizes anew the productive genius of American industry." Cochrane said that there should be no problem meeting the three-hundred-ship level set by President Roosevelt in 1943. "You may be justly proud of your contribution to the success of the DE program."[19]

Cochrane and Gibbs shared more than a desire to carry out the president's wishes, however. They possessed a similar work ethic, with Cochrane known to work seven days a week and well into the night during the war years, taking plenty of work with him when he left each evening. An inspiring and strong leader, Cochrane was meticulous in his demand for professionalism, insisting on thorough staff work from the more than six thousand people working in the Bureau of Ships. Earning the nickname "the shirt sleeve admiral," Cochrane frequently would leave off his coat and cap with the gold braid to drop in to drafting rooms and shops to check the progress of his projects. Prior to the United States' entry into the war, Cochrane, who has been credited with coming up with the first design for a DE, traveled to England to study that country's submarines as well as its convoy vessels, which focused on antisubmarine rather than antiaircraft configurations. A direct outgrowth of that visit would be his strong support for the mass production of destroyer escorts as a means to stop the German U-boat slaughter in the North Atlantic.[20]

Another way that Gibbs was able to save time, energy, material, and money was to build scale model ships before the plans for the full-sized vessels were sent to the shipyards. Although building models was not new to the shipbuilding industry, Gibbs' models, which were one-eighth the full-sized ship, reproduced precisely to scale all aspects of the hull, fittings, pipes, ducts, wires, valves, switches, gauges, and even cooking equipment. Every detail of the completed vessel was faithfully reproduced in the model, allowing engineers and draftsmen an opportunity to visualize all aspects of the proposed ship, and correct problems, before the plans were sent out to the shipyard. First, a temporary model of wood or plastic was constructed; further along in the design process, it was replaced with a finished model of wood, plastic, and metal. Even the engine room was reproduced in exquisite detail.

In fact, Harold Bowen, a strong supporter of Gibbs and head of the Navy's Engineering Bureau, said that the models were so astonishingly accurate that it was safe for draftsmen to obtain actual dimensions from the models, and that it was easier for the pipe shop to lay out its piping from the model instead of laying out templates in the actual ship. So impressed was the Navy Department, that it actually started to require shipbuilders to provide both models as well as the actual ships, much to the chagrin of some shipbuilders who thought the practice wasteful and expensive.

Because destroyer escorts used four different power plants to propel the vessels, Gibbs had four separate models built, each one having a different engine room. Representatives of the shipyards where the full-sized vessels eventually would be built also came to Gibbs and Cox's New York City office to study the models, which were used to answer any questions and save valuable time once the plans arrived in the shipyard and production began. As mass production of the full-sized ships got under way, most of the issues already had been addressed and changes made at the scale model stage. Some of the models were as long as twenty-six feet and accurate to one-sixty-fourth of an inch. If there was a bad idea or a mistake in the blueprints, they would likely show up in the model.[21]

In order to speed the production of destroyer escorts, Gibbs and Cox assumed the role of central procurement agent in addition to designing the vessels, which would be built in a number of private shipyards. According to maritime historian Frank O. Braynard, this was the first time the Navy entrusted the planning, purchasing, and building of a multiple ship program entirely to a private organization. Other "firsts" marked the DE project, including having large prefabricated portions of the ships put together outside the shipyard, where they later would be transported for assembly.

The Shipbuilders Council of America lauded the prefabricated aspects of the new ships, saying that it had helped American shipyards to break world speed records for production. "With a hull put together in thirteen prefabricated sections, some of which weighed 84,000 pounds, the destroyer escort is slightly smaller than the World War I destroyers, and is about 300 feet long with a 35-foot beam," the council noted, adding, "More than thirty-six skilled trades are needed in the construction of a single destroyer escort vessel. In a great many of the shipyards now constructing them, women workers are shouldering their full share of the precise work that goes into the building of the hardest hitting ship of its class ever made."[22]

"The Battle of the Atlantic was at its worst while these ships were being built," Braynard observes, pointing out that one convoy of sixty ships was attacked by German submarines six days after sailing. Only five of those vessels survived the trip across the Atlantic. Gibbs accelerated procurement of materials and expanded prefabrication of ship sections, cutting construction time from one year to seven months. In fact, the HMS *Fitzroy*, a destroyer escort built for the British in the Bethlehem Steel Corporation's Hingham,

Massachusetts, shipyard set a new national record when it slid down the ways only eight and a half days after its keel was laid. That shipyard also set another record producing ten destroyer escorts in a single month.[23]

In order to keep the ships rolling out at a rapid pace, Gibbs and Cox determined that many of the available pipes, valves, and fittings met commercial standards but not necessarily the more stringent Navy standards. If it were to meet the accelerated deadlines set by President Roosevelt, the company argued, it should be allowed to use the materials meeting commercial standards, which were more readily available. Gibbs and Cox considered this decision of "extreme importance" in allowing it to maintain the rapid timetable set for destroyer escorts as well as for the construction of landing ships.[24]

Seventeen shipyards across the nation undertook construction of the DEs, working around the clock and using mostly inexperienced men and women to mass-produce these trim but deadly new warships. Although more than 1,000 were ordered, only 563 actually were constructed because, as U-boat activity in the Atlantic began to subside, some 442 of the planned DEs were cancelled, with resources being diverted to the construction of other vitally needed vessels.[25]

The course of the war in the Atlantic might have been different if destroyer escorts had been constructed when they first were suggested. Unfortunately the United States had none of these little warships in its fleet when Germany declared war on it and had little ability to protect the merchant ships being torpedoed and sunk by U-boats right off the East Coast. "The Battle of the Atlantic has taken a turn for the worse," the *New York Times* asserted in February 1942. "Largely because of increased sinkings off the Canadian and United States coasts." The article went on to say that Allied resources to battle the Germans and Japanese were stretched to the limit. Secretary of the Navy James Forrestal, a neighbor and friend of FDR back in New York State and a former administrative assistant to the president, stepped in and urged Admiral Stark to start construction of destroyer escorts, which, reluctantly, the general board finally agreed to initiate, even though Navy operations put them in sixth place on the priority list behind all other vessels, except submarines.

Although the cost of constructing a DE was said to be half that of a conventional destroyer, it took some time for regular Navy folks to adjust to the new and unique kind of warship. "Old Navy men who see them for the first time are apt to stare and scratch their heads," Ashley Halsey Jr. observed in a September 1943 *Proceedings* magazine article, adding, "The hull is conventional, but the superstructure borders on the weird—something between a submarine conning tower and a tank turret." Halsey added, "Wheelhouse, bridge, and charthouse are all sheathed in blank steel except for two slit ports and some small portholes. A shielded anti-aircraft gun is about where the wheel should be, and forward of it are two all-purpose guns on stepped-down platforms."

The DEs' engines, termed "iron sea horses" by the *New York Times*, were chosen for the ships because of their toughness, adaptability, and simplicity of operation. Mass-produced at remarkable speed, they were said to be capable of reversing themselves in a matter of seconds, to be able to wheel the vessels around at unbelievable angles, and to have enough speed to outmaneuver U-boats.[26]

Time magazine, in a February 1943 article, called destroyer escorts "highly efficient" but noted that they were too late in coming to the Battle of the Atlantic. "The destroyer escort situation is worse, since only a handful have been delivered. As a result a single destroyer often convoys 15 hapless merchantmen across the Atlantic *v* the ideal setup, which would be closer to one escort for every three freighters." The magazine correctly placed the blame for the delay in building DEs squarely on the shoulders of the Navy brass in Washington. The "main reason for the lag in escort ships has been a series of Washington miscalculations," *Time* noted, adding, "First, the Navy underestimated the real job. Then there was a drive for landing barges. The merchant shipping program itself has put enormous train on all ship suppliers. More recently, the synthetic rubber program and high-octane gasoline program collided with the escort program for parts." *Time* concluded: "This week it looked as if Washington would give the escort program a real green light. It was too late to stew over past mistakes. The real challenge to business—for on the success or failure of gear maker and instrument maker may rest the outcome of the Battle of the Atlantic."[27]

Sen. Harry Truman also weighed in on the Navy's failure to accelerate the construction of destroyer escorts in an April 1943 report on Navy and merchant ship construction, applauding the "magnificent job" by the Navy in building a first-class fighting fleet but stating it was done at the expense of protection of vessels carrying vital cargoes to overseas battlefronts. In Truman's report, he criticized the Navy for being "slow to realize" the menace of the German submarines. "Some sinkings were unavoidable," the Truman report stated. "But a large part of the loss would have been prevented had we had an early and large production of sub-chasers and destroyer escorts." The report concluded, "Such losses will be prevented when more of such ships have been delivered and commissioned." The senator, who would be tapped the following year to run as FDR's vice president, admonished the Navy to be "less conventional and conservative in its thinking . . . and spend less time propounding explanations as to why unfortunate situations have occurred."[28]

The Roosevelt administration was quick to respond to Truman's criticism, although one wonders whether FDR—himself a strong proponent for the construction of escort vessels—might privately have agreed with some of the conclusions reached by the senator. Navy Secretary Knox defended the Navy's action, saying the destroyer escort program had been ready to start but that other needs overshadowed the ability to start turning out the smaller vessels. Knox blamed the delay in moving ahead with DE construction on the need to build invasion barges, by diversions of materials to the synthetic rubber and high-octane gasoline programs, as well as on the aircraft program. "It was a matter of stress on different things at different times," he stated.[29]

Truman's report came about a month after Knox's announcement that "several score" of destroyer escorts already were on the water battling Nazi U-boats, and that several hundred more were on the way. Knox referred to them as a "small destroyer" with enough firepower to shoot it out with submarines on the surface, as well as antiaircraft guns and torpedo tubes for antisubmarine duty. "It is a specialized craft," the Navy stated, "with a definite job to do."[30]

Two months later, Navy Under Secretary James Forrestal told workers at the Philadelphia Navy Yard, where eighteen DEs would be built, that the U-boat menace would be eliminated within four to six months thanks in part to the rising tempo of construction of DEs. "Next year," Forrestal said, "destroyer escorts will become the largest single class of warships in the United States." He added: "That is the answer which you and workmen like you in other shipyards will give to Hitler and his wolf packs."

Indeed, six months later Forrestal, in remarks to the employees of Consolidated Steel Corporation in Orange, Texas, where more than 20 percent of the destroyer escorts were being constructed, said the new vessels already were taking a toll on the German submarines. "I cannot tell you in equal detail about the destroyer escorts you have built," Forrestal told employees.

"As you know, President Roosevelt and Prime Minister Churchill have put special restrictions on news of the anti-submarine war, and properly so, because we want to keep Hitler guessing about what has hit his wolf packs. But this I can say: Your DEs from this yard have been in the battle of the Atlantic for weeks. They have gone in slugging at the slightest hint of a sub, and I believe you can count on them to bring you some scalps."[31]

One can only speculate how differently the Battle of the Atlantic might have been—and how many merchant ships and sailors' lives might have been saved—if the Navy brass had listened to Cochrane back in 1941, and even to Roosevelt a year earlier. Robert H. Connery, a Naval Reserve commander assigned as historian to Forrestal's office, stated it very simply in a book coauthored with Robert G. Albion, Navy Department historian during the war years: "The delay in DEs was inexcusable for the need for this type should have been obvious from the submarine experiences of World War I. By mid-1940, Britain's desperate need for escort vessels should have brought some action." Sadly, for Britain and the United States, it did not.[32]

Despite a continuing institutional bias by some conservative Navy brass against new and novel vessels, such as destroyer escorts, the tough little ships proved their worth as they quickly became critical to the reversal of German supremacy on the Atlantic. Beginning in 1943 destroyer escorts sunk more enemy submarines than any other type of vessel, earning the reputation as the United States' most important antisubmarine vessel plying the dangerous waters of the North Atlantic. Manned by a "green" crew of valiant young sailors, these warships courageously confronted the perils of an enemy unseen as they swiftly discharged their duties in a daring run along the edge of the abyss.

4

Away All Boarding Parties

"**C**ease firing," the skipper ordered. Minutes later, the ship's loudspeakers broadcast a command not heard on a Navy vessel since 1815. "Away all boarding parties," the captain barked, as wooden whaleboats hurriedly were lowered over the sides of three destroyer escorts and into the choppy waters of the North Atlantic. The 26-foot diesel-motor vessels were on their way to rendezvous with a large, black Nazi submarine, lying dead ahead like a giant beached whale, foundering and spurting sea water from its damaged sides.[1]

When sailors from the destroyer escorts USS *Pillsbury, Jenks,* and *Chatelain* scrambled on board their boats, they were excited at the prospect that they soon would capture a Nazi U-boat, something that had eluded American forces over the course of the entire war. Although they were about to make naval history with the first capture of an enemy vessel at sea since the War of 1812, that did not cross their minds as they plowed through heavy seas off the coast of West Africa. "We had a job to do, and that's what we were thinking about," said Wayne M. Pickels, boatswain's mate on board the *Pillsbury*, one of the nine-man boarding party who climbed on board *U-505* and descended into the eerily dark and cramped quarters of the German submarine.

It all began on a peaceful Sunday morning in June 1944, bright and clear with a stiff wind blowing. The destroyer escorts were part of a group of ships under the command of Daniel V. Gallery, skipper of the carrier USS *Guadalcanal*, churning through the North Atlantic on its way to search for Nazi submarines in the area around the Cape Verde Islands. "Hunting submarines is big game hunting," Captain Gallery noted, "but 99 percent of the time it is a most monotonous and discouraging occupation. Your planes scour the ocean continuously, day and night. The gun crews practically live at the stations. For a month at a time nothing may happen except, perhaps, a false alarm or two, when the lads get desperate and begin imagining things. Then, just about the time you decide that there are no submarines in the ocean, all hell busts loose."[2]

"I had just come up to the bridge after attending divine services," Gallery wrote, "when the radio loudspeaker announced: 'USS *Chatelain* to task-group commander. I have a possible sound contact.'" Gallery, who was planning to depart for Casablanca for refueling, was not alarmed as sound contacts were not uncommon in the North Atlantic. Sound gear often would pick up submerged whales, which appeared similar to a submarine on the sonar screen. Alarms would sound as sailors rushed to their battle stations and prepared to open fire on the suspected submarine. Suddenly a whale would surface, eye the convoy of ships, and blow before descending once again into the depths of the ocean.[3]

But this was no whale. Gallery ordered his carrier away from the scene as the destroyer escorts *Pillsbury*, *Pope*, *Flaherty*, *Chatelain*, and *Jenks* swiftly sped to the site of the contact to subdue the submarine. The *Chatelain's* captain, Dudley S. Knox, reported, "Contact evaluated as sub. Am starting attack," as the DE dropped its first depth charges.[4]

Two wildcat fighters launched from the carrier flew over the site, hoping to spot the U-boat. They did. The submarine, which had made the mistake of rising to periscope level, now tried to make a run for it, but the fighter planes fired their machine guns into the water to mark the sub's location for the *Chatelain*. The fighter planes radioed the U-boat's position and the destroyer escort swung around, chasing the submerged vessel, continuing to fire depth charges. "We struck oil," Knox jubilantly radioed. The submarine, with its damaged hull and jammed rudder, began to surface some seven hundred yards from the *Chatelain*. Gallery did not want this one to get away, so he broadcast over the loudspeaker, "I want to capture this bastard, if possible—I want to capture this bastard, if possible."[5]

"Match pointers," ordered the gun commander on board the *Pillsbury*, which along with the *Jenks* had joined their sister ship in the attack. Boatswain's Mate Pickels, whose battle station was on the 40-mm gun, was using non-armor-piercing bullets so the submarine would not sink. Pickels, along with sailors from the *Chatelain* and *Jenks*, commenced firing their deck guns at the *U-505*'s conning tower, as the fighter planes, swarming overhead, peppered the vessel's deck with machine-gun fire.

Captain Harold Wilhelm Lange gave the order to his crew of fifty-nine men to abandon ship. The submarine's hatch popped opened and German sailors scrambled to get off the vessel, diving into the churning ocean waters to avoid the hail of bullets coming from the destroyer escorts and airplanes. Lange and his first officer, Paul Meyer, both were hit by antiaircraft fire before diving over the side. But the gunfire barrage was short lived as the order to cease fire came within minutes.[6]

"Away all boarding parties," the loudspeakers blared, as the wooden whaleboats were lowered over the side heading to the first rendezvous and capture of an enemy ship at sea in more than 129 years. "Save us, comrades, save us!" the German sailors, struggling in the water, yelled as the American whaleboats sped toward the U-boat. The *Pillsbury*'s engineer, Zenon Lukosius, shouted back that help would be on the way soon as the whaleboat passed the German sailors bobbing in the heaving seas. The crew of *Pillsbury*'s whaleboat had been ordered to board the submarine, while whaleboats from the *Chatelain* and *Jenks* were on their way to pick up German sailors.

Arriving at the submarine, the crew of the *Pillsbury* whaleboat noticed one German sailor dead on deck, killed by wildcat gunfire as he attempted to train the U-boat's deck guns on the approaching whaleboats. Hans Fisher, one of the original crew of *U-505*, was the only sailor on either side killed during the historic capture. Now, the job of these young American sailors, none of whom had ever set foot on board any type of submarine, was to descend into the vessel's cramped quarters and search for the booby traps and explosive devices that they expected the Germans had rigged before jumping overboard. On a runaway course at six knots, in a tight circle to starboard, *U-505*'s valves had been opened by the German sailors and the boat was flooding with seawater. The American sailors also feared that explosive charges had been set to scuttle the boat, sending it with all of its secrets to the bottom of the sea.

The *Pillsbury*, in what Gallery calls "the wildest seagoing chase I've ever seen," took off after the submarine, darting around outside of the circle while the destroyer escort's whaleboat cut across inside the circle. "It looked for all the world like a rodeo with a cowboy trying to rope a wild horse," Gallery noted. The boarding party, led by Lt. Albert L. David, leaped from the wooden boat on board the submarine, holding on tightly to prevent slipping on the wet deck and into the water. Now their job was to climb up the conning tower ladder and plunge through the hatch and attempt to coral the submarine and stop the boat from exploding and sinking.[7]

But the boarding party was not certain that all the Germans were off the boat, so the men took precautions to make sure any Germans left on board the sub could not close the hatch and dive the boat with the Americans on top. Pickels brought along a heavy tool box and thirty feet of chain on board. "Before anybody went down the hatch," he recalled, "I was to lower the tool box down into the control room and secure the chain topside in case the Germans were on board, [so] they couldn't close the hatch on us," Pickels said. But as the U-boat rolled side to side, Pickels lost his chain overboard when he tried to rescue the gunner's mate, Chester Moscarski, who also slipped and fell in between the submarine and the whaleboat as the sailors jumped on board. Fortunately, they had brought along another chain and were able to secure the hatch before entering.

Overcome by the strong stench of diesel when they entered the submarine, Pickels and his shipmates likened the odor to that of a mix of diesel, oil, bilge water, kitchen, and "outhouse" smells, all combined to produce an unforgettable stink. Armed with Tommy guns, sailors rushed through the narrow passageways of the vessel, rapidly flooding with seawater, in search of any Germans still on board. The Germans were gone, but a crew member had opened the seawater intake valve and removed its cover. A steady stream of seawater was pouring into the compartment. Engineer Zenon Lukosius hurried to find the cover to the sea strainer. Of course, the sailor knew that the Germans often booby-trapped the valves so they would explode if an attempt was made to close them. Tension filled the air and everyone held their breath as Lukosius said, "Here goes nothing" and replaced the cap, which the Germans had tossed nearby in the corner of the control room. Seawater stopped entering the submarine.

Racing through the boat, sailors looked for explosive charges that could sink the vessel at any moment. Torpedoman Arthur Knispel, the first American sailor to enter *U-505*, hurried through the submarine looking for the demolition bombs. He found six bombs that had been rigged by the Germans before leaving the boat and yanked the wires off each of them. What Knispel did not know was that the boat's chief engineer, Joseph Hauser, whose duty was to set the timers for the demolition charges as ordered by Lange, had failed to do so. The engineer, in fact, had quickly climbed up the conning tower ladder and jumped into the water right behind the captain and his first officer, Paul Meyer, leaving his mission unfulfilled. U-boat sailors, many still in their teens, were—like their American counterparts—young and inexperienced, which may account, in part, for the engineer not carrying out the captain's demolition order. Once Lange and Meyer left the boat, panic may have overtaken the crew, who no longer had an officer directing their actions.[8]

Captain Lange recalled the moment he knew *U-505* was doomed, which, because of a series of failed missions and low morale, had become known as an unlucky boat. "When the boat surfaced," Lange said in a statement given while prisoner on board the USS *Guadalcanal*, "I was the first to the bridge and saw now four destroyers around me, shooting at my boat with caliber and anti-aircraft." After being wounded by shrapnel, Lange said, "I gave the order to leave the boat and to sink her. My chief officer, who came after me onto the bridge, lay on the starboard side with blood streaming over his face. Then I gave a course order to starboard in order to make the aft part of the conning tower fire lee at the destroyer to get my crew out of the boat safely."

Lange lapsed into unconsciousness. Later he awoke to find his crewmen scrambling with their life jackets on the submarine's deck. The captain does not remember going overboard, but he did recall ordering his men to give three cheers for what he thought was his sinking boat. But thanks to the quick and heroic efforts of the American destroyer escort sailors, the boat did not sink, and it, along with its valuable cargo was saved, providing a windfall for Allied intelligence.[9]

Rushing through the boat, Wayne Pickels and the other sailors grabbed confidential documents and other material, stuffing it into canvas sacks and tossing them topside, after which the top-secret cargo was loaded into the waiting whaleboats. "I made at least four trips with bags loaded with data," Pickels said. "Once we cleaned out the radio room, the last thing they gave me was the Enigma machine," he said, noting that the code encryption device resembled an old manual typewriter. Pickels passed the last bag and the Enigma machine topside. But when Ernest Beaver, whaleboat bow hook, took the machine, he remarked that the boat already was overloaded and was going to toss the Enigma machine overboard. "I don't think anybody will want this old radio," Beaver said, not knowing the importance of the device, as he prepared to drop it into the ocean. Phil Trusheim, the boat coxswain, realized the value of the "old radio" and told Beaver to stow it away with the rest of the loot.[10]

After the radio room was cleared out, the captain's cabin was next. Pickels broke open Lange's locked cabinets and desk and retrieved all the books, manuals, charts, code books, paperwork, and other documents, placing them in a canvas sack before sending it topside. "I got his fountain pen," Pickels said, describing a Mont Blanc pen that he slid into his pocket and brought home to America. They also retrieved several pairs of binoculars and a German pistol in the cabin but were told to place the name, rank, and serial number of the owners on the items, which they promised would be returned to them after the war. "They wanted to keep [the capture of the boat] a secret," Pickels said, and they thought that news of the capture might leak out if any of U-505's items were kept by the sailors. Mission accomplished, the USS *Jenks* was speeding to Bermuda with all of the submarine's top-secret loot, and the carrier, with its German submarine in tow, was ordered to Casablanca, some one thousand miles away.[11]

"Coming on the eve of 'Overlord,' the capture of U-505, with everything from acoustic torpedoes to her most secret code books and tactical publications intact, proved one of the war's major windfalls for Allied intelligence," noted historian Philip. K. Lundeberg, who also served as ensign on board another destroyer escort, the ill-fated USS *Frederick C. Davis*. The capture of the submarine proved to be a veritable goldmine of information—more than a half ton of documents and equipment—and remains one of the most significant events in World War II.[12]

The *Pillsbury* suffered serious damage as it came alongside the U-boat in order to pass over some pumps so the crew could remove the water flooding the submarine's control room. The ship drew too close to the submarine's diving planes, which pierced the thin hull of the destroyer escort's engine room, and seawater flooded the DE's engine compartment. With the ship now out of commission as far as the towing plan was concerned, that duty would fall to Gallery and his carrier. U-505, the Nazi vessel that had sunk at least eight vessels during the war, was now a war prize, sporting a giant American flag placed proudly on top of the sub's periscope.[13]

Hooking a cable from the carrier to the submarine was not without its own risks. *Chatelain* signalman Frank P. DeNardo and his whaleboat crew delivered the tow rope and attached cable from the carrier to the submarine. The whaleboat crew attached the cable to U-505 but neglected to pull the rope out of the water. The line wrapped around the shaft of the whaleboat, stalling the engine. As the wooden boat bounced around in the water, it was clear that somehow the rope would have to be removed from the shaft if they ever hoped to get the engine started.

Knife in hand, DeNardo dived overboard into the choppy seas, swimming under the boat to cut the line. After he came up for air a couple of times, he was told that the carrier was signaling them. Climbing back in the whaleboat to answer the signal, the coxswain jumped into the choppy seas in order to finish the cutting job. Mission complete, the engine kicked over and the whaleboat and its crew headed back to the *Guadalcanal* and some much welcome dry clothes.[14]

As night fell sailors on board the *Pillsbury* went to work making repairs to its damaged hull and flooded engine room. Pickels said they used a canvas and fiber collision mat, similar to a giant bandage, to patch the gashes made by the submarine's diving planes. Once the work was complete, the destroyer escort caught up with the carrier, but much to everyone's surprise, the tow line to the submarine broke around midnight, setting *U-505* free.

"Our pleasant dreams were rudely interrupted at midnight when the towline broke," Gallery said. The *Pillsbury* was assigned to continue circling the submarine all night to ensure that it remained stationery until daylight, when the carrier returned with a stronger tow cable. Once the new cable was in place, the carrier received orders to change course and head to Bermuda, some 2,500 miles away, where Navy officials believed it could better hide its prize catch. Gallery gave the order, and *Guadalcanal* started what would be a nerve-wracking fifteen-day journey towing *U-505* slowly across the Atlantic Ocean, through the primary submarine travel lane, en route to its secret hideaway in Bermuda.[15]

Aware of how excited the young sailors were to tell everyone they had captured a German submarine, Gallery issued a top-secret, one-page order to all members of the task force group in which he called the capture of *U-505* "one of the major turning points in World War number two *provided* repeat *provided* we keep our mouths shut about it. The enemy must not learn of this capture." He added, "I fully appreciate how nice it would be to be able to tell our friends about it when we get in, but you can depend on it that they will read about it eventually in the history books that are printed from now on." Gallery went on to say, "If you obey the following orders it will safeguard your own health as well as information which is vital to national defense." He concluded with this crude yet clear directive that left no room for confusion: "Keep your bowels open and your mouth shut."[16]

Meanwhile the USS *Chatelain* had its own special cargo—some thirty-eight prisoners from *U-505*, along with the submarine's skipper, Captain Lange. Joseph Villanella, son of an Italian immigrant who shined shoes for a living in New York City, was a radarman on board the destroyer escort and said each prisoner was given a shopping bag containing clothes, underwear, toothbrush and toothpaste, soap, and towels. Villanella said they were warned not to take any souvenirs from the Germans in order to protect the secret capture. Although Villanella did keep a diary of his wartime exploits, following orders to keep the secret, he made a one-word entry in his diary for the *U-505* capture: "Sub" was all he wrote. But the young radarman did decide to "rescue" one souvenir—an article of clothing from one of the prisoners. He kept a pair of swimming trunks with the name *REH* marked inside, belonging to *U-505*'s machinist's mate, Werner Reh.[17]

Three *U-505* prisoners, including Paul Meyer, the boat's executive officer, came on board the USS *Jenks*, which had been assigned to transport the submarine's loot to Bermuda. Arthur Overacker, then a twenty-three-year-old sonarman from the little town of Milford Center, Ohio, will never forget seeing the Germans as they stepped on board his vessel. Meyer, who had been wounded in the head and shoulder as he followed Lange out of the conning tower, was clutching a small item close to his chest when he was helped on board the *Jenks*. "He was holding a picture frame when he came aboard," Overacker said. Sailors grabbed the frame from the first officer only to discover it contained a photograph of his wife. They dried it off and returned the picture to Meyer, who was rushed to sick bay to treat his scalp and shoulder wounds.[18]

With its treasure trove of top-secret materials, the destroyer escort sped at flank speed to deliver its cargo to Bermuda in four days. Overacker said they were going so fast that the sonar, designed to locate German submarines, would not operate properly. "We never slowed down," he said, even though the captain, J. W. Dumford, was warned several times by his crew that, if they did not slow down, they would run out of fuel. Dumford acknowledged the advice but continued to rush at top speed to his destination. "When we came into Bermuda, we came in on fumes," Overacker recalled.

U-505's confidential documents, code books, and two Enigma machines were loaded into waiting trucks and taken to a Navy seaplane for transport to

Washington, D.C., where eager intelligence officers poured over the material. Dumford went along to provide Washington officials with a firsthand account of the capture. The boat's acoustic torpedoes and other equipment was inventoried and loaded onto various ships, including the USS *Slater*, that left for Norfolk. Prisoners also were transported to the United States and held incommunicado at a camp in Ruston, Louisiana.[19]

Although the destroyer escort USS *Frost* had played no role in the capture of *U-505*, one of its crew members had a previously unknown connection to the submarine's skipper, Captain Lange, who had been transported to a military hospital in Bermuda following his boat's capture. Nineteen-year-old Robert Storrick, signalman on board the *Frost*, developed a close relationship with Lange while the young sailor was recuperating from surgery for mastoiditis in the same hospital where the submarine captain secretly was being held.

Growing up in Washington, Pennsylvania, Storrick had tried to join the Army Air Corps in 1943 but was turned down because he had a "bad heart" according to doctors. That same day, Storrick recalled, he walked across the hall and joined the U.S. Navy, immediately boarding a steam train in Pittsburgh for training at the Navy facility in Sampson, New York. Storrick scored high enough in a battery of tests to be a chosen as a candidate for the Navy's V-12 officer's training program and was sent to Cornell University to study mechanical engineering.

Eventually he received his orders to board the USS *Frost* waiting at Pier 92 in New York City. The ship left for submarine training off Bermuda and later was assigned to patrol west of the Azores. Although he didn't know it at the time, Storrick soon would leave his ship after developing a serious ear infection, causing severe pain and swelling. The sailor was sent to the hospital in Bermuda where a mastoidectomy was performed. The disappointed teenager was ordered to stay behind to recuperate as the rest of his shipmates left to join a convoy escorting the USS *Quincy* with President Franklin Roosevelt on board, on his way to the last summit meeting with Winston Churchill and Joseph Stalin at Yalta.[20]

Storrick was about to be introduced to Lange, the captain of the captured *U-505*, secretively held in the same hospital where he was recuperating. The young DE sailor was assigned to perform orderly duties for Captain Lange, who was recuperating from injuries received during the historic capture of his submarine. "I took him to breakfast every day in the officer's mess or solarium, pushing him in his wheelchair," Storrick said. "I had no idea who he was except he was a German captain. They never told me, and I never learned who he was until after the war." For the next five weeks, Storrick said, he was with Lange from the time he first woke up until it was time for bed. "The only time we were apart was when I had to go get my own meals because I (not being an officer) had to eat separately, of course."

The German told him he had worked for eleven years at the Philadelphia Naval Yard prior to the war and only returned to Germany after Adolph Hitler summoned all German nationals home, threatening to harm their relatives if they did not return. "He was angry at Hitler for having to go back to Germany. He was not a Hitler lover," Storrick said, noting that upon his arrival in his homeland, he was inducted into the German navy without delay.

Lange spoke English well. Together they listened to war reports on the shortwave radio in the hospital's officer wing solarium. Lange would translate the German broadcast for Storrick, and they were amused at how differently the American and German radio reports, both laced with a heavy dose of propaganda, portrayed the war. "When we compared the reports, it was like two different wars were being fought," Storrick noted. "It was comical. We said we shot down one hundred of their planes, and they said we shot down twenty-five, and the reverse was true." He said the pair engaged in a lot of small talk but stayed away from subjects dealing with the United States, President Roosevelt, or specific details about U-boats, even though the young American sailor questioned the captain on technical aspects of German submarines. "We are not to talk about that," Lange politely replied.

After the captain had healed sufficiently, he was sent to the United States by airplane. The day he left Bermuda, Lange was wearing dungarees with a big *P*, for "prisoner," emblazoned across his back. Parting was bittersweet for the Nazi captain and American sailor. "I actually saw a tear in his eye—here he goes from captain to a lowly prisoner of war, and heading for where he didn't know," Storrick said.[21]

Capture of an enemy submarine with its treasure trove of top-secret documents and equipment had never been a stated goal during the Battle of the Atlantic. The orders for Allied forces was to find and sink the U-boats, sending their valuable secrets to Davy Jones' locker. Destroyer escorts were good at that, as the record shows. In fact, Gallery's boys had done just that when it discovered another German submarine about three months before its encounter with Captain Lange and his ill-fated boat.

It was Easter Sunday eve when the USS *Guadalcanal*, with Gallery in command, and his destroyer escorts were combing the waters between the Azores and Gibraltar for German submarines. As night fell, Gallery decided to launch four night-flying Avengers, even though they had little experience landing airplanes on the baby flattops in the dark. "It was a scary business," Gallery noted. "We went at it gingerly, but it worked out well." Gallery pointed out that the radar in the airplanes was able to determine "something" was down there, but it could not differentiate between an enemy submarine, an Allied ship running without lights, or a Portuguese fishing trawler. But on this night the airplanes would have the good fortune of a full moon to help guide their flight.[22]

As midnight approached, the first three bombers returned to the ship without spotting anything. "Secure operations until sunrise," Gallery ordered as the Avengers returned empty-handed. However, when the last plane landed on board the carrier, the plan quickly changed. "Cap'n, I almost got him," the pilot announced to a startled Gallery and his officers, who were crowded in the ship's combat information center. The pilot was quizzed as to whether he really had spotted a submarine, to which he exclaimed that he was absolutely certain since he looked right down the sub's conning tower and saw the lights on inside the vessel, about forty miles from the *Gualdalcanal*. Gallery ordered planes back in the air and within a short time, one of the planes had found the 1,120-ton submarine, *U-515*. The sub was surfacing to charge its batteries, about fifteen miles from the first sighting. Gallery ordered the destroyer escorts to the area.

By now the submarine was only fifteen miles from the Allied ships, which were closing in fast on their target. The airplanes continued to transmit additional sightings as the U-boat tried to surface. The destroyer escorts USS *Pope, Flaherty, Pillsbury,* and *Chatelain* rushed to the site and closed in for the kill. Dropping depth charges throughout the morning, the DEs continued to pick up sonar contacts but were not able to hit their target. The U-boat captain had taken his boat deep, some eight hundred feet down. Next he launched several sonar decoys—canisters containing a compound of calcium and zinc that produced a massive amount of underwater bubbles, simulating the echo of a submarine—in order to fool the DEs' sonar. It worked. "This chap that we were after was obviously a tough customer who knew his business," Gallery said, noting that the U-boat's Captain Werner Henke, whose submarine sunk more ships than any other U-boat commander after 1942, was able to maneuver his boat with great skill to avoid being hit by one of the depth charges.[23]

The pummeling the boat received from hedgehogs and depth charges finally took its toll on the damaged vessel. With water and oil pouring in and with significant damage to the boat's engine room, the submarine finally began to surface. Joseph Villanella, radarman on board the USS *Chatelain*, raced to his battle station in the radar shack that day. The *Pope* was picking up contact with the submarine and then losing it. His ship then picked up contact and continued to join with the *Pope* in firing depth charges. "We were the only ship in the immediate area when the sub came shooting out of the water bow first and laid on top of the water. We knocked the hell out of it," Villanella said. The other DEs rushed to the scene and joined in the assault. "We threw everything at it," Villanella remembered, adding that the hatch opened and Germans started pouring out, jumping into the churning waters.[24]

Two German sailors rushed out of the conning tower and ran over, aiming the submarine's deck cannons directly at his ship. Roger Cozens, sonarman on board the USS *Flaherty*, said the Nazi sailors were within range of the deck guns from the *Flaherty* and *Chatelain*, and as the DEs took aim at the submarine, the Germans quickly abandoned their efforts and jumped into the sea to avoid being shot. The other members of the crew followed suit. "We then spent several minutes sinking *U-515* with cannon fire," Cozens remembered. He added, "We shot it full of holes and it sunk. Later, it was realized that we might have boarded and saved *U-515* or at least its important documents."

Henke, *U-515*'s thirty-five-year-old commander, still hoped to make a run for it. But once he surfaced and realized the destroyer escorts were surrounding him, he knew his fate was sealed. "All hands, abandon ship," Henke ordered as destroyer escorts started shelling the surfaced boat. Wildcat fighter planes also continued to dive, strafing their machine guns at the submarine and the crew who were floundered in the waters below. The submarine finally sunk, and sixteen German sailors went along with it to their deaths. Some forty-four survived, many suffering bullet and shrapnel wounds. They were taken prisoner on board the *Chatelain*.

Henke, who was tough and smart and had become a national hero for sinking some twenty-six Allied and merchant vessels, still demonstrated a defiant spirit, even though he had been defeated and his boat sunk. As the crew from the *Chatelain* picked him up in their rubber life raft, the U-boat

After sinking a U-boat, most DE skippers would attempt to rescue the German sailors, who then were taken on board, fed and clothed, and had their injuries attended to by the pharmacist's mates. Here sailors from the USS *Chatelain* leave the ship in a raft to rescue survivors after the *U-515* was sunk on Easter Sunday 1944. As Captain Werner Henke, the U-boat skipper, was picked up, he tried to capsize the raft twice. After boatswain's mate Victor Coleman, with a raised oar, threatened the captain, Henke settled down. *Photo taken by Joseph Villanella; courtesy the photographer*

captain tried twice to capsize the small raft, according to Joseph Villanella, who watched from his ship's deck. "After several attempts [to capsize the raft]," Villanella said, "Henke was threatened by B.M. Coleman, who raised his oar and would have clobbered him if he hadn't quit." The captain gave up and was hauled on board. Once on board the *Chatelain*, he was escorted to the ward room, where he protested to the DE captain about excessive firing upon his men. "You didn't have to kill so many of my men, we would have surrendered," Henke declared.[25]

Wayne Pickels, the USS *Pillsbury*'s boatswain's mate, was on the fantail of his ship when they first picked up contact with the submarine, which fired an acoustic torpedo at his destroyer escort. "It [the torpedo] came to us," he said, "and when it crossed our wake, it made a turn and followed us." The captain zigzagged to avoid the torpedo, which used the sounds of the ship's propellers to hone in on its target. But it still followed the ship. "Here comes one of those

SOBs with ears," one of Pickel's shipmates yelled as the torpedo continued on course toward the ship. The ship outmaneuvered the deadly fish, and "the torpedo with ears," fooled by the DE's "foxer gear," passed harmlessly into the ocean. Henke had four of the acoustic torpedoes on board his boat.[26]

Over the course of the battle in the Atlantic, the goal was to sink, rather than capture, Nazi U-boats. Although capturing them, as was done in the case of *U-505*, could have provided a wealth of important information about tactics and deployment—and may have resulted in the saving of Allied lives—it was not until Gallery and his men made history by keeping the boat afloat and seizing its valuable cargo. Around the same time that *U-505* was captured, destroyer escorts sunk another German submarine, which, it turned out, was laying mines off the harbor of Nova Scotia.

A light south wind was blowing over calm seas as the sun set on 5 July 1944. The USS *Thomas* was prowling the North Atlantic in a zigzag fashion near the Grand Banks, one hundred miles southeast of Sable Island. The destroyer escort was part of a hunter-killer group, a collection of Allied warships whose mission was to seek out and destroy Nazi U-boats. Suddenly the sonarmen on board the USS *Baker* heard a series of "pings" indicating the American fleet was not alone. A U-boat was dead ahead, 1,200 yards. The USS *Thomas* quickly sped at full speed to assist its sister DE.

Racing to their battle stations, sailors on board the *Baker* fired a series of depth charges in the area where they thought the U-boat was moving. Within a short time a large black vessel broke the ocean's surface and tried to make a run for it. The destroyer escort fired all its guns at the German boat, *U-233*, and launched a full pattern of depth charges in the U-boat's path. American sailors reporting a huge geyser of water and fuel oil spewing upward from the enemy vessel. Even though it was severely damaged, the U-boat took off on a high-speed escape as flames and smoke poured from its conning tower. There was only one way left to stop it.

"We are going to ram!" Capt. David M. Kellogg ordered. Charlie K. Field, the twenty-two-year-old only son of an Indiana telegraph operator, was assigned to the *Thomas* as a yeoman and assumed additional responsibilities as the captain's talker, the sailor whose duty was to pass the captain's orders to the crew, usually by sound-powered telephones in those days. As he conveyed the captain's order to ram, Kellogg told the engine room to be ready to reverse the engines quickly upon contact with the U-boat. Field repeated the order: "It's flank speed, not full speed, and then back-up." An apprehensive Field, who had been at sea for only about six months, didn't quite know what to expect. "We could sink, since other ships ramming have sunk," he recalled thinking.

With seawater splashing over the bow of the racing ship, the destroyer escort bore down on the U-boat at flank speed, firing its 3-inch, 20-mm guns to keep the German sailors from manning their deck guns. "Suddenly, within seconds, we hit the sub with our bow about twenty feet aft of the conning tower and drove right into her water tight pressure hull, breaking the U-233 in two," Field recalled. There was a "horrendous blow" as the steel ships collided and the U-boat rolled on its port side, disappearing into a sea of white foam and sending thirty-two sailors to an ocean grave. Some twenty-nine German survivors, including the boat's badly injured commander, Captain Hans Steen, were fished from a sea littered with debris, bodies, and blood. The *Thomas* suffered damage during the ramming, including a badly bent lower stem.[27]

Shivering from the cold, the German sailors were glad to be helped on board the vessel. For many U-boat sailors, not unlike their American DE counterparts, this was their first time at sea, some barely out of their teens, having little or no experience on the water, let alone engaging in deadly naval combat. Although Field said the Germans feared the Americans would torture and kill them, in fact, the enemy sailors—after being stripped and searched—were given hot showers, blankets, dry clothes, hot soup, coffee, cigarettes, and an "alcoholic stimulative where necessary" before being transferred to the escort carrier, the USS *Card*, where the thirty-six-year-old U-boat captain later would die from injuries sustained during the battle. Two secret Nazi code wheels were found on the prisoners. The captain was buried at sea with full honors.

U-233, commissioned only ten months earlier and on its first patrol, was a large mine-laying boat that had sailed from Norway some forty days prior to this encounter, traveling mostly submerged across the North Atlantic. Surfacing in Canadian waters, its job was to lay sixty-six moored mines off the harbor in Halifax, Nova Scotia, a mission cut short by the swift action of the American hunter-killer group. The group, which sailed from Norfolk after being alerted to the mine-laying U-boat's route by Allied codebreakers, consisted of the *Thomas*, *Baker*, and *Card*, as well as the destroyer escorts USS *Bronstein*, USS *Bostwick*, and USS *Breeman*.[28]

This was not the first time the USS *Thomas* and its sister DEs would find U-boats prowling very close to the East Coast of the United States. In fact, U-boat commanders frequently targeted Allied merchant ships silhouetted against the glow of U.S. coastal cities. Lighted buoys also helped U-boats locate merchant ships, making them easy targets for the submarines.

In a little over eight months following the Pearl Harbor attack, 609 Allied ships traveling in American waters were sunk by 184 U-boats, sending more than 3 million tons of vital supplies and material to the bottom of the sea. Allowed to continue unchecked, the U-boats threatened to cripple all commerce along the North American shipping lanes. Brazenly operating along America's shores, coastal residents frequently watched ships burning in the nearby distance. Field himself was shocked one Sunday while on liberty when he took his wife and oldest daughter to Miami Beach for some sun and surf. Instead he and other beachgoers watched in horror as a U-boat torpedoed and sunk an Allied ship.

Back on board his ship, Field was about to come face to face with the fury of Hitler's marauders once again. One calm evening on 29 February 1944, radarmen on board the *Thomas* reported contact with a submarine in the North Atlantic. All hands hurried to their battle stations, manning the guns and getting ready to fight. Although this turned out a false alarm, a couple hours later sonar picked up another signal, and this time it was the real thing. A U-boat was racing on a direct course for the destroyer escort, closing fast at only eight hundred feet.

The PA crackled to life, calling all hands to battle stations. The night sky suddenly lit up as the USS *Bronstein* fired a series of star shells, revealing the surfaced U-boat running straight for the *Thomas*. Captain Kellogg ordered a hard turn to port as the DE set a new course. "No sooner had we straightened up on the new course, than we sighted in the dark sea, two fluorescent trails of light caused by two torpedoes fired at us by the U-boat," Field said. "They went by us on either side," he said, adding that "we up on topside sweated for a few minutes, and realized how very, very close we had come to being blown out of the water!"[29]

The submarine quickly disappeared under the dark sea. But the destroyer escorts were not about to let this one get away. As the midnight hour approached, the DEs still followed the U-boat on sonar as it moved invisibly beneath the waters. The ships fired hedgehogs and dropped depth charges in order to flush out the U-boat. The submarine was patrolling the North Atlantic together with other U-boats in search of Allied vessels. Sound echoing indicated that there were more than one U-boat prowling beneath the Allied convoy. "We gained then lost, then regained contact with the subs," Field said, noting that the dangerous hide-and-seek operation went on until the wee hours of the morning of 1 March. Before dawn it would come to an explosive, history-making end.

Around 3:30 AM the *Thomas* laid a pattern of depth charges, producing a huge explosion beneath the water. The end had come for *U-709*, a combat submarine commanded by twenty-six-year-old Captain Rudolf Ites. Fifty-two hands and the captain were lost. Later that morning the USS *Bronstein*, commanded by Sheldon Kinney, would sink *U-603*, another combat submarine, commanded by Captain Hans-Joachim Bertelsmann. None of those fifty-one crew members survived.[30]

But dangerous times were not yet over for Field and his rookie shipmates. On 16 March, Captain Hans-Joachim Brans, the twenty-eight-year-old commander of *U-801*, a combat vessel, was en route for West African waters when he ordered the submarine to surface so the crew could brush up on some gunnery practice. Unfortunately for Captain Brans, two Navy Wildcat fighters, launched from a carrier escort, spotted the German vessel and began firing on it. One German sailor was killed and nine were injured, including the captain. In an emergency dive *U-801* made a quick escape from the Navy planes. Later that night, under the cover of darkness, Brans brought the U-boat to the surface to bury his dead crewman. He also radioed to *U-488*, one of several submarine milk cows used to supply fuel and provisions to other submarines. Brans said he needed the boat's doctor to treat him and his wounded crewmen.[31]

That radio transmission, however, would spell the beginning of the end of their mission. The message was intercepted and Navy Wildcat fighters were sent out to find the submarine. A little after dawn on St. Patrick's Day they found the U-boat west of the Cape Verde Islands and repeatedly bombed it. The U-boat dived to 984 feet to escape the onslaught. The hunter-killer group, including the USS *Thomas*, USS *Bronstein*, and destroyer USS *Corry*, rushed to the site and began tracking the submarine. Sonar contact was made and the ships immediately started pounding the boat with depth charges and hedgehogs. Suddenly the U-boat surfaced off the *Thomas*' port beam. The destroyer and the *Bronstein*, fresh from two U-boat kills earlier in the month, sprayed the surfaced submarine with gunfire. Apparently not all crewmen on the U-boat received the captain's order to abandon ship and scuttle the boat, as many stayed with the vessel as it sunk to the bottom of the sea. Forty-seven survivors were rescued by the *Bronstein* and *Corry*.[32]

David M. Graybeal, a rural Virginia high school teacher turned DE sailor, was serving as assistant engineering officer and supply officer on board the USS *Snowden* in the summer of 1944. As the *Snowden* and other members of its hunter-killer group were planning to head back to port in order to receive a fresh supply of depth charges, they picked up something on sonar northwest of the Azores. *U-490*, a milk cow commanded by thirty-five-year-old Captain Wilhelm Gerlach, was unaware of the DEs' presence and was caught by surprise. Allied ships launched a barrage of depth charges and hedgehogs. Captain Gerlach ordered an emergency dive to 1,000 feet, out of reach of the DEs' depth charges. Although the U-boat was certain it could escape, the hunter-killer group tracked it for fifteen hours, pounding it with depth charges and hedgehogs along the way.

As night fell the frustrated DE commanders decided to lure the U-boat into revealing itself. The three destroyer escorts, the USS *Snowden*, USS *Frost*, and USS *Inch*, all departed the area. The U-boat, assuming the ships had given up, surfaced a little after midnight on 12 June. The DEs were waiting and started firing star shells, brilliantly illuminating the submarine. They pounded it with gunfire. Graybeal of the *Snowden* said the U-boat captain sent a message in English to the American ships: "Save our crew." The ships trained their searchlights on the vessel, as crewmen climbed out and jumped into the water. All sixty crewmen were rescued.[33]

"We were eager to get it [the submarine]," Graybeal said. "As a matter of fact, it was my job to go over and go aboard to see what I could find down there by way of valves that were open and so on. I took a couple of seamen with me." Graybeal started to collect his gear as the whaleboat was readied. "Away the whaleboat," Capt. A. Jackson Jr. ordered. But suddenly orders changed. The U-boat was starting to sink. There would be no inspection of the vessel, which took all its secrets to the bottom of the sea. Only the crew survived.[34]

"They were virtually frozen when we got them aboard," Graybeal said. "They were wearing coverall kind of things and so we stripped them as quickly as we could and put them in a shower to keep them from dying of being frozen." Graybeal described them as looking like they were eighteen or nineteen years old, "just like a lot of our crew." Although they interrogated the sailors, he said they were "very well trained," aware they only needed to provide name, rank, and serial number. "They'd just repeat that again and again," he added. Reflecting on the German sailors, Graybeal said that "there weren't hard feelings then. I mean, we'd been trying to kill each other all right, but the sea is the great enemy, and so sailors from all over the place feel like we have something in common. We got them on board, we saw they had something to eat, and they got some clothes. They seemed like nice guys."[35]

Field recalled one Nazi psychological tactic that proved unnerving to him and his shipmates. While traveling in the vast loneliness of the North Atlantic near the Azores, the ship's radio shack picked up a radio broadcast playing popular music: "Welcome back, DE-102, to your station," an announcer interrupted. "We'll be visiting you shortly and help you find the bottom of the ocean."

The broadcaster was Axis Sally, who played American hit parade tunes and spewed plenty of Nazi propaganda from her radio station in Germany. While the sailors enjoyed hearing the popular music and her seductive voice, they were less fond of some of the messages. Field said they were puzzled over how she knew their location, unless a U-boat had spotted the ship through its periscope. "How did she know, and who's watching us out here?" his shipmates wondered with a certain amount of anxiety and trepidation. Axis Sally, in fact, was an American-born woman, Mildred Gillars, who had joined the Third Reich as a military propagandist, broadcasting her messages from Germany to American sailors and soldiers around the world.[36]

In addition to the weather, enemy submarines, and the likes of Axis Sally, sailors also had to cope with loneliness and homesickness as they traveled the vast oceans of the world. One welcome relief was a letter from home—from a mother, father, or sweetheart. Sailors would wait anxiously for word from home, which frequently was delivered via a mail sack in a breeches buoy to the ship. The young bluejackets quickly lined up to see whether the sack contained a letter or package addressed to them.

For Earl Charles White Jr., a twenty-year-old radioman on board the destroyer escort USS *Halloran*, virtually every mail call brought news, advice, love, and encouragement from his home in Brighton, New York, where he had graduated high school in 1943 before enlisting in the Navy. In meticulously written letters, his father, Earl Charles Sr., began each with "Hello Son" and asked, "How is every little thing with you today?" followed by "the best

I hope." The remarkable collection of more than fifty letters, painstakingly preserved for more than half a century by the young sailor, were all written in careful longhand, beginning in late 1944 and stretching to 28 September 1945, when young Charles returned home, wounded but alive, from his duty in the Pacific theater.

White wrote his son, sometimes several times a week, about his plans to plant a victory garden and other events going on back home, encouraging him and letting him know just how proud he and his family were of their young Navy man. The letters detail simple things—things that young Charles must have missed—like the robins returning in spring to the neighborhood, the activities of Cokey, the family dog, the bowling league, his siblings buying an orchid for their mother at Easter, little sister Patty's first time away at summer camp, or playing a round of golf at the Oak Hill Country Club, where the family also swam, dined, and celebrated holidays.

The letters were filled with plenty of details about the family, including many of the wartime sacrifices required on the home front. Charles Sr. writes his son about having a steak for dinner—courtesy of a friend and a very rare treat since he said beef required red points under the rationing program, and they didn't have too many of those ration stamps. Meat rationing, which went into effect in 1943, required red ration stamps to buy fresh, frozen, cured, or canned meats. Charles about he and his son never liking canned fish. "Remember how we used to stick up our noses over canned tuna fish or salmon—well right now we can't buy it and it is a delicacy." He explains to his son why he has not been able to send him any pipe tobacco: "Can't get it—tobacco for pipes is as scarce as cigarettes." After Easter, he promises, he may be able to send him some the next time they mail a "care box" from home, which regularly included copies of the daily newspaper sports pages that Charles carefully folded and saved each day for his son.

In a 21 March letter, Charles Sr., who operated a lumber business in East Rochester, New York, is struck by his son's thoughtfulness in sending his little sister, Patty, twenty-five dollars for her birthday—five for her and twenty so she could get some new clothes, a big help for families struggling to keep their children fed and clothed during the lean war years. "All I can say about it is that you are a 4-0 brother, pretty nice of you, believe me—I know Pat thinks you are pretty nice—Mother and me think you are tops—but it is a lot of fun making people happy. I mean, you are missing the expression on their faces when you do these things, son, but there will come a time when you won't—but I can tell you it is well appreciated and damn fine of you."

Charles' ship, the USS *Halloran*, spent its entire time in the Pacific, serving as a screen for replenishment forces as well as during the invasion and capture of Iwo Jima. As part of the Okinawa assault forces, the *Halloran* repelled six attacking Japanese aircraft, splashing one and damaging two others while narrowly being missed by a Japanese torpedo. It would not be so lucky on 21 June, when a kamikaze attacked the *Halloran* and, although the ship's gunners shot it down, an exploding bomb killed three men and caused significant damage to the ship. Charles Jr. received a Purple Heart for injuries sustained during that attack, which reportedly killed his fellow radioman, who had just switched seats with White before the assault.

Charles' little sister, Patty, wrote her big brother on 30 August, the day before she was about to start the fifth grade. "When you come home will you take me fishing. Please. I want to go so badley [*sic*]," Patty wrote. "Dad is going to take me swimming later. I wish you were going with me. When you come home will you dive off the high diving bord [*sic*]. One of the fish died. Now we have one." Her P.S. states: "Say helo [*sic*] to some of the boys on the ship."

The White family, like so many other American families, worried about their young sailors and soldiers and gathered around the radio every day to hear broadcasts about the war while anxiously watching their mailboxes for some word. "Waiting, waiting, and then a letter—then all smiles for a few days," Charles Sr. wrote. A father's longing to see his son—"to have you home with us, to eat and talk with us"—comes across in so many of the letters, which are representative of the anguish and pain felt by millions of American families during the war.

"I can't tell you, son how many times my thoughts are of you lately, guess I am getting a little homesick to see my boy," Charles Sr. wrote. "At night, at home, when I am all alone, everyone gone to bed—I just try to picture you, what you are doing, where you are, how you look, and if you have changed much." He added, "Well, son, every day brings it just one day nearer to the time we will be together again and one happy day that is going to be—so we will just keep saying it won't be long now." He signed each letter "As ever, your Dad."[37]

Letters like these from the home front helped sustain America's young DE sailors, the vast majority of whom were still teenagers away from their homes and families for the first time. Lonely and worried mothers, fathers, wives, and girlfriends would write letters—sometimes every day—sharing their feelings and telling how they long to have their boys back home. Since they were not able to telephone, letters became the only way to communicate with their men at sea. Hearing about the events in their hometown, the comings and goings of their parents and siblings, and the pride their families had in them for the important work they were doing, helped to give these young sailors hope that they would someday—in the not too distant future—be back home with their family and friends, even while Nazi U-boats and Japanese kamikazes and suicide submarines were trying their best to keep that dream from being fulfilled.

Although the DE sailors may not have been prepared for the loneliness, homesickness, or especially the unsettling propaganda of Axis Sally, most had undergone intense and very specialized training at the new Subchaser Training Center on Biscayne Bay in Miami, Florida. The Navy took over eleven hotels—much to the chagrin of the local chamber of commerce—to house and train sailors in the techniques of submarine fighting. Ballrooms and warehouses became makeshift classrooms. The Naval Reserve officers and recruits would undergo a seven-day-a-week training regimen for about two months at the school, whose commandant was Lt. Cdr. E. F. McDaniel. Having just completed grueling escort duty on a destroyer in the North Atlantic, the tough, no-nonsense commander was ready to whip the sailors into shape before sending them out to battle enemy submarines.

Grover Theis, a magazine writer who was allowed to sit in on the classes, said McDaniel was "a far cry from the layman's conception of a ripsnortin', fightin' seadog type of man, who usually is pictured as a cross between a walrus and an English bulldog. Probably most of the trainees class him at a glance as the professor or clergyman type. They soon find out that appearances are deceiving." Regarded as a "mean, lean, thin-lipped officer whose eyes burned with hatred for the enemy," McDaniel started the school on 8 April 1942 with 50 pupils. By the time 1943 had drawn to a close, more than 10,000 officers and 37,000 enlisted men had received training in antisubmarine warfare. Students from fourteen foreign navies, battling on the side of the Allies, also attended the school. Some 360 foreign officers and 1,374 foreign enlisted men passed though the facility.[38]

Originally dubbed the "Donald Duck Navy" because of the small size of the vessels on which his sailors would serve, McDaniel ran a tight ship

Loneliness and homesickness were common among sailors who were at sea for long periods. They eagerly looked for news from home and lined up when the mail sacks arrived. Here the USS *Liddle* comes alongside its sister ship, the USS *Kephart*, to transfer a sack of mail. Using a rope and pulley system, sacks of mail, supplies, and even people were transferred between ships. *Photo taken by Harold S. Deal; courtesy Jeff Deal*

and pupils underwent a strenuous curriculum of classroom instruction—ten hours a day, seven days a week—and hands-on field experience on board the school's training ships, even doing battle with friendly "enemy" submarines. McDaniel insisted on hiring only instructors who had actually hunted submarines so they could convey real-life techniques to the pupils. "The course work at SCTC was highly concentrated and demanding with much homework," recalled James Edward Day, who would eventually be assigned to a sub chaser and, later, to the USS *Fowler*. "At least we didn't have to do a lot of marching and drilling or worry about keeping our rolled up socks in straight rows in our dresser drawers."[39]

Recruits already had gone through boot camp, and this training was highly specialized and designed to teach sailors how to detect and destroy enemy submarines. A specially constructed "dark room" was built atop a Miami warehouse to train pupils in a variety of aspects of submarine detection, including real night darkness, false dawn light, and other conditions and illusions they might encounter at sea. Because there are no dry docks at sea, recruits were taught to use their ingenuity and skill in making repairs to their ships. Although not every sailor made it through the grueling training, those who did soon would find themselves on board tiny sub chasers, patrol boats, converted luxury yachts, or the United States' newest class of warships, the destroyer escort. The pupils were taught to think fast, act fast, and snap to their battle stations instantly on command. An engine instructor in a Miami factory, who had gone through the long school of seamanship in Scandinavia, praised the raw recruits, saying, "Listen, there ain't any boys anywhere like those boys. The European system by which I was brought up made us go up by slow stages and after a good many years, we were pretty good. I ain't criticizing my ancestors, but these boys can absorb enough so much faster that they'll quick be good enough for the job. You got to hand it to these kids."[40]

President Roosevelt's twenty-nine-year-old son, Franklin D. Roosevelt Jr., arrived in Miami early in 1944 for two and a half months of specialized officer training at the SCTC. Lieutenant Roosevelt, scheduled to take command of one of the new destroyer escorts under construction at Federal Shipbuilding and Drydock Company in Newark, New Jersey, would undergo intense classroom instruction as well as fieldwork designed to make him an expert at detecting and destroying enemy submarines.

Like other soon-to-be DE commanders, Roosevelt would embark on a six-day officer's training cruise off the coast of Florida. Designed to provide the maximum amount of training in the shortest period of time, the cruise covered topics such as ship handling, convoy control, formation steaming, damage control, ship armament, and antisubmarine instruments. The DE also would come under "friendly" attack from torpedo bombers and submarines.[41]

School ships departed Miami on Monday mornings at 8:30 and remained training at sea until returning to port Saturday morning. Even though this was a training cruise, crews were in a state of readiness because German U-boats were traveling within sight of Miami Beach and certainly would not shrink from an opportunity to sink any American ship. Because there were no facilities on board for doing personal laundry, students were instructed to bring enough clothing to last for one week, plus towels and toiletry articles. Bedding, furnished by the ship, would be washed on board, and students would pay thirty-five cents for each load. Students also were charged five dollars for the meals they would eat during the six-day cruise. After completion of the training, Roosevelt and the other students soon would learn the identity of their ship command. On 10 April 1944, FDR Jr. received his orders to report to Norfolk for a one-week indoctrination before heading to Newark for his new ship, the USS *Ulvert M. Moore*.[42]

5

The Only Man on the Place

lying three miles above the earth, the twin-engine German bomber unleashed its new secret weapon on two unsuspecting American warships cruising below on the Mediterranean Sea. One of the 3,400-pound missiles exploded on the light cruiser USS *Philadelphia*, injuring several crewmen, but spared the ship serious damage. The second American warship, the USS *Savannah*, did not fare as well. The missile ripped through the hull, piercing the armored gun turret roof as it passed through three steel decks and landed in the lower handling room, where it exploded. A gaping hole in the ship's bottom, a ripped open seam on the port side of the American cruiser, and scores of dead and injured sailors were left in its wake.

Sailors rushed to seal off flooded and burned compartments, but secondary explosions in the gun room slowed fire-fighting efforts. Working around burning debris, blood, and the lifeless bodies of their shipmates, crewmen hurried feverishly to put out the fires and keep the ship from sinking. Once the fires were extinguished and the ship's list corrected, the light cruiser limped back to Malta for emergency repairs, assisted by two salvage tugs. Casualties were high on board the *Savannah*, with 197 American sailors dead and 15 wounded.[1]

German scientists invented this new weapon—a radio-controlled glide bomb—referred to by the Luftwaffe as the Fritz X; it was designed as an antiship weapon and already was making great strides destroying Allied ships, including destroyers, battleships, cruisers, troop ships, and even a British hospital ship. In fact, following Italy's truce with the Allies, the Germans used a glide bomb to blow up an Italian battleship, the *Roma*, slicing it in two parts and sending its 1,255 sailors to the bottom of the Mediterranean. Its sister ship, the *Italia*, was also hit by a missile but was able to return to Malta. The Germans also successfully used the bomb to disable the British HMS *Uganda* and HMS *Warspite* and to sink the HMS *Spartan* and HMS *Janus*.[2]

The remote-controlled glide bomb had fins and would appear to glide as the pilots in the airplane high above the target visually controlled its movement using radio signals. Flares or battery-powered lamps on the tails would help the pilots guide the missile in a meteor-like dive to its target. With an armor-piercing warhead packed with 660 pounds of explosives, the weapon could reach speeds in excess of six hundred miles per hour with a range of eight miles. The Luftwaffe's bombers had to drop the bombs from high altitudes for them to achieve the maximum range, which kept the planes well out of reach of the ships' antiaircraft guns. Clearly the Allies needed to find a way to counter this deadly new weapon, which threatened to send more and more Allied ships and crews to watery graves.[3]

The solution, it turns out, would come from the genius of a young American who got his early education in a one-room schoolhouse in Running Water, South Dakota. George Gowling was born in Mitchell, South Dakota, and moved to Running Water when he was in the fourth grade, eventually finishing high school in Springfield. Later he worked for the Bell Telephone Company before joining the Naval Reserve in November 1942. Having graduated with an electrical engineering degree from South Dakota School of Mines and Technology, the Navy decided to put Gowling's training to good use. He was sent to the University of Arizona for a month of additional high-tech training before being enrolled in Harvard and MIT graduate schools for advanced training in "ultrahigh-frequency technique." Finishing his training in August 1943, Gowling was assigned to the "counter measures" unit of the Naval Research Laboratory in Washington, D.C.

It was there that Gowling first learned of the existence of Germany's new glide bomb, which was causing great damage to U.S. and Allied ships traveling in the Mediterranean area. "This is the number one problem for the Navy right now," he was told, and his assignment was to determine how these new missiles were controlled and to develop an effective countermeasure to them, something the navies of both the United States and Britain had been trying, unsuccessfully, to do for more than a year.

A pretty tall order, thought Gowling, but one he undertook with great enthusiasm. At that time there was wide but unproven speculation about how the missiles were controlled, ranging from infrared to high-frequency radio waves, according to Gowling, who said the Navy—perplexed by the new weapon—even issued bulletins advising that if a ship were attacked by a glide bomb, sailors should turn on their electric razors in what would turn out to be a useless attempt to jam the bomb's signal. "That was pretty pathetic," he recalled thinking.

So Gowling went right to work. The young officer was placed under tight security, watched day and night by agents from the FBI, as he went about his task, first at the Naval Laboratory and later on board the destroyer escort USS *Frederick C. Davis* assigned to the Mediterranean, a major theater of war in 1943–44. After the Allies successfully took control of North Africa in May 1943, American and British forces moved ahead to invade Sicily in July. But the Axis would not give up without a fierce fight and, armed with their deadly new weapon, would be a potent force with which to reckon.

In addition to the electrical engineer from Running Water, another very bright young man, Frank McClatchie, also was working at the laboratory on designs to build a spectrum analyzer to be installed on board destroyer escorts to assist in countering the glide bombs. McClatchie was a German-born American whose father was an inventor doing pioneering work on early tape recorders and vacuum cleaners. So technical genius ran in the family, and young Frank, who had to learn to speak English once his parents returned to the United States in 1930, also started working for the telephone company after graduating from high school in Compton, California. "I was curious about radar," McClatchie said, "and the only way to learn about it was to join the Navy." Of course, because he was German born, the young telephone company technician was thoroughly investigated by the FBI to ensure he was not a spy. Once Gowling and McClatchie, who remarkably were not acquainted while working at the lab, perfected the device to counter the glide bomb, it was time to try it out in the field.[4]

When Gowling and his four assistants boarded the *Davis* in November 1943, no one, including the ship's captain, knew the details of their top secret mission, and the crew was instructed not to ask questions. "They didn't know why I came aboard, or what I was doing there," Gowling recalled. He said they had two radio receivers and a companion unit with a lighted screen showing the frequency of the signal coming into the receivers. When a receiver was tuned to a certain signal, it would appear as a vertical line in the center of the companion unit. Signals that were lower or higher than that frequency would appear as blips on either side of the vertical line on the screen.

As part of his research, Gowling studied photographs of some of the new bombs that had been damaged during battle and noticed what appeared to be an antenna on the bomb. "I didn't tell anyone, but from that I had a fairly good idea what frequency it might be," Gowling said. When they tuned the receiver to the suspected frequency, which was higher than he expected, the bomb's frequency appeared on the screen. But his job was not yet finished. The Germans were using twelve different frequencies for their bombs, so Gowling and his men had eleven more to discover. The former Bell telephone man said he took notes as one of his assistants worked the companion unit and the other two men handled the receivers. Eventually, they were able to determine each of the twelve frequencies used by Germany's secret weapon.

The next step was to build a transmitter to jam the German bomb signals. Gowling took his discovery and ideas on board the USS *Vulcan*, a repair ship traveling in the Mediterranean, and asked a Western Electric employee on the ship to build a variable frequency transmitter to his specifications. "I didn't tell anyone about this," Gowling remembered. Back on the *Davis* the young lieutenant installed the transmitter in the radio shack and climbed to the top of the mast himself to install the antenna, as the ship swayed from one side to the other. His invention worked. When he and his men jammed the signal, Germany's new secret glide bomb, which had been launched at the convoy of American ships, abruptly veered away from its target, traveling erratically before eventually falling harmlessly into the sea amid applause and cheers on board the destroyer escorts.

Gowling quickly provided the details of his discovery to the Naval Research Laboratory in Washington, which, using his specifications, built two units each more powerful than the Gowling prototype for installation on the *Davis* and another DE, the USS *Herbert C. Jones*. Thanks to this invention, Gowling said no ship escorted by either of these DEs ever was hit by one of the German glide bombs. For years after leaving the Navy, Gowling remembered receiving an annual letter from the FBI warning him of the penalties for disclosing details of his discovery to anyone. Until now it has remained his secret. "They never released me to this day," he said. Although Gowling was the actual inventor of the jamming device, he insists it was a "team effort" by him and his four assistants, radar men James A. Combs and Frank A. Frazer and aviation radio technicians Richard L. Youmans and Evan Powers, all of whom worked with Gowling on the receivers and companion unit used to identify the German bomb frequencies.[5]

In January 1944 the *Davis* and *Jones*, both equipped with the new jamming device, arrived in Naples, Italy, to assist amphibious forces with the invasion of the beachhead at Anzio. Their role was to provide protection from submarines and radio-controlled bombs, which they carried out with extraordinary results.

"The Germans didn't take this sitting down," he said, noting that once they became aware that the Americans had developed a jamming device, they sometimes would leave frequencies on for bombs that were not in the air in order to make it more difficult for Gowling and his men to pinpoint the actual bomb's frequency. Gowling said the Germans knew what was happening on board the *Davis*, adding that Axis Sally, radio propagandist for the Third Reich, would sometimes make oblique references to the work he and his men were doing. "I understood the significance of what she was talking about," he said, when she spoke about the jamming device, although he added that most of the others on board his ship did not.[6]

"Let's all concentrate on Frau Meier," a German pilot was overheard by a *Davis* radioman monitoring transmissions from four Nazi planes flying overhead. The DE radioman was fluent in German and knew that "Frau Meier" was German slang for "gossipy woman," a term Axis Sally had used in her radio broadcasts to describe the *Davis*. Within seconds the German bombers peeled off and headed straight for the DE. Although the planes dropped thirteen bombs, ringing the *Davis*, the only damage from the attack was a shrapnel injury to the shoulder of a crewman and some shrapnel holes in the superstructure on the ship's port side. The *Davis* had one more advantage, according to gunner's mate William Riemer: There were six German patriots on board who had defected to the United States and would monitor German radios to determine when bombers left their bases—in essence, an early warning system for the *Davis*.[7]

The *Davis* and *Jones* stayed in the Mediterranean for the duration of the Anzio operation and were very successful at stopping the glide bombs from reaching their marks. During the twelve-day period, 22 January to 2 February 1944, twenty-six radio-controlled glide bombs were launched, and the DEs were able to divert all of them with the jamming device; during the period 2 February through 7 February and 12 February through 14 February 1944, there were thirteen glide bombs launched at Allied ships in the Mediterranean. No ship was hit by the bombs, thanks to Gowling's work, and the success of the Allies at Anzio is due in no small part to the work of Gowling and his men. The task force battle report credits the two DEs with spectacular success in protecting the Allied ships from the radio-controlled bomb, noting that "the efficiency with which the *F.C. Davis* and *H.C. Jones* jammed radio-controlled bombs is an outstanding achievement on the part of these vessels."

Gunner's mate Riemer also recalled the *Davis* being threatened by German frogmen, who attempted to attach limpet mines to the bottom of the ship to blow it up. Watches were set up on the port and starboard sides of the ship, and crewmen dropped quarter-pound blocks of TNT over the side, hoping the explosion who discourage German swimmers from coming too close. None of them ever succeeded in harming the *Davis*.

Gowling believes the DEs were chosen for the jamming work because they were more maneuverable than destroyers, had a shorter turning radius, and were able to move into position to jam the signal more quickly. Jamming devices later were installed on other Allied ships, including the Normandy invading fleet. Germany made a total of 1,386 glide bombs from April 1943 to December 1944, when manufacturing was discontinued since Gowlings' invention of the jamming device rendered them mostly useless.[8] Despite this major success for the Allies in the Mediterranean, however, U-boats in the North Atlantic remained a problem for the Allies, albeit a diminished one from December 1941 to the end of 1942, when German submarines sunk some two thousand Allied ships, sending more than 9 million tons of ships and cargo to the bottom of the sea.

Although the United States now was turning out new ships at lightning speed—with American shipyards building more than 6 million tons each year—Hitler's U-boats still had not given up hope of winning the Battle of the Atlantic, as evidenced by their continued presence in the North Atlantic shipping lanes. Destroyer escorts, radar, sonar, and other antisubmarine measures were making great stride in turning the "hunters" into the "hunted" to be sure; however, U-boats still posed a very real danger to ships at sea. In fact, another one thousand Allied ships were sunk by U-boats from September 1942 to the end of the war.[9]

U-boats routinely would prowl the coastal waters of America, making traveling around offshore waters a dangerous experience. Admiral Döenitz's young and fearless U-boats captains were skilled and cunning adversaries and frequently took what some might consider great risks traveling in shallow waters near America's shores, sometimes even attacking in the daylight hours. But the Nazi submarines had little to fear because the U.S. Navy was not prepared for the U-boat attacks, which accounts for the large number of Allied ships sunk in the United States' own home waters. The first U-boat, *U-85*, was not sunk until May 1942 off Cape Hatteras, North Carolina, by the USS *Roper*, a World War I–era four-stack destroyer. All forty-six sailors on board the U-boat were killed. By stark comparison, the Nazis already had sunk six hundred Allied vessels during the same period.

On 12 June 1943 twenty-year-old Elmo Allen was at his duty station in the radio shack when the USS *Edgar G. Chase* was dispatched to Jupiter's Inlet off West Palm Beach, Florida, to investigate a confirmed U-boat sighting. The DE, accompanied by the destroyer escort USS *Reuben James* and two Coast Guard cutters, raced full speed to a point east of the inlet. The ships searched the area for hours, but no U-boat was found.

Suddenly the klaxon sounded and all hands rushed to battle stations. The *Reuben James* reported "submarine contact." Another false alarm. Three hours later, though, things would change dramatically. The *Chase* sonar operator, Thomas L. Hardwicke, reported "contact" with a strong propeller noise detected. "Loud and clear," reported Hardwicke, noting the U-boat was 1,600 yards away, moving from left to right. Contact was lost again, as a Coast Guard cutter on the attack cut across the DE's bow. A few minutes later, they picked up the signal again, with the sonar operator shouting, "Echo Clear, range 1,600 yards."

"Fire hedgehogs," Capt. John J. Morony of the *Chase* ordered, making a quick course change, as he pursued the submarine at a speed of twelve knots. When the ship closed within two hundred yards of the submarine, twenty-four hedgehogs were launched. Twenty-three explosions were heard under the water, indicating that the weapons had struck something solid. To make sure, eleven depth charges were rolled off the ship, and tremendous underwater explosions were heard, and the sea rose up, splashing over the ship's deck. Sonar contact was lost. A strong pungent odor of diesel fuel was reported in the water, and several men on the DEs reported seeing clothing, splinters, and other debris floating in the water. After searching for another twenty hours, the DEs were ordered to return to port. They were sure the U-boat had been sunk, but there was little evidence to support their belief.[10]

Years later the evidence finally was found. The U-boat they were pursuing was *U-190*, under the command of Captain Max Wintermeyer. The submarine had been dispatched from the German base at Lorient, in occupied France, on 1 May on a mission to sink Allied shipping off the East Coast of the United States, from Virginia to the Florida straits. Years after the war ended, during a chance encounter in Hoboken, New Jersey, between the former U-boat commander, now skipper of a German supertanker, and the *Chase*'s former engineering officer, Lt. Robert Shanklin, it was learned that the German submarine had survived the assault and, as the DEs searched the area, had stayed submerged during the entire twenty hours, exceeding the twelve-hour limit for a submarine to remain safely underwater.

The U-boat commander ordered complete silence on the part of his crew, as the submarine sat motionless on the bottom of the sea. No movements were allowed on board the boat for fear they would be detected by the DEs. U-boat crewmen simply sat silently at their duty stations, waiting for the Allied vessels to leave the area. Unfortunately for many of the German sailors, this cat-and-mouse waiting game would turn deadly, as oxygen supplies became depleted and sailors started to become incapacitated. After the American ships finally called off their search and the boat was able to depart the Florida coast, most of the crew were too ill to perform their duties, and they scarcely were able to make it back to their French base.

Captain Wintermeyer, speaking of destroyer escorts to Lieutenant Shanklin, his former adversary, admitted, "I hated those damn things," and recalled that the encounter off the Florida coast was "the worst experience I had in all of World War II." He said, "They kept us down there for 20 hours—I thought we were kaput and then they went away and we came up for air." It could not be learned whether the presence of debris in the water after the attack had been discharged by the U-boat from its torpedo tubes to fool the American ships into thinking they had destroyed the boat, a tactic often used by U-boats, or whether, in fact, some damage did occur as a result of the DE attack.[11]

By the fall of 1944, Admiral Döenitz was trying to rebuild his U-boat force, which had been suffering since the Allies had been making great headway in curtailing U-boat successes in the North Atlantic, due in no small part to the arrival of the destroyer escorts and stepped up air patrols. Several submarines, so-called nuisance boats, were still prowling the North Atlantic, particularly in the area of the Cape Verde Islands. But the intense Allied attention in the area was starting to make Döenitz rethink whether he should establish a base in Penang, off the Malay Peninsula, as the Japanese had suggested, allowing more direct access to Allied prey in the Indian Ocean and the South Atlantic.

Captain Karl Albrech, the thirty-seven-year-old commander of *U-1062*, a torpedo supply boat, was about to leave Penang in July 1944, after delivering forty torpedoes to the Axis forces there. The U-boat had arrived at the Far East location in April, unloaded its torpedoes, and stayed before embarking on its return journey in order to repair its broken air compressor. The three-month visit was not a pleasant one for the Germans, however, especially because of the unpalatable food available. U-boat sailors were used to a heavy diet of sausage, dark bread, and sauerkraut, not the Japanese fare of rice garnished with vegetables and tinned fish. Unable to stand eating the rations provided, the Germans set up their own small factory to prepare food more to their liking.[12]

By the time July arrived, the crew of *U-1062* was more than ready to go home, and they happily started the long trip back to France. But Albrech and his crew of fifty-five soon would run into something a lot more unpleasant than rice and fish. Tenth Fleet intelligence indicated that the U-boat was planning to rendezvous with *U-219*, headed to the Far East, and they were in the vicinity of the Cape Verde Islands. Three destroyer escorts sped to the scene the morning of 30 September. The USS *Fessenden*, USS *Douglas L. Howard*, and USS *J. R. Y. Blakeley*, all part of the hunter-killer group with the escort-carrier *Mission Bay*, arrived at the location southwest of the islands and started to search. It wasn't long before sonar picked up *U-1062*, and *Fessenden* launched a full pattern of hedgehogs. Fourteen seconds later four underwater explosions were heard and a geyser of water erupted. The *Fessenden* followed up with seventeen depth charges. As night fell a large oil slick covered the area of attack, indicating that Albrech and his crew likely had succumbed.[13]

Ernie Pyle, the celebrated World War II newspaper correspondent who earned a Pulitzer Prize in 1944 for his riveting stories about life as an American GI, took a ride on a destroyer escort, the USS *Reynolds*, as the little ship carried the famous journalist—who later would write about his adventures—from Iwo Jima to Guam in February 1945.

"Drenched from head to foot with salt water," Pyle wrote of his experiences on board the *Reynolds*. "Sleep with a leg crooked around my rack so I won't fall out. Put wet bread under my dinner tray to keep it from sliding. Even got my Jesus-shoes ordered." He continued, describing destroyer escorts for his readers: "A DE, my friends, is a destroyer escort. It's a ship long and narrow and sleek, something like a destroyer. But it's much smaller. It's a baby destroyer. It's the American version of the British corvette." His column, which, although it was mailed back to his newspaper from somewhere in the Pacific, was never published.[14]

"They are rough and tumble little ships," Pyle wrote. "Their after decks are laden with depth charges. They can turn in half the space of a destroyer. Their forward guns can seldom be used because waves are breaking over them. They roll and they plunge. They buck and they twist. They shudder and they fall through space." Living on board a DE was certainly a challenge, Pyle wrote, but getting on board one of these little ships in the middle of the vast ocean was an even more hair-raising adventure.

Transfer between ships was accomplished by use of a breeches buoy, consisting of a canvas sack, a heavy line, and a bunch of strong sailors to ensure that you made it. Ships would use this method to transfer sailors, mail, movies, and supplies among other items, between ships. Sometimes the cargo in the sack would end up in the drink when the line would unloosen from the clamps, allowing the cargo to drop into the water. "To help give you an idea what this operation is like," Pyle wrote, "suppose you ran a rope from the roof of your house to the roof of your barn, and left a little sag in it. Then you put a pulley on the rope, hang a sack to the pulley, get into the sack, and then slide from the house to the barn. Fun, eh?"[15]

Pyle, who transferred from the carrier USS *Windham Bay* to the *Reynolds*, remembered the cold winter day when the larger ship came alongside of the destroyer escort, which was disappearing behind the giant Pacific Ocean waves. The wind was howling as they readied the reporter for his nerve-wracking trip between the two warships. He was strapped in a life jacket and then placed inside the canvas sack: "When they're all set, the sailors shoot a line across from ship to ship. They actually shoot it, with a rifle, for you could never throw a line that far in these winds."

Transferring men between ships on the high seas was a hair-raising experience, especially for the person in the so-called breeches buoy. The sailor climbed into the heavy canvas sack, which had leg holes, making it resemble a pair of breeches. He was hauled across the water using a pulley system and the arms of some very strong sailors. Sometimes the sailor ended up in the drink. *Photo taken by Harold S. Deal; courtesy Jeff Deal*

Pyle, who said he could not swim a stroke, continued: "On one ship the line is made fast. But on the other it runs through a pulley, and behind the pulley is a long line of sailors holding to the line. An order is shouted. Then men on the heavy line pull it up taut, raising me off the deck. Half a dozen hands lift me over the rail. Another order. The men on the other ship run with their lines, and I'm on my way across." On the way over, Pyle wrote, "you whiz up and you whiz down, just like you were a yo-yo. Sometimes your sack almost smacks the water," which, in fact, is designed so that if the bag falls into the ocean, the passenger would automatically be provided with a flotation device—little comfort for the individual who is dangling in the air as he is pulled across the open waters. "Finally, you arrive on the other side. A dozen hands grab your sack, and pull you onto deck, and steady you until you've got out of the devilish contraption. You heave a great sigh of relief."[16]

Owen Nicholson, a twenty-year-old sonarman on board the *Reynolds*, watched as Pyle arrived on his ship and said the reporter told him that, in spite of the countless dangerous battles on which he had reported, the transfer between the two ships was one of the most frightening trips of his life. Nicholson, an early high school graduate in Denver, Colorado, who had just started college as the war broke out, volunteered for the Navy and, after boot camp, was assigned to the *Reynolds*, originally built for the British. After being redesignated as an American destroyer escort, the *Reynolds* spent its entire career in the Pacific theater.

It was a cold and windy late afternoon, and all the enlisted men on board the *Reynolds* knew was that they were to come alongside the carrier to "transfer a man" to their ship, unaware that they were about to meet the most famous reporter of World War II, according to an entry Nicholson made in his wartime diary. "The officers were all lined up waiting for him," Nicholson said. "After Ernie Pyle shook hands with all the officers, he told them he was going to eat with the men." Nicholson said Capt. Marvin Smith and the other officers all were "quite miffed" that the famed journalist chose to eat with the enlisted men rather than dine with the officers, who had a special meal prepared in anticipation of his arrival. But Pyle was "a regular guy," Nicholson said. "He was interested in what you [the enlisted guys] thought, and what you were going through."[17]

Pyle, best known and most beloved for his stories about regular GIs, seldom wrote about or spent time with officers during his time as a war correspondent. Nicholson recalled one supper with the journalist, who was on board three days and two nights, when he held up a piece of bread to the light to show Pyle the weevils. "We told him that was how we got our protein. Ernie got a kick out of that." He said that a provision ship in his convoy gladly sent over flour when the *Reynolds* ran out. "They were glad to get rid of it" because the flour was full of weevils. But he did remember that, while Pyle was on board, the sailors were given the best food in a long time.

Pyle seldom slept while on board, Nicholson said, instead choosing to spend as much time as possible with sailors, sitting in a corner on deck, talking to them during their watches, and recording his conversations in a little notebook. "He was the most engaging individual I had ever met." Nicholson wrote in his diary, "Ernie Pyle is a swell, regular guy. He won't even talk to the officers, but spends his entire time talking to the enlisted men. You can talk to him just as any enlisted man and he talks back just as if he's one of us."

Pyle told the sailors they were on a "luxury cruise" compared to the fellows in Europe, Nicholson wrote. He said his shipmates asked Pyle whether the European or Pacific wars were the worst places to be, to which Nicholson said Pyle replied, "War is hell, wherever it is, but at least in Europe the guys are on the front lines, then they get relieved for a few days. They could go back to civilization and could steal some chickens and get some wine and at least have some semblance of normalcy before they'd have to go back to the front." Comparing the men in the European theater to the DE sailors, Pyle noted that the boredom on board a DE in the Pacific was "uncanny." He told the sailors "You go to sleep at night, you see the water. You get up in the morning and see the water. That is something that few people can understand."[18]

Pyle obviously enjoyed, and was proud of, his three days on board the *Reynolds*, as evidenced by the words he wrote: "We mothered ships that were big and slow. We were tiny in comparison. We ran 'way out ahead, and to the side. We and DEs like us formed the 'screen,' and there was nothing bigger than us in it. We felt like strutting." The reporter went on, comparing the DEs' role to that of a little boy: "We felt like the little boy of the plains left at home for the first time to protect his mother from the Indians—the only man on the place!"[19]

6

Blood Frozen in My Veins

"Right standard rudder," shouted Lt. John F. McWhorter as the American warship dropped out of formation to investigate a possible sonar contact astern of the vessel. Steaming on that foggy April morning in 1945, some six hundred miles northwest of the Azores, the USS *Frederick C. Davis*, or "Fightin' Freddy," as it was affectionately nicknamed, was part of a fourteen-ship hunter-killer group dubbed Operation Teardrop providing a picket barrier to stop Nazi U-boats from sneaking into U.S. coastal waters.

Americans still had not recovered from the near-panic of a few months earlier when New York City mayor Fiorello LaGuardia had warned of possible rocket attacks on the Big Apple. Although Germany's U-boat force was greatly diminished by spring of 1945, residents in U.S. coastal cities still feared the Third Reich had a secret new weapon—robot rocket bombs—which could be launched from submarines to destroy coastal communities.

In fact, prowling silently below the water that very morning was one of Hitler's U-boats, on its way to the United States. Although it did not carry robot rocket bombs, the snorkel-equipped vessel was listening intently for evidence of any propeller sounds from Allied vessels above. "Propeller noises from several ships. Some turning fast, some slowly grinding," twenty-eight-year-old Captain Paul Just stated as he ordered *U-546* to periscope depth so he could investigate. "On the horizon stands a large dark square. I know this silhouette from the last trip: aircraft carrier," he noted, adding that there were no escorts visible, nor planes in the sky.

The carrier quickly disappeared over the horizon and Just ordered his boat below, where he could listen and observe undetected. He wanted to locate and sink that carrier. Soon the German captain would hear the telltale sound of propellers and again would rise to periscope level. He saw six destroyer escorts "slim and beautiful, as they cut through the waves as with a knife" but realized they were "a magnificent, but treacherous picture." The captain knew what he had to do.

Just continued to observe the ships, now steaming directly toward his location. His crew readied torpedoes. "Perspiration is on my forehead . . . my breath stops, my mouth is dry," the captain said, describing the moment they were about to fire on the American ships. As *U-546* launched its torpedoes, the captain realized what would be in store for him and his crew once the remaining DEs seek revenge: "Hell awaits us."

As Lieutenant McWhorter swung the *Davis* about to investigate a possible enemy submarine, his sonarmen picked up *U-546*'s signature about 650 yards away. The DE captain rushed to the bridge as the crew readied weapons for attack. It was too late. The acoustic torpedo fired from the submarine was about to hit its mark

The missile plowed into the port side of the destroyer escort a little forward of midships, followed by a massive explosion, making a shambles of the flying bridge and instantly killing Lieutenant McWhorter and everyone else on the bridge. The ship's young captain, James R. Crosby, was cut in two by a steel shroud. Sleeping crewmen in the aft living section of the ship were thrown from their bunks while other crewmen in the forward sections were killed instantly or flung overboard. The mast broke near the yardarm as the ship crumpled and buckled straining to remain afloat.

Ruptured fuel lines fed fires that burned out of control. The wardroom was ablaze as other compartments in the forward section of the ship flooded in a matter of seconds. Within five minutes of the attack, the ship's buckling quarterdecks were deeply submerged and the *Davis* broke in two. "We knew she was going down quickly," Ens. Philip K. Lundeberg recalled thinking after leading a group of repairmen hurriedly through the ship, dogging down hatches and securing valves in a valiant but vain attempt to keep the ship from sinking. By the time the ensign gave the order to abandon ship, many of the men already were in the water, some thrown overboard by the torpedo blast, while others remained trapped inside the burning, twisted wreckage as it plunged to the bottom of the sea.[1]

Levi Hancock, acting chief boatswain's mate from Savannah, Georgia, had just left the mess hall, one compartment away from where the torpedo hit, and was climbing up the ladder. "I was blown off the ladder and woke up on a sister ship," Hancock said. When fished from the icy waters, he was clinging to a timber, dazed and struggling to remain afloat. Hancock lost his left leg, and his right knee was crushed and mangled. He lost some teeth and had severe lacerations on his face. "A corpsman on the sister ship sewed my lip back on," Hancock said, noting his dungarees were in tatters, resembling a hula skirt. The twenty-year-old country boy from Savannah, who had learned about the water while working summers on a shrimp boat, quit high school so he could make the Navy his career. He never would realize that dream but would survive to return to Georgia, where he would spend the rest of his life on crutches. "I was lucky to be alive," he said.[2]

Nineteen-year-old Roy Adcock, who left high school in 1943 to join the Navy, was the ship's cook and had just settled down in his bunk around 8:00 AM after being on duty for twenty-four hours. He was jarred awake by a crash that seemed to send shock waves throughout the ship. "I was asleep in the top bunk and I wound up on the deck," Adcock said. The lights on the ship went out and the steam pipes were bursting as the young sailor headed aft and up a ladder to get to his battle station. "I thought an airplane had hit us," Adcock said, as he looked up to see the mast broken off and dangling. "My battle station was the number one 3-inch gun," he recalled, noting that as he rushed to get there, he was surprised to see the deck awash and burning red hot from the inferno below.

Adcock grabbed a life jacket handed out by a shipmate, strapping it on quickly before jumping over the side into the iceberg-laden waters. Although he was not a swimmer and, in fact, had never been on the water before joining the Navy, he used the doggy paddle to reach a floater net, a type of life raft fashioned by floats tied together with lines. He clung to the net in the freezing water, hoping one of the other DEs would pick him up. The USS *Otter* rescued Adcock and eleven other crew members. Eight survived. "I was froze to death. I woke up aboard the ship in an officer's bed, covered with thirteen blankets," he noted. "They said my blood was frozen in my veins." He added that part of his feet have no feeling to this day. "I don't know how we made it."[3]

Ens. Ruloff F. Kip knows what saved his life that day. A radar officer on the sister ship, the USS *Pillsbury*, Kip was on temporary assignment to the *Davis* the day of the attack. He had been sent to the DE to repair some radar equipment and had retired to his cabin after finishing his midnight watch.

Sailors on board DEs in the North Atlantic had a lot more to contend with than Hitler's U-boats. Ice, freezing rain, snow, bitterly cold temperatures, heavy seas, and howling winds often made life on board these ships almost unbearable. But the teenage sailors, seen here on board the ice-encrusted USS *Thomas* on a 1945 trip to Iceland, had a job to do—and they did it despite harsh conditions. *Courtesy the Destroyer Escort Historical Museum*

Ensign Kip shared that tiny cabin, once used to store potatoes, with Ensign Lundeberg. He decided to catch some sleep before continuing his work on the radar equipment. "When the torpedo hit," Kip said, "drawers jumped out and there was a great deal of broken glass about." With lights out all over the ship, Kip had difficulty orienting himself, especially since he had only recently arrived on board and was not yet familiar with the whole ship. He rushed to follow Ensign Lundeberg, who made a "bee line" for the door.

When Kip, dressed only in his skivvy shirt and shorts, realized that the ship was in serious trouble, he rushed back to the cabin to get his heavy, flax wool sweater for warmth. He had received the "letter sweater" for track while studying engineering at Princeton University in 1943. Kip put on the sweater and quickly made his way topside, passing a grotesque sight of battered and bloody men with badly burned faces being helped into life jackets. Jumping overboard into the icy waters, Kip made his way to a floater net, where another crew member was clinging for his life.

Within a short time the USS *Flaherty* came alongside the floater net and fired empty depth-charge cases for the sailors to grab on to and inflated a number of rubber life rafts, which were dropped overboard. Although some *Davis* survivors were taken on board the ship, the rescue was cut short as the *Flaherty* received a positive sonar contact with a U-boat that appeared to be heading directly for the ship. The DE sped off at flank speed to pursue the U-boat, leaving Kip and many of the other wounded floundering in the frigid waters.

A little later the USS *Hayter*, fresh from its work with the USS *Otter*, *Varian*, and *Hubbard* in sinking *U-248* three months earlier, arrived to complete the grim work of sorting out survivors from the dead bodies floating in the water. Kip swam toward the DE and grabbed a life ring thrown from the ship. The next thing he remembered was waking up in a bunk in the wardroom, shaking from shock. A pharmacist mate later told the ensign that the Princeton sweater saved him from hypothermia as he floated in the freezing waters.[4]

Peter Karetka, a signalman on board the *Hayter*, grew up in the Depression years in Holyoke, Massachusetts, where his father worked as a slip cutter in the Whiting Paper Mill. After leaving school in the ninth grade to study auto mechanics at vocational school, he spent time in the Civilian Conservation Corps. Once he turned eighteen he decided to join the Navy so he could see the world. Enlisting in November 1940 and following eight weeks of boot camp, he was assigned briefly to a carrier before being assigned to a destroyer, the USS *Hughes*. In 1944 he was transferred to the newly commissioned destroyer escort *Hayter*, after two months of training in sub-chaser school in Miami.

"I saw the *Davis* get hit," said Karetka, who was stationed on the bridge that foggy morning in April 1945 in the North Atlantic. "She split in two, it couldn't have been more evenly cut than if someone measured it from the center and then started cutting it in half." Prior to the hit, as his ship was turning starboard, Karetka said the *Davis* broke out its black pennant indicating that they had made sonar contact with a submarine. Within seconds the torpedo sliced the ship in half. Watching through his long glass, Karetka saw the men from the *Davis* starting to dive overboard as the crippled destroyer escort started to sink. He said sharks immediately showed up, and Lieutenant Stratton up on the forecastle of his ship used a rifle to shoot the sharks as they attacked the men in the icy waters. "I would hear them squeal as the sharks hit them," the signalman said.

Karetka alerted Capt. Fred Hughey, pleading with the skipper to save the men. The captain told him to round up some volunteers and head out to rescue as many men as possible. Four men, including Karetka, lowered the whaleboat over the side and rushed out two hundred feet to pick up survivors. They rescued twelve men from the *Davis*, including one sailor whose face had been seared by steam. "There was no skin on his face," Karetka said, who noted that he still has nightmares about that sailor's burned face.

DEs were outfitted with wood-hulled motor whaleboats used when crewmen had to leave the ship for rescue operations or to investigate, for example, debris on the water following an attack on a suspected U-boat. After being lowered into the water, sailors from the USS *Liddle* prepare to pilot the twenty-six-foot craft through heavy seas. *Photo taken by Harold S. Deal; courtesy Jeff Deal*

Ensign Lundeberg, the young officer who initially tried to control damage on board *Davis* after the explosion, was asleep following his midnight watch when the torpedo hit. "It sounded like a collision," he recalled, and he and his damage-control team hurried forward to secure hatches and watertight doors to prevent the ship from sinking. Once he realized that the ship was going down, he went topside and was shocked at how the *Davis* had caved down in the middle. Although sailors are trained to jump overboard when abandoning ship, the *Davis* was so far down and the decks so flooded by then that he said, "I simply walked right into the water," which by now was only two feet below the deck.[5]

Of the 192 men on board, only 77 survived, including 3 officers, Ensign Lundeberg, Ensign Kip, and Robert E. Minerd, the ship's assistant communications officer and the senior surviving officer. When the torpedo hit, Minerd was in the Combat Information Center (CIC) leaning over the dead-reckoning tracer, while he tracked the U-boat. Everyone else was killed in CIC, probably when they were catapulted to the overhead, sustaining fatal head injuries, Lundeberg theorizes. Although Minerd was stunned from the torpedo's impact, he was still able to break open the door to the pilot house where he discovered the helmsmen, legs crumpled up in his trousers. Minerd gallantly carried him to the door of the outer bridge, where he barely had time to fit the crippled shipmate with a life jacket before both were swept over the side of the ship.[6] The *Davis*, which only a year ago had successfully "jammed" the German glide bombs and shot down thirteen enemy airplanes in the Mediterranean, earned a final, albeit dubious, distinction as the last American warship sunk in the Atlantic in World War II.

Lundeberg, who later in life became friends with Paul Just, commander of *U-546*, confirmed that the commander was not initially planning to attack the *Davis* but, having sighted a carrier about five hundred yards in the distance, decided to try and sneak through the destroyer escort picket barrier in order to attack. Lundeberg said Just gambled at moving through the line of escorts at periscope depth and almost made it until sonar contact was picked up by the *Davis*. Recognizing that he had been caught, Just ordered the torpedo launched against the destroyer escort at near-point-blank range.[7]

Even as the floating remains of the *Davis* disappeared beneath the icy waters of the North Atlantic, its sister destroyer escorts were on the hunt to find the U-boat and destroy it. Within thirty-seven minutes of the *Davis* hit, the USS *Flaherty* picked up a positive sonar contact and the other DEs moved in for the assault. Hedgehogs were launched and sailors on board listened and waited for an underwater explosion signifying the submarine had been hit. There was no explosion—and this U-boat commander was no amateur.

The U-boat went deep and silent. The battle would last all day and into the early evening before the U-boat finally was forced to surface. Captain Just was highly skilled in his efforts to evade capture over the next twelve hours. The captain ordered all men not on watch to lay in their bunks to conserve oxygen and keep activity and noise to a minimum. "They are probably rescuing their comrades and their dead," Just said. He circled around the area as his wake distorted the ships' sonar signals and ejected air slugs from his torpedo tubes to confuse the DEs. He even was able to jam the DEs' sonar by sending out his own signals and dove deep beneath the temperature gradient. "I let U-546 sink to 150 meters," Just wrote. "At 200 meters is the absolute limit. We stay at 150 to have a few more reserves. [Propeller] noises are getting louder, they are coming!"[8]

"You know these guys were pretty smart down below. They knew how to evade," remembered Pellegrino Soriano, a sailor on board another DE, the USS *Janssen*. "They had all kinds of devices that would clutter up . . . our sounding gear. But our sound people . . . were getting pretty smart after a while. We could almost tell what kind of evasive maneuvers that the sub was thinking."[9]

The battle finally came to an end as one of the DE hedgehogs wrecked the submarine's bridge and punctured the vessel's pressurized hull, rupturing the batteries and releasing chlorine gas, killing all sailors in the forward section of the U-boat. Just described the scene below: "There is no longer a water jet coming into the boat, it is an avalanche of white gushing mass. Tons of weight are added to the boat within a short time. Our feet are losing ground. We all hold on as good as we can; don't fall back. Everywhere it cracks and rattles, it is totally dark. We cannot see each other any longer. Objects are flying like projectiles to the back wall. Is this the end?"

Indeed it was. The captain finally relented and the German boat broke through the white-capped waters as all the DEs opened fire. But Captain Just was not yet done fighting. Broaching the surface, he launched a torpedo at the *Flaherty*. It missed. "That stinker fired a torpedo at me!" exclaimed the DE's skipper. The DEs continued their barrage until, finally, the submarine started to sink. German sailors, rushing to escape the vessel, jumped into the frigid Atlantic. "Cease fire, the sub is sinking," Just said.

Rescue operations continued for nearly two hours as the DEs were able to save thirty-two crew members and the U-boat skipper. Twenty-six Germans died. After interrogation it was learned that *U-546* was one of six U-boats launched by Hitler in the waning days of the war in a final attempt to disrupt the East Coast shipping lanes. They were fitted with a new device called a snorkel, which allowed them to remain submerged; they only needed to surface periodically to run their diesel engines and recharge the boat's batteries. The device also permitted fresh air to be drawn into the boat. But following interrogation it was determined that, despite East Coast fears, there were no plans to rocket bomb American cities.[10]

Seaman Soriano of the *Janssen* recalled a lot of anger on the ships toward the German sailors, who were frightened about what the Americans might do to them after sinking one of the DEs, killing 115 American sailors. But Soriano said the skipper warned the crew that the prisoners would be fed and clothed and their injuries would be attended to, and if they died, they would receive a proper burial at sea, just as an American sailor would receive. "It was quite moving," Soriano said. "I was quite impressed with that, that we believed [that] and we did what we believed. We never maltreated them. It gave us a whole new outlook that these people were human, they were afraid."

"Who is Truman?" asked one of the prisoners taken on board the USS *Pillsbury*. President Roosevelt had just died and Harry Truman was the new American president. The prisoner, in broken English, continued, "Let us go and we'll go help you defeat the Japs, then we'll go to Russia and wipe them out too."[11]

The sinking of a ship, such as the USS *Frederick C. Davis*, forced the teenage sailors to grow up very quickly. Watching your shipmates die a brutal and bloody death, witnessing your ship—your home away from home—explode in a violent fire storm as you are tossed into a raging and cold sea, made these young recruits come of age very rapidly. Although many of them had voluntarily signed up to serve, they certainly never had any of this in mind when they enlisted.

Following the Japanese attack on Pearl Harbor, thousands of teenagers rushed to join the military to avenge Japan's assault on America. Sixteen-year-old Warren J. Kerrigan was leaving the Fabian Theater at Washington and Newark Streets in Hoboken, New Jersey, when he heard the news of the attack. He wanted to join up right then, but he waited until he graduated from high school.

"We were mad about what happened and wanted to do something about it," Kerrigan said. He lived at 314 Monroe Street, directly across the street from young Frank Sinatra, who was nine years older than Kerrigan. But young Kerrigan had some very unfortunate luck when his entertainer father, an Irish tenor returning from a gig, was killed by a drunk driver. Kerrigan was only fifteen. Growing up in Hoboken without a father was difficult, Kerrigan said, describing himself as a "dead end kid." He said the U.S. Navy changed all of that, giving him structure and teaching him about authority and the importance of following orders."[12] Assigned to the USS *Frost*, Kerrigan and his shipmates went on to distinguish themselves by sinking five German submarines, a record number of "kills" in the Atlantic Ocean for any destroyer escort in World War II. The ship received a presidential citation for outstanding combat service, earning seven battle stars over the course of the war.

In the beginning the story of the USS *Frost*, named flagship of the escort division group, was routine and uneventful, making a safe Atlantic Ocean convoy crossing in very heavy seas from New York to Casablanca in November 1943. The most notable incident during that cruise involved an emergency surgery that was needed by a seaman on board one of the merchant ships, performed by the physician on board the *Frost*, who used the ship's dining table as an operating table. Conditions for surgery were not the best, for either patient or doctor, who wielded his scalpel as the tiny ship tossed and rolled on the heavy seas. The operation was a success and the seaman was put ashore to recuperate once the convoy reached its destination.

Boredom was pretty standard for sailors on board destroyer escorts, and watching movie films help to fill that void and provide sailors with a taste of what was going on back home. "Radio City Music Hall" as it became known on some ships, consisted of a big white screen and a 35-mm projection machine showing feature films wherever they could find some space—a chow hall, a sleeping compartment, and, in the warmer weather, the forecastle or fantail of the vessel. Sailors rested in chairs, laid on the deck, or reclined on kapok life preservers watching Humphrey Bogart and Lana Turner "dance a jig" on the screen as the tiny ship rolled and bounced on the turbulent North Atlantic.

Sailors on board DEs were up before 6:00 AM, lining up for a hearty breakfast of bacon, French toast, or pancakes. Afterward, they cleaned up, got ready for inspection, and received instructions for the day's work. Roll call was taken to ensure that no one had fallen overboard during the night. Here officers inspect sailors on board the USS *Liddle*, making sure the sailors' shoes are properly shined. *Photo taken by Harold S. Deal; courtesy Jeff Deal*

The Navy leased about three hundred films a year for viewing by sailors at sea. Before the war they obtained three copies of each film; however, after the war began and the number of ships and demand for feature films increased dramatically, the Navy leased twenty-one copies of each film, which were circulated and traded between ships. A few ships had other ways to deal with the dullness of the day-in, day-out monotony of escorting vessels across the sea, and the USS *Frost* was one of those ships with a recipe for breaking up the dull routine.

Five crew members formed a musical group dubbed the "Fantail Five," entertaining the crew and officers with music of the 1940s, often before evening movies were shown on the fantail of the ship. Alfred Chickini, radarman, played trombone; Greg Eckholm, sonarman, played trumpet; A. J. Browning, sonarman, played saxophone; Chief McElfrish, boatswain's mate, was the drummer; and John Brinkman, sonarman, played clarinet. Two band members were professional musicians who went on to play in the "big bands" following the war, Kerrigan said. In fact, in 1945, while the *Frost* was docked

Many ships had mascots on board. The dogs and cats brought friendship and some happiness and fun to the crew, reminding them of the pets they may have left behind. Sailors on board one ship even sewed their ship's dog his own life jacket in case they needed to abandon ship. Here the USS *Pettit*'s mascot gets ready for his evening meal. *Courtesy Martin Davis and the Destroyer Escort Historical Museum*

in Manhattan, they were invited to play on the New York City radio station WNEW's *Make Believe Ballroom*, later cutting a record called *Muskrat Ramble*. The *Frost*'s Lt. Stanley Mosky called the Fantail Five a "fantastic and talented bunch" who helped crewmen and officers alike pass the time on the vast and lonely North Atlantic. They were good for morale.[13]

Most destroyer escorts were not so fortunate as to have a five-piece band on board, but the USS *Bates*, commissioned at the Hingham Shipyard in September 1943, had something even a little better: Eddy Duchin, piano prodigy and renowned "Magic Fingers of the Radio" bandleader, had been assigned to the ship as an officer. Duchin had his record collection with him, and the *Bates* also had a small piano so he could entertain the crew and officers at sea, and sometimes when his ship was in port.

Joining the Navy because he "always liked ships," Duchin was a graduate of the Massachusetts School of Pharmacy and received his basic training at the Great Lakes center, where he also assisted with the Navy band. Later he received specialized instruction at the sub-chaser center in Miami before serving as executive officer on board a coastal patrol ship (PC) prior to his assignment to the *Bates*. Although his band was one of the most popular in the country, appearing on radio shows with Ed Wynn and George Burns and Gracie Allen, Lieutenant Duchin—who longed for sea duty—said, "I've put my music aside for the duration. My band is broken up." Fortunately for the crew of the *Bates*, the piano player turned naval officer would often relent and spend some time entertaining the sailors.[14]

But the *Bates* and *Frost* were the exceptions. "It was pretty dull at sea," Kerrigan said unless, of course, one of Hitler's U-boats showed up. And that's just what happened on 26 April, when the hunter-killer group was steaming in the early morning hours near Cape Verde Islands. The *Frost* picked up an exceptionally loud and clear echo, indicating that a submarine was dead ahead about 1,000 yards. Crew members rushed to battle stations as the *Frost* and USS *Huse* raced toward the location, closing at about 220 yards. The *Frost* fired its hedgehogs, resulting in a tremendous underwater explosion just ahead of the ship, which was jarred and rocked from the shock waves. Two more severe explosions followed, indicating the crew had hit its target. But no oil or debris, usual signs of a hit, were visible. But it wouldn't take long for the crew to receive confirmation when later that afternoon an airplane from the group's carrier spotted a large oil slick in the area of the attack.

To cut down on boredom at sea, some ships had talented crew members who got together to play music. On the USS *Frost*, the Fantail Five entertained the crew. In 1945, while the ship was docked in Manhattan, the group was invited to play on radio station WNEW's *Make Believe Ballroom* and later cut a record, *Muskrat Ramble. Courtesy the Destroyer Escort Historical Museum*

"Smelled like an oil refinery," was how the area was described, the brown slick covering a seven-mile-long area and a thick yellowish brown emulsified oil continued to bubble up to the surface for days. The submarine sunk by the *Frost* later was identified as *U-488*, one of the Nazis' milk cows, used to carry provisions, diesel fuel, ammunition, and even mail from home to the other U-boats. Taking out these types of submarines was a high priority for the Allies because, without fuel and supplies, the U-boats would be "dead in the water." *U-488*'s Lieutenant Studt and his crew of sixty-three German sailors were entombed 560 feet below the ocean's surface.[15]

With the first U-boat "kill" under its belt, the *Frost* returned to New York in May for repairs, maintenance, and much-needed shore leave for its crews. But there was still a war going on, and after a two-week period, the destroyer escort was again at sea on its second hunter-killer mission. This time they would be heading to the Azores where the Germans had set up a picket line of

U-boats stretching to Newfoundland, providing meteorological information for German command as well as intercepting convoys with supplies for Gen. Dwight D. Eisenhower's European campaign.[16]

Meanwhile another milk cow, *U-490*, commanded by Captain Wilhelm Gerlach, was on its way to provide supplies and fuel to submarines along the picket line. The supply ship carried no torpedoes and spent most of its trip underwater, using the snorkel device to avoid having to surface and risk detection. On 11 June, according to *U-490* crewman Kurt Bunzel, after five weeks underwater, the boat dove to a depth of eighty meters "with the hope of spending a peaceful Sunday in the middle of the Atlantic." Bunzel said that "extreme caution" was needed because the submarine was asked to surface the day before and radio its position to headquarters. Transmitting that signal, it would turn out, was the beginning of the end for *U-490*, as it was intercepted by the Americans' high frequency/direction finding equipment, commonly referred to as Huff Duff, which zeroed in on the radio frequency used by German submarines.[17]

Armed with the submarine's probable location, the hunter-killer group sped toward the site, where it was about to disrupt the German submariners' peaceful Sunday morning. The *Frost* picked up the first contact between Flores and the Flemish Cap and quickly deployed its foxer gear. The *Frost* did not know this U-boat, a supply sub, had no torpedoes. As the *Frost* began firing hedgehogs, *U-490* crew member Bunzel said the boat immediately dove to 200 meters, although they wanted to dive deeper but feared the boat would be unable to sustain such greater depths. The boat eventually did go deeper, coming to rest about 280 meters below the surface, very close to its maximum safety limits.

"The ribs began to croak," Bunzel said, as the U-boat "lay defenseless." He recalled that the "attack lasted all Sunday til midnight. During that time more than three hundred depth charges exploded in our immediate range, and although the crew was shaken up and already thought their final hour had arrived, the boat proved the quality of German workmanship for which we were all very thankful."[18]

The *Frost* pounded the submarine with depth charges from morning to night Sunday, never receiving confirmation that it had been sunk. Sonar confirmed that the ship was there but not moving. Frustrated and exhausted, the

Frost decided to deceive the boat into thinking the Americans had left. The order was given and all the DEs steamed away from the site. "We reduced our speed going out, and went out a few miles and just stopped dead. We came back very slowly and there they were, like sitting ducks," Kerrigan said. *U-490*, with its batteries depleted and convinced the Americans had left, finally surfaced to use its diesel engines to recharge the boat's batteries. "About 2 a.m. the command was given to surface," Bunzel wrote. "Very quickly and with the hope that the enemy would not notice. We surfaced without equalizing pressure. On opening the hatch by the commander, the situation turned to our disadvantage, the boat lay immediately to one side and shivered once more after a powerful explosion."[19]

The night skies suddenly brightened as the DEs, quietly waiting in the nearby distance, fired star shells illuminating the U-boat, which had surfaced almost between the *Frost* and USS *Snowden*. "Guys started jumping overboard," Kerrigan said, adding that the submarine sent a message by blinker signal to the Americans—"SOS. Please Save Us"—as the crew of sixty sailors started diving into the icy, dark waters. The *Frost*, *Snowden*, and USS *Inch* continued firing their deck guns at the submarine as they raced toward the vessel, illuminated by the ships' powerful searchlights. Suddenly the U-boat began its scuttling operation to prevent the Americans from capturing it and all its secret documents. The boat's Kingston valves were opened, flooding the vessel, which quickly disappeared below the ocean's surface.

The *Frost*'s Huff Duff radioman, Frank Musumeci, remembered looking overboard at the screaming and shivering German sailors, some in yellow life rafts and others struggling to stay afloat in the pitch-black icy waters. For a moment William Creech, the ship's twenty-year-old signalman, thought they might have sunk an English submarine. When one of the submariners called up, "How are the Brooklyn Dodgers doing?" another shouted, "Are you English or Americans?" fearing that they would not fare as well if taken prisoner by the English. "But humanity won out," Musumeci noted, adding that all sixty sailors were rescued. Musumeci, who grew up in a poor family in New York City's lower East Side, also was struck by the fact that the German sailors "looked like us," were young—many just teenagers—and spoke English. He said some were previously merchant mariners and told the crew about their experiences in Charleston and Savannah during those years. He said they did not expect to be rescued.[20]

"High waves and the endless depth of the sea around us. Under those conditions the crew drifted slowly, scattered because of the high sea, in the dark Atlantic, expecting to die there," *U-490* crew member Kurt Bunzel remembered. "The enemy had turned away and thus our last hope disappeared in the dark of night. The stars above us were shining brightly and dark was the hope of ever seeing our home and families again."

"Then a miracle happened," Bunzel noted. "After about two hours, dark silhouettes of ships appeared on the horizon." The Americans had returned to rescue the U-boat survivors. "The hostility was put to rest and humanity took over. The shipwrecked were rescued after the old sailors tradition in peace time." The prisoners were given dry clothes, food, and coffee and would live to once again see their families.[21] Warren Kerrigan's ship took on board thirteen German survivors, including Gerlach, the executive officer, and the boat's engineering department. Gerlach spoke English, and the prisoners were treated with respect.

Ship Storekeeper Robert Holman, who grew up in rural South Carolina and learned about the water paddling a rowboat on a fish pond, thought the U-boat encounter was most unique. "Not a man was so much as scratched on either side, no one was hurt," he recalled, adding that the Germans appeared certain that the Americans would simply shoot them while they struggled in the water. That did not happen.[22]

After delivering the German prisoners to Casablanca and picking up fuel, ammunition, and supplies, the *Frost* and its hunter-killer group were once again at sea in search of Nazi U-boats. Meanwhile, twenty-five-year-old Captain Gerth Genmeiner and his crew of fifty-seven on board *U-154* were at sea as well on their way to America, taking a southern route to Cape Hatteras, North Carolina, where the boat had been ordered to disrupt Allied shipping.[23]

Prowling the waters east of the Azores, the USS *Inch*, one of the hunter-killer group, picked up a sonar contact with Genmeiner's boat. The German skipper ordered torpedoes fired at the DE, narrowly missing their mark. The *Inch* launched a hedgehog attack and quickly was joined by the *Frost*, which also fired hedgehogs and depth charges in order to strike the enemy below. The two ships pounded the U-boat for about an hour and a half until a violent underwater explosion rocked the small vessels. The DE sailors knew the target had been hit. Within minutes oil, shattered wood, and glass floated to the surface, along with other debris, including jackets with military insignia, German cigarette lighters, and, what usually was considered proof positive, human remains.[24]

After the successful U-boat sinking, the hunter-killer group proceeded west to New York Navy Yard, where the ships were repaired and overhauled before, once again, being ordered to sea in search of enemy submarines. But the American sailors soon would come face-to-face with an enemy far more unpredictable, far more deadly than any Nazi submarine, an enemy for which even a larger vessel such as an American destroyer was no match, let alone a ship the size of the *Frost*.

It was September in the Atlantic and the tropics were brewing up a storm. The destroyer USS *Warrington* departed Norfolk, Virginia, escorting the USS *Hyades*, a refrigerated provision ship known to sailors as a "beef boat," on its maiden voyage, its skipper on his first command. The ships were heading to Trinidad and the Panama Canal when, two days out of Norfolk, they ran into heavy weather off the coast of Florida. As night fell winds gusted up to one hundred miles per hour, blinding rain slowed the ships to four knots, and seventy-foot waves crashed over the decks, forcing the destroyer to heave to or stop while the larger and heavier provision ship continued on its way.

The storm worsened by dawn's light with the destroyer rolling heavily as water started pouring into the vessel's vents. The ship lost electrical power as well as the main engines. Steering control was lost on the bridge. The pounding waves had smashed open the ship's bulwark in two places. The *Warrington* radioed the *Hyades*, swept some seventy-five miles away by the storm. The radio was silent, and by noon the skipper came to the grim realization that all hope was lost. A simple SOS was sent along with three words: We need assistance. Finally, the order to abandon ship was given, and within the hour the crew had jumped overboard as the ship, now lying on its starboard side, sank below the waves some 450 miles east of Vero Beach, Florida. Clinging to makeshift life rafts for nearly forty hours, the survivors were tossed around in the mountainous seas as sharks circled them in search of a human meal.

The *Frost*, along with the destroyer escorts *Huse, Inch, Snowden, Swasey, Woodson*, and *Johnnie Hutchins*, were on their way through the heavy seas to re-cover survivors. The *Hyades* also returned to help. But the sailors were not pre-pared for the macabre scene they were about to discover. "The smell of death was everywhere," Warren Kerrigan, the *Frost*'s quartermaster, said. "The stink

was awful. Bodies were everywhere, you could see them up to the horizon."
Kerrigan never understood why the captain of the *Warrington* sailed right into
the hurricane despite some fourteen weather warnings.

Fishing out mutilated bodies, Kerrigan and his shipmates were sickened
by the sight of sailors who had been chewed on by the sharks, which frequently ripped through the floater nets to get at the men. The water was covered
with blood, debris from the ship, and human remains. As the sailors pulled the
lifeless bodies on board, sharks jumped out of the water trying to get one last
bite. *Frost* signalman William Creech, who grew up on a tobacco farm in Ten-
nessee, remembered the bodies being placed in canvas shrouds and holding an
American flag over them as the fallen sailors were slid into the sea.

"This scene was far worse than any submarine sinking," Kerrigan said.
John "Bo" Keally said those rescued by his ship, the *Johnnie Hutchins*, were
covered with sores from seventy-two hours in the salt water. "They froze at
night and roasted during the day." Only 5 of the ship's 20 officers were res-
cued, along with 68 of the crew of 301 men. The survivors were dropped off in
Bermuda, where the ships replenished their supplies before returning to New
York for maintenance and, later, additional antisubmarine training exercises in
Guantánamo Bay and Bermuda.[25]

Although the U-boat menace in the Atlantic had been reduced by January 1945, when President Roosevelt took the oath of office for the fourth and
last term as president, several German submarines still were prowling the East
Coast of the United States looking to disrupt commerce and sink any Allied
vessel they could find. Three days after delivering his fourth, and briefest Inaugural Address, an ailing Roosevelt and his top advisors boarded the heavy
cruiser, the USS *Quincy*, bound for Yalta and his last wartime conference with
Allied leaders. With a stiff west wind sweeping across the North Atlantic, the
president's ship carefully plied the submarine net gate and headed out into the
open sea where the Nazi wolf packs roamed. They were joined by a number of
other escort vessels, including the *Frost*, *Swasey*, and *Snowden*, which had been
dispatched from training exercises in Bermuda.[26]

That trip across the Atlantic was relatively dull for the crew of the *Frost*,
now more accustomed to the thrill of matching wits with prowling U-boats.
Kerrigan said the crew was never told that President Roosevelt was on board
the cruiser. The relative calm would not last for the *Frost*, however. After completing its presidential escort, the DE returned to the United States for main-

tenance and then was ordered back to sea. Steaming out of Hampton Roads in March, the ship and its convoy were traveling through heavy seas and gale-force winds on a mission to stop a group of snorkel-equipped U-boats from reaching America.

Frank Musumeci of the *Frost* was about to experience something that he would never forget. The decks of the little destroyer escorts were awash with seawater as the convoy plowed its way through the turbulent ocean. The young sailor remembered people calling it "western ocean weather at its worst," as gale-force winds tossed the warship around like a cork on an ocean that at times seemed ready to swallow up the tiny vessel. One lurch at dinner reportedly rolled tables, benches, mess furniture, and food on board the convoy's bigger and heavier carrier, the USS *Croatan*, first to port, then to starboard. At least a hundred sailors were injured.[27]

Meanwhile nine Nazi U-boats were sailing from Norway on their way to America, where intelligence authorities, armed with the German enigma machine, already had decoded the messages. The U.S. Navy knew the U-boats were coming and they were ready to give them an American welcome. Two of the six snorkel-equipped U-boats were headed for U.S. waters as part of the operation Admiral Döenitz termed "Seewolf." *U-1235*, commanded by thirty-three-year-old Captain Franz Barsch, and *U-880*, commanded by twenty-seven-year-old Captain Gerhard Schotzau, left Norway with orders from Admiral Döenitz to "attack ruthlessly and with determination."[28] Through the rough North Atlantic waters they moved swiftly, heading to a point north of the Azores where a reception party of destroyer escorts was waiting. With heavy seas running, forty-mile-per-hour winds, and fog lying low to the water, conditions were not good for airplanes to spot the submarines or for surface ships to fight them. Nonetheless the U-boats came and the destroyer escorts were lined up to stop them.

Shortly before midnight on 15 April, first contact was made by the USS *Stanton*: A U-boat was moving toward the picket barrier, about 3,500 yards away, on a collision course with the *Stanton*. The carrier escort, the USS *Croatan*, quickly moved away from the area. All hands scrambled to battle stations on board the *Stanton* as it quickly steamed toward the contact point. The DE illuminated the seas with its intense searchlights, piercing through the thick fog. There, drenched in searchlight beams was *U-1235*, sitting in the fog on the surface because the water was too rough for use of its snorkel gear. The U-boat quickly dove as the DE crews readied hedgehogs for attack. The USS *Frost* sped to the area to assist in the assault. For the next two hours, the two destroyer escorts battered the submarine with repeated hedgehog attacks, launching the bombs into the heavy seas. An hour past midnight, two tremendous undersea explosions rocked the DEs and could even be felt by the carrier escort some twelve miles away. The U-boat was destroyed and all hands lost.[29]

As seas continued to build on that stormy night, the USS *Frost* made radar contact with another submarine, *U-880*, a mile and a half east of where the previous German boat plunged to its death only forty minutes earlier. At first they thought it must be *U-1235* but soon learned that it was the other Seewolf submarine, *U-880*, trying to make a run for it while surfaced on the rough waters. With fog so thick that star shells failed to illuminate the surfaced U-boat, the DE shone its powerful searchlight, revealing the boat.

The ship opened fire, but with heavy seas they could not accurately aim the guns or position their ship to ram. The U-boat captain took his boat below the waves. Hedgehog crews on board the *Frost* and *Stanton*, faces stung with the biting salt spray splashing over the bow, prepared their weapons for attack. The hedgehogs were launched in an elliptical pattern, and at about 2:00 AM a violent explosion was heard. *U-880* had followed in the footsteps of its sister Seewolf submarine. A huge oil slick appeared signaling the demise of the German submarine.[30]

Destroyer escorts continued to prove their worth as they sailed the gale-swept North Atlantic in search of enemy subs and the public started to embrace the little ships as they continued to make headway in the battle against Nazi U-boats. In fact, a stained glass window in the chapel of the Norfolk Navy Base depicted the Virgin Mary holding a destroyer escort in her arms. The design came from Wilbur H. Burnham at the suggestion of a Catholic chaplain in charge of the chapel. After the window stirred up a great deal of controversy, however, it was ordered to be "altered" by the chaplain at the Norfolk Naval Base.

Some Navy officials didn't think these novel new warships would last six months, and even the *New York Times* took a jaundiced view of the new little vessels: "DEs have been coming off the ways for some time now," the newspaper began in an 11 April 1943 article. "Old Navy men who see them for the first time are apt to stare and scratch their heads. The hull is conventional, but the superstructure borders on the weird—something between a submarine conning tower and a tank turret. Wheelhouse, bridge and charthouse are all sheathed in blank steel except for two slit ports and some small portholes. A shielded anti-aircraft gun is about where the wheel should be, and forward of it are two all-purpose guns on stepped-down platforms."[31]

Although some regarded destroyer escorts as slightly more seaworthy than a rubber raft, others said they were actually bigger and better than four-piper destroyers, America's best destroyers in World War I. The DEs surpassed World War I destroyers and flush-deck destroyers in both tonnage and beam and were longer than the standard World War I destroyer (nine feet shorter than the flush-deck vessel). Another important feature of the DEs was their cost. They could be built for $5 million each, about half the cost of a standard World War II destroyer, and turned out in much less time, four months compared to nine months for a destroyer. In summary the Navy said that the DE program would produce "twice as many ships for the same money in half the time," an excellent bargain for perilous and economically difficult times.[32]

But this is not to say that the diminutive size of these warships was not a challenge for the young men serving on board. In fact, the ships pitched and rolled, sometimes as much as 45 degrees or more, which means they were nearly lying on their side on the ocean surface. Fiber rugs were fastened to steel decks with scotch tape so they would not slide, ash trays were tied to stanchions with wires, and there were hand railings along the entire length of the narrow decks. Chairs were welded down in the radio shack. Sailors had trouble airing their bedding on board, even on sunny days, when spray still washed the deck. At times the weather was so rough and the ships pitched so badly that they could not cook on board. During bad storms, bakers said the bread dough ran to one end of the pan, with the loaves coming out only half as long as usual.[33]

For David Graybeal, pulling double duty as assistant engineering officer and supply officer on board the USS *Snowden*, it was like being married to the ship. "There are good times and there are hard times and those destroyer escorts in the North Atlantic were heavy sea rollers . . . and we were dealing with some seasickness, and about equally bad was getting bruised. Sometimes we rolled more than 45 degrees from vertical, which would mean that the bulkhead was more level than the deck," he said, adding, "I've seen men's feet patterns on the bulk head where they would put their foot up there to keep from falling over. You'd be walking along and all of a sudden the ship would throw you into one of those iron stations or something. I was always bruised in some way or another."[34]

Seaman 2nd Class Martin Davis recalled the seasickness. "It was horrible," he said in describing several trips across the North Atlantic. "I was totally seasick the entire way over. It was made worse by the fact that when I first got aboard the ship didn't have enough bunks for all of us, and so the three of us that came out of boot camp slept on hammocks." When Davis slept in the hammock, he would hit his head against the overhead as the ship pitched, rolled, and bounced around the ocean. "I had to carry a pillow on my face," he said.[35]

The USS *Reuben James* radioman, John Lampe, who dropped out of school at seventeen to join the Navy, remembered the remedy given sailors experiencing seasickness on board his destroyer escort. "The first night out you would get the greasiest pork chops, or the greasiest food there was . . . because that would put a lining on your stomach," Lampe said. "It would keep you from ripping up your stomach." The first time he got seasick, Lampe was strapped in his bunk to prevent being tossed out as the ship rolled. A short time before he was to take the midnight watch, a shipmate came in and told him it was time for him to go on duty, to which Lampe said, "I don't feel well. I don't think I'm going." The sailor pulled the radioman out of his bunk and dragged him to his watch station.[36]

Arthur C. Fleischmann Sr., signalman on board the destroyer escort USS *Gantner*, remembered the violent squalls in the North Atlantic as his little ship made seven North Atlantic crossings in 1943 and 1944. Often, Fleischmann said, the escorts could not even see the other ships in the convoy because of the rain, snow, fog, and surging seas, which flooded the decks, sometimes even washing sailors overboard. A great deal of time was spent by DEs herding their ships back into formation, especially at night when the ships seemed to drift away more frequently.

Lt. Robert M. Bavier Jr., executive officer on board the *Gantner*, said the ship often would roll as much as 45 degrees from the vertical, swinging through an arc of 90 degrees, all in less than ten seconds. "Add to this motion the pitching thrown in simultaneously, and you'll see why we had to hold on," Bavier said. "Everyone had bruises to show for the storm, and sometimes more." Bavier said it always felt good to get below after a trick topside: "To hot

USS *Liddle* signalman Joseph A. Paradis from New York City prepares to send a Morse code message by flashing light to a ship in his convoy on the North Atlantic. Sailors often used flashing lights to communicate with other ships. Signalman Paradis was killed a year later when a kamikaze crashed into the *Liddle* in the Pacific at Leyte Gulf. *Photo taken by Harold S. Deal; courtesy Jeff Deal*

tea or coffee, a dry bunk, or just listen to the radio playing—sometimes soft and peaceful, to lead us away from our little world suddenly gone mad, and at the other times blaring out as if in accompaniment to the plunging, lurching and dancing of the ship."[37]

Standing watch all night was another major adjustment for many of the young DE sailors, most of whom were used to getting a full night's sleep in the comfortable beds at home. Instead of sleeping in the safety of their own bedrooms, the young sailors now would have to stay awake all night, watching

Sailors also used signal flags and the semaphore system to communicate with nearby ships. Each uniquely colored and patterned flag signified different letters, numbers, and definitions, and the semaphore system used the angle of the signalman's outstretched arm to represent letters in the alphabet. This means of daytime signaling was preferred because enemy vessels outside the circle of visibility would not be able to intercept the messages. *Liddle* signalman Yadon sends a message to another ship. *Photo taken by Harold S. Deal; courtesy Jeff Deal*

for enemy vessels, which often would sneak up and strike when least expected. Between continents lay three thousand miles of lonely ocean, with its storm-tossed swells and the deadly German wolf packs prowling silently beneath the waves.

"The average day started at 5:30 in the morning," recalled Charles Lovett, who grew up in Atlantic City, New Jersey, before enlisting in the Navy at the age of seventeen and serving on board the USS *McNulty*. "The boat's mate would get on the PA system and blow his whistle and say, 'Now here this, clean sweep down, forward aft.' That was our cue to get out of the bunk and get the brooms and sweep down. That was the start of our day." Lovett's "bunk" was a hammock, which he said did not provide very comfortable sleeping accommodations. "You couldn't turn around, you had to lie on your back all the time," he said.[38]

Fueling at sea also posed its own special set of dangers, both for destroyer escorts and for the oilers from which they were obtaining their fuel. Great care had to be taken to avoid collision of the DE's flying bridge with the oil tanker as the two ships would steam along at the same speed. "It was messy," recalled

Capt. Kenneth H. Hannan, skipper of the USS *Swearer*. "We get alongside and get down to ten knots and throw out a line holding us to the oiler." Hannan would stand by the helmsman and help to guide the ship alongside. The six-inch hose was then stretched between the two vessels, and 90,000 gallons of black oil, which in steam-powered DEs was heated to 250 degrees, flowed under pressure through the hose. "It took a couple of hours to fuel us."

Frank McClatchie, that bright young German-born American technician who had assisted in developing the countermeasures to foil Hitler's new secret glide bomb, recalled one day that they were trying to refuel on the stormy North Atlantic. McClatchie was on board the USS *Neal A. Scott*, where he had been assigned as a radio technician after his stint in the Navy laboratory, when the destroyer escort ran low on fuel. As fuel was being delivered to the DE through a fuel line to an aircraft carrier, a U-boat showed up.

The carrier ordered an emergency termination of the fueling, creating what McClatchie termed "a real mess" as axe-wielding sailors quickly severed all cables and the fueling hose between the two ships as black oil sprayed all over the ship. Of course, because of its proximity to the carrier, the *Scott* could not maneuver to fire upon the U-boat, which was readying its torpedo to launch against the carrier. Fortunately for the carrier and the rest of the Allied convoy, another destroyer escort showed up and fired at the submarine, later identified as *U-1228*, which then made an emergency crash dive. Although the submarine escaped, this would not be the last time *U-1228* and the *Scott* would meet on the high seas.

The next morning the *Scott*, still low on fuel, was approached by the *Frederick C. Davis* with orders to take its station in the picket line while the *Scott* sailed back to Nova Scotia for refueling. "We had just gone over the horizon," McClatchie said, "when we heard over the TBS [talk between ships] radio that the *Davis* had taken two torpedoes amidship and sunk in a couple of minutes." McClatchie recognizes a certain irony in the sinking of the *Davis* by *U-546*, noting, "It was the *Davis*, the very ship that took the torpedoes meant for the *Neal A. Scott* . . . and my very first spectrum analyzer went down with her along with the men."[39]

Radio Technician McClatchie would soon find himself riding on board the German submarine that had foiled his DE's attempt to refuel only a short time earlier. In May, after the war with Germany ended, *U-1228*, commanded by twenty-five-year-old Captain Friedrich-Wilhelm Marienfeld, was just off

Refueling on the North Atlantic in heavy seas was often a difficult and messy job. First the DE had to draw close to the oil tanker, with both vessels steaming at the same speed. Then a six-inch-diameter hose was hauled from the oiler to the DE, where sailors would catch it and proceed with refueling. In steam-powered DEs the black oil came though the hose at 250 degrees and pressurized to one hundred pounds per square inch. DEs usually could take about 95,000 gallons of fuel in one hour. *Photos taken by Harold S. Deal; courtesy Jeff Deal*

the Grand Banks in the North Atlantic. The skipper already had jettisoned torpedoes and some secret documents when the USS *Neal A. Scott* showed up to take control of the submarine. The German-born McClatchie, the only DE crew member fluent in German, was assigned to a thirteen-man boarding party, and although other officers on board the whaleboat were senior to the radio technician, he quickly became the man in charge. He could speak the language, after all, and would be able to communicate with the submarine's crew, none of whom could speak English.

Twenty-eight of the U-boat crew members along with two officers were loaded into the whaleboat and sent back to the *Scott*, where they were held as prisoners of war. The remaining crew members and officers were herded into the torpedo room as the American crew took over the petty officers' quarters. "Fancy quarters they were too," McClatchie remembered, adding that the quarters were replete with "wooden paneling and a swastika emblazoned on the punch bowl."

"The German captain and I did not hit it off well," the radio technician said, adding, "When I interrogated him as to numbers of crew and how many are needed to operate the sub, he pretended not to understand me and became quite difficult to get along with." When McClatchie ordered Captain Marienfeld off the sub, the captain "turned purple in the face and sputtered in German, 'If this was a German Navy taking over an American ship, they certainly would not remove the captain from command of his ship.'" Reluctantly the German captain climbed into the whaleboat and was taken back to the DE. McClatchie then spoke with the submarine's executive officer, who "had no trouble understanding me and we got along just fine for the remainder of the trip."

The American boarding party thoroughly searched the submarine, opening every locker and cabinet. Some confidential documents and a decoding device were found. A single box of hand grenades also was discovered and tossed overboard. McClatchie radioed the DE captain that the U-boat was secured and ready to follow the DE to Portsmouth, New Hampshire. The radio technician communicated with the *Scott* using Morse code, with a key word sequenced by prior agreement to let the captain know the American crew was still in charge of the submarine. The boarding party also attached a chain with a lock to the conning tower, dropping the chain down the hatch with a lock securing the opposite end. "This would insure that the sub could not dive with us in it because the main hatch could not be closed," McClatchie said.

McClatchie was amazed at the submarine's periscope, a type he had never seen before on any other vessel. "It was a solid installation," he said. "You would place your eyes to the glass, push a button and the periscope would go up. You could move 360 degrees without ever moving off your seat." McClatchie believes the unique periscope design was lost forever when the submarine was scuttled by the U.S. Navy about nine months after its surrender. "It was a terrible loss," he observed.

He also remembered the German radio operator showing him a rather primitive handheld device that was used to detect a destroyer escort's presence. "That's why we could never catch their boats when they were on the surface," he noted. "It consisted of a funnel with a germanium crystal at the apex and a two tube audio amplifier and batteries on a belt with earphones on his head." McClatchie said the operator would come on deck of the submarine and turn around slowly, listening for a distinctive DE radar signature. If it was detected, the U-boat would crash-dive.

Although the boarding party kept enough German sailors on board to operate the boat, they neglected to keep the cook and had to fend for themselves during the six days. "In every nook and cranny," McClatchie said, "there were stored cans of food." The trouble was that none of the cans had labels, so the Americans had no indication of what was inside each can. Indented in cans' lids were numbers, obviously identifying the contents, but the Americans had no key for the numbers, so each time they opened a can, it was a surprise. McClatchie kept a list of numbers and foods, carving them on the wall of the petty officer's compartment. Not that it mattered, though, because McClatchie said during the trip, the Americans mostly subsisted on Schnapps, which they mixed with cherry juice.[40]

As the U-boat was returning to Portsmouth behind the *Scott*, a Navy blimp showed up with movie cameramen hanging out all of the windows taking pictures of the victorious U.S. Navy bringing in its captured German U-boat. Presumably the footage would be used on the Movietone news, the international cinema newsreel company whose films were shown in theaters during feature films. Because the ship and submarine happened to be in the middle of the Gulf stream, the weather was pretty warm and the "conquering heroes" were relaxing and sunbathing on the destroyer escort's foredeck, not quite the image the Navy wished to convey to the American public. The film never made it to the big screen.

7

Off the Shores of New Jersey

Unseasonably warm breezes blew over the ocean as the lights of Point Pleasant reflected and danced on the tranquil waters. Residents of this New Jersey beach community were returning from work and preparing their evening meal, unaware of the danger lurking nearby offshore. Prowling silently along the coast was one of Adolph Hitler's U-boats, commanded by twenty-seven-year-old Captain Helmut Neuerburg, who, along with his crew of fifty-five sailors, had traveled to U.S. shores to sink some ships in the final months of World War II.

With the North Atlantic nearly flat calm on that overcast evening in February 1945, the USS *Crow*, one of thirty destroyer escorts manned mostly by Coast Guard men, was escorting a convoy from New York to Liverpool, England. Joined by seven other escorts, the vessel was traveling along at fifteen knots when, a little after 4:30 PM, Sonarman Howard Kenneth Denson heard a "ping" indicating a possible U-boat was in the vicinity, about sixty-five miles off the coast of New Jersey.

The *Crow* chased the submarine for more than three miles as the U-boat dashed away from the East Coast in a frantic run for deeper water. Closing on its target, now only eight hundred feet away, the ship suddenly lost the sonar signal. The DE fired twenty-four hedgehogs. Multiple underwater explosions jarred the ship, indicating that the missiles had hit something solid. The *Crow* then dropped depth charges over the side. Air bubbles and an oil slick surfaced. More depth charges were fired, and more air bubbles and oil were seen. The *Crow* called for help and the USS *Koiner* left the convoy and rushed at flank speed to the site.

Realizing that by leaving the convoy the destroyer escorts left their charges vulnerable to other U-boats that might be prowling the American coastline, they radioed for a hunter-killer group to assist in searching for the U-boat. As they waited the DEs continued to bombard the area with depth charges. The *Koiner*'s commander lowered a whaleboat over the side to investigate the dark water near the attack site. The whaleboat crew returned with an oil-soaked rags, confirming that the substance on the water was oil.

After three hours the DEs returned to their convoy, and although the commander and crew of the *Crow* were convinced they had been pursuing and sunk a German submarine, the skipper of the *Koiner* did not agree. Of course, sailors from the *Crow* argued that the *Koiner* had arrived thirty-nine minutes after the initial pursuit by the *Crow* so did not witness the U-boat turning and speeding into deeper water. The final official assessment was that the object was likely an existing wreck or "nonsub" since the *Koiner* did not see any discernable movement.

Disappointed, the crew of the *Crow* never accepted the final assessment. They knew what they saw, and they were convinced that they had been chasing a moving target. Later the German command agreed with the *Koiner* skipper, stating that they had no U-boats operating off the coast of New Jersey in February 1945. Since neither DE submitted an antisubmarine warfare report on the incident, when the time came for the U.S. Navy to make its final assessment, it sided with the *Koiner* and ruled that the ships had not been pursuing a U-boat.[1]

Fast forward forty-six years. In the fall of 1991 a pair of adventuresome Atlantic wreck divers made an incredible discovery about sixty-five miles off the coast of Point Pleasant, New Jersey, in the general vicinity where the USS *Crow* believed it had pursued and sunk a German submarine. Some 230 feet below the waves off New Jersey's sandy beaches rested what appeared to be a German submarine with the skeletal remains of its crew still inside. In subsequent dives, crockery bowls dated 1942 and marked with an eagle and a swastika, and a dinner knife with the name "Horenburg" carved in the wooden handle, were recovered. Martin Horenburg was the chief radioman of *U-869*, a German submarine presumed to have been sunk off Gibraltar. A box of spare parts also were recovered bearing a brass plate inscribed *U-869*. The divers speculated that the submarine had been sunk by one of its own torpedoes, which had gone astray, circling back and smashing into the U-boat.

Captain Neuerburg took command of *U-869*, a conventional combat submarine, sailing from Kristiansand, Norway, on 8 December 1944. The boat was to serve as a weather boat for the Ardennes offensive and, later, disrupt shipping operations off the coast of New York. By the end of three weeks, the boat should have reached New York, but German command never received a report from the submarine indicating it had arrived at its destination. Several radio messages to the U-boat went unanswered. By January, having heard nothing from *U-869*, Germany was certain the boat had met its end. However, on 6 January, *U-869* radioed German command advising that it was about six hundred miles southwest of Iceland. Concerned that the boat might not have enough fuel to patrol New York, German command asked for a fuel report from the submarine. It failed to reply to this request.[2]

Twenty-two-year-old Howard Denson, who had joined the Coast Guard right out of high school, was manning the sonar that early evening off Point Pleasant and was the first to detect the U-boat. "Clearly," Denson recalled, "it was a moving target." At first, when Denson heard the telltale "ping" indicating a metallic object below, he was not alarmed as he had detected a number of possible submarines while serving as sonarman on board the *Crow*. However, when the signal grew stronger and started moving, the skipper called all hands to battle stations as he swung the destroyer escort toward the suspected U-boat and started the chase. "There was no doubt that the submarine was moving," he said.

The dark sonar shack had no windows, of course, so Denson could not observe as hedgehogs were launched and depth charges fired. The chase lasted about an hour, the crew manning their battle stations the entire time. Finally, after being ordered to return to the convoy, the *Crow* and *Koiner* took about six hours to catch up with the collection of ships heading to England.

This kind of excitement was just what young Denson had hoped for when he climbed the old wooden steps of the Woolworth building back in Seymour, Indiana, to enlist. He wanted to join when he was seventeen years old, but his mother wouldn't sign for him. Finally, after he became eighteen, he no longer needed anyone's permission. He walked into the recruiting area over the store and saw booths for the Marines, Merchant Marine, and Coast Guard. The Marines were taking people right away, whereas the Coast Guard didn't call you for a month, which appealed to him. He rejected the Merchant Marine even before he arrived at the Woolworth building because he remembered the newspaper headline of merchant ships torpedoed and sunk right off the New York coast. "That wasn't for me," he said. Now, serving as sonarman on board the *Crow*, he was face to face with the same U-boats that were sinking Allied vessels in clear view of residents living along the East Coast, wreaking havoc on Atlantic shipping.[3]

Harold Muth, gunnery officer with Denson on board the *Crow* during that fateful night in February, said the navigator came rushing up to the CIC to use the dead-reckoning tracer to plot the German submarine's track. The pinging and echoing indicated a strong target, which continued to move away after the DE first picked up the signal some 1,200 to 1,500 yards from the convoy.

Muth, an experienced sailor who had served three years on antisubmarine duty on board the 165-foot Coast Guard cutter *Triton* prior to his assignment on the *Crow*, immediately left his temporary duty as watch officer in the CIC and rushed to his battle station, where he supervised the firing of hedgehogs at the target below. "It was a moving target," Muth said, adding that his ship chased the U-boat more than three miles before launching the hedgehog attack—another reason he is certain the target was moving. The sonar equipment on board, he noted, was not capable of picking up a target outside of one and a half miles. Once the submarine was discovered it made a run for it, with the DE finally overtaking it some three miles away. "Clear echoes and Doppler showed the target was moving," Muth said.[4]

Several underwater explosions were detected and an oil slick, diesel fuel, and air bubbles appeared on the water's surface, indicating to the crew of the destroyer escort that the U-boat had been struck. When the *Koiner* launched its whaleboat and oil samples were recovered, the crew of the *Crow* considered it confirmation that they had sunk the boat. However, because the *Koiner* arrived after most of the action was over and its skipper was senior to the captain of the *Crow*, he issued the ruling that the target was stationary, and the *Crow*'s skipper did not wish to challenge his senior officer. Of course, Muth's view is a bit different. "The target was stationary," the gunnery officer admits, "because the *Crow* made it stationary."[5]

Lacking concrete proof that they had sunk *U-869*, they had to wait nearly half a century for confirmation and credit for the "kill." But twenty-four-year-old Ens. George King knows what actually happened that February day. King, who served as officer of the deck during the incident, is certain they were chasing a submarine, and he witnessed the oil and bubbles on the water's surface after the hedgehog attack. When the *Koiner* ruled the target "nonsub."

King told his skipper, Lt. John M. Nixon, he was wrong. "We're doing what we're told to do," Nixon told the ensign. And the matter was settled—at least for that day.[6]

Herbert Guschewski was a radio operator on *U-869* but was taken off the boat with pleurisy just before it set out on its final voyage. Guschewski, who also had served on *U-602*, said that misguided torpedoes—so-called circle runners—that circle around and hit the submarine from which they were launched were not common. "That happened once in 100 boats, if ever," he noted. He, like most others, had believed the boat and its crew perished off Gibraltar in some 13,000 feet of water at the hands of the USS *Fowler* and another French escort. Now he acknowledges that his comrades died in as little as 230 feet of water off the coast of New Jersey.[7]

The location of the wrecked submarine is only about four and a half miles from the position of the *Crow's* attack, a difference experts say could easily be attributed to navigational error. In addition a Coast Guard report noted that if the submarine had traveled at average speed, after its last known contact, it would have arrived on 11 February at the exact location of the *Crow's* attack. The commander of the *Koiner* was correct, the Coast Guard analysis said, that he was bombing a wreck—a wreck, however, that was only one hour and thirty minutes old. "It's highly likely that the attack on February 11, 1945 was responsible for the sinking of U-869," the report stated. "The attack most probably prevented the submarine from attacking a ship in convoy CU-58. It's time to give these aging heroes the recognition they deserve."[8]

"I was in my carpenter's shop in the stern," Robert Quigley, the ship's carpenter's mate, said. Suddenly there was a tremendous explosion that "seemed to lift the entire stern of the ship out of the water." His first thought was that the *Crow* had been hit by a torpedo, and he rushed to his battle station on the number one gun. Once on deck, shipmate Theodore Sieviec yelled, "We're attacking a submarine, this is the real thing." Quigley said that several hundred yards of diesel oil covered the ocean, and air bubbles were everywhere, indicating that the submarine had been hit.[9]

Eighteen-year-old Gunner's Mate Sieviec gazed over the side and saw the bubbles and watched as the oil spread across the ocean. Sieviec, who was assigned to the number two gun, holds the distinction of firing the first hedgehog at *U-869*, and he was sure the bubbles and oil meant the bomb hit its mark. During the attack, six of the hedgehogs failed to launch, so he hauled each of the 75-pound bombs across the deck, lifting them, one by one, and tossing them over the side of the ship. "The bubbles were moving," during the attack, indicating that the target was moving also, Sieviec said, convinced they were pursuing a submarine and, in fact, had sunk the boat.[10]

Now, after all these years, the men of the *Crow* have a powerful new ally in their quest to receive credit for sinking the German submarine. The leading German authority on U-boat losses during the war has revised his official assessment and concluded that *U-869* was most likely sunk by the actions of the *Crow* and *Koiner*. In his reassessment Axel Niestle has amended the loss of *U-869* "to show that it was sunk on 11 February 1945 by a series of Hedgehog and depth charge attacks from the destroyer escorts USS *Howard D. Crow* (Lt. John Nixon) and USS *Koiner* (Lt. Cdr. Charles Judson) in position 39 degrees 33' N/73 degrees 02W."[11]

"No U-boat is known to have survived a direct hedgehog hit, thus *U-869* is likely to have been seriously damaged by it," Niestle noted, adding, "Possibly unable to control the inrush of water, the bottomed boat was later destroyed by a series of depth charge attacks, which is likely to have caused the reported damage to the boat's hull." He concludes that the Allied A/S Assessment Committee, which ruled *U-869* had met its demise near Gibraltar, may have used "incorrect information derived from signal intelligence, which denied the presence of a German U-boat anywhere near the position of attack at the given date."

Niestle believes that Captain Neuerburg never received the radio message from U-boat command to steer to the Gibraltar area and instead continued toward its original destination, the East Coast of the United States. The area where the wreckage of *U-869* was discovered is "almost identical" with the original patrol area assigned to the submarine, according to Niestle, lending more credence to the claims of the crew members of the *Crow* that they attacked and sunk a U-boat in that vicinity. With twelve antisubmarine attacks recorded in this area during February, only one attack was listed within a twenty-five mile radius of the wreck site of *U-869*, the German researcher concludes.[12]

Battling the enemies of his country was just what young Robert Quigley was looking for when he signed up for the Coast Guard after Pearl Harbor. Following the Japanese attack, the seventeen year old quit school and joined several of his friends who wanted to do their duty to defend America. "That's what our generation did," he said. Unfortunately when he tried to enlist in the

Navy he was turned down because of high blood pressure. The Air Force said no too. Then he tried his luck with the Merchant Marine, where he also was rejected for the same reason. Finally, when a dejected Quigley was leaving the Merchant Marine recruiting office in Boston, he noticed colored footprints on the sidewalk and an attached message: "Follow these footprints to action." He did just that and arrived at the Coast Guard recruiting office, where a doctor, after taking his blood pressure, told him to go outside, walk around, and then come in and lay very still on the cot for a time. When the doctor took his blood pressure again, he passed. The proud teenager was now in the U.S. Coast Guard and was ready for some action.[13]

And action was what Ernest Hughes of Saratoga Springs, New York, was hoping for when he piled into his father's 1936 Oldsmobile and headed for Glens Falls to sign up. His father, who worked at General Electric Company in Schenectady, and his mother, a worker in the Van Raalte Knitting Mills in Saratoga, had hoped their seventeen-year-old son would finish high school before joining up; however, after a few older neighborhood kids joined the Navy, young Ernest quit school and enlisted too.

After filling out the paperwork, Ernest and his father then made the trip down Route 9 to Albany, New York's capital city, where the young sailor-to-be would join hundreds of other recruits ready to fight for their country. Hughes and the other recruits then boarded a troop train from Albany to boot camp in Sampson, New York. After basic training, Ernest was shipped off to the Great Lakes Training Center, where he received specialized instruction in engineering before being assigned to another new U-boat fighter, the USS *Holton*, being commissioned in New Orleans. Cold winds and snow of the Great Lakes chilled the recruits, required to attend night school, with classes starting at midnight and running until 5 AM, when they were given breakfast. They had to teach around the clock because there were so many recruits needing training. Hughes' engineering and damage-control training would soon pay off.[14]

On the *Holton*'s second duty escorting a convoy of ships across the Atlantic to the Mediterranean, young Ernest Hughes got a taste of just how dangerous a job convoying could be, regardless of whether the ships encountered any German submarines or bombers. In the mid-October 1944 crossing, all hands rushed to their battle stations as the sailors prepared for what they assumed would be a nighttime fight with an enemy submarine about four hundred miles off the African coast.

Hughes, part of the damage-control party, finished a routine inspection to ensure all hatches were secured and came out of a forward hatch to the sight of bright orange and yellow flames soaring high into the dark night skies. He, like his twenty-seven-year-old captain, John B. Boy, thought the ships, on the starboard quarter of the convoy, likely had been torpedoed by an enemy submarine. Captain Boy ordered his ship to proceed closer to the burning vessels for a better assessment. But what they found had nothing to do with an enemy submarine. Instead the SS *Howard L. Gibson*, an American Liberty ship, had veered off course and collided with a British tanker, the SS *George W. McNight*, a regular danger when so many ships were moving so closely together across the dark waters of the North Atlantic.[15]

"We saw a flash of fire," Boy remembered. "We didn't know if it were torpedoed, so we took off for the ship." Once they determined that the Liberty ship had plowed into the bow of the tanker, Boy ordered his DE alongside and readied the hoses to start pouring water on the roaring flames, maneuvering dangerously close to the burning vessel. Although the crew on both ships were fighting the fire, once they realized that they were doing little to kill the flames, the sailors starting to abandon ship, lowering lifeboats and rafts into the dark and turbulent waters. The *Holton* picked up the sailors, and after being briefed on the ship's condition, Captain Boy decided to assemble a repair party to go on board the flaming ships. After fighting the fires all night, they finally extinguished the flames.

Once the smoke cleared, Hughes, who jumped to the burning ship to help fight the fire, remembered seeing a body lying on the charred deck. "He looked like he had been fried to death, like a fried egg," Hughes said. The sailor's remains literally had to be scraped from the deck. A second sailor was presumed thrown overboard when the ships collided. Both were buried at sea the following morning. Several other crewmen suffered serious burns on the face and hands and were being treated on board the destroyer escort. "This type of experience turns you into a grown-up fast," Hughes said.[16]

Collision on the high seas was not uncommon during the war, when hundreds and hundreds of vessels were traversing the North Atlantic, many of those vessels manned by mostly "green" crews and commanded by skippers with minimal experience at sea. Traveling darkened to avoid detection by the enemy only heightened the danger of ship collisions. Bronx native Norman Taylor learned firsthand about what happens when ships collide on the cold

Escorting large numbers of ships across the North Atlantic was a dangerous and difficult job for the DEs. Just keeping the larger ships from drifting apart or colliding, particularly at night, kept the escorts very busy. Looking out from the USS *Liddle*, a convoy of ships is visible as far as the eye can see. The *Liddle*'s depth-charge racks are in the foreground. *Photo taken by Harold S. Deal; courtesy Jeff Deal*

and dark ocean. Taylor, whose father pulled him out of school at fifteen to work for forty-nine cents an hour in the New Haven Railroad machine shops, decided he had enough of that type of work after two years, and signed up for the Navy. Boarding what was referred to affectionately as the "Black Diamond Special" because of the soot spewed out by the coal-burning train, seventeen-year-old Taylor and his fellow recruits were spirited out of New York City to their new "home" at the Sampson training facility.[17]

After basic training and advanced gunnery instruction, Taylor was sent to the Brooklyn Navy Yard to await his ship, the USS *Weber*, returning from convoy duty in England. Taylor boarded his new ship, moored in the navy yard, and was assigned to chip paint while awaiting his first convoy duty. This would be the first time the seventeen-year-old Bronx kid had ever been on the water, and he was in for some wild ride.

Taylor said, "I had the midwatch" on one particularly black night on the North Atlantic crossing from Norfolk, Virginia, to Sicily in late October 1944. "I was up on the 20-mm gun, when all of a sudden this fishing vessel comes across our bow." Taylor said the five-hundred-ton Portuguese fishing trawler, trying to sell fish to ships in the convoy, crossed from right to left directly in the path of his ship. "We hit him right in the middle. We climbed up over top of him," Taylor said. The collision ripped a twenty-eight-foot gash in the DE.

Taylor was thrown from the gun tub to the deck below. There was complete mayhem as the ship's crew rushed to reverse the engines to get the DE off the top of the sinking fishing trawler. The Portuguese fishermen were frantically trying to cut the lines holding the lifeboat so they could escape to safety before their vessel sank. Taylor said he would never forget the eerie sound of the two ships scrapping together: "It was a wailing, screeching sound, as we reversed, buoyancy returned to the fishing boat and she popped up out of the Atlantic with her lights still on."

The Portuguese sailors piled into the lifeboat and headed for safety on board the DE. They watched as the hatches on their trawler sprung open, releasing their catch of thousands of pounds of fish. With each wave washing over the fishing vessel and the initial crash damage, the hatch covers began to break loose and the contents flowed out into the sea. "When she pulled apart, you could see under the hull, fish and fish and more fish," Taylor recalled. The fishing vessel disappeared below the ocean's surface. The *Weber* took the fishermen to Gibraltar, where the vessel also underwent repairs. Taylor said the only casualty, besides the fish, was a single caged canary on the trawler.

Robert Hoenshel, executive officer on the Coast Guard–manned destroyer escort USS *Marchand*, was on the bridge during one North Atlantic crossing when the convoy encountered a severe gale. With mountainous waves and torrential rain, visibility was near zero as his ship escorted a convoy to Ireland. Without warning there was a tremendous explosion as two ships, unable to see each other in the thick fog, collided.

The American tanker, the *Murfreesboro*, was carrying 125,000 barrels of high-octane gasoline en route to the British Isles when a Panamanian ammunition ship, the *El Coston*, plowed into it. The tanker exploded in flames but remained afloat. The *El Coston* was not so fortunate, sinking with a loss of nine crew members. Although the tanker was towed to port and salvaged, some sixteen Navy gunners and twenty-nine crew members, including the captain, died in the flames that engulfed the ship.[18]

But most of the action on the North Atlantic had more to do with submarines than fishing trawlers, something that William C. Stanback would soon discover after boarding the USS *Gandy* in January 1944 as an ensign or, as the captain called him, "the most junior of all junior officers." Born in the small railroad town of Spencer, North Carolina, Stanback eventually went on to the University of North Carolina, where he joined the Naval Reserve and became what affectionately was called "a 90-day wonder," skipping boot camp and going directly to midshipman school in New York City. Unlike many others who went on board destroyer escorts, Stanback loved the water and had learned to sail as a boy in Salisbury, North Carolina.

His skills would be put to the test on what he calls "his first day of the war," when on a foggy spring morning his ship helped sink a submarine before breakfast. "I was seated at breakfast when we could feel the distant explosion and general quarters was sounded, and we went out searching," Stanback said. The *Gandy* headed for an area about seventy miles south of Nantucket Island, where *U-550*, commanded by twenty-six-year-old Captain Klaus Hanert, had risen to periscope depth and fired a salvo of three torpedoes at the *Pan Pennsylvania*, a tanker that was in a convoy of twenty ships en route from the Caribbean via New York to Northern Ireland. The tanker burst into flames and eventually sunk, along with its cargo of 140,000 barrels of gasoline and seven airplanes on its deck.[19]

The Coast Guard–manned destroyer escorts *Joyce* and *Peterson* rushed to the area and, after picking up a sonar contact of the U-boat, fired depth charges that ruptured the air and fuel lines on the submarine, causing flooding and other damage. The submarine captain surfaced and decided to fight it out with, what he thought, was a single destroyer escort. He was wrong. Not only were the *Joyce* and *Peterson* there, but the *Gandy* had just arrived to recover survivors from the sunken ship and also search for the U-boat. Captain Hanert's boat, now surfaced in broad daylight, readied its guns for firing at the American escorts.[20]

"Instead of surrendering, they tried to man their guns and they shot at us, and we shot at them, and the captain said ram," said Stanback, who was on the bridge during the attack, which injured some of the *Gandy* crew. "Full speed ahead, ram," the *Gandy* captain ordered, as the destroyer escort hit the submarine well aft, on the starboard side, causing minimal damage on the DE due to its reinforced bow plate. All three DEs then opened fire on *U-550*. Realizing all hope was gone, Captain Hanert ordered his crew to abandon ship and scuttled the submarine, preventing a capture and boarding at sea. Thirteen survivors, including the captain, were picked up by the *Joyce*.[21]

Milton Stein, another 90-day wonder who also had lots of experience on the water as a boy growing up along the California coast, reported for duty on his birthday in September 1943 on board the USS *Brough*. Stein's decision to join the military came at the end of his third year at UCLA, when he saw a notice in the newspaper about the Army Air Corps and left college to join up. Although he did fine in his pilot training, the Air Corps was only taking a limited number of recruits and he was not one of the ones selected for further training. So he turned to the Navy, where he signed up for the V-7 program in which he could become an officer provided he had at least two years of college.[22]

After training on board a battleship and a short stint on board a Liberty ship, Stein was assigned to a brand-new destroyer escort, the USS *Brough*. Although the *Brough* saw little enemy action, it did experience some serious problems following the shakedown cruise. Upon arriving at the ship, Stein quickly discovered that he was the only officer with deep-sea experience as well as battleship knowledge, most of the other officers having been reassigned from desk jobs to go to sea. Following the traditional shakedown cruise in Bermuda, the ship encountered a severe storm with gale-force winds in the North Atlantic that had severely damaged the ship's gun shield. Without changing course the captain went forward to inspect the damage and was immediately struck down by a giant wave. He hit his head on the deck and died instantly. Stein moved up to the second in command once the executive officer assumed the captain's duties, and after the newly installed captain was transferred to another ship, Stein became the *Brough*'s skipper.[23]

But it seemed that all of the *Brough*'s troubles were not yet over. The day after taking command, twenty-five-year-old Captain Stein said his ship was ordered to join a hunter-killer group. "As was customary, we tested all gun circuits," Stein said. "A new seaman aboard was talking to someone while leaning on a K-gun drum. The gunner's mate on deck mistakenly signaled all clear to the bridge and the firing button was pushed." The K-gun was fired, carrying the new seaman with it into the sea, exploding on contact. The seaman's body later was recovered and he was buried at sea.[24]

German U-boats, enemy aircraft, raging seas, and mistakes by an unseasoned crew were not the only threats American sailors had to face on the high seas. Another unseen and deadly danger lurked just beneath the oceans waves and could quickly send a ship and its crew to the bottom of the sea. The crew of the USS *Rich* learned that lesson the hard way, only eight months after the ship was commissioned in Bay City, Michigan, when it was ordered to provide screening for the Utah Beach bombardment group at the invasion of Normandy in June 1944.

Built in eighty-seven days at the DeFoe Shipbuilding Company in Michigan, one of two of the seventeen DE shipyards without direct ocean access, the newly minted destroyer escort *Rich*, with its skeleton crew, was towed down the Mississippi River to the Gulf of Mexico for its final outfitting, with commissioning ceremonies on 1 October 1943. After its shakedown cruise it was assigned to escort and patrol duty, making three successful transatlantic crossings. On 12 May 1944, it would make its last.

During the Normandy invasion the following month, the *Rich* provided screening for the heavier ships that were supporting the troops landing on Utah Beach. Six destroyer escorts were dispatched for the initial invasion, including the USS *Maloy*, *Blessman*, *Amsbury*, *Borum*, and *Bates*, which was assigned with the *Rich* to provide screening for the bombardment group.[25] *Bates* soundman Tom Eddy kept a personal diary of the invasion. After arriving in Plymouth, England, on 31 May, Eddy observed that the harbor was filled with scores of landing ships and troop ships. On Friday, 2 June, Eddy wrote, "Catholic priest came aboard today and heard confessions and gave communion to Catholic members of the crew. Feel 100 per cent better now."

At this point Eddy learned the job expected of his ship for the upcoming invasion. "Our mission," he wrote, "is to take over two islands before the main force can take over the beach. Task considered dangerous one since we will have to go through unswept waters. Our mission is complete we will screen USS Nevada. Next job is to be part of picket line. Danger from 'E' boat attacks." E-boats, as they were referred to by the Allies, were German fast-attack craft used in coastal warfare.

The next day Eddy received a shipboard promotion to second class soundman. "Almost resembles a going away gift," he wrote in his diary with a sense of foreboding. "Would have liked to be able to show it to Mom and Dad. May get that chance eventually." On 5 June he wrote, "Got underway this morning for Northern France. Expect to reach it tomorrow morning. Big things are in the making. Dread the thoughts of operating the sound gear during the battle."

Eddy and his crewmen soon would be in the thick of battle as they approached the Saint-Marcouf Islands, an area found to be uninhabited but filled with land mines, wounding many soldiers as they set foot on the beach. The injured were taken on board the *Bates* for treatment. "As we came in," Lt. Cdr. Henry Wilmerding Jr., *Bates'* executive officer said, "we could see anti-aircraft fire against the paratroops being landed."

The Allied invasion fleet, which totaled thousands of ships, more than 2,400 of which were American naval vessels, pounded Utah Beach with gunfire and unloaded thousands of troops, while C-47s dropped paratroopers behind enemy lines and German fighter planes bombarded the invading naval forces with gunfire. Of course the Allies had been successful at leading Hitler to believe their invasion would take place at Pas de Calais rather than Normandy, which was chosen in part because of its proximity to the relatively undamaged ports of southern and western England, and in close range of English fighter plane bases. About 124,000 U.S. naval officers and men participated in some fashion in the invasion, with some 87,000 men on board landing craft and smaller escort vessels. Another 15,000 men were on board combat vessels and 22,000 attached to the amphibious bases in Europe.

"Missed death notice twice this morning," Eddy wrote in his diary. "Once when shell made a very close miss and secondly when three Spitfires stopped German aircraft as it was diving to strafe us. Hope our luck will continue to hold out."

Wounded soldiers were brought on board ship for medical treatment before being transferred to the USS *Joseph T. Dickman*, a former passenger ship taken over by the Navy during the war. The next day, about 4:00 AM, a bomb narrowly missed the *Bates*. "Slept through it all," Eddy wrote. On the third day of the invasion, the USS *Meredith* stuck a mine and started to list badly, taking on water. The *Bates* rushed to the scene, mooring near the crippled ship's bow as sailors leaped across to safety. Injured and dead sailors also were taken on board. The American destroyer went down so quickly that tugs alongside quickly had to cut lines in order not to get swallowed up as the ship sank.

Although the *Bates* came under heavy fire during the invasion, it escaped any direct hits. Wilmerding's biggest impression, he said, was the complete lack of confusion during the initial landings on the beach. "It ran like a piece of well-oiled machinery," he noted. "I was impressed by the silence on all the ships. Everything ran like a railroad timetable. There were no orders given. Radios were not used. There was absolute silence with people moving around like a bunch of ghosts."[26]

As the battle raged on, one American destroyer, the USS *Glennon*, struck a German mine about three miles northwest of the Saint-Marcouf Islands in the morning hours of 8 June. Although the ship suffered damage to the stern, its captain, Edward Michel, was confident that it would not sink. One sailor standing on the fantail of the tin can when the mine hit was thrown forty feet into the air before splashing into the ocean. He suffered two broken legs, but he, along with other sailors who were swept overboard in the explosion, was rescued. Minesweepers rushed to the scene, as German salvos were launched at the injured ship. When the *Rich* arrived to offer assistance, putting a whaleboat overboard to rescue sailors floundering in the water, the destroyer's captain said no help was needed, warning the destroyer escort to "clear area cautiously; live mines." But the warning came too late.

"The *Rich* circled the damaged destroyer and had just begun rescue operations when an underwater explosion shattered its stern. The smoke had hardly cleared when another blast smashed its bow and it went down," a horrified Lieutenant Commander Wilmerding said.[27] The *Rich*'s sonarman, Dan Schmocker, was on the flying bridge when they struck their first mine, blasting the young sailor fifty feet into the air. "When I went up in the air, I remember seeing other guys up in the air. I was just spinning," Schmocker recalled, adding that the blast was so powerful that it blew off his helmet, earphones, shoes and socks, and his girlfriend's class ring. Both his legs were broken.[28]

The first mine exploded off the *Rich*'s starboard beam. Three minutes later a second mine went off directly under the ship, blowing off fifty feet of the *Rich*'s stern. Two minutes later a third mine exploded under the ship's forecastle. Lt. Clarence Ross was at his station in the deckhouse midships when the first blast came. "I hurried up to the bridge and told the captain it appears that we hadn't been damaged," Ross said. "I returned to my station and had no sooner arrived than there was another explosion that picked up the whole ship and shook it like a dog with a rat in his mouth."

A "rending, crushing, breaking sound" was heard, meaning only one thing: The ship had been hit and was badly damaged. Ross rushed out on deck and was shocked to see one-third of the *Rich* gone. He could see the half-submerged stern of his ship floating away. Although the engine room was starting to flood, Ross thought the ship could still be saved. The captain told him he should do what was necessary to keep what was left of the vessel afloat. "As I was running down the passageway there was another explosion," which threw the young lieutenant up to the overhead, knocking him unconscious. When he awoke, he opened the door and found no one standing.

"The mast was lying over the bridge and the bow was partially submerged. The sailors on the forecastle were a tangle of bodies," Ross said, adding that when he climbed up an outside ladder to the bridge, he found everyone dazed and either lying down or holding on to something. Captain Michel appeared to be in shock. The executive officer, Lt. Cdr. William Pearson, severely injured, told sailors to attend to others before him. Everywhere people were groaning and crying for help. The ship had begun its death throes.[29]

Donald Lawrence, water tender on board the *Rich*, was a fireman on board the USS *Patterson* during the Japanese attack on Pearl Harbor, having joined the Naval Reserve in 1936. When the first explosion hit the *Rich* on that 8 June morning, Lawrence was in the fireroom. Plunged into darkness, he heard escaping steam and knew that somewhere in that darkness was a "thin, stabbing finger of steam so hot it can sear the flesh off the bones." He found a flashlight and was able to locate the source of the escaping steam. Lights then came back on—but not for long. "We didn't have much time to think about what damage might have occurred, because no sooner had the lights come on again than we were thrown to the deck by a second explosion. Again we were plunged into darkness, and again that hissing of steam in the inky black told us a steam line had ruptured somewhere," Lawrence said.

Groping their way through the maze of machinery below, the sailors finally found a ladder, climbing to the hatch above—just as the ship was rocked by a third explosion. Once on deck they realized that the end was near. Remarkably Lawrence said there was no panic as the ship slowly sank beneath the waves. "Those who were unhurt had only one thought in mind—to care for those who needed help," he recalled. "Every man did something. Some went about the ship administering morphine to the more painful cases. Others got the wounded onto stretchers and over the side to the waiting PT's, and when there were not enough stretchers, volunteers descended to the officers country and brought up mattresses on which the wounded could be transported."

Most of the wounded were transferred to the waiting torpedo boats and Coast Guard vessels swarming around the wreckage. Bodies and parts of bodies were everywhere. Water had mostly covered the *Rich*'s main deck as the gunnery officer went about his duty to ensure that the depth charges were set to "safe" so that, when the ship sunk, the ash cans would not automatically detonate, injuring sailors struggling in the water. "The ship began to roll, slow-ly and as though reluctant to give up its hold on life," Lawrence said. "Those in the water turned on their backs as they swam, to watch the ship. The little DE went down, all the time slowly and gracefully, with her colors still flying." Lieutenant Commander Pearson, who had told sailors to care for others first, went down with the ship. The captain was injured but survived. The ship sunk within fifteen minutes of striking the first mine. Ninety-one sailors lost their lives that day, with the remaining seventy-one suffering injuries.

Meanwhile, sailors on board the *Glennon*, the destroyer the *Rich* was assisting when it struck the mine and sunk, were busy trying to lighten the ship in order to free the ship's fantail, which had been anchored by its starboard propeller following the blast. They pumped fuel forward and jettisoned depth charges. Sailors even rushed forward "sallying ship," an old-time method in which they rush from side to side or stern to bow in order to use their body weight to help extricate the ship. It did not work.

Finally, on 10 June, additional crew members returned to the ship with equipment they thought would help free the crippled destroyer. But the Germans were not about to allow that to happen. A fired salvo hit the vessel amid-ships, cutting off all power. The Germans continued firing until finally the order was given to abandon ship. The ship rolled over and sunk, with twenty-five crewmen lost and another thirty-eight injured.[30]

Mines were a serious hazard for sailors at sea, and especially so during the Normandy invasion, since Hitler had ordered mining along the British coast as far back as 1939 in planning his attack on France and ordered the installation of offensive mines along the French coast two years later. Mine-sweepers were kept very busy detonating these underwater dangers. On 7 June alone, thirty mines were detonated near the boat lanes near Utah Beach. Some mines, whether of the magnetic or pressure variety, were deployed by surface ships, set by U-boats through their torpedo tubes, or dropped by Luftwaffe's aircraft. Mines could be attached to anchors allowing them to float at a prede-termined depth. Others could lie in wait on the seabed in shallower water.[31]

The primary goal of mine laying was to cut off the flow of troops and supplies from England to the Continent, noted historian Clay Blair, explain-ing that a secondary aim was to disrupt or shut down British merchant ship-ping and unleash a psychological terror among the populace. The Germans certainly can claim some success in that effort. Within a short time of the

Germans mining the seacoast in the fall of 1939, three freighters were sunk and the new British heavy cruiser *Belfast* had suffered severe damage in the Firth of Forth on 21 November. The battleship *Nelson* was mined while entering Loch Ewe on 4 December.[32]

Minesweeping operations took on a higher priority, and scientists were tasked with finding a way to detonate the magnetic underwater bombs. As Winston Churchill noted, "The whole power and science of the Navy were now applied; and it was not long before trial and experiment began to yield practical results." Within three months they devised a method using two wooden vessels, sailing on a parallel course about 300 feet apart, each dragging two buoyant electrical cables. One cable constituted a negative electrical pole, the other a positive one. Energized by a current from the two ships, the saltwater completed the electrical circuit, creating an intense magnetic field almost ten acres in size, safely exploding the mines in that area.[33]

In addition to the wooden minesweepers, the British developed a technique for "degaussing" or neutralizing the magnetic fields of the ships, reducing their vulnerability to the magnetic mines. At first they clamped a big, permanent electrical cable around the ship's hull and energizing it with shipboard current. Later they discovered that they could achieve the same result by passing a very powerful electrically charged cable along the hull while the ship was in port, providing "degaussing" for about a three-month period.[34]

But the Germans were not the only ones to use mines during the war. Japan also utilized them, as James Mitchell, an eighteen-year-old New Jersey native, eventually would discover. Mitchell, who enlisted in the Navy while still attending high school in Newark, needed his mother to sign for him since he was too young to join on his own. The Navy wasted no time in calling him to duty once school ended. Mitchell attended high school graduation ceremonies on Friday night and arrived at boot camp in Sampson, New York, in the wee hours the following Tuesday morning after taking an overnight train Monday from Grand Central Station in New York City.

For Mitchell and this round of recruits, boot camp lasted much longer than normal because all of the service schools and available slots on ships were filled and there was a long waiting list to get in. Consequently the regular six-to-eight-week training lasted thirteen weeks. Eventually he was shipped off to Fort Lauderdale, Florida, for training in radar before being sent to Pier 92 in New York City in November 1944 to await his ship, the USS *Roche*, commissioned nine months earlier.

On 26 November the *Roche*, with young radar striker Mitchell on board, was under way on its first North Atlantic convoy crossing, which, fortunately for its newly minted crew, was uneventful. "If you were over twenty-five years old, they would call you 'pappy,'" Mitchell said, recalling the young age of his fellow sailors. "We were all just a bunch of kids." Although the *Roche* did not sink any U-boats on its several crossings, Mitchell does remember some concern when they picked up a signal that, upon investigation, turned out to be a big wooden platform with a wire-wrapped pole in the middle, obviously placed as a decoy by the Germans. After the discovery, the ship beat a hasty retreat back to the convoy.[35]

In May 1945 the *Roche* was ordered to the Pacific—the beginning of the end for this destroyer escort, which had made several successful Atlantic crossings, safely escorting hundreds of ships with supplies and troops from America to England. After passing through the Panama Canal and picking up supplies in San Diego, it sailed to Pearl Harbor for additional training. In August, en route to Eniwetok, word was received of the Japanese surrender. Later it was assigned to antisubmarine patrol looking out for any Japanese submarines that might not have received word of the surrender.

On one assignment to escort a troop ship, the USAT *Florence Nightingale*, with the first occupation troops on their way to Japan, they were rendezvousing somewhere in the middle of the Pacific Ocean, escorting the ship into Tokyo Bay. Mitchell said the harbor was full of floating debris—wooden crates, logs, and a variety of garbage. He was on the flying bridge when someone on the bow spotted a floating mine in the midst of all the debris as the tide was going out. "He yelled and was pointing" at the mine as general quarters was sounded, Mitchell recalled. "They gave a left full rudder, and it skidded along the starboard side of the ship, almost got beyond the fantail—but not quite, when it detonated."

The violent explosion lifted the tail end of the ship almost vertically and turned the ship's fantail into a mass of twisted steel, nearly blowing it off completely. Three men were killed and dozens of others injured, including one of Mitchell's good friends, William Weiss, a seaman from Pittsburgh who was part of a working party that had just mustered on the fantail. Thanks to the quick action of the repair parties, the ship remained afloat. But the *Roche* would not live to sail another day. Judged too costly to repair, it eventually was decommissioned and sunk off Yokosuka.[36]

Word that hostilities had ceased also came too late for one of Hitler's U-boats, which was traveling very close to the East Coast of the United States just twenty-seven hours before Germany surrendered. In broad daylight on 5 May 1945, twenty-four-year-old Captain Helmut Fromsdorf was sailing *U-853* within four miles of the Rhode Island coastline near Point Judith when, at periscope depth, he spotted the SS *Black Point*, an aging collier carrying 7,500 tons of soft coal through what was thought to be friendly waters. No escorts accompanied the ship on the final leg of its journey from Newport News, Virginia, to Boston.

Traveling alone into the shallow continental shelf waters of Rhode Island Sound, the freighter suddenly was blown apart by a tremendous explosion, opening up a forty-foot hole in its stern. It sank within a half hour. A torpedo had smashed through the starboard side of the vessel, just aft of the engine room. Although the *Frederick C. Davis* remains the last American warship sunk in the Atlantic during the conflict, the *Black Point* was the last U.S.-flag merchant vessel sunk in U.S. waters during World War II.[37]

"We were having dinner in the wardroom," said William Tobin, gunnery officer on board the destroyer escort USS *Atherton*, which had just completed a successful transatlantic crossing escorting a Liberty ship from Gibraltar to New York and was south of Block Island on its way to Boston. "The radioman came down and told the captain they were picking up traffic about a torpedoing off Point Judith." The twenty-three-year-old Yale graduate, who grew up as a grocer's son in Waterbury, Connecticut, rushed to his battle station as Capt. Lewis Iselin ordered the destroyer escort to the scene along with another destroyer escort, the USS *Amick*, and the USS *Moberly*, a Coast Guard frigate.[38]

Tobin's ship already had defused its weapons in anticipation of docking in Boston Harbor, but now it was back to battle. "We rearmed our weapons and headed down the Narragansett channel, and when we got there lots of small boats were in the harbor," Tobin said. "We got to the scene of the torpedoing that was only three miles off shore, between Block Island and Point Judith." The SS *Black Point* was no longer visible, but debris and thirty-four survivors were in the water. Rescue operations were under way by the local boats.

Realizing there was little left for them to do, the captains of the *Atherton*, *Amick*, and *Moberly* quickly headed south to the open ocean in search of the Nazi U-boat that had torpedoed the ship resulting in the death of twelve merchant sailors. "With startling accuracy," as the *New York Times* reported, the *Atherton* picked up a sonar contact in about twenty minutes, believed to be the submarine silently sitting one hundred feet below on the bottom of the ocean. After passing over the suspected contact, Captain Iselin of the *Atherton* and Capt. Leslie B. Tollaksen of the *Moberly* ordered weapons deployed. "That's a pig-boat down there, all right! Hold your hats boys! We're going in!"

Atherton gunner's mate Preston Davis, who had joined the Navy after graduating from high school in Arlington, Virginia, in 1943, dropped the first round of thirteen magnetic depth charges. One exploded within minutes, indicating that it hit either the submarine or some other metallic object below the water. Since the eastern seaboard was littered with scores of shipwrecks, Davis could not be certain. The *Atherton* pounded the water with depth charges and hedgehogs for hours, well into the wee hours of the next morning. Tobin said his ship dropped five patterns of depth charges and three or four patterns of hedgehogs, periodically losing and then picking up sonar contact with the submarine. During the course of the barrage, the *Amick* was ordered to leave the scene and escort a merchant ship on its way from New York City to Boston. The destroyer USS *Ericsson* arrived to assist in the search for the U-boat as the bombardment continued, rattling the windows of the distant Block Island post office.

As the fog lifted in the early morning hours, debris believed to have come from *U-853* was strewn about the water, including oil, wood, escape lungs, a wooden flagstaff, a rubber life raft, a rubber patch with German writing indicating how to use a life raft, a crushed cigarette tin, and the submarine captain's hat. Although the oil and wood debris could have been discharged by the U-boat to trick the Navy vessels into thinking the submarine had sunk, the *Atherton* sailors were convinced that their depth charges and hedgehogs had hit their mark based on the other debris. Later a diver from a Navy salvage ship descended to the ocean floor and found the submarine's conning tower smashed and a great split in its side. Bodies of *U-853* sailors also were strewn about some one hundred feet below the ocean's surface. *U-853* would be the last German submarine sunk by the United States in the Atlantic during the war.[39]

Although there were no survivors of *U-853*, sailors on board the *Atherton* remember taking on board a Nazi prisoner of war suffering from a burst appendix just hours before the encounter with *U-853*. Twenty-two-year-old Carl Barth joined the Navy right out of high school and went on board the

Atherton as a signalman. The only water he saw before joining the Navy was the Ohio River. The Kentucky-born sailor took a message from a merchant ship that there was a German POW on board who was seriously ill while the destroyer escort was on its way back from delivering a convoy to Gibraltar.

"The only doctor of the whole group of ships was on our ship," Barth said, "so we went alongside the merchant ship and put a line across, put him [the doctor] in a bag, and hooked onto a pulley up and sent him across to the other ship." Barth said that once the young doctor, Lt. Maurice Vitsky, who was Jewish and a recent graduate of a Virginian medical school, examined the prisoner, Franz Krones, he ordered him returned to the *Atherton*, where he could operate on him. "We brought them both back. This was the doctor's first major operation, and all he had were meager operating facilities and a pharmacist mate to assist," Barth remembered.

With a surgery textbook in front of him and the assistance of twenty-year-old pharmacist mate Thomas J. Ciaccio, the young doctor opened up his German patient and removed the ruptured appendix. However, infection had spread and it was clear that the German's life was hanging in the balance. "He put handfuls of sulfur into the wound," Tobin, the gunner's mate, remembered. "We didn't have much penicillin, so he put in handfuls of the sulfur [*sic*] powder along with a deep drain." Five days later, the doctor was forced to reopen the incision and install a deeper drain. "It was touch and go for awhile," said Tobin, the youngest officer on board. But the patient survived and the last time the *Atherton* sailors saw him, he was being off-loaded on a stretcher in Boston, heading for a Navy hospital, where he did recover.[40]

Captain Iselin showed uncommon caring not only for the German prisoner but also for his entire crew. From all accounts, in fact, the captain had the utmost respect and loyalty of his crew due in no small part because of the personal interest he showed in his men and his willingness not to ask them to undertake an assignment he was not willing to do himself.

Iselin, like many DE skippers, knew how to instill loyalty in those under his command. Most of his crew were in their late teens, with one sailor being fifteen years old and another only thirteen. An incident that continues to this day to be retold by crewmen from the *Atherton* illustrates the skipper's innate ability to earn the admiration of his young crew. "I was on watch that day," said the ship's signalman, Carl Barth, describing an incident in early 1945 that would forever leave an impression on the entire crew of his ship. The *Atherton*

Unlike larger ships, most DEs did not have a doctor on board. Sailors had to rely on pharmacist's mates for most routine medical care. For more serious illnesses, sailors would be transferred to larger ships. Pharmacist's mate Milfred Poll treats a minor wound to a sailor's finger while the USS *Liddle* escorts a convoy through the North Atlantic. *Photo taken by Harold S. Deal; courtesy Jeff Deal*

had left the shipyard where it had been serviced, and once out to sea Barth noticed that the steel antenna atop the mast, some ninety-three feet above the water, was flopping back and forth in the wind. Someone in the shipyard had forgotten to tighten the bolts.

Barth immediately reported the problem to the officer on deck, who called Captain Iselin. Watching the swaying antenna, Iselin noted that if it continued to flop back and forth, it would not be long before the bolts sheared off and the twelve-foot steel antenna came crashing down. Obviously someone had to go up and tighten the bolts, Iselin said. Barth suspected he might be selected by the captain to climb the mast and secure the bolts. "The skipper called for the ship fitter to bring up a set of crescent wrenches," Barth said. "The captain stuck those crescent wrenches in his hip pocket and climbed the mast himself."

"That day, every man who was not on watch was out on that deck praying that he would get down safe," Barth said. "From that day on, that man could ask us to do anything." Barth said that Iselin took a real chance climbing the mast himself. "Captains don't do that," he noted. Barth said he should have sent either him or a ship fitter up to do the job, but "that's just the kind of man he was."[41]

Gunnery officer Tobin was standing below, watching in astonishment as Iselin climbed the mast. "I get paid more than you do," Iselin reportedly told Radioman Carl Heitzel, who also assumed he might be asked to tighten the bolts. Iselin put the wrenches in his back pocket and ascended the ninety-three-foot tower, swaying back and forth as the ship rocked on the heaving seas. "It must have been lunch time [in the shipyard] or the end of the day, and somebody just forgot to tighten the bolts," Tobin said. "The captain was an experienced sailor and was not a neophyte, but he never bragged about it. He was a good navigator. He didn't know much about gunnery. He didn't know much about engineering. And he would let the officers who were in charge do what they have to do. But he was on top of everything."[42]

"A fine officer is what makes a ship," Tobin said. "A ship is a ship. It's a lot of steel put together in a form. One DE is just like another—it's the people aboard that make the difference. Lieutenant Iselin was a fine officer."[43]

8

Sailors in the Shadows

The sixty-year-old black woman rose when it was her turn to speak. Mary McLeod Bethune, one of seventeen children whose parents were born into slavery in rural South Carolina, was far from her southern roots on that memorable day in 1935. She was standing in the Oval Office at the White House, about to address the president of the United States.

"Now I speak, Mr. President, not as Mrs. Bethune but as the voice of fourteen million Americans who seek to achieve full citizenship," she began. "We have been taking the crumbs for a long time. We have been eating the feet and the head of the chicken long enough. The time has come when we want some white meat."[1]

Bethune was part of a delegation called to the White House to review the year-old National Youth Administration (NYA) created by President Franklin Roosevelt to assist young Americans, many of them minorities, struggling with economic and social issues. Bethune had devoted her life to improving the social, economic, and educational position of African Americans, receiving a great deal of publicity and scores of accolades for her work. She had been selected as a member of the NYA's advisory board by Aubrey Williams, its social activist director, and now had a chance to give Roosevelt a firsthand accounting of the state of affairs for minorities in the United States.

Bethune, who met and became friends with both Sara Delano Roosevelt, the president's mother, and First Lady Eleanor Roosevelt a year earlier, urged President Roosevelt to continue advocating for the nation's minority population, encouraging him to open more doors for blacks so they could contribute their talents in government and in business. "Because they already have a reassuring and hopeful belief that there is somebody in the White House who cares!" she told the president. Roosevelt, said to be visibly touched by Bethune's words, leaned across his desk and grasped her hands in both of his. "Mrs. Bethune," he said, "thank you for the informal knowledge you have placed at our disposal in these important days of beginnings in a new field. I'm glad that I'm able to contribute something to help make a better life for your people. I want to assure you that I shall continue to do my best for them in every way."[2]

A week after her historic White House visit, Bethune received a letter asking her to return to Washington to meet again with Roosevelt. She rushed to the capital, meeting first with Aubrey Williams, who told her that the president, impressed by her earlier presentation, decided to create an office of minority affairs within the NYA and wanted her to become its director. She accepted the position and pledged to do her best under the leadership of Williams, who already had many powerful enemies, particularly among southern conservatives, for his liberal views on civil rights. As she was leaving the Oval Office, Roosevelt, looking at Bethune but speaking to Williams, said, "Aubrey, Mrs. Bethune is a great woman. I believe in her because she has her feet on the ground—not only on the ground but in the deep, plowed soil."[3]

Roosevelt developed a fondness for Bethune and met with her regularly on matters relating to minorities, sometimes to the chagrin of some of his less-enlightened White House staff, and would be hearing a lot more from her on integration of the military once it appeared that the United States was headed to war. Although he may have agreed with some of the views of both Bethune and Eleanor Roosevelt, the latter also a staunch advocate for minorities, FDR was first and foremost a political pragmatist who understood the strong sentiments against blacks held by many southerners, including some who worked closely with him in the White House, and the ramifications integration could have at the ballot box. While Bethune may have made a deep impression on FDR, it would take more time—and more relentless convincing and even threatening by other prominent minorities—before Roosevelt would initiate decisive action allowing African Americans to fight side by side with white Americans. But their day would come.

Walter White, an African American with skin so light he could pass for a white man, was one who would make additional headway with Roosevelt on the issue of ending segregation in the armed forces as well as in American industry. As a thirteen-year-old boy, White survived the 1906 race riots in Atlanta, Georgia, and twelve years later became assistant secretary of the National Association for the Advancement of Colored People. Soon he would follow Bethune's path to Roosevelt's White House door.

Race relations in America were becoming increasingly strained as blacks were not only segregated in the military but also banned from jobs in the industrial plants providing wartime equipment and materials. As the situation started to approach a flashpoint with a major protest march planned for Washington, Franklin Roosevelt was urged in the summer of 1941 to meet with White and Asa Philip Randolph, a Harlem street orator and head of the Brotherhood of Sleeping Car Porters, the first black labor union, which helped lay the groundwork for the civil rights movement. Those requests were rebuffed.

Instead Eleanor Roosevelt was dispatched by the president to New York City to meet with White and Randolph, urging them to call off the rally. She told them of her fear of violence should a demonstration occur, particularly since the Washington police force was made up mostly of southerners. Randolph, who had moved to Harlem from Florida as part of the black migration north, told the first lady that there would be no violence unless the president "ordered the police to crack some black heads."[4]

When Eleanor reported to FDR that the rally was still on, the president relented, agreeing to meet with the march organizers. During the White House meeting, White and Randolph urged the president to issue an executive order abolishing discrimination in the armed forces as well as in America's industries. White, who at the time was being courted by supporters of Wendell Wilkie to throw his support to the Republican presidential candidate, pointed out to the president the irony of the American military being trained to fight against Hitler's theories of race while the Army and Navy were practicing a similar philosophy. He also said that inefficient and prejudiced southern officers were handicapping the armed services by making it unattractive for bright white northern recruits, let alone African Americans, to stay in the services, where they were forced to tolerate the backward ways of the southern officers.

Roosevelt turned to Navy Secretary Frank Knox, who attended the meeting, for an explanation. "We can't do a thing about it because men live in such intimacy aboard ship that we simply can't enlist Negroes above the rank of messman," Knox said. "Hold on Frank," Roosevelt replied. "We've got some good Negro bands in the Navy. Why don't we make a beginning by putting some of these bands aboard battleships? White and Negro men aboard ship will thereby learn to know and respect each other and then we can move on from there." Knox said he would look into the president's idea, a small and some might say condescending step, but no one really expected much from Knox, a friend of Theodore Roosevelt who had all but eliminated blacks from any rank above messman. "Experience of many years in the Navy has shown clearly," Knox wrote earlier, "that men of the colored race in any branch than the messman branch, and, promoted to the position of petty officer, cannot maintain discipline among men of the white race. . . . As a result, teamwork, harmony and ship efficiency are seriously handicapped."[5]

Realizing that the only way to stop the demonstration was to agree to an executive order, President Roosevelt asked White and Randolph to prepare a draft order they felt would help remedy the situation, and suggested they retire to the Cabinet Room and get started right away drafting the order. Over the next week several drafts were developed, some of which White said emasculated the order to the point of it being worthless. A final draft was agreed on, and it, which would become Executive Order 8802, was issued by Roosevelt on 25 June 1941, seven days after the first White House meeting. Roosevelt's directive specifically banned discrimination on account of race, creed, color, or national origin in industries holding government contracts for war production and in vocational training for jobs in war industries.

In announcing Roosevelt's order, the *New York Times* carried a story on page twelve headlined "President Orders an Even Break for Minorities in Defense Jobs." The president noted that "the democratic way of life within the nation can be defended successfully only with the help and support of all groups." Executive Order 8802, however, would amount to a sea change in American industry, where people like the president of North American Aviation flatly stated, "We will not employ Negroes. It is against company policy." Or as Kansas City's Standard Steel Corporation declared, "We have not had a Negro worker in twenty-five years, and do not plan to start now."[6]

Although the order did nothing to eliminate segregation in the armed forces, it was seen as a historic step forward in ending discrimination in America's industries. Roosevelt understood that no single executive order would end deep-seated racial feelings, but it certainly would set the stage for further advancements for minorities. The order was met with ridicule and criticism in many quarters, particularly from some industries and southern railroads, which refused to follow the president's directive. But eventually they would comply or risk losing lucrative government contracts.

Six months later, in an address to the nation, Roosevelt touched on racial discrimination, stating, "We must guard against divisions among ourselves and among all the other United Nations. We must be particularly vigilant against racial discrimination in any of its ugly forms," the president said, cautioning, "Hitler will try again to breed mistrust and suspicion between one individual and another, one group and another, one race and another, one government and another." Whether or not he recognized the impact of his words, Roosevelt was echoing the same sentiment expressed in that June 1941 meeting in the White House with White and Randolph: How can America rail against Hitler's discrimination when we permit it to go on here at home?[7]

Change, however, came at a snail's pace in the military, given the resistance on the part of Army and Navy brass, military officers, and a large majority of white sailors and soldiers. Some contended that discrimination in the military simply reflected the social segregation of blacks throughout the nation. Once again Eleanor Roosevelt, sometimes acting as a moral conscience for her husband, may have provided the catalyst sparking a small, incremental change in the attitude of the United States' military brass by opening up the ranks of the Army Air Corps to black pilots, who Army officials had contended would not be capable of learning the technology necessary to fly an airplane.

In early 1941 the first lady traveled to the Tuskegee Institute, founded by Booker T. Washington in 1881, and visited the field where the civilian pilot training program was under way. It was there she met Charles Alfred Anderson, son of an African American chauffeur in Pennsylvania and an accomplished pilot, having taught himself to fly in the 1920s. Later he was tutored by a member of the German air force in World War I and received the first commercial pilot license ever awarded to an African American. In 1934 Anderson and another African American pilot embarked on a thirty-five-day interracial goodwill flight sponsored by the Tuskegee Institute to South America, with scheduled stops in the Bahamas, Cuba, Caribbean, Nicaragua, Brazil, San Salvador, Guatemala, and Mexico. They had made similar flights across the United States and Canada.[8]

"I remember her [Eleanor Roosevelt] telling me that everybody told her we [blacks] couldn't fly," Anderson said. He said the first lady told him, "I see you flying all right here. Everybody that's here is flying. You must be able to fly. As a matter of fact, I'm going to find out for sure. I'm going up with you." The first lady brushed off concerns by Secret Service agents over her safety as she and Anderson headed to the small plane sitting on the runway.

When she climbed into the Piper Cub and the pair made an hour-long flight over Alabama, Eleanor Roosevelt made history. "Well, you can fly all right," Roosevelt reportedly told Anderson after they landed. The African American flyer credits the first lady with convincing her husband to open up the Army Air Corps to blacks. In January 1941 the *New York Times* announced that the first African American pursuit squadron would be organized in the Army. Two months later the Army called for thirty-three volunteers on a "first come, first served" basis for an African American unit in the Army Air Corps, which would be known as the 99th Pursuit Squadron and was to be formed in the fall at Tuskegee. Pilots were required to have two years of college or the equivalent and to undergo six months of training.[9]

Although the color barrier was starting to crumble ever so slowly in the Army, the Navy was another matter. Knox, who had agreed to explore Roosevelt's suggestion to install African American musical bands on battleships so that whites and blacks could get to know one another, never took any action on it. Later the president asked the Navy's general board to develop a plan to enroll 5,000 minority recruits. The Navy board told Roosevelt it would not comply with his request, telling the president that the current role played by "these people" in the military is sufficient. The board believed that integration simply would not work because white men would not accept a black in position of authority over them, felt they were the superior race, and refused to allow blacks into intimate family relationships leading to marriage.[10]

Race relations in the United States continued to boil, with riots and brutal beatings starting to erupt in the nation's larger cities, and at the same time the Navy's staunch opposition to integration started to thaw ever so slightly. Faced with a need for manpower to fight a war at sea that they were unprepared to wage and a president who was becoming less tolerant of the military's recalcitrance with regard to race, the Navy's brass relented and finally opened up enlistment to blacks for ranks above messman in the spring of 1942. The Navy's action amounted to an acknowledgment that the days of segregation were numbered.[11]

Although certainly a product of his times and a political pragmatist at heart, a hint of Franklin Roosevelt's true feelings about race and intolerance can be gleaned from his own writings years before he ever became president. Back in 1928, when FDR, running for governor of New York State and working as a part-time columnist for the *Standard*, a newspaper in Beacon, New York, touched on the subject in a column titled "Between Neighbors." Roosevelt, discussing political parties, bigotry, and the KKK, related a story where he was the guest of honor three years earlier at a chamber of commerce banquet in a small city in Georgia. He said the community was almost pure Scottish and English Protestant ancestry.[12]

"I sat on the right of the mayor of the town and on the other side of me sat the secretary of the chamber of commerce, a young man born in Italy, and a Roman Catholic. Just beyond sat a Jew who was a member of the executive committee," Roosevelt recalled. "I turned to the mayor and asked him if the Ku Klux Klan was strong in the city. He said 'yes, very.'" Then I asked if most of the members of the chamber belonged to the Klan, and again he said 'yes.'"

"If this is so," a puzzled Roosevelt asked, "why is it that the secretary is a Catholic and that a Jew is on the executive committee?" Roosevelt said the mayor "turned to me utterly surprised and answered: Why, Mr. Roosevelt, we know those men. They are intimate friends of ours, we respect them and like them. You know this Klan business doesn't apply to people you know!"

Adding his own personal commentary, Roosevelt wrote: "I often wonder if those unfortunates who are working in open defiance of that article of the Constitution of the United States which guarantees religious liberty are also opposed to the great commandment, 'Thou shalt love thy neighbor as thyself.'" He concluded the column with these words: "Think it over."[13]

Twelve years after Roosevelt wrote those words, religious and racial discrimination still existed throughout the nation, particularly in many of the southern states, which still held pre–Civil War views about the rights of minorities. There was strong opposition to minorities in the military, frequently by members of Roosevelt's inner circle. In 1940 the regular Army had only five black officers, three of them serving as chaplains, and no black man ever had attended Annapolis. Following World War I, enlistment of blacks in the Navy had been discontinued, although recruitment of messmen may have been kept open formally. But in actual practice, only Filipinos were recruited into the messman branch from 1919 until 1932.

By 1932 the total enlisted force in the Navy was 81,120 men, of which only 441 were listed as African Americans, the majority of whom were messmen. Most of the remainder were musicians assigned to the station band in St. Thomas in the U.S. Virgin Islands. In his private diary, Roosevelt's interior secretary Harold Ickes questioned whether African Americans could qualify as pilots. "There is some doubt," Ickes wrote, "whether they [blacks] can qualify as first-class aviators, but the president wants them to be given a chance in this branch of service, and on ground aviation work they are to have their full ten percent proportion."[14]

Roosevelt suggested to Secretary of War Harold Stimson that, with regard to African Americans drafted into the military, they be proportioned into the various services based upon their proportion in the general population, which at that time was 10 percent. "Negro leaders are very much concerned," Ickes wrote, "because they anticipate that conscripted men of their race will all be turned into labor regiments. The president is opposed to this and said so."[15]

But the president saying blacks should have a chance to serve, and even his groundbreaking Executive Order 8802 opening up employment to blacks, did little to stop the clashes between blacks and whites in the streets as well as in the Army and Navy training centers. Militancy within the black community increased and thousands of blacks streamed from the Deep South to the promise of industry jobs in the North. Although Jim Crow was still alive and well, the shift toward some semblance of equality had begun, and soon African American sailors would be doing more than loading ships or serving meals to white officers. In fact, for the first time since Reconstruction the federal government was about to revive the principle of racial equality, leading some to proclaim Roosevelt's New Deal the "Second Reconstruction."[16]

Benjamin Garrison grew up in Columbia, South Carolina, with rigidly segregated schools, drinking fountains, bus stations, and train stations. He had to sit separately from whites in the balcony of movie theaters. If blacks wanted a meal in a southern restaurant, they were forced to go to the back door, he said, where they would be given their meal in a brown paper bag. It all seemed normal to Garrison, having spent his entire life in the South. "I didn't realize until later how this should not be," Garrison said. "The adults shielded us from this—they never taught us to hate anybody."

Garrison's father was a musician and his mother taught adults to read and write under the auspices of FDR's literacy program. After graduating Booker T. Washington High School in 1942, Garrison enlisted in the Navy prior to being drafted. Boarding a train in Columbia, Garrison arrived the next day at the massive Great Lakes Naval Training Center, where he would join other blacks in Camp Robert Smalls, a segregated facility, the Navy's first for training African Americans, named for a black Civil War hero and located on the other side of the tracks from the main training facility.[17]

Tenth-grade student James Graham followed a similar path. He was born in tiny Lake City, South Carolina, and attended a segregated one-room school before joining the Navy in 1942. Graham originally wanted to join the Army Air Corps, but once he learned that they did not accept blacks, he signed up with the Navy after being assured that he would not have to serve as a mess attendant as previous African Americans were required to do. After an overnight ride on a segregated steam train from Columbia, Graham was sent to Camp Smalls.[18]

For Adolph Newton, a seventeen-year-old runaway from Baltimore, Maryland, who forged his parents' signature to enlist, the experience at boot camp was a real awakening. Newton skipped school that day and climbed aboard the Liberty Limited bound for Chicago and the promise of a new life. Upon arrival he and the other African American recruits were herded into the back of an open truck on its way to their barracks at Camp Smalls. As the truck passed other camps in the base, Newton remembered white guards at those camps taunting, "You're gonna be sorry" and "You had a good home but you left." Until a full complement was present, the black recruits were told they would be issued no clothing or bedding. Instead they would keep their civilian clothes and be forced to sleep on the floor.

"I had always taken a warm bed for granted," Newton said, "but that weekend I found out just how important a mattress and blankets are. The floor was my mattress, and my overcoat was my blanket." He shivered himself to sleep each night in the drafty barracks on the windswept shores of Lake Michigan. "I felt every board in the floor; they seemed to cut right into my back. I eventually settled for rolling halfway onto my side."[19]

Eventually a full complement of recruits arrived, but Newton and the other boots were in for another surprise. They would not be sleeping in beds but would be in hammocks. It took some skill not only to get in and out of a hammock but also to keep from falling out of one while asleep. "Bodies were hitting the floor for a week," Newton said.

For sixteen weeks Newton and his fellow sailors-in-training would be examined and tested and would learn to march, shoot a rifle, and tie knots. In short they would get a taste of discipline, Navy style. "Each morning," Newton recalled, "we had to march down to the drill hall for a personal inspection. Here each trainee was inspected to see if he had shaved, bathed, put on clean underwear, and pressed his uniform."[20]

Newton remembered lectures from the camp's admiral in which the officer warned the African American boots that they had to be "better than good." The admiral told them that there were no written guidelines for integrating the Navy, that this was brand-new territory, and that they were certain to face problems both from fellow white boots as well as white officers. He said the only way to overcome these obstacles was to study hard and use their heads—being "good" would not be enough, he said. The African Americans had to be better than good in order to survive military life.[21]

James Graham was all of ninety pounds when he arrived at Camp Smalls. The Lake City, South Carolina, kid was excited that the Navy was finally allowing blacks to do more than clean and cook, and he was ready to learn all that he could with the hopes he would soon be at sea. But training for the Camp Small boots went longer than expected. Usually, the training at Great Lakes would take six or eight weeks, but for the recruits in Camp Small, the time stretched to sixteen weeks because, the way Graham saw it, "they were trying to figure out what to do with us."[22]

In the beginning white petty officers were assigned as company commanders. Gradually blacks were brought in as assistant company commanders until, finally, they were put in charge of some of the training. Unfortunately some of those black commanders had little experience on how to train recruits, themselves having served only as mess attendants. This was all new to the Navy, and there was still plenty to be worked out, so Lt. Daniel W. Armstrong, son of the Civil War general and founder of the Hampton Institute in Virginia, was appointed overall commander for the training of all African Americans at the facility.[23]

As the number of blacks continued to stream into the Navy, two addi-tional camps were used for the overflow. Armstrong, a southerner and Annapolis graduate, believed that blacks should be segregated and have "special" treatment, a policy many white officers failed to embrace. They contended that all recruits should be trained according to the same standards. But Armstrong was the boss, and according to the official naval station history, many stabbings and barrack fights between blacks ensued and might have been reduced had Armstrong allowed officers to use "impartial firmness" in disciplining the black recruits, just as they did with the white men.[24] Armstrong believed that because of differences in background, blacks were not qualified to compete against white recruits in some disciplines, although this certainly proved not to be the case as many Camp Smalls graduates excelled in service schools, and went on to provide exemplary service in all advanced specialized schools with several eventually becoming officers. The first black Navy officer was appointed in 1942, nearly 150 years after the founding of the Navy.

Camp Smalls set up segregated service schools for gunners, radiomen, quartermasters, signalmen, yeomen, storekeepers, cooks, and bakers in September 1942. The following month schools were set up for aviation machinist and aviation metalsmiths, said to be the most successful of the segregated service schools. A new $200,000 building was built the following spring to house these schools, which ironically gave the African American recruits better classrooms, laboratories, and equipment than was available for the white Great Lakes recruits. Some seven thousand blacks entered the Camp Smalls service schools during the three years they were in operation.[25]

Eventually the government studied the segregated service schools and determined that they were operating inefficiently. Some of the schools had only four or five students, which obviously was a waste of valuable resources. Segregation was found to be a "useless luxury," in the government's words, so integration in service schools was introduced on a small scale in 1944. The experiment proved an immediate success and that the black students were "well liked and well treated, did well in their classes and had no complaints to make." The color barrier crumbled a little more with the gradual integration of the service schools, a precursor to integration of the entire facility, which got under way in the summer of 1945.[26]

James Graham, that ninety-pound seventeen year old from Lake City, South Carolina, has clear memories of his days in Camp Smalls. He has an especially vivid one involving President Roosevelt, who decided to visit Great Lakes. Roosevelt was revered by the majority of blacks throughout the nation and the idea that he was coming to Camp Smalls was very exciting for the black recruits. "We waxed the floor and cleaned the barracks for two weeks when we heard he was coming," Graham said. "President Roosevelt was coming to pay us a visit!" The day of FDR's arrival, all of the troops were standing at attention in the barracks awaiting the arrival of their commander in chief. To the great disappointment of the black recruits, the president did not stop.

"I just happened to be standing near a window and I saw the [presidential] limousine swoosh by," Graham said. The president, it turns out, was not snubbing Camp Smalls but simply had a tight schedule, traveling more than 8,750 miles by train and automobile inspecting facilities throughout the nation. He didn't have time to meet any of the recruits in the facility as the top-secret two-week trip was designed to inspect training and industrial locations and was not specifically aimed at garnering publicity for the president.

Daisy Suckley, the president's cousin and close confidante, accompanied him on the cross-country tour that fall, and she recorded her thoughts on the Great Lakes stop in her daily diary. It was a dreary and rainy day when the presidential train arrived in the wee hours of Saturday morning, 19 September 1942. "Sailors & marines stood silent guard on the tops of buildings & about every hundred feet on the ground in the light of . . . flood lamps. We shifted back and forth on sidings & finally stopped," Suckley wrote.[27]

Suckley and the rest of the contingent piled into the presidential car and toured the base. "The station is . . . not quite finished yet, 68,000 men," FDR's cousin wrote. "We saw (the men) doing their various daily duties—a company doing setting-up exercises, a couple of blocks further a group of Negroes raking a yard & singing in unison, two or three companies singing as they march, another jumping over obstacles & in & out of trenches, etc., etc. We drove about 35 miles around the station before returning to the train. A group of nurses in white uniforms saluting just as well as the men."[28]

For seventeen-year-old Thomas Howard, boot camp would be the first time he was away from home. Howard, son of a hog carrier in East St. Louis, Illinois, quit Lincoln High School to join the Navy in the summer of 1942. After an eight-week stay at Camp Smalls, he was selected to go to gunnery school at Great Lakes and served as a gunnery striker for the next six weeks. With training complete Howard was sent to Cape May, New Jersey, and assigned to a converted minesweeper, which patrolled the Delaware Bay area. He would remain there through 1943 until finally being assigned to the USS *Mason*, the first Navy warship manned by a mostly black crew.

When he went on board the *Mason* in March 1944, Howard was excited about the prospect of serving on an American warship and was ready to take his post as a gunner. Unfortunately all the gunnery posts were filled and he was assigned general seaman duties swabbing the deck. "I didn't like my duties at first," Howard said. So when a vacancy in the galley occurred, he jumped at the opportunity, turning in his mop for a serving tray. "I was close to the good food," Howard remarked, noting that he never did get the gunnery job for which he was trained and instead served in the mess his entire time on board the destroyer escort serving chow to enlisted men.[29]

Benjamin Garrison, the nineteen year old from Columbia, South Carolina, followed a similar path from Great Lakes to minesweeper patrol along the East Coast. After boot camp and specialized training as a signalman, Garrison was sent to Lockwood Basin in East Boston, Massachusetts, and assigned to a wooden boat patrolling Boston Harbor for submarines each night. Later Garrison was assigned to the USS *Puffin*, a minesweeper patrolling Boston Harbor and the coast of Maine. Then he got the call to report to the *Mason*, about to be commissioned at the Boston Navy Yard.[30]

James Graham was selected for radio school after completing Great Lakes. Eventually he would find his way to Cape May, New Jersey, along with classmate Thomas Howard, and be assigned to a minesweeper, the USS *Blue Jay*, a converted yacht patrolling the East Coast. He would spend his next year looking for mines and doing what he considered longshore labor work along the docks. When he received the call to go on board the *Mason*, Graham was more than happy to comply.[31]

A driving blizzard with bitter winds and freezing temperatures greeted the recruits as they arrived at the Boston Navy Yard and boarded their shiny new USS *Mason* in March 1944. Although gale-force winds were blowing off the water, Graham said the cold really did not bother the new recruits, who were excited about being the first African Americans to serve as full-fledged sailors on board a Navy warship. Graham recalled that the ship, getting the finishing touches before commissioning day, had no heat or electricity.

What would be a groundbreaking event for African Americans, the Navy, and the nation was recorded in the 21 March 1944 edition of the *New York Times*. The seventy-five-word article headlined "New Navy Crew Mostly Negroes" appeared on page ten of the newspaper. "The destroyer-escort *Mason*, first United States naval vessel with a predominantly Negro crew, was com-missioned today at Boston Navy Yard," the *Times* article noted. "The crew of 204 includes forty-four whites. Later the vessel will be manned entirely by Negroes specially trained for destroyer-escort duties."[32]

The momentous occasion received a bit more publicity in the *Norfolk Journal and Guide*, one of the leading black southern newspapers. "First Negro-Manned Naval Vessel Is Commissioned," headlined a story appear-ing on page two of the 25 March 1944 edition. During the ceremonies at the Boston Navy Yard amid a driving spring snowstorm and bitter cold tempera-tures, Republican Massachusetts governor Leverett A. Saltonstall and Boston mayor Maurice J. Tobin, a Democrat who eventually would succeed Salton-stall as governor, spoke as the crew stood at attention. "There was moisture in the eyes of some of its colored workers who, with their white comrades, braved the bitter cold to witness the ceremony," the newspaper reported. A sense of pride was evident among the blacks present as well as a realization that this would be their opportunity to show the Navy and the American people that they were every bit as capable as white sailors.[33]

Lt. Cdr. William M. Blackford, from a prominent Virginia family, was selected as skipper of the *Mason*. From all accounts, Blackford, who was white, as were the ship's other officers, was admired and respected by his crew, who used terms such as "great man, competent, understanding" to describe him. There is no evidence to suggest that the Navy knew that the skipper's great-grandmother was a well-known southern abolitionist when he was assigned to the *Mason*, and although some speculate that her views on slavery were carried through the generations, Blackford was not a "crusader," according to his son.[34]

Once at sea Blackford wrote a letter to his parents, which read in part, "I think the crew is better than average and is developing some spirit. There has been a lot of bunk said about Negro crews. We can't see that they are any different from others if treated the same, but will know more later. They are anxious to make a name for themselves. [They] actually work harder."[35]

Although James Graham admired Blackford and contends that the skip-per was only interested in running a good ship, the sailor felt that the *Mason* was "programmed for failure." Graham said "they didn't want us to succeed," and his ship received a high level of attention from base officers as well as from officers on other ships. "There were always inspections" by these officers whenever the ship was docked. While nothing was ever found to be amiss, Graham and his shipmates saw this activity as part of the overall view held by Navy officials that the ship would not succeed.[36]

But if that was truly the attitude of the Navy brass, the courageous black sailors on board the *Mason* were about to prove them wrong. Following a routine shakedown cruise off Bermuda, the ship left Charleston in mid-June escorting a convoy bound for Europe, arriving at Horta Harbor, Azores, in July. Although it was against the rules, James Dunn, the ship's signalman, kept a day-to-day detailed diary of his time on board. "We are getting underway at 0340," Dunn wrote in his 14 June entry. "Each man is on his special sea detail. ... None of the boys seems to know what we are going to do. About 0600 we see some merchant ships coming out of port. Then we knew that the real stuff was here at last."[37]

On board the *Mason* for its first convoy across the German submarine hunting grounds was Thomas W. Young, a reporter for the *Norfolk Journal and Guide* and the first African American war correspondent reporting from a Navy ship. Young described the transatlantic trip as an "odyssey" that was both "the fulfillment of a promise and the answer to a question." He said the cruise, in which the *Mason* and the other destroyer escorts safely escorted the convoy with its vital war supplies to Europe, fulfilled the promise the Navy made to send black sailors into combat on board a warship. In addition Young said the cruise helped to answer the question regarding what was happening to the African American sailors who had been trained in the Great Lakes and Hampton Naval Training centers.[38]

Although there were some U-boat contacts made during the crossing, the submarines left the convoy alone. But high seas, gale-force winds, and subfreezing temperatures frequently caused severe damage and loss of life on board the tiny DEs, which were tossed around like corks in the heavy seas. As water heaved up on deck it quickly turned to ice, coating the steel deck, making walking treacherous, and encasing the lines with thick ice. As the ships rolled and pitched, it was easy for a crewman to slip on the icy deck and wind up overboard.

Elmo Allen, radioman on board the USS *Chase*, had quit school in his senior year to join the Navy. Allen had tried three times, all unsuccessfully, to join the Navy since he was sixteen years old. Each time the recruiter had told him he was too skinny. But when March 1943 came around and the war raged on, the Navy jumped at the chance to signing up the still-skinny Jackson, Michigan, kid. "By that time, they were glad to see you," Allen said, because manpower needs were becoming critical in the war. But Allen, who was ready to do battle with the Nazis, never could have imagined that one of the greatest and most destructive enemies he would be facing would be the weather.[39]

Hurricane season had just arrived in the North Atlantic in the fall of 1944 when Allen and his shipmates were ordered to New York City to prepare for a special assignment: shepherding a ragtag collection of seventy-six U.S. Army vessels from New York City to Falmouth, England, some 3,500 miles away. The invasion of France already was under way and the Allies were pushing toward Germany. Although the U-boat strength in the North Atlantic was reduced by this time, there still were a few Nazi submarines lying off America's shores waiting for an opportunity to strike Allied vessels. But on this trip the weather would steal the show from the U-boats.

Besides the destroyer escorts *Chase* and *O'Toole*, three other DEs would provide escort duty for the convoy, the USS *Powers*, USS *Bermingham*, and USS *Mason*, that new American warship manned by a mostly black crew who were about to call upon all their skills and training to survive the dangerous crossing. They had no way of knowing just how much they would be tested in the weeks ahead. The fleet oiler USS *Maumee* and seagoing tug USS *Abnaki* were assigned to the trip as well. The mission was to deliver this strange collection of Army vessels, manned by civilians, to the staging area in England for use in the war zones in northern Europe. The route would be through the unpredictable and stormy North Atlantic, made even more dangerous by an active hurricane season.[40]

In fact, as preparations were under way for this latest crossing, a category-three hurricane, with winds of up to 150 miles per hour, already was devastating parts of the American coastline, causing more than $100 million in damage and a loss of forty-six lives. Called the "Great Atlantic Hurricane" of 1944, the storm packed a wallop, producing seventy-foot waves and resulting in the sinking of five ships, including two U.S. Coast Guard cutters, a minesweeper, and an American destroyer, the USS *Warrington*, with the combined loss of 344 American sailors.[41]

Lt. Cdr. Russ V. Bradley, skipper of the destroyer escort *Chase*, viewed this storm as an "evil omen" of what might be in store for his convoy, designated Convoy N.Y. 119. A few days after the hurricane had become extratropical and merged harmlessly with another storm near Greenland, Convoy N.Y. 119 got under way. "The sea that day was mirror calm," Captain Bradley remembered. "It gave us no hint of what was to come." The Army vessels consisted of fourteen steel railroad car floats, fourteen wood cargo barges, twelve large sea-going tugs, fifteen small harbor tugs, fifteen self-propelled harbor oil barges, one Panamanian tramp with a Greek crew, and two British net tenders.[42] The civilians chosen by the Army transport service to operate the vessels were "the last scrapings available from the exhausted wartime manpower pools." Some consisted of misfits, unable to find other jobs on conventional merchant ships, with many either too old or too young for military service.[43]

The DEs would have their work cut out for them. The trip across the North Atlantic would not be quick, as the escorts had to keep their speed below five knots in order not to lose the motley collection of Army vessels, most of which were not accustomed to sailing on the high seas. Bradley remembered seeing the *Queen Mary* steaming at twenty-five knots across the Atlantic, carrying troops to England. The ocean liner made three round-trip crossings before Convoy N.Y. 119 would even arrive in England.[44]

"The first two weeks were a constant scramble to herd the unruly units back into the convoy," Bradley wrote. "Even modest bad weather broke up the formation, but mostly it was an endless series of equipment failures, sick crew members or just plain inability to do what was required." On one night of moderately rough seas, one of the tugs lost its bilge pumps and developed a bad list. Before any help could be given, the vessel turned over, dumping its crew of twelve into the dark ocean waters. Eleven of the twelve were rescued. This was only the first—but would not be the last—casualty of the trip.[45]

With ninety-mile-per-hour winds and seas building to heights of sixty to eighty feet, the vessels of Convoy N.Y. 119 were in for some real trouble. "The poor little tugs and oilers could do nothing but run with the waves, hang on, and try to survive," Bradley said. Elmo Allen, radioman on board the *Chase*, said it was "like riding the Coney Island roller coaster standing up." He said the crew was "hanging on for dear life," noting that "the DEs had no internal passageway, making it all but impossible to go fore and aft with the chance of winding up overboard."[46]

Bradley said this trip made him realize how sturdy the destroyer escorts were: "The angry crest would tower over our bridge—itself 40 feet above the waterline, and lift the stern sky high." He added, "We had to hang on with both hands and she whipped and twisted and dropped like a stone each time a crest passed under." Bradley recalled "the slide down into the trough was unnerving with dark and heaving water all around, and it seemed most likely that the ship would break up or else dive right under the water. After a night and day of this, however, through a sort of numb fatigue, we thought perhaps we would make it."[47]

And they did—at least most of them. The casualty list included nineteen men lost at sea, three small tugs, eight steel car floats, and five wooden cargo barges. The remainder of the convoy made it into England on 20 October, more than a month after departing New York City. On the final approach there was an incident, Bradley remembered, involving the destroyer escort *Mason*, the African American–manned warship. With a seventeen-foot crack in its deck plates, the *Mason* was starting to take on water—some twenty-one inches reported in the chain lockers—but was dispatched to speed ahead toward Lizard Head, England, escorting a group of twenty smaller craft before they faltered in the heavy seas.

The tiny warship led the tugs, oil barges and other small vessels to port on a fourteen-hour trip through the treacherous channel with its fifty-foot waves and ninety-mile-per-hour winds. Upon arriving safely the crack in the ship's deck was welded and, within a couple of hours, the *Mason* was back on the water, plowing through fifty-foot seas to assist the remaining members of the convoy—a courageous move by the captain and his crew of the little DE, especially given that two larger British destroyers assigned to assist the convoy chose not to venture out onto the angry seas.[48]

Mason signalman Lorenzo A. DuFau remembered the day they headed back out to sea to help the rest of the convoy. "The calm that was among the crew members in the midst of this conflict was remarkable. We would resort to trying to humor each other rather than being in fear. But fear was there," he said. "There was no way to swim to get out of there because the ships couldn't come near each other and the nearest line was straight down. So if the end came, we'd hope that we were at peace with our Maker."[49]

In his 16 October diary entry, James Dunn, the *Mason*'s signalman, said the sea was still raging and pitching the ship from side to side as the tiny escort tried to round up ships in the convoy "like a shepherd rounding up his sheep." The howling winds and raging seas reminded Dunn of the earlier days of the convoy when it plowed through the cyclonic North Atlantic: "You couldn't stay in your bunk at all. All the ships are having a very hard time, especially the small Army tugs. One of them sank last night . . . also a boy fell over the side of one of the destroyer escorts and hasn't been found since." Dunn went on to write, "People shouldn't condemn a sailor so much for what he does while in port, because you don't know the hell he goes thru at sea."[50]

After safely escorting the vessels to port, Dunn also recalled when the *Mason* was ordered to return to sea to search for the other ships as well as survivors. "The weather is still very bad and a terrific storm is coming up," Dunn wrote. "The two British ships started back with us but later turned back because the sea was too rough. But we had to keep going." Dunn added, "It didn't look as thought we were going to make it but with the help of the Lord we made it safely. We have never been in a storm as rough as that one."[51]

Nineteen-year-old *Mason* radioman Ben Garrison, who was "elated" to have a chance to serve as a full-fledged sailor, will never forget Convoy N.Y. 119, which he described as a "hair-raising" experience. Garrison said the quartermaster told him the ship took a 70-degree roll during the crossing. The young sailor, who was in his foul-weather gear with a wool jacket and long johns, said as the water washed over the deck it would freeze on contact. Lines were caked with thick ice, making them difficult to handle. They had to be especially careful walking on the slippery decks, he said, because if a sailor went overboard no one would be able to rescue him in the raging seas.[52]

Thomas Howard, the eighteen year old who trained as a gunner's mate but spent his time in the ship's mess, remembered gripping onto the ship's cable guardrails to keep from being tossed overboard. "The waves were astronomical," Howard recalled. "That was the day of all days," he noted in recalling Convoy N.Y. 119. Howard said the *Mason* would sink down and then lurch back up as the ship pitched from side to side.[53]

For their heroic efforts, the crew of the USS *Mason* was recommended by Captain Blackford as well as the convoy commander, Cdr. Alfred L. Lind, to receive a Navy commendation, a commendation that, despite their courageous steadfast devotion to duty, was not awarded to the black sailors who served on board the *Mason*, owing almost certainly to the racial prejudice of the time. After all, if the *Mason* was "programmed to fail," as some of its crew believed—and it instead excelled—the Navy brass would have found it easier to bury the commendation recommendation than to admit they were wrong. It would take more than half a century before the U.S. government bestowed upon the

Mason crew members who were still alive the honor they had earned—and been recommended for—way back in 1944.[54]

Even though the men of the USS *Mason* wore the uniform of the U.S. Navy, racial prejudice was felt every day. In fact, Ben Garrison recalled an instance when he and his white shipmates were on board a ferry in Virginia. They sat down at the lunch counter and placed their order. The white waitress eyed Garrison warily but did bring him his hot dog and Coke. Within minutes, however, a white man came from the kitchen and, using a racial epithet, told Garrison to leave. "I had to persuade my shipmates not to defend me," Garrison said, adding that he quietly picked up his lunch and left the counter.

Martin Davis, pharmacist's mate on board the USS *Pettit*, labels as "horrible" the treatment of blacks on board DEs. "When I first got aboard the ship I saw these black fellows and they were all segregated," he recalled. "They were all living in one location of the ship and they were serving as cooking personnel, officers' stewards, and they were treated by the officers like servants." Davis said the treatment carried over off the ship as well. "If you ended up in a southern port, if you ended up in Norfolk, Virginia, or anyplace in the South, these fellows had to get in the back of the bus."

Davis recalled one instance while his ship was docked in New York. In South Beach, he said, Italian prisoners were being held, and when Italy surrendered, the POWs were given American military uniforms with a green patch that identified them as "Italy." Davis said he would never forget what happened while in port. "The saloon keepers were serving Italian POWs but were refusing to serve American black servicemen."[55]

Cassin Craig was a white supply officer assigned to the *Mason*. The Philadelphia native had graduated from high school and college before the Navy sent him to Harvard Business School for additional training. Craig said he was assigned to the ship and was not aware until he boarded that the ship was manned by a predominantly black crew. Craig came on board in November, following the Convoy N.Y. 119 crossing, and made three convoy crossings to North Africa later that month. "They were good sailors," Craig said in describing the black crew, noting that the white officers were unexpectedly impressed by the African American sailors, although he did detect racial tension on board ship, particularly on the part of some of the white officers.[56]

War correspondent Thomas Young, who rode along on one of the *Mason*'s first missions, said the ship served as a "floating laboratory" that showed how easily workable the principles of democracy are when given a fair trial. "Here is being tested the ability of its men in uniform to live and work peacefully and harmoniously and effectively," Young wrote, "irrespective of previously applied patterns of separation." Young noted that the *Mason* was just like all other American warships. Bunks were assigned according to the sections in which the men work rather than their racial identity. The chow hall had no separate tables for whites and blacks. "The men line up for their meals, first come first served, and sit where there is a vacant seat to eat them," he wrote. "Any other arrangement obviously would carry over into the way these men work and fight together. Such an effective and high spirited team could not exist otherwise."[57]

The *Mason*'s sailors would not soon forget their visit to Northern Ireland, where they received a warm and hospitable welcome. In Thomas Young's article on the trip, headlined "Irish First to Treat USS *Mason* Crew Like Real Americans," he said if the ship ever went AWOL, it was a fairly safe bet that search planes would locate it in the Irish Sea. "We were overcome by their friendliness," Thomas Howard remarked.[58]

"Funny," one sailor mused, "how I had to come all the way across the ocean to a foreign country before I get to enjoy the feeling of being an American." Compared to wartime Boston, Philadelphia, Norfolk, or San Diego, Young remarked, this Irish port was poor, dull, and half starved. But the black sailors on board the *Mason* found it kind and pleasant. After almost six weeks at sea, the sailors walked the streets and frequented the pubs and dance halls, where a large, friendly group of local women helped bring back memories of home. "It was the first time in my life that I've been treated like a real American," one *Mason* sailor remarked.[59]

For Seaman William Bland of the *Mason*, Ireland was an experience like no other. "All the boys on the *Mason* were raised right here in this country, in the United States, and we couldn't go to a movie show or sit down at a counter in Woolworth's even," he recalled. "We had to go around to the back. And the next thing you know, we were on the ship, and we were scared. Then we went to Ireland and the Irish people didn't look on us as our skin color. They looked on us as Americans—as American fighting men."[60]

9

Coming Right at Me

Steaming northwest in Manila Bay, three destroyer escorts were screening an American carrier on a sunny January afternoon in 1945. Suddenly eight Japanese suicide planes came in low and out of the sun, racing toward the convoy. Sailors on board the DEs rushed to their battle stations, manning their antiaircraft guns, firing at the kamikazes headed for a collision course with the American ships.

Once the DEs started firing, four of the planes quickly scurried away, but four others kept strafing the convoy with gunfire as they flew directly toward it in their suicide mission. While the DEs splashed three of the planes, one continued to evade the sailors. Heading directly for the USS *Stafford*, the kamikaze plowed into the destroyer escort's starboard side amidships, lodging between the engine room and fire room. The crash opened up a twelve-by-sixteen-foot hole in the hull of the ship, which started to lose its way and take on water at an alarming rate.

Franklin D. Roosevelt Jr., skipper of one of the DEs, the *Ulvert M. Moore*, immediately realized that the *Stafford* needed help, its engine room flooded and fires erupting on its deck. Captain Roosevelt radioed the group commander, "443 is dead in the water. We're going to assist her." He quickly broke formation and dashed to the aid of his sister ship while calling for help over his radio.

The escort group commander barked back, "442, I don't give a damn if your father is president of the United States, get back in formation as ordered immediately!" Captain Roosevelt did not answer and instead proceeded to the *Stafford*, where he started to pull survivors from the water. Later Roosevelt was reprimanded for leaving the formation by the superior officer, who warned the young skipper, "Just because your father is president of the United States you will still obey my orders!" FDR Jr. reportedly told his superior, "No, I'm going to save my buddies." And he did just that. Roosevelt's ship was able to rescue fifty-four men and three officers, assisted by the destroyer USS *Halligan*, which rescued additional men. Two sailors on board the *Stafford* died and twelve were wounded. The ship survived.[1]

Dale Anderson, torpedoman on board the *Ulvert M. Moore*, was stationed on the torpedo tube during the attack on the *Stafford* when three kamikazes headed straight toward his ship. "They were flying real low and close to the water," Anderson said, adding that one of the suicide planes was heading directly for his position on board the *Ulvert M. Moore*. "I could see him [the Japanese pilot] sitting in the plane with his goggles on. He was coming right at me, there wasn't anything I could do." Reciting the Lord's Prayer, the nineteen-year-old country boy, who had never spent any time on the water before being assigned to the DE, knew what was about to happen as the plane banked for a direct collision with his ship. But the ocean intervened. Much to Anderson's surprise, one of the kamikaze's wings hit a rising wave, tumbling the plane into the water. Plane and pilot disappeared below the churning ocean waters.[2]

"Captain Roosevelt was a very good skipper," *Ulvert M. Moore* torpedoman George Lawson said. Lawson, a Missouri boy drafted into the Navy right out of high school, also had never been on the water before boarding the *Moore*. "As long as all the ship work was completed, he got us a lot of leave," he said, adding that FDR Jr. took good care of his men and would allow them R&R time when the ship lay over on one of the Pacific islands. "They let us go over on the beach and let each of us have one or two cans of beer," which was stored in an undisclosed location somewhere on the ship. "We never knew where it was stored," Lawson recalled—not that sailors didn't try to find the alcoholic stash.

Lawson and fellow torpedoman Anderson agree that although he was well liked by his men, Roosevelt ran a tight ship. Lawson said that Captain Roosevelt held a captain's mast for dozens of sailors who failed to wear their life jackets on deck as required. Many of the sailors tried to hide when officers started to collect names, but Anderson did not. He acknowledged that he had neglected to wear his life jacket and, as a result, received a more lenient sentence when Roosevelt convened the mast. "I got off pretty easy, just a couple hours extra duty," he recalled.³ Roosevelt was "good at maneuvering," unlike the *Kendall C. Campbell*'s Captain Johnson, who Richard Warner, the ship's executive officer, said ran their ship into the stern of a tanker tied up at the dock in Panama, opening up the tanker "like a can of tuna." Meanwhile, he said, "young Roosevelt just slides right in ahead of us."⁴

Fifth-born child of Franklin and Eleanor, FDR Jr. also was known among the men for gallantry and loyalty to his shipmates as well as to his sister ships. Prior to his service on board the destroyer escort, Roosevelt was on board the destroyer USS *Mayrant*, where he served as executive officer when, on 1 August 1943, while moored at the dock in Palermo Harbor, Sicily, the ship came under heavy aerial attack. Several bombs landed close to the ships and others struck a trainload of ammunition and nearby gasoline and explosives storage facilities. As flying bomb fragments and shrapnel wounded two men on the bridge, partially amputating the leg of one, Roosevelt grabbed a wounded mess attendant and hauled him down an outside ladder to a field dressing area below. Shrapnel hit Roosevelt's shoulder as he carried the man, but he still managed to slide down the rest of the ladder to get his shipmate to safety.

When Roosevelt returned to the bridge and started to light a cigarette, he noticed something that he would never forget. Pulling out his old Zippo lighter from the shirt pocket near his heart, Roosevelt noticed a large dent on the lighter, apparently made from a fighter plane bullet. He always believed the lighter saved his life. FDR Jr. was awarded a Silver Star and Purple Heart for the 1943 incident.⁵

Theodore Barnhart, signalman on board the USS *Seiverling*, one of Roosevelt's sister DEs, revealed a story about Captain Roosevelt that appears to have gone unnoticed in the history books. Although it was known that Roosevelt did not attend the funeral of his father, who died on 12 April 1945, few appear to know the specific details as to why he refused to be with his mother and siblings for funeral services in Washington, D.C., and Hyde Park, New York, where the president later was buried in the rose garden of his estate. On the day the president died, Barnhart was standing watch on the bridge in the early morning hours when the radio shack sent up a message that President Roosevelt had died. "I put the heading on it, read it, and read it again," Barnhart remembered. The stunned signalman went down to the radio shack and asked them, "What the hell are you trying to do, get me in trouble?" Once the authenticity of the message was confirmed, Barnhart returned to the bridge and relayed the message by flashing light to the *Ulvert M. Moore*, notifying the DE captain that his father—the president of the United States—had died.

Lt. William H. Bell had the deck watch on board the *Moore* when he received the message from the radioman about 2:00 AM. Bell immediately called for his relief watch officer and headed to Captain Roosevelt's cabin to relay the news of his father's passing. "I proceeded to Frank's cabin, and as gently as I could, I awakened him from a deep sleep. When he was awake I sat on the side of his bunk and handed him the message, the news of the death of his father, President Franklin D. Roosevelt. Frank read and reacted by slumping forward as he sat, head in hands. I put a hand on his shoulder, and we silently grieved together. Finally, the president's son turned his head toward me and calmly said, 'Thank you, Bill. I'll be all right. Get back on watch.'"

The *Seiverling* then relayed another message to Barnhart from the task force commander: Roosevelt's ship was to come alongside the carrier where an airplane was waiting on the catapult to take him to the Philippines, where he would be rushed to Hawaii and then to Washington, D.C., for his father's funeral. Barnhart relayed the task force commander's order to Roosevelt's ship.

"About fifteen minutes later I got a call from Roosevelt's ship with a message for the carrier," Barnhart said. "Roosevelt refused to come along side the carrier because he had shipmates who also had lost their parents, and they were not allowed to leave the ship, and he didn't feel he should be treated any different than his shipmates," said Barnhart, who along with Roosevelt was part of a task force on its way to the invasion of Okinawa. "I always thought his family should know why he refused to attend his father's funeral," the signalman noted, adding that "he was a great enough man not to take advantage of his position." Roosevelt's group was ordered to delay flying their flags at half staff in honor of the president until the battle was over so FDR Jr. would not be distracted from his responsibility of running his ship.[6]

In June, once both destroyer escorts had been relieved of duty in Okinawa, they proceeded to Guam for refueling before departing for Ulithi. No liberty was to be allowed while in the harbor—unless, of course, your name was Roosevelt. FDR Jr., along with another officer and a Navy or Red Cross nurse, piled into a Jeep and wandered into a portion of the island called "no man's land," an area not yet cleared of Japanese soldiers. The three reportedly were held down by gunfire for several hours.

Meanwhile, once the ships were fueled and ready to leave, a vigorous debate ensued about whether they should depart the area without Captain Roosevelt. "The brass wanted the exec officer to take 442 to sea because they wanted to get the carrier out of the harbor," Richard Warner of the *Kendall C. Campbell* remembered. "But somebody thought better of the situation. So instead of leaving in darkness, it was well into the morning when Frank returned and off we went."

Barnhart met Roosevelt a few times when their ships were in port and he was assigned to deliver messages from his captain. He regarded FDR Jr. as "a fine gentleman, an all-around Navy man. He was a good officer who took good care of his men." Barnhart said that if Roosevelt's shipmates wanted a can of beer after dinner, the skipper likely would have provided one for them. Because the Navy was dry, Roosevelt once was asked what he would do if someone complained that he was providing beer to his men in defiance of Navy regulation. Barnhart said Roosevelt replied, "I'd tell them to talk to my father."[7]

Barnhart said Roosevelt had a good sense of humor. He remembered the first message he ever received from FDR Jr.'s ship. "We were in Pearl Harbor," Barnhart recalled, when a "PVT," or private message, was relayed from Roosevelt to the *Seiverling*'s captain, Francis Adams Jr., a descendant of the same Adams family that had produced two American presidents. At first Barnhart did not see the message, but then he noticed the signal light was being bounced off a cloud. The message to Captain Adams: "Meet you on the beach for a short snort 15 minutes. Roosevelt." Barnhart said the two captains were close friends in spite of Adams being the son of Charles F. Adams, secretary of the navy under former president Herbert Hoover. When Roosevelt's ship was having some mechanical troubles, Barnhart flashed a message from Captain Adams to Roosevelt: "Do you need a good Republican sailmaker? Adams."

Daniel Sutelle, a twenty-two-year-old native of the little town of Ambridge, Pennsylvania, was a pharmacist's mate on board the *Seiverling* and recalled when his ship was docked alongside the *Moore* and *Yosemite*, a destroyer tender in Pearl Harbor. Son of a steel-mill worker in the community of about five hundred people, Sutelle always liked the water and was interested in medicine, so he was pleased to be handling medical matters on board the ship.

Once, while Sutelle was talking to one of Roosevelt's officers who had come on board the *Seiverling*, the *Moore*'s PA system sounded: "All hands now hear this, lay back to the fantail the skipper wants to speak to you." Sutelle and the other officer went up to the torpedo deck, where they could peer over the 5-inch gun to see what was happening on the fantail. "We went up there and here comes FDR. He was about six two, a big handsome guy," Sutelle remembered.

"Men," Roosevelt began, "I had to go over to the Pearl on business, and I was only gone about two hours, and I had left a bottle of scotch in my quarters." Roosevelt continued: "When I came back, it was gone. I'm going to give whoever took that bottle fifteen minutes to put it back, and if he does, nothing untoward will happen." A crusty old fireroom chief, with a greasy hat and rumpled uniform, called out to Roosevelt, "Ah for Christ's sake, cap'n, give 'em a break. We could all use a drink about now." Sutelle said the captain did not hear the chief's remarks. Roosevelt's bottle of scotch was never returned.[8]

Roosevelt's ship, the *Ulvert M. Moore*, saw plenty of other action in the Pacific. The day before the attack on the *Stafford*, Torpedoman Dale Anderson, who was drafted into the Navy "the minute I turned eighteen," recalled the kamikaze attack on the *Ommaney Bay* in the predawn hours of 4 January, when the convoy was steaming through Sulu Sea. A twin-engine kamikaze, which had not been detected by radar or even by the lookouts on deck, crashed into the escort aircraft carrier only a thousand yards from the *Ulvert M. Moore*'s starboard bow. A heavy explosion rocked the *Ommaney Bay*, and large fires broke out on its starboard side. Fully gassed airplanes on the flight deck exploded. Water pressure, power, and bridge communications were lost as sailors fought the raging flames in heavy black smoke while dodging ricocheting ammunition from the 50-mm guns.

Seriously wounded sailors were strapped to cots and covered with kapok life jackets before being lowered into the white-capped seas, where two swimmers were assigned to take care of each sailor. As another explosion rocked the carrier, two sailors from the destroyer escort USS *Eichenberger* picking up survivors were killed by flying debris. Because of the flames and debris, it was difficult for the rescuing ships to get too close to the burning vessel. As flames soared high into the dark skies, Roosevelt's ship rushed to the aid of the burning vessel, and the *Moore*'s crewmen were able to rescue fifty sailors, with ninety-five lost. Many others suffered flash burns and shock. The water was red with blood and black with oil as the bodies of scores of corpses of American sailors bobbed up and down in the debris-littered sea. "There were plenty of bodies floating in the water," Anderson said. "We couldn't do much with them."[9]

William Bell, the officer on board the *Ulvert M. Moore* who delivered the news to Captain Roosevelt of his father's death, grew up in Schenectady, New York, and went on to Princeton University following graduation from high school. He majored in economics and worked as an apprentice with J. P. Morgan in New York City following college graduation in 1939. The next year he enlisted in the Navy and, on Pearl Harbor day, received the call to report for duty in two days. Although Bell had failed the eye test, he was found to be a good candidate for naval intelligence. His first duty was taking applications from prospective naval officers. Later he got his wish and was assigned to sea duty for two months with the Canadian navy on board a corvette near Halifax. Eventually, in spite his eyesight, he was reassigned to the sub-chaser school in Miami before boarding the *Ulvert M. Moore* as a junior lieutenant in 1944. It had become obvious that the Navy needed all the men they could recruit to fight America's enemies on the high seas.

"I was impressed and bewildered," is how Bell remembered the day he boarded the destroyer escort. "I had a lot of responsibilities and wasn't sure I was trained enough." He met Captain Roosevelt, whom he recalled as "a big man with a great deal of naval experience. He had a grand personality and we just hit it off right away. His courage and ability were of the highest." Bell said that Roosevelt spoke often of his family, noting that "he adored his mother" and was "very proud of his father." He stated that FDR Jr. felt that his older brothers, Jimmy and Eliott, had taken "cushy" jobs in the war effort with a high rank and "he and his brother John were out to vindicate the Roosevelt name." Bell recalled that FDR Jr. wanted to get out and fight and, at times, some of the officers on the ship wished their captain wouldn't volunteer so quickly for so many dangerous missions.

"We had an Ivy League ship," Bell said, noting that he was a Princeton graduate, Roosevelt was a Harvard graduate, and the executive officer, Bobby Whitney, was the son of the president of J. P. Morgan, where Bell had worked prior to the Navy. Other officers hailed from Princeton and Yale University, Bell said. "We had a grand time."[10]

"While we were off Manila Bay, our radarman detected a surfaced ship coming out of the bay," Bell said, noting that it turned out to be a Japanese submarine. The vessel, which was believed to have senior Japanese military officers on board, quickly submerged, and Captain Roosevelt was ordered to go after the submarine and destroy it.

As the *Ulvert M. Moore* raced through the rough seas to intercept the submarine in the darkness of a moonless night, sonar picked up the submerged vessel and Bell ordered firing of the hedgehogs. A second firing of hedgehogs ensued, followed by a third, which was followed by a distinct "crack" and bubbling and hissing noises, indicating the submarine had been hit. "There was a terrible explosion, right at our stern," Bell said, and oil came to the surface, followed by a "geyser of flames" reaching fifty feet into the dark night skies. Sailors noticed the strong odor of diesel oil, what appeared to be a life jacket, small boxes, pieces of deck planking, and a considerable amount of paper appearing on the water's surface—all strong indications that they had hit their mark. Sailors on board said Roosevelt had hoped to sink the submarine on 30 January so he could present the "kill" to his father as a birthday gift. Unfortunately for FDR Jr., the sinking came two days too late.[11]

While the role of destroyer escorts in World War II has largely been overlooked, the part they played in the Pacific war is even less well understood, with most DE accounts instead focused on the essential role the little ships played in defeating German U-boats in the North Atlantic. Although they were critical in helping to turn the tide of the war for the Allies in the Atlantic theater, destroyer escorts in the Pacific performed roles far and above what their original designers envisioned. In addition to escorting convoys and antisubmarine work they performed in both the Atlantic and Pacific, they also protected the Pacific fleet's replenishment forces, served on picket duty battling the Japanese kamikazes, and even fought head to head against Japanese warships during the Battle of Leyte Gulf. To be sure, destroyer escorts participated in every major Pacific battle, fending off Japanese submarines and relentless kamikaze suicide squads and valiantly fighting against the world's largest battleship.

The USS *Day* was escorting a collection of fifteen tugs, including the large *Whippoorwill*, and fifty-five tows from San Pedro Bay in the Philippines to Lingayen, where the equipment on the tows would be used to build a torpedo boat base. Jim Larner, a farm boy who quit school to join the Navy, was on board the destroyer escort and was asleep at the range-finder deck that morning because it was too hot to sleep below. A Japanese bomber suddenly appeared over the ship's fantail and flew right over the tow. Two bombs were released, missing the destroyer escort by about fifty feet. The explosion of the bombs jarred awake Larner, the fire-control striker, and he rushed to his battle station on the aft director.

"By the time I had the cover off and swung around on target, the Jap had turned around to make another bombing run," Larner wrote in his shipboard diary. "The forward 5-inch mount was manned and was turned onto automatic. When I pressed the firing key we got off one shot, way off target, but it at least told the Jap that his sneak attack had not worked and we were ready. He immediately cut off his second attack run and left us." The ship safely escorted its charges to their destination, although Tokyo Rose, the Japanese radio propagandist announced, "USS *Day* was sunk today."

In the greatest naval battle in history, the Battle of Leyte Gulf, destroyer escorts once again had their mettle tested and emerged victoriously proud fighters just as they had in battling the Nazi U-boats and German fighter planes in the Atlantic theater. Their heroic story unfolds just before dawn on 25 October 1944 off the island of Samar in the western Philippine Sea.

A mighty force of four Japanese battleships, nine heavy cruisers, one light cruiser, and ten destroyers steamed from the northwest out of the San Bernardino Strait and circled around the eastern side of Samar, surprising both themselves as well as a small fleet of three American destroyers and four destroyer escorts—the USS *Samuel B. Roberts, Raymond, Dennis*, and *John C. Butler*—in place to screen six escort carriers providing air support for General MacArthur's troops fighting to liberate the Philippines. None of the American vessels carried anything larger than a 5-inch gun compared to the imposing Japanese warships, some of which carried 18.1-inch guns. A true David versus Goliath engagement—described by the *New York Times* as one of the most heroic episodes in American history—was about to begin.[12]

Robert Copeland, commanding officer of the six-month-old destroyer escort USS *Samuel B. Roberts*, affectionately known as "Sammy-B," was on his way to the wardroom for a cup of coffee when a lookout called out to Ens. Dudley Moylan: "Surface radar reports that they have a contact, Sir, bearing about three-three-zero approximately thirty or forty miles away." The ship's radar, which had been having some problems, showed a fuzzy, dense area on the screen. Copeland looked toward the area of the sighting and noticed a dark storm cloud or thunder head in the distance. "Well, there's a storm over there," Copeland said, "but there could be something inside of it, so keep an eye on it."[13]

As Copeland started to descend the ladder toward the wardroom and some hot coffee, a lookout shouted, "Object on the horizon. Looks like the

In the Pacific theater DEs often were called upon to perform duties far beyond what was envisioned by their designers. They participated in the greatest naval battle of all time at Leyte Gulf. Here the destroyer escort USS *Butler* (*background*) and destroyer USS *Heerman* make smoke to hide U.S. vessels from the Japanese fleet. The heavy black smoke shielded the carriers from the view of enemy ships as well as from Japanese kamikazes trying to make suicide runs. *U.S. Navy photo, courtesy the Destroyer Escort Historical Museum*

mast of a ship." And over the misty horizon came not one ship but an enormous armada of Japanese warships, including the 68,000-ton *Yamoto*, the world's largest battleship, closing in at thirty knots on the American fleet. At first it was thought the Japanese ships were fleeing following the battle at Surigao Strait the previous evening. The captain and his officers had listened intently to the garbled TBS radio chatter the night before, which stretched well into the early morning hours, and they were certain the Americans had vanquished the Japanese fleet.

Sonarman Whitney Felt recalled hearing over the loudspeaker that morning that they could see the "remnants" of the Japanese navy in the distance. Felt looked astern and saw the ships, which appeared as tiny dots on the horizon. But the dots started to get larger and larger. "Why, I wondered, if the ships were fleeing, were they getting larger?" Felt said. "Suddenly," he recalled, "there were white puffs of smoke visible from the enemy ships, and moments later I could hear a whistling sound I'd never heard before, and almost immediately there were huge splashes nearby in the water, strangely colored green and blue and yellow." Outnumbered and outgunned, the tiny American fleet was under attack—and odds were they would not survive.

Clearly not designed to battle these mighty warships, the DEs and their carriers were ordered to change course and head away from the mainland and the fast-approaching mammoth Japanese vessels. Combat air patrol planes from the carriers flew directly over the warships, which opened fire on the American aircraft. By changing course, the American carriers hoped to launch their bombers, the only way they—staggeringly unmatched in firepower and speed—could hope to fend off the powerful enemy warships. The airplanes, though, were not outfitted with the armor-piercing weapons to fight ships and instead were armed with general-purpose, light bombs for use on the mainland in their support of MacArthur.[14]

The overwhelming Japanese force commenced firing, the first salvo splashing between the *Roberts* and *Fanshaw Bay*, the escort carrier serving as the flagship of the fleet with Adm. Clifton "Ziggy" Sprague on board. Geysers of rainbow-colored water shot high in the blue sky as the Japanese shells, dyed a different color for each specific ship, rained down on the American fleet. "We took off on the new course," Copeland said. With orders to scramble all planes on the carriers, many of the aircraft needed to be refueled and rearmed in order to battle the Japanese warships. Sailors frantically rushed to get the planes ready. "Any plane that couldn't be made operational right away was pushed over the side to make room," Copeland recalled.

The fleet started making smoke in order to hide from the Japanese. White smoke, a chemical concoction generated on the fantail, swept around the ships while heavy black smoke poured out of the big burners in the boiler fire boxes. The escorts sped away but could only go as fast as the slowest carriers, which shook and trembled as they cranked their engines up to nineteen knots. With their giant guns roaring, the Japanese warships raced in hot pursuit toward the American fleet at speeds of twenty-six to thirty-five knots. The Japanese continued pounding the ships with high-caliber shelling, some of the missiles getting a little too close for comfort. It wouldn't be too long before they would catch and annihilate the Americans.

Running through a heavy rain squall, the destroyer escorts were hidden briefly by the driving rain and smoke still pouring out of the ships, but not before some of the carriers were hit by Japanese shells. The USS *Gambier Bay* took direct hits from the cruiser *Tone* and became the first casualty of the battle, reportedly the only American carrier sunk by surface gunfire. Next the enemy made direct hits on the destroyers USS *Hoel* and *Johnson*, both of which sank, along with the carriers *Gambier Bay* and *St. Lo*, the latter having lost its previous name, USS *Midway*, only two weeks earlier when the name was taken for a giant new attack carrier.

Armor-piercing shells went right through the thin-skinned DEs, flooding compartments and causing minor damage. Sailors on board would not fare as well as their ship. Percell Worley, a machinist's mate on board the USS *Dennis*, which had earned praise for splashing two Japanese aircraft in the battle at Morotai, was at his battle station in the forward mess hall, manning the battle phone circuit for the ship. Suddenly an 8-inch armor-piercing shell from the *Tone* burst through the port side of his compartment, barely missing him as it whizzed through the chief's quarters, exiting just above the waterline on the starboard side. Two more shells hit the ship, knocking out one of the *Dennis'* two 5-inch guns and a 40-mm gun director.

A shell ripped through the leg of fire controlman William Curtis, a professional hockey player from Boston stationed in the 40-mm gun tub. He bled to death despite valiant efforts by the pharmacist's mate to save him. This direct hit also took the lives of two Pennsylvania natives, both in fire control—John Sambo, who left the Scranton–Wilkes-Barre area to join the Navy, and George Grater of Philadelphia.

Charles Davis, another fire controlman, was in the shower room on the main deck when the battle heated up. A small piece of shrapnel came through the deck and entered his chest, collapsing his lung. He later died. Boston native Maynard Emery, in the damage-control unit near the forward mess hall, was just getting a drink of water when an 8-inch shell pierced the ship on the port side near the forward bulkhead, just above the waterline, passing right through the passageway and out the starboard hull. A small piece of shrapnel hit him in the right temple, instantly killing the young sailor.

"Grazi, get up on the 40-mm," an officer yelled at nineteen-year-old Fred Graziano, the torpedoman striker who was "scared stiff" but followed orders. He served as a third loader, passing ammunition. Graziano believes that his 1,500-ton ship actually sunk a 10,000-ton Japanese cruiser, although official credit was not awarded the *Dennis*. Quitting school in the tenth grade, he

Gunner's mates ready the 40-mm gun on board the USS *Liddle*. The guns were capable of firing 140 rounds per minute, reaching 19,000 feet high to down enemy aircraft. When DEs were assigned to the Pacific, torpedoes and hedgehogs were removed and the 3-inch, 50-caliber guns were replaced with more efficient 5-inch, 38-caliber guns. Additional 40-mm and 50-mm antiaircraft guns also were added. *Photo taken by Harold S. Deal; courtesy Jeff Deal*

had always wanted to join the Coast Guard but was too young and his parents wouldn't sign for him. Once the Nyack, New York, native received his draft notice, however, he quickly signed up for the Navy, and his parents sadly watched their only son go off to war.

A mailman on board the *Dennis*, nineteen-year-old Charles W. Touzell had just settled into his bunk for some shuteye when the PA crackled calling all hands to battle stations. He raced to the 20-mm gun, but the carrier *Gambier Bay* already had been hit and was dead in the water. The *Dennis* made two torpedo runs on the Japanese ships. "We missed on the first run at 2,400 yards. We broke through the smoke again and closed on the cruiser to 1,800 yards and fired our two remaining torpedoes," said Touzell, who also had quit high school in Philadelphia and joined the Navy.

Before the DE could take cover again in the smoke, the Japanese would unleash another, even more deadly barrage against the small ship. "The cruiser hit us four times with 8-inch armor-piercing shells. We lost five shipmates in the attack, but managed to stay afloat," Touzell said. "After our second torpedo attack I believe one of our fish had struck the cruiser as I heard a real large explosion and saw a fire ball through the smoke." Touzell, like his shipmate Graziano, believes they sunk that cruiser.

Nineteen-year-old Syracuse, New York, native Donald Derwoyed, serving on board the destroyer escort USS *Raymond*, had just finished the midnight to 4:00 AM watch as a water tender in the number two fireroom. After a couple of hours sleep he heard the call for chow. Returning from breakfast to his bunk area for a little more rest, Derwoyed soon would be called topside, where he would be fighting for his life against a massive Japanese armada. "I was sitting on my foot locker when I heard Capt. [Erin] Beyer announce over the ship loudspeaker, 'The whole Jap fleet is fifteen miles astern of us. Anyone off watch can go topside and watch the show. We won't engage any of them. Admiral Halsey's going to take them on.'" But before the sailor could head topside, a more-urgent sounding message came over the loudspeaker: "Man your battle stations! They are firing on us! You are all a good bunch of boys— God bless you all!"

Derwoyed dashed up the ladder to the fantail and his battle station on the 20-mm gun, where he served as a loader. He looked to the rear and saw the Japanese warships firing on the *Gambier Bay* as he rushed to his station. Shells were splashing in the water all around his ship. "I could see the cruisers and battleships firing on us and all the shells were landing in the water, but not one shell hit us." A startled Derwoyed then looked over the side and noticed a wake heading for his ship. He understood its significance: A torpedo was on its way. "I was between the 5-inch gun and the bulkhead and watched the torpedo go right underneath us," he recalled. "If the torpedo had been set about three feet higher, we would have been blown to smithereens."

Shipmate Vern Kimmell, a fire controlman, was as shocked as anyone on board when the unsuspecting Japanese fleet stumbled upon the equally unsuspecting American fleet. "It was a total surprise," said Kimmell, who was then twenty years old and had joined the Navy while still in high school in Vincenes, Indiana, determined once he graduated to follow in the footsteps of his father, a sailor during World War I. As the lead fire controlman on the 5-inch gun, Kimmell believes the *Raymond* scored at least forty-eight hits on one of the Japanese cruisers. He credited his captain's skillful ship handling for keeping the *Raymond* safe as the ship zigzagged through the water in a mad dash to avoid being hit by the Japanese torpedoes. "We were one lucky bunch," he noted, adding that during the attack no one showed any fear: "We had a role to play and we were just thinking of getting our job done."

"I was washing my hands and thinking about eating breakfast," recalled Howard W. Fortney, chief electrician's mate on board the *Raymond*, when the alarm sounded. "My battle station was midship repair. I remember closing the watertight door on the starboard side of the ship, just past the wardroom, and I looked out and saw the lineup of Japanese battleships on the horizon." As he witnessed the shelling of the aircraft carriers, Fortney said he was certain the entire American fleet would be wiped out within a half hour. "I didn't see how we could escape."

Firing was fast and furious. The destroyer escorts were pitted against an enemy that was bigger, faster, and more powerful—defying all odds of survival. Firing more than 1,413 rounds at the Japanese fleet, the barrel of the 5-inch gun got so hot that the paint on it bubbled up, turned brown, and peeled off. "It was really a miracle that we were able to make the torpedo runs and not get hit," Fortney said. "I did pick up two or three pieces of shrapnel on deck but nobody was injured at all. The *Raymond* was not damaged."

"The picture of a DE making a run on a cruiser or a battleship was pretty pathetic," the *Raymond*'s Lt. Robert L. Johnson Jr. later wrote in a letter to his wife. "I was pretty scared anyway, I guess; my knees didn't seem to [be] acting quite right, and there was a cold, tight feeling in my stomach. I didn't see— none of us did—how we could come out of this spot alive. It was a foregone conclusion that they'd sink everyone of us inside of a half hour. . . . I thought about you, darling, and wanted very much to live; but I didn't see how it could be arranged."

With the *Gambier Bay* mortally wounded, the order was given to make a torpedo run on the Japanese fleet. The die had been cast and there was no turning back. The *Raymond* followed orders, making a beeline for the Japanese cruiser. "We cut back through our own smoke, heading for one of the cruisers on our starboard quarter," Johnson wrote. "Our after-gun was masked now but the forward gun kept pounding. George and I looked at each other, smiled and shrugged. The smile said, 'so long, fella!'; the shrug said, 'It can't be helped.' It's funny how quickly you get used to the idea of dying, and how, once you've made up your mind to it, it seems very impersonal."

But Lieutenant Johnson and the crew of the *Raymond* would not be dying that day. Dashing through the churning waters alive with Japanese torpedoes and enemy gunfire hammering the American ships, the *Raymond* closed fast on the target looming ahead. The DE was pounded with incessant gunfire as the Japanese tried to force the *Raymond* to retreat, spraying its forecastle with shrapnel and chunks of twisted steel. But the DE kept coming. "The cruiser ahead seemed huge and close." Johnson said. "Stand by torpedoes," the captain ordered. "Left full rudder."

The little destroyer escort heeled over sharply and turned to unmask the torpedo tubes. "Fire when ready!" the captain exclaimed. With binoculars trained on the cruiser, Johnson saw a "big flash forward on him and a geyser of water. Somebody's fish connected; maybe ours, maybe not." The *Raymond* sped back and rejoined the formation. "Somehow, unbelievably, we made our run, fired our fish, and came back! We had steamed into the teeth of the enemy's guns and we were still afloat!"

Nineteen-year-old AG Kessinger, machinist's mate on board the *Raymond*, missed seeing a lot of the action since he was in the engine room making sure the bilges were not leaking as the shelling continued. Kessinger, whose parents gave him the first name AG, hailed from the small town of Ewing, Texas, where his father operated the steam equipment in a saw mill. One of seven children, Kessinger quit Biboll High School to join the Navy in 1942. Because of the critical need for personnel, he spent only twenty-eight days in boot camp before being assigned to the USS *Temptress*, a 206-foot patrol gun boat operating along the East Coast, where he didn't see much action. A few months later Kessinger was assigned to the *Raymond*, after a brief stint in destroyer escort school in Norfolk, Virginia. Now this Texas farm boy would be smack in the middle of the greatest naval battle in history.

"I was in the after engine room and walked out on deck and just as I got out the captain announced that there was a Japanese fleet back of us and they were firing on us," Kessinger said. "His next words were 'Man your battle stations.'" Kessinger said that in the first hour some two hundred Japanese shell bursts splashed in the vicinity of his ship. Although the battle seemed to last forever, it was less than three hours before it ended. Like many of his shipmates, Kessinger credited his captain's ability as a good ship handler for keeping the vessel safe. "He knew how to chase splashes," the sailor said.

When the order was given for the destroyers and destroyer escorts to turn around and fight, most of the sailors shared the view of the *Raymond*'s Lieutenant Johnson: They would not be going home to their families. "Little fellows, make a torpedo attack," Admiral Sprague told the DEs. "My God, how are we going to do this?" Copeland, commander of the *Roberts*, recalled thinking. He understood that the firepower of the destroyer escorts or even the American destroyers would be no match for the giant Japanese warships. But he had his orders.[15]

"My hands were ice cold from fear," recalled Lt. Everett "Bob" Roberts, the *Roberts'* executive officer, as Copeland gave the command to launch a torpedo attack against the mighty Japanese fleet. "I computed the course to bring us within launch range. . . . I wished he had ordered me to find a course that would be an escape route," Roberts said. "We launched the torpedoes and fired our 5-inch guns at a very close range." In fact, the destroyer escort was said to be so close—only 2,500 yards away from the enemy vessel—that the Japanese cruiser's 8-inch gun could not be aimed low enough to hit the little ship. The *Roberts* scored some decisive hits with its 5-inch guns against the towering enemy vessels.[16]

Jack Yusen, the eighteen-year-old son of a New York City garment worker whose battle station was the 40-mm forward gun, continued firing as the Japanese rapidly closed in on the American fleet. "I could see the [Japanese] shells," Yusen said, adding that the enemy at first was too far away for the reach of the DE shells. But he recalled dozens of Japanese shells exploding nearby with the plumes of colored water swamping his little ship, which rolled and shuttered with each exploding round.

Thoughts of home and life swirled through the young sailor's mind as he did the job he was trained to do, even though he and his shipmates believed they were fated for disaster. "This will be the last time I will be around," Yusen recalled thinking as the massive Japanese fleet bombarded the Americans. He said that 275 rounds were fired from the 5-inch gun forward and another 300 rounds from the 5-inch gun aft. "The 5-inch shells would bounce off the Japanese hulls," he said, but the shells were able to cause some damage topside on the enemy cruisers, two of which reportedly were knocked out of commission by the American fighters.

Radioman Richard Rohde's battle station was the windowless radio shack where, hunched over the desk with headphones on, he was transcribing messages coming in over the TBS radio. The nineteen year old from Staten Island whose father had lost everything in the Great Depression always received messages in code. On that day he was startled to get his first "plain language" message simply stating, without using the typical secret code, that the American fleet was under attack by a massive Japanese force and needed help from any ship that could provide it.

Although Rohde could not see the action from the dark radio room, he didn't need his eyes to know what was happening. "My other senses worked fine," he said. He could hear the unmistakable sounds of battle, feel the little ship as it shuttered and shook with each incoming shell, and smell the gunfire and the smoke as the Sammy B and the other destroyer escorts tried to hide from the massive Japanese force while gallantly pounding them with their 5-inch guns. But the Japanese warships were not ready turn tail and run from these diminutive American ships and started to score hits of their own with their armor-piercing shells, which, although they passed through the destroyer escort's thin hull, found their way to the ship's engineering spaces. Air in the combat information center fouled, filled with asbestos from insulation jarred off the piping. Steam lines ruptured, scalding several firemen to death as a shell pierced the number one engine room. Another shell at the water line opened a huge hole in the port side and ocean water started pouring in. Faced with a vessel that was about to sink, Captain Copeland gave the order to abandon ship.

Gunner's Mate Paul Henry Carr, captain of the aft 5-inch gun, ordered his crew to fire every available shell at the oncoming Japanese ships. The barrel of the gun overheated and, when a Japanese shell knocked out power on the ship, combustion gases could not be discharged from Carr's weapon. Carr fired six more shell even though he knew that, at any moment, the shell might explode because of the accumulation of dangerous combustion gases. It didn't matter to Carr—he had a job to do, and his job was to keep firing at the enemy.

Then the unthinkable happened. The seventh shell "cooked off" and blew the mount apart, catapulting Sam Blue, the fuel setter, overboard. Carr, standing right next to the exploding mount, was ripped open in a wound stretching from his neck all the way down to his groin. Rushing across the deck, which was covered with burning oil, rescuers arrived at the gun and found Carr on his knees holding a 45-pound projectile in his arms, still trying to load it into the mangled breech. "Although he was ripped open from his neck to his spleen, his mind was still saying, 'Load, fire, load, fire,'" Yusen said of the Oklahoma boy who was devoted to doing his job. His shipmates gently removed the shell from his bloody arms, and Carr died a hero a few minutes later.

Sailors were thoroughly trained on what to do with confidential documents to keep the information from falling into enemy hands. Care must be taken to either destroy or throw overboard all special decoding equipment, even as sailors are frantically trying to get to lifeboats before their vessel sinks below the waves. The main deck of the *Roberts* was scattered with dead and dying American sailors. "I ran up to the bridge, which was crowded with refugees from the lower deck," Tom Stevenson, then a twenty-two-year-old lieutenant, said. "A shell hit just aft of the area and we were knocked down by the concussion; the flags bags were on fire. . . . By the time we were operating at half power and it appeared we were going to be ok." But that would not prove to be the case. The ship, just six months old, was about to begin its final minutes of life.

Stevenson, whose father ran the T. J. Stevenson steamship company in New York City, was the ship's communications officer and, unlike the majority of the "green" crew, had some seagoing experience, having served eight months as a deck boy on a Norwegian merchant ship, earning an expert helmsman certificate. But none of that experience prepared him for what was to come. Although he was stationed in the combat information center, the blast had driven him from his battle station as scalding steam and asbestos fibers poured through the air vent.[17]

Once Captain Copeland gave the order to abandon ship, Stevenson quickly began his sad but necessary duty. "I went down into the radio shack and tried to destroy the electric coding machine," Stevenson said. Unfortunately he had failed to previously attached a hand grenade to the side of the machine as he was supposed to do in the event destruction was ordered. He never thought he would need it, and now had no way to destroy the equipment.

But Soundman Howard Cayo happened by with a Thompson submachine gun and sprayed the machine with .45-caliber slugs, rendering it useless. "I took the [metal decoding machine] wheels and threw them overboard," Stevenson said. As the crippled ship continued its death throes, Stevenson next had to climb down through the hatch and head through a dimly lit passageway to the ship's safe to remove the secret documents. Joseph Nabors, a signalman, went along to assist. "But I had trouble opening the safe because my hands were shaking," Stevenson said. Finally able to dial the right combination, they removed all of the secret documents, including the Leyte Gulf invasion plans, placed them in weighted bags, went topside, and threw them overboard. There were still more bags of documents to retrieve, but Stevenson made the last trip below by himself since Nabors decided he had better get himself overboard before it was too late.[18]

In his great haste to grab the last bags and haul them topside, Stevenson not only forgot his wallet and college ring, in his room adjacent to the area where the safe was located, but also neglected to weigh down one of the bags of secret documents. The captain was on deck when Stevenson threw the last bag over the side. The unweighted bag of secret documents floated to the surface. "You better get that bag," Copeland told Stevenson, who jumped over the side, grabbed the bag, and, instead of returning to the sinking ship, swam toward one of the floater nets where some of his shipmates were struggling to hold on. Stevenson, whose legs were bleeding from shrapnel, held onto the bag and collected knives and other heavy materials from the sailors to weigh it down before letting it drop to the ocean's bottom.[19]

Tullio J. Serafini at forty-four was the oldest man on the ship and served as a first-class radioman. He was an Italian immigrant who, along with his family, came to America and settled in coal-mining country near Carbondale, Pennsylvania. The burly 220-pound no-nonsense sailor had served in World War I, after lying about his age in order to join, and left his family and a good job to reenlist in order to again serve his adopted country. He said America had been good to him and his family and he wanted to return the favor.

This time, however, returning the favor would carry a hefty cost. When the "abandon ship" order was issued, Richard Rohde, the nineteen-year-old radioman who traded a blue uniform with silver buttons he wore as a page at the Guarantee Trust Company in Manhattan for the chambray shirt and dungarees of the U.S. Navy, was more than happy to leave the radio room filling with scalding steam and asbestos.

"As I stepped out of the radio shack standing next to my chief radioman, Tullio Serafini, all of a sudden there was a big explosion," Rohde said. "We both got hit. I looked at him. He had no shirt on and all I could see was blood. He was hit in the shoulder and stomach and all down the one side. I thought, no way is this man going to live." As Rohde looked at his own leg he saw a gaping hole in his dungarees and what resembled hamburger meat oozing out of the hole. He looked away and quickly made his way down the ladder and over to the rail. Rohde removed his shoes and, being a disciplined Navy man, set them neatly side by side on the deck of the sinking ship before climbing over the rail and jumping into the water, ablaze with patches of burning oil.

"I started to swim away from the ship as quickly as I could, and my life belt had been hit by shrapnel and would not work," Rohde said. He noticed a tiny life jacket floating on the surface. The miniature kapok life vest had been sewn by shipmate Sam Blue for the ship's mascot, a mixed breed dog named Sammy B, who perished in the explosion. "I grabbed it and put it under one arm, and it provided a little bit of buoyancy." Rohde, who was swimming with great haste, stopped for a moment to catch his breath. He lifted his head out of the water and was startled to see a Japanese destroyer towering right in front of him, still firing at the *Roberts*. Realizing he was in a very bad location, Rohde quickly changed course and swam around to the other side of the ship and found a life raft with eight men on top, along with a floater net, which had been fastened in a makeshift fashion to the raft. Some forty or fifty men were clinging to the net.[20]

"I'll never forget that sinking feeling when the ship went down. All of a sudden we were alone," Rohde said—no food, except for a few malted milk tablets, and no American ships in the vicinity to rescue the injured sailors. With most of the water casks hit by shrapnel and contaminated, the sailors had little to drink. Rohde had always liked his food salty, so he made the mistake of taking a few swigs of sea water. The next thing he knew he was swimming away from the net heading toward a "tunnel" he believed would lead him to a drinking fountain under the sea. Finally, his shipmates brought the hallucinating sailor back and tied him to the net to keep him from swimming off again.

Drifting in two separate groups, the exhausted survivors used a buddy system to watch one another so they could grab some sleep. "It was horrible at night," Rohde said. "It wasn't cold but there were big seas running with big swells. We couldn't see anything." The sailors were all covered with fuel oil, which Rohde believes saved them from serious sunburn and, perhaps, sharks, which might not find the smell of fuel oil too inviting. "When you looked at us all you saw was our white eyeballs and teeth," Rohde said. "You couldn't wipe it off."

Everyone seemed to have a different idea on how to keep the sharks away. Some said kicking their dangling legs and making noise would keep them away. Others said such activity instead would attract the hungry creatures. In hopes that it would repel the sharks, a few sailors wanted to spread a yellow dye on the water, stored in an emergency kit on the raft and to be used as a rescue signal for planes. But if they used it up they wouldn't have it to signal rescuers. The tired and demoralized men debated and argued. No one was certain what to do.

As the Sammy B's stern sunk below the waves, Jack Yussen looked up to see a Japanese cruiser suddenly appear, doing about twenty knots and headed right for the American sailors clinging to the net. "All you could see was that giant bow wave, and we were yelling and screaming, sure he was going to run us down." But the big cruiser made three passes around the life net, with the swells from each pass swamping the net, dumping the men into the water. The ship did not hit the survivors. A crewman on board had a motion picture camera and was filming the sailors struggling to stay on the raft. Then, much to the surprise of the sailors, as the ship made its final lap, the Japanese captain was standing on port wing saluting the American sailors. That would be the last human being the DE sailors would see for more than fifty hours.

"The next morning, when the sharks came around, that was a horrible, horrible thing," Yusen said. "They hit one our boys right off the bat, and we had to cut him loose." Once the sailor's body floated away from the raft, the sharks followed and gave the sailors a short reprieve from any further attacks. Night fell once again. Men started to hallucinate. Some sailors, hallucinating from drinking salt water, swam or drifted away from the group never to be seen again.

"The next morning, I was dozing on the net when I felt something on my leg," Yusen remembered. "There was a shark, pushing my leg with its snout. He went away, and a few seconds later he hit a guy two down from me." After the attack they pushed that sailor away from the group. Yusen believes he was spared because he had more oil covering his body than some of his other shipmates. Bob Roberts, the ship's executive officer, described one shipmate as "fastidious and regular," who decided to swim away from the group—out of the oil patch that covered the water— in order to defecate. "When he lowered his pants a shark nudged him," Roberts said. "Quickly, he scrambled back to the group in the oil patch."[21]

"We did a lot of praying," said Ernest Glenn Huffman, a nineteen-year-old North Carolina boy who had spent ten years of his life in an orphanage after his mother died when he was only five years old. "I was more afraid in the water than when the battle was going on," Huffman said, noting that sailors were trained to do their jobs in the heat of battle and with little time to think about other things. Huffman said that he saw one shark during the fifty-hour ordeal but that it didn't bother the sailor who paired up with Whitney Felt as they took turns watching each other when they slept. Felt, who was a sonarman, remembered the first night as "forbidding" as the tired and injured sailors simply struggled to stay alive. "To many," he said, "it was the longest night they ever experienced." The second night did not seem as long or tedious as the first, he said, since the men were "exhausted beyond belief" and slept with their heads held barely above the ocean by their life jackets.[22]

All of the survivors believed they would be rescued immediately after the Sammy B went down. Spirits were buoyed when a Navy plane flew over and dipped its wings at the sailors struggling to stay afloat in the hot afternoon sun. Captain Copeland, who did not know how to swim, was on the raft and saw the plane come in about forty or fifty feet off the water as the pilot gave the sailors the "thumbs up" signal. "That brought us from the depths right up to the peaks," Copeland said. "We said, 'Oh boy, we've been sighted and there will be help on the way.'" But help never arrived on that first day, and by early evening the dejected men had become discouraged as they faced the prospect of a lonely night on the open ocean without food and water—and their hope of a rescue dashed.

Realizing that he and the other officers needed to set a good example or the exhausted men would lose all hope, Copeland organized his group into teams of two and they started to paddle due west toward the island of Samar, which they figured was about thirty miles away. "We weren't in bad shape physically," Copeland said, "but after fifteen minutes of paddling both he [the ship's executive officer, Bob Roberts] and I were completely exhausted. The other officers and chiefs took turns and paddled in fifteen minute stints throughout the night. By the next morning the group jubilantly sighted land—the mountaintops of Samar.

"We got close enough to Samar to see palm trees silhouetted against the sun," said Dudley Moylan, who said the good swimmers moved to the inshore side of the floater net and started swimming. "Two guys on the raft paddled while everyone in the water on the offshore side kicked." Battling tide and current, the group never made it to shore, although Copeland believes that, at one time, they may have been as close as five hundred to one thousand yards from the beach. They were swept back out to sea—so far back, in fact, that when dawn broke, they could no longer see land.[23]

Even the best-trained officer has his breaking point, and for Captain Copeland it finally came on that day off Samar. The thirty-five-year-old captain, who had been trained as a lawyer at the University of Washington while enlisted in the Naval Reserve, "just folded up," in his words, once they failed to reach the beach. "I didn't go completely out of my head," Copeland said, "but intermittently my thoughts and mental perceptions got quite vague and befuddled. I lost all muscular control of my head and hands and my muscular coordination was completely gone."

Copeland felt he was a drag on the men and should be allowed to drown, but Bob Roberts, his executive officer, overruled his captain and made sure he was placed on the raft where he would be safe, watched throughout the night. After several false sightings of white lights during that night, help finally would arrive the next morning.

"On the third day," radioman Rohde recalled, "we saw a ship." They wondered whether the ship was friendly or another Japanese vessel. "They spotted us and they came over ever so slowly and they had their guns trained on us." Someone from the ship yelled at the oil-covered sailors, "Who won the world series?" Rohde said one of the survivors yelled back, "Don't ask such goddamn fool questions. Pick us up!" Someone else finally answered, and PC-653 proceeded to pick up the bedraggled sailors.

Rohde recalled that the decks of the patrol craft, which had been busy picking up other survivors, were crowded with men. Once on board Rohde was given a bowl of oatmeal. "Nothing ever tasted better than that," he said, noting that they also gave him a shot of Canadian Club whiskey, which "really warmed me" after more than fifty hours in the water. Rohde, whose oil-soaked clothes were removed, recalled that they laid him out on deck directly over the engine room. "My butt was right on a rivet and it was hot," he said. Later, when he was treated in a military hospital, he had to lie on a ring because of the painful burn inflicted from the hot rivet, a scar he still carries today.

Too exhausted to climb up the net dropped over the side of the patrol craft, two sailors helped Seaman Glenn Huffman up the net. With nothing to eat or drink for more than fifty hours, Huffman weighed ninety-six pounds. "I laid on the anchor chain and fell sound asleep," he said. Communications Officer Stevenson was shocked to discover that Tullio Serafini, the radioman from Carbondale, Pennsylvania, whose side was ripped open by the blast, was still alive. Hoisted on board the patrol craft by a wire bucket, Stevenson said,

"Tullio, you made it! I gave him his wallet back, but he died the next day and I never saw him again."[24]

Vern Kimmell, fire controlman on board the *Raymond*, was relieved—and surprised—when the Japanese fleet finally started to retreat. "Our rate of fire during the engagement was such that, when the Japanese turned around and headed north, we had 32 rounds of 5-inch ammunition left," Kimmell said. "At our rate of fire, we would have exhausted all of 5-inch ammunition in another thirty minutes. We would have been defenseless if the Japanese had stayed on scene." Kimmell said that they had fired every type of ammunition on board, including star shells, antipersonnel shells, dual-purpose ammunition. "Anything that went through that 5-inch barrel we fired." The other destroyer escorts were in a similar predicament. Franklyn "Jeff" Conley, signalman on board the USS *John C. Butler*, which continued making smoke to conceal the Americans, said they fired everything they had at the Japanese fleet. Although they never fired their torpedoes, they did pound the battleships and cruisers with their 5-inch guns and even resorted to firing star shells as their ammunition supply dwindled.[25]

The Japanese left, Kimmell believes, because they became convinced the tiny American fleet was part of Admiral Halsey's larger group and they didn't want to tangle with his immense firepower. In Robert Johnson's letter to his wife, the *Raymond* officer expresses his bewilderment as to why the Japanese retreated. "For some reason," he wrote, "the whole Jap task force began to retire. When they got out of range of our guns, they stopped and lobbed a few more salvoes in our general direction, but they seemed pretty half-hearted about it and I think it was more face-saving than anything else."[26]

Kimmell appears to have been correct as to why the clearly superior Japanese fleet retreated from a group of American vessels they easily could have defeated. In fact, Admiral Tomiji Koyanagi, chief of staff to Vice Admiral Takeo Kurita on board the Japanese battleship *Yamoto*, offers some insight about that October day in 1944. Clearly the Japanese fleet was as surprised to encounter the American vessels as the Americans were to see pagodas coming over the misty horizon. "Just as day broke at 0640 on the 25th and we were changing from night search disposition to anti-aircraft alert cruising disposition," wrote Koyanagi, "enemy carriers were sighted on the horizon. Several masts came in sight about 30 kilometers to the southeast, and presently we could see planes being launched."

Koyanagi was excited. "This was indeed a miracle," he said. "Think of a surface fleet coming up on an enemy carrier group! We moved to take advantage of this heaven-sent opportunity. *Yamoto* increased speed instantly and opened fire at a range of 31 kilometers." They vastly overestimated the size and power of the American fleet, which they believed included four or five fast carriers guarded by one or two battleships and at least ten heavy cruisers. Little did they suspect that they would be doing battle with a small American fleet comprised of escort carriers, destroyers, and destroyer escorts.

As the furious battled raged on, the Japanese became convinced that they were fighting American cruisers when, in fact, they were much smaller destroyers. Admiral Koyanagi praised the Americans' efficient use of smoke screens and rain squalls making them visible to the Japanese battleship for only short intervals. "We pursued at top speed for over two hours," he said, "but we could not close the gap, in fact it actually appeared to be lengthening. We estimated that the enemy's speed was nearly 30 knots, that his carriers were of the regular large type, that pursuit would be an endless sea-saw, and that we would be unable to strike a decisive blow." The Japanese called off pursuit. "Giving up pursuit when we did amounted to losing a prize already in hand," the admiral noted. "If we had known the types and number of enemy ships, and their speed, Admiral Kurita would never have suspended the pursuit, and we would have annihilated the enemy." Fortunately for the Americans, they left before realizing their error.[27]

When the battle ended, said Jeff Conley, who was on board the *John C. Butler,* the captain gave each sailor a beer. "I had gotten my bottle of beer and came out on the starboard side, about a mile from the *St. Lo,* when I saw this airplane coming in." At first Conley thought it was one of the American planes returning to its "nest" on board the carrier, but he soon would realize his mistake. "It turned out that it was a kamikaze, and it went right into the stern of the *St Lo,* and there was a tremendous explosion." Howard Fortney of the *Raymond* watched in horror the enormous power of the fiery explosion as the suicide plane crashed into the ship, igniting its torpedo and bomb magazines and blowing one of the vessel's giant aircraft elevators hundreds of feet in the air. The ship, which had scored a direct hit on one of the Japanese destroyers, was engulfed in flames as dense black smoke poured from it. Its slowly turned on its side and sank beneath the waves. One hundred and fourteen men died.

Jumping into the churning, oil-filled water, Conley and shipmate Bob Turner swam out to rescue crew members from the carrier. Sharks were circling the mortally wounded ship and its dead and injured crew, many struggling in the water with others burned beyond recognition. Conley spotted two sailors quite a distance away, frantically waving for help. Neither sailor knew how to swim and their kapok life jackets were torn and filling with water. They were about to drown. Conley convinced the first one to remove his jacket, which was providing no buoyancy because it was filled with water. The sailor climbed on Conley's back and he swam back to the cargo nets, which had been lowered over the side of the *Butler*. Conley, exhausted from firing 198 rounds at the Japanese fleet, swam out to assist the other sailor. "He didn't want to give up his life jacket and I told him, 'You get rid of the jacket or you're going to sink. God bless you.'" With great reluctance, the weary sailor unstrapped the life jacket, climbed on Conley's back, and was carried back to safety. The bodies of dead sailors were piled up on the fantail of the ship, and once their dog tags were removed, the valiant young men were buried at sea. More than four hundred of the *St. Lo*'s crew were rescued.[28]

Meanwhile, while the battle at Samar was under way, additional American warships, with troops, planes, tanks, and supplies on board, were moving in support of MacArthur's return to the Philippines. The USS *Coolbaugh*, a destroyer escort commissioned only a year earlier in Philadelphia and code-named "Pigsticker" during the invasion, was steaming toward Leyte, battling a fierce typhoon along the way. Once the winds and seas subsided and the invasion got under way, the kamikazes showed up.

"We were attacked by thirty Jap planes," wrote Robert L. Goggins in the diary he secretly kept while at sea. Goggins grew up in Lincoln, Nebraska, where his father drove a bread truck. He quit school at seventeen to join the Navy, and after a cold and snowy eight weeks at boot camp in Great Lakes, he was assigned as a gunner's mate on board the *Coolbaugh*. "Twenty-seven were shot down by our planes, and one shot down by the carrier *Santee*." One of the kamikazes came out of the clouds and made a dive on the *Santee*. Loaded with a 1,000-pound bomb, the plane crashed through the flight deck on the port side, coming to rest on the hangar deck. The explosion blew a hole fifteen by thirty feet in the ship. Fires erupted and compartments started to flood. Sixteen men died and twenty-seven were injured, but the ship did not sink. The enemy had more in store for the crippled carrier. Japanese submarine *I-56* took aim at the ship, firing a torpedo into its starboard side. No casualties occurred from the torpedo strike, and the Japanese quickly discovered that this converted tanker was one tough customer.[29]

Within seconds of the attack on the *Santee*, the kamikazes took aim at another carrier, *Suwannee*, originally built as an oiler and recommissioned in 1941 as an aircraft carrier. Gunners on board the carrier hit at least three suicide planes, but the third one rolled over and dove eight thousand feet, crashing directly into the ship's flight deck and opening a ten-foot hole. The carrier exploded in flames when the kamikaze's bomb detonated in the mess hall, ripping a twenty-five-foot gash in the hangar deck. Dozens of sailors were thrown overboard.

"We picked up ninety-one survivors who were blown off the *Suwannee*," Goggins wrote, adding that some had burns the size of a hand on their back and many were injured by shrapnel. "Our pharmacist mate, Robert Wicks, worked all day and night on the burned and wounded sailors." Goggins rescued one man clinging to an empty ammunition case in the water. He was being held up by three of his shipmates to keep his head out of the water. "When he climbed up the floater net and started to go forward with the rest of the badly injured," Goggins wrote, "we could see that his whole back had been blown out—just a mass of blood." He died later that evening and was buried at sea.[30] The *Coolbaugh* and several other ships left the Philippines with injured sailors and the crippled carrier and headed to the island of Palau, where the wounded could be transferred to the USS *Bountiful*, a hospital ship, for treatment and repairs could be made to the carrier.

Not every destroyer escort struck by a torpedo or hit by a kamikaze succumbed. In fact, sailors on board one little ship, the USS *Chaffee*, lived to tell about the night in January 1945, when a Japanese bomber launched a torpedo that plowed directly into the destroyer escort's bow without causing any loss of life and resulting in only minimal damage to the ship. Albert R. Pincus was a twenty-one-year-old electrician's mate on board the *Chaffee* when the ship joined a group of escort vessels ordered to protect the battleship USS *Pennsylvania* during operations in Lingayen Gulf. Pincus, whose Russian immigrant parents ran the Pinky's Candy store in Brooklyn, New York, skipped school one day and went with two of his classmates, Whitey Robbins and Willie Levine, to the Navy recruiting station in Brooklyn and signed up after being turned down for the Army Air Corps because of a problem with depth perception. After boot camp at Great Lakes, Pincus eventually found himself on board the USS *Chaffee*.

While *Chaffee* was anchored in Lingayen that January in 1945, three Japanese torpedo bombers came out of the night sky and headed directly for the battleship. Two of the aircraft were shot down but the third peeled off and disappeared into the darkness. With the threat apparently over, most of the ships secured from battle stations—most, that is, except for Pincus' ship, whose captain was overly cautious. He felt the third plane would return to finish the job. And he was right. "About ten minutes later the third betty came back, and we could see it silhouetted in the moon," Pincus said. "Full speed ahead," shouted the skipper. "The captain swung the fast little ship around and headed right toward the betty, and without our running lights, we were invisible in the black of night."

Pincus said that the pilot was startled as the DE appeared in his path, dropping his bomb right in front of the ship. "The fish landed so close to us that the spray, when it hit the water, wet the officers and men on the bridge. It then hit us in the bow, right at the boatswain's locker, but below the water line, going clean through the bow and out the other side." The forward compartment quickly flooded with seawater and the ship began to list out of control. The ship hit a coral reef, damaging the propeller. But it did not sink. The kamikaze was shot down.

The next morning the fleet commander came on board the damaged destroyer escort to thank the crew and officers for saving the *Pennsylvania*. The battleship sent over lots of ice cream and cake for the men, as well as some spare parts so repairs could be made to the ship. Pincus said he would never forget that morning when the fleet commander personally thanked the *Wiseman's* captain, William F. Jones, for saving the battleship from the kamikaze attacks. With an "Ah shucks, commander, we're just doing our duty" attitude, the young skipper thanked his superior officer for the praise—but he and his men were a lot more grateful for the ice cream and cake.[31]

10

Pink Streaks of Afterglow

A s Douglas MacArthur continued his assault on Japanese forces in the Philippines, additional ships were on their way to provide fuel and supplies for the battle-weary American troops. Unknown to this collection of American destroyer escorts, destroyers, carriers, cruisers, and oilers, they were about to face a relentless and savage foe ready to show the young sailors there was more to fear in the Pacific than just the Japanese.

Sailors on board seven destroyer escorts, part of the convoy sailing westward toward the Philippines, would be battling an enemy for which they were no match, despite their training and, for many, experience battling the ruthless Nazi U-boats in the Atlantic. Unsuspecting of the danger that lay just over the horizon, the destroyer escorts USS *Bangust, Waterman, Sesson, Swearer, Lamons, Tabberer*, and *Weaver* continued their westward advance as the skies turned dark and brooding, the ocean churned up, and the winds began to howl.

Mother Nature was their new foe, and she was about to deliver a deadly blow to the American forces, unleashing a violent typhoon that would cause more damage and loss of American lives than occurred in the Battle of Midway, a turning point in the Pacific war. Faced with an enemy far more devastating than any Japanese torpedo, there was very little these teenage sailors or their young skippers could do about it.

"We had no warning of this storm, and all of a sudden the barometer started going down," Capt. Henry Lee Plage of the destroyer escort USS *Tabberer* said. "It was every man for himself, practically, after that." The tiny destroyer escort, struggling to stay afloat, lost steerage a couple of times as the ship's mast, which towered ninety-three feet above the water line, cracked and buckled. Crawling across the deck on their bellies, sailors held on to the deck as the ship pitched and rolled more than 70 degrees, lying nearly on its side in the raging seas. The twenty-nine-year-old skipper, respected and loved by his teenage crew, could no longer keep sailors stationed on any of the weather decks for fear they would be injured by the falling mast and other debris or swept overboard by the mountainous ninety-foot waves and to a certain death in the shark-infested waters. Visibility was zero and torrential rain drenched the sailors as 150-mph winds howled, tossing the small ships around as though they were nothing more than balsa-wood models.

"I was on the helm trying to decide if we got hit should I go over the side with my shoes on or off," said Walter Roberge of the USS *Swearer*, then sixteen years old. "It was a horrendous thing," said the sailor, whose mother had forged his birth certificate a year earlier so he could enlist before he was of age. As he held on to keep from being thrown overboard, Roberge may have wondered in retrospect whether he had made a good decision back then. "I was thrown across the CIC and into the plot board, severely bruising my ribs."[1]

Forty-five-thousand-ton battleships were rolling as though they were tiny canoes running a series of white water rapids. Some of the American vessels would not survive. "I can tell you, it's one hell of a feeling to hear over the TBS when you are in a terrible typhoon that three destroyers, slightly larger than the ship you are on, have floundered and sunk by turning broadside," said Richard B. Hillyer, then a seventeen-year-old sailor on board the USS *George*. "It was the longest night of my life."[2]

"A check of the inclinometer shows our rolls were up to 73 degrees, both starboard and port," only 2 degrees short of the maximum roll the gauge can record, Roberge said. "Eating was next to impossible. The cooks fixed us some sandwiches and coffee and we did the best we could under the circumstances." Roberge recalled that he feared leaving the bridge since he knew below decks would not be the best place to spend the night. A veteran of the North Atlantic, Roberge said the hurricanes in that ocean were like a "stroll in the park" compared to the Pacific typhoons.

Some of the destroyers were riding high in the water when the storm hit since they had pumped out their bilges in preparation for fueling, which had to be aborted. The ships lay on their sides, stacks flat against the mountainous swells on the ocean's surface. Trying to make its way through a confused mass of vessels, in the driving rain and zero visibility, the *Swearer* came face-to-face with a carrier directly in its path.

"The captain orders full right rudder full ahead of the port screw, and full reverse of the starboard, and out of the carrier's way," Roberge recorded in the diary he secretly kept while on board. "It is to no avail! We are locked in irons. We just keep going on the same course. We just cannot steer clear." As the little ship moved on a collision course with the carrier, the larger ship suddenly spotted the little DE in the heavy fog and rapidly turned to port, just missing the *Swearer*. "Had they not," Roberge said, "we surely would have been cut in half."[3]

Although destroyer escorts were found to be relatively good at staying afloat, Captain Plage said the ships did roll—"like the very devil." Plage recorded a 72-degree roll on the *Tabberer*. Once the ship's mast toppled, its radio, radar, and electronic identification equipment ended up on the bottom of the ocean. They had no communication with the other ships or with Admiral Halsey, who feared the destroyer escort had been lost in the violent storm.[4]

As bad as conditions were for the *Swearer* and *Tabberer*, things were even worse for several other American vessels battling the fury unleashed by the ferocious storm, said to be the worst to hit the Pacific in fifty years. Bulkheads creaked and groaned as they struggled to stay afloat. Airplanes, securely lashed with rope and wire to the steel decks of their carriers, were ripped loose and tossed about the deck. Air intakes ruptured and fires erupted as the monstrous waves continued to pound the ships.

The violent storm would take its toll. Three American destroyers and more than one hundred aircraft were lost, and nearly eight hundred men were swept into the angry seas. Most would never be seen again. Twenty-eight ships were damaged, some heavily, as the little DEs were tossed around like corks on the roiling seas. Adm. William "Bull" Halsey, on board the USS *New Jersey*, either misread or failed to heed the weather warnings, and to this day his actions remain controversial. In his autobiography, however, he makes it clear that he understood how dangerous such a storm is for small Navy vessels.

"What it was like on a destroyer one-twentieth the *New Jersey*'s size, I can only imagine," Halsey said. "I was told that some of them were knocked down until their stacks were almost horizontal and were pinned there by the gale, while water rushed into their ventilators and intakes, shorting the circuits, killing their power, steering, lights and communications, and leaving them to drift helplessly." Certainly the sailors on board the tiny destroyer escorts could have provided the admiral with ungarnished eyewitness accounts of just what it was like on board those vessels tossed around during the storm, later named "Halsey's typhoon" or Typhoon Cobra.

Once the storm subsided it was time to look for survivors. In what Halsey described as the "most exhaustive search in Navy history," more than one hundred ships spanned out across the heavy seas looking for American sailors, most of whom were suffering from exhaustion, dehydration, and shock and were confronting the mortal danger of an ever-expanding collection of hungry sharks lured to the area by the smell of blood from injured sailors.

Chief Radioman Ralph E. Tucker, ordered by Plage to rig an emergency antenna on the ship so he could communicate with the other vessels in the fleet, suddenly heard a cry and noticed a pinpoint of light off the ship's starboard bow. "Man overboard," Tucker shouted, and the skipper swung the ship around and headed for the light. "It was quite close to us," Plage said, "and as we approached it, we heard voices out of the water. . . . We came around, the seas of course still very rough . . . [and] we put our search light on him and came alongside to pick him up."[5]

The rescued sailor had been swept off the USS *Hull*, a destroyer that, along with the USS *Spence* and USS *Monaghan*, was overcome by the storm. The *Hull* toppled on its side, and as seawater rushed into the pilothouse, the destroyer sunk below the raging seas. The *Spence* broke in half and drifted away. The *Monaghan*, which had hosted President Roosevelt during a Caribbean cruise in 1936, imploded on itself. Sailors on the destroyer were praying out loud that they might live as the crippled ship groaned and then sunk beneath the waves, taking 90 percent of its crew to their graves.

William Fairlee was a twenty-one-year-old milk truck driver from Schenectady, New York, when he decided to enlist as a machinist in the Navy. Assigned to the USS *Bangust*, Fairlee said his ship, alongside the *Monaghan* when the destroyer imploded and sunk, was shaken to its very core during the storm. Fairlee, in the aft crew quarters that morning, heard something rolling around the fantail of his ship. "I looked out and saw it was a depth charge," he said, and although it was not armed, the machinist felt uncomfortable letting it roll about the deck. Fairlee and some of his shipmates hurried topside and tried to stay standing on the swaying vessel while they pinned the depth charge against the life line, cut the line, and shoved the charge overboard.

Henry Eugene Davis, a fire controlman on board *Bangust* who had left school in the tenth grade to enlist in the Navy, was on the bridge as eighty-foot waves of green water poured over his station, swamping the ship. Although his vessel suffered some minor damage during the storm, Davis was shocked by the degree of rolling experienced by the ship. The decks were painted red and the red paint extended about six inches up the bulkhead, after which the color was changed to white. "I remember seeing footprints on the white paint. The men were walking on the walls," he said, adding that he and many of his shipmates doubted they would survive the ferocious storm. "I sort of got religion during that period."

"Like babes in the woods" was how one sailor on board the USS *Melvin H. Nawman* described his shipmates since they never suspected that the building seas foretold what would be one of the worst typhoons in Pacific Ocean history. Despite the weather, sailors did have to eat in order to keep up their strength, often standing up gripping the ship while gulping down their meal before the next wave knocked them over. "You hooked a leg around something, the messboy handed you a piece of bread which you buttered from a dish he had in his free hand," the *Nawman* sailor wrote to his mother. "Next you picked up a piece of unpleasant looking boloney that was skidding around the pantry table and slapped it on the bread."[6]

As the storm started to subside and radio communications were reestablished, Captain Plage was ordered to speed to the rendezvous point but ignored those orders and stayed in the area searching for survivors. "To hell with that," he said, "we are going to stay here." When he picked up the survivor from the *Hull*, he was not aware that two other destroyers had sunk as well. The next day the *Tabberer* picked up the *Hull*'s commanding officer, Capt. James Marks, described by Plage as "pretty far gone, very weak, he couldn't help himself at all. We had to drag him aboard."

"Finding the survivors was our first concern, getting them aboard was the next task," Plage said. "We tried to head into the wind and head right for the man, trying to cut down on our roll, but we found the seas were so high that I was afraid if we got too close to him and tried to bring him alongside, we might have the bow thrown into the man and push him under or crack his head; so the only thing we could do was to come in upwind . . . and let the wind blow us down to him."[7]

Sailing his ship into the teeth of the storm, the skipper risked his own life and the lives of his teenage crew in an all-out effort to rescue as many men as possible. Shining the ship's powerful twenty-four-inch searchlights on the waters, Plage understood that these bright beacons might attract Japanese submarines in the vicinity. But the skipper felt strongly that it was his duty, and the duty of his men, to rescue as many Americans as they could find, regardless of the risk. And he did just that over the next two days. Maneuvering the warship close to sailors struggling in the water, they threw a line over the side with a loop on the end instructing them to place the loop around their torso and under their arms. Sailors could then be pulled on board the ship. Cargo nets were dropped over the side and a couple of sailors, donned in life jackets, were stationed at the water line to assist survivors to climb the nets.

Boatswain's Mate Louis Purvis, a rugged twenty-two-year-old New Jersey native, was one of the sailors assigned to pluck survivors from the churning waters. Assisting sailors up the net, Purvis noticed a man in the water who seemed to be unconscious some distance away. Swimming out to save the sailor, Purvis discovered that the man actually was dead. Ripping off the sailor's dog tags he swam back to the ship when, without warning, his lifeline became tangled on the sonar dome beneath the ship, yanking him under the vessel that was pitching and rolling on the raging seas. Pulled under the ship twice and coming up only briefly for a gulp of air, he broke free and swam under the ship, coming up on the other side. Sailors quickly pulled him on board. "Dammit," he said, "I bet I'm the first sailor to be keelhauled in two hundred years."[8]

Sharks circled the injured and bleeding men struggling to stay alive on floater nets and makeshift rafts. The sun burned their skin red as they shivered in shock, delirious from the salt water, praying that help would arrive. Some of them would not make it. Joseph McCrane, an officer from the *Monaghan*, climbed on board a raft after being swept over the side of his sinking vessel. He found Joe Guio, one of his ship's gunner's mates, badly injured, naked, and shivering in shock. McCrane held the West Virginia native in his arms to keep him warm as Guio lapsed into unconsciousness. Darkness fell.

"Guio awoke and asked me if I could see anything, and when I told him I could see the stars, he said that he couldn't see anything," McCrane noted. "He then thanked Melroy Harrison, seaman second, for pulling him aboard the raft and then he thanked me for trying to keep him warm. He laid his head back on my shoulder and went to sleep."

"About a half hour later I had a funny feeling come over me," McCrane said, "and I tried to wake him up only to find that he was dead. I told the rest of the fellows and we decided to hold him a little longer before we buried him." Twenty minutes later, McCrane said they had their first burial at sea. "We all said the Lord's prayer as he was lowered over the side." More burials would follow that evening as delirious sailors, thinking they saw land, houses, and loved ones, slowly succumbed. One man swam away from the raft and disappeared forever into the night.[9]

As the *Tabberer* approached one exhausted man, treading water but unable to reach a life raft, an enormous shark slid down a wave within six feet of the sailor. Men on board ship opened fire with their rifles and the shark retreated. Robert Surdam, who had given up a career in commercial banking in Albany, New York, to become the ship's executive officer, fearlessly jumped over the side without a life jacket to save the sailor. He fastened a line around the man, now unconscious, and hauled him on board the ship, where he was revived.[10]

The *Tabberer* saved fifty-five men, forty-one from the *Hull* and fourteen from the *Spence*. The *Swearer* rescued nine men and the *Robert F. Keller* picked up another thirteen. The rest of the American sailors would remain at the bottom of the sea. The ships proceeded to Ulithi, arriving on Christmas Day, with little to celebrate except that—thanks to the courage, determination, and seamanship of these valiant DE sailors along with men from several other American ships—ninety-eight men would live to see another Christmas.

For seventeen-year-old Henry Eugene Davis, that Hayward, California, boy who had dropped out of school in the tenth grade to join the Navy, the typhoon was an experience he will never forget. Davis and his ship, the *Bangust*, were veterans of battling more than just the weather. About six months before the typhoon, the ship was on patrol about seventy miles northeast of the Marshall Islands when a radar contact was made of an unidentified surface object in what would be the first enemy action for the eight-month-old destroyer escort.

A little before midnight on 10 June 1944, radar picked up an unidentified object some twelve miles away. Rushing to battle stations, sailors readied weapons as the *Bangust* headed toward the suspicious object. Davis' battle station was on the gun rangefinder, "the highest and most visible target on the ship." The destroyer escort fired a star shell spread to illuminate the object, thought to be either a small fishing boat or enemy submarine. The *Bangust* also sent Morse code via underwater sonar to the vessel requesting identification. Instead the vessel dove, confirming to the Americans that they had encountered a Japanese submarine. "We made three hedgehog runs, but they were not successful," Davis said, adding that the submarine's captain was very skillful at taking evasive maneuvers to avoid being hit. "On the fourth run, we nailed him with the hedgehog." The submarine, later identified as *RO-42*, exploded right beneath the destroyer escort, violently rocking the *Bangust* and jettisoning various pieces of equipment into the air.

"It shook the hell out of the ship," Davis recalled. "At first we thought we had been torpedoed and we immediately called for damage-control reports. We had split a seam on the underpart of the ship from the force of the explosion." Five subsequent explosions followed. The strong odor of diesel oil was detected and air bubbles and pieces of cork floated to the surface. At dawn an oil slick two miles long and half mile wide was discovered. Throughout the morning, oil continued bubbling to the surface until it covered an area ten miles in diameter.

Then the sharks showed up—at least two dozen of them circling the area where the explosion had occurred. For Lt. Leonard Andrews, the sharks came a little too close for comfort the morning after the attack. As he leaned over the side of the ship to get a better look at the debris in the water, a gust of wind blew off his hat, which landed on the water's surface. But Andrews could forget about retrieving it. "It was gobbled up almost instantly when it hit the water," Davis said, adding that the officer was more than a bit irritated since he had been working at getting the shiny gold braids on his new cap to look a little more "salty."[11]

Although destroyer escorts originally were designed to escort convoys and fight Nazi U-boats on the North Atlantic, they also would end up battling the Japanese submarines as they plied the waters of the Pacific Ocean. In fact DEs, sometimes assisted by other American warships, were responsible for sinking some twenty-six Japanese submarines in the Pacific as well as one found lurking in the spring of 1943 in the mid-Atlantic southwest of the Azores.

The destroyer escort credited with the most "kills" of Japanese submarines was the USS *England*, which sunk six Japanese boats in just twelve days in May 1944, a feat unparalleled in American naval history. On the evening of 17 May 1944, a group of destroyer escorts, the USS *England, George,* and *Raby*, was on routine patrol between the Marianas and the Japanese-held Truk when the *England* received a radio message from Admiral Halsey that a Japanese submarine was spotted heading south from Truk toward the Solomons. The destroyer escorts were dispatched to investigate the submarine, suspected of carrying supplies to Buin on the island of Bougainville, still in Japanese control. But their search was about to turn up more than one submarine.

The American vessels steamed northwest, making sonar sweeps along the way. At first they didn't find anything. The next day the *England* picked up a sonar contact 100 feet deep south of Bougainville, quickly moving in for the kill. After several hedgehog runs at the submarine, whose captain took the boat down to 324 feet to avoid the missiles, they hit pay dirt. A violent underwater explosion occurred, lifting the *England* clear out of the water—an explosion so severe that sailors on board were sure they had been torpedoed. But within a short time, large amounts of oil, debris, bags of rice, broken furniture, cork, and even a mattress bubbled to the surface, confirming that the submarine had sunk. Sharks quickly arrived to survey the area for human remains.

This was the beginning of what would be twelve days of high drama in which the *England*, not yet six months old, would sink five more submarines stationed as part of a Japanese scouting line to alert them of any American advancement toward the Marianas, Palau, or the Philippines. Even if the submarines were sunk, the Japanese reasoned, they should have enough time to get a message to Tokyo of the advancing forces. But the USS *England*, along with the *George, Raby* and, later, *Spangler*, was about to unravel the Japanese plan.

When all was finally ended, six Japanese submarines lay at the bottom of the ocean, Tokyo's scouting line had been eliminated, and American forces were free to move ahead to the Marianas, Saipan, Tinian, and Guam with Japan sending its forces to the island of Palau, where they assumed incorrectly that the Americans were heading.

John A. Williamson, the executive officer on board the *England*, who also served as an instructor at the antisubmarine school in Miami, said that the efforts of the *George, Raby*, and *Spangler* were "instrumental in gaining contact and tracking submarines." While those destroyer escorts were not credited with firing any of the hedgehogs that resulted in the sinking of the Japanese submarines, according to the executive officer, they did track them, provide vital information to the *England*, and even made some runs on the boats. Williamson, whose ship received a presidential citation, believes the *George* and *Raby* should receive some type of award because they were with his ship the entire time of the six sinkings. Sailors on board the other ships contended that sinking the six boats was the result of a "combined effort" and that all four destroyer escorts should have received presidential recognition.[12]

While the *England* and the other destroyer escorts scored a major victory that would forever be recorded in the annals of American naval history, there were still plenty of Japanese submarines stalking American vessels in the Pacific, and it would not be long until another destroyer escort would be embroiled in combat with one of the largest of them.

Robert Currie, a twenty year old from Newtonville, Massachusetts, who had joined the Navy in 1942 would find himself on board a destroyer escort, the USS *Riddle*, about to come face to face with a so-called I-boat, one of Japan's large submarines, constructed based on Germany's U-boat design. Currie, who wanted to be a pilot, arrived at the federal building in Boston to join the Army Air Force but was turned down because he only was a high school graduate. So he flipped a coin to see whether he would try to enlist in the Marine Corps or the Navy. Heads, it was the Navy, and he was off to boot camp in Newport, Rhode Island. Rushed through training because of America's desperate need for sailors, he was selected to go to quartermaster school followed by officers' training school. But that isn't what Currie had in mind. "I wanted to go to sea," he recalled, and he was afraid that if he didn't get out to sea soon, the war would end and he would never see any action.

After a brief teaching duty at Sampson, the young quartermaster eventually got his sea duty on board the *Riddle*, where he finally would see the action for which he had been yearning since boot camp. Independence Day 1944 would be that day. The *Riddle* and the destroyer USS *David W. Taylor* were screening a group of six oil tankers and an escort carrier in the vicinity of the Marianas. A tropical breeze helped make this beautiful Fourth of July even better. Seas were calm and the sun was shining. All seemed right with the world until Currie heard the words, "Contact. Bearing 250 degrees, range 1,900 yards!" Sonar had picked up something metallic deep in the water. Battle station alarms sounded as the *Riddle* swung around to investigate.

"I was on the bridge and heard the ping," Currie said, certain they had found a submarine. "The convoy took an emergency sharp turn to the left and we started making some runs on it [the submarine]." Despite firing depth charges and hedgehogs, all was quiet beneath the water—the submarine was obviously taking evasive actions to avoid being hit. The USS *David W. Taylor* joined the attack. "They dropped some depth charges and there was a big explosion," Currie recalled. Oil and debris floating to the surface. Both vessels were credited with the "kill."[13]

While destroyer escorts continued to rack up a respectable number of submarine "kills" over the course of the war in the Pacific, vengeance was to be enacted by Japan. On a rainy evening in October 1944, the USS *Eversole* was about to meet its match in the Leyte Gulf area, about three weeks after another destroyer escort, the six-month-old USS *Shelton*, was torpedoed by a Japanese submarine, *RO-41*, off Morotai. Although sailors on board the *Shelton* rushed to save the injured ship by throwing heavy equipment overboard in an effort to stay afloat, it was too heavily damaged by the torpedo, which hit the fantail and blasted away the starboard propeller. It capsized and sunk while under tow. Thirteen of the *Shelton*'s men died and twenty-two were injured.

Three weeks later, 28 October, was a rainy and very dark night in the waters of Leyte Gulf. "I was asleep when all of a sudden without warning I was thrown out of my bunk," the *Eversole*'s Daniel R. Gallagher said. "It was pitch black and I didn't know what happened." With blood streaming from his forehead, the nineteen-year-old sailor stood up and tried to feel his way through the dark after-steering compartment when a second explosion knocked him off his feet. "There must have been men yelling but I don't remember as I was in shock." The teenager, clawing his way through the dark, found the ladder and climbed topside. "The ship was one foot from the water on the starboard side," Gallagher said. He scrambled to the railing to jump overboard.

But Gallagher could not swim. He had no life jacket and most of his shipmates already were in the water. "I was scared and in shock," he said. Suddenly, seemingly out of nowhere, a life jacket slid down the deck, landing right in front of his feet. "God let that happen as it saved my life." Hastily strapping it on, he quickly dived over the side and started to make his way to a life net, bouncing in the churning waters about eighty feet away.

Stanley G. Skebe, the machinist's mate, had just showered after finishing the eight-to-midnight watch. Skebe and shipmate Ray Jambois retired to the after crew quarters to get some sleep, but it was so hot in that compartment that Skebe picked up his clothes and life belt and went to the machine shop, where it was cooler and where shipmate Jack Neumann offered his cot to the sailor while he stood watch. Skebe lay down on the cot and fell fast asleep.

"The next thing I knew I was lying face down on the deck with my head against the hatch coaming," Skebe said. "I don't know how long I had been lying there, but I did hear someone say, 'There's a body here' and felt several men step over me as they went out of the machine shop." His shipmates thought he was dead. "The lights were still on forward when I finally was able to get up."

Covered in blood, the terrified sailor strapped on his lifebelt as he watched shipmates slide down ropes into the dark ocean. He quickly followed, swam to the cork life raft, and hung on in the pouring rain as he watched his seven-month-old ship break in two and slip silently beneath the seas. It was gone in fifteen minutes.

Drenched in oil in the predawn gloom, the injured sailors clung to the life raft praying and hoping to be rescued. Suddenly they saw a light in the water and thought the ship's whaleboat was on its way to save them. They started yelling for help until they realized it was no whaleboat. *I-45*, the Japanese submarine that had torpedoed their ship, had surfaced and Japanese sailors were on deck firing machine guns at the American sailors struggling to stay afloat in the water. They strafed the men with 20-mm gunfire for some twenty minutes, although the darkness and rain kept them from hitting the American sailors. Suddenly a tremendous underwater explosion, possibly a Japanese antipersonnel bomb deposited on the ocean floor, accomplished what the Japanese gunfire had failed to do.

"My communications officer was instantly killed about five feet from me," Capt. George Marix of the *Eversole* wrote. "I was seized with very bad cramps and lost all control of my bowels." The skipper, who had been the last to leave the sinking ship after giving an injured sailor his life jacket, said that unconscious men started to drift from the floater net and he and his officers swam them back to the net, placing them on board. He estimates thirty men died from the underwater blast.

When the destroyer escorts *Richard S. Bull* and *Whitehurst* showed up, the submarine quickly submerged. The *Whitehurst* tracked the boat and, after getting a strong sonar contact, fired hedgehogs into the ocean. A thunderous underwater explosion followed, signaling that the submarine had succumbed. As daylight dawned, debris from the Japanese boat confirmed the "kill." Eighty *Eversole* sailors died and 136 were rescued, all injured and struggling in the water for a harrowing two hours until help arrived.[14]

Six months later the Japanese would exact their revenge on the USS *England*, which had set a record sinking six Japanese submarines the previous

May. While patrolling near Kerama Retto off the southwestern coast of Okinawa in May 1945, the destroyer escort was attacked by three kamikazes, one crashing into the *England*'s bridge, instantly killing sailors in the CIC and engulfing the ship in flames that incinerated the wardroom, captain's cabin, ship's office, and pilothouse. Some thirty-seven sailors died and twenty-five were injured, but the men in the ship's damage control, spraying water on the inferno as well as dousing those of their fellow shipmates whose clothes were on fire, extinguished the flames and managed to keep the vessel afloat. The *England* would survive and was towed into Leyte for temporary repairs, but it would never again see battle.[15]

Submarines, kamikazes, and stormy weather were not the only worries for the American fleet. The Japanese were trying out a new weapon called a *kaiten*, a one-man human torpedo capable of delivering a powerful 3,400-pound bomb directly into the underbelly of a warship. Ranging from 48 to 55 feet in length, the midget submarines, with their expendable operators, could travel at speeds from twelve to thirty knots and had a short periscope so the sailor could locate his target. In November 1944 a *kaiten* was successful at sinking an 11,000-ton American oil tanker, the USS *Mississinewa*, and soon one would take aim at the destroyer escort USS *Underhill*.

Richard Graves, a twenty-five-year-old Chico, California, native was an ensign on board the destroyer escort USS *Rall* that November in 1944. The *Rall*, commissioned seven months earlier, had provided escort service to oil tankers during the assault of Leyte Gulf and was now anchored along with several other warships in the relatively safe Ulithi Harbor awaiting repairs and orders for the next engagement. They would not wait long—for that engagement, it seems, would be coming directly to the harbor and the American vessels anchored there.

Graves grew up in the San Francisco Bay area and did a lot of sailing on his brother's sailboat during his younger years. "I loved the Navy and loved sailing," he said, which is why he selected that branch of service, although he acknowledged that the unattractiveness of trench warfare played a role in his decision, just as it had for many teenagers enlisting in the sea services. On the afternoon of 19 November, Graves and some of his buddies were off duty from patrolling the harbor entrance and were enjoying a delightful time swimming and sunning themselves in the lagoon, protected by moveable submarine net gates and ship lookouts. Beating down on their skin, the warm sunlight felt good, giving the men a welcome reprieve from the rigors of battle. But the reprieve would soon come to an end.

A bit "fuzzy headed" the next morning, Graves and his shipmates were jarred awake at dawn when the captain called everyone to battle stations. It seems that Japanese midget submarines had managed to sneak into the harbor and one crashed into the USS *Mississinewa*, an American oiler anchored there. Sailors on board the tanker were going about their normal morning chores and had no idea that their ship, supposedly safely moored inside a heavily protected harbor, was about to become a flaming inferno. Its tanks had been filled to capacity with 404,000 gallons of aviation gas, 9,000 barrels of diesel oil, and 90,000 barrels of fuel oil. It was a perfect target, a virtual powder keg, for a human torpedo. The ship exploded in a cauldron of flames.

"It was a terrible blast, and I had no idea what was going on," Graves said. "As soon as the anchor cleared the bottom we were underway" in search of the midget submarine. But it was too late—the damage already was done. The *Mississinewa* was burning uncontrollably, and as the flames spread, more explosions followed as thousands of gallons of fuel ignited. Flames reached one hundred feet into the sky and, within three hours, the six-month-old vessel turned over and sunk, reported to be the first victim of the deadly new *kaiten* weapon. Fifty sailors, including three officers, died in the explosion.

The destroyer escorts USS *Halloran* and *Weaver* joined the *Rall* and two destroyers as they searched the harbor for other submarines that might have snuck through the net. Lookouts on board the *Rall* spotted a swirl in the water near the cruiser USS *Mobile* and dropped three depth charges, as did the other DEs. An underwater explosion followed.

"We came about and saw the swirl in the water," said William Shumate, a nineteen-year-old fire controlman on board the *Rall*. "We dropped the depth charges and two men were blown to the surface." They tried to retrieve the bodies of the two Japanese sailors blown out of the *kaiten*, but were unsuccessful. Shumate said the water's surface was blue and pink in color as hundreds of dead fish floated near where the depth charge had exploded.[16]

Although *kaitens* were certainly a deadly weapon, the Japanese were not able to sink too many American warships with these human torpedoes, an underwater version of a kamikaze. But for the twenty-one-month-old destroyer escort, the USS *Underhill*, its first contact with one of these suicide submarines, unfortunately, would be its last. Steaming about 150 miles northeast of

Luzon, the DE, along with several other escort vessels, was escorting seven landing ships and a merchant ship from Okinawa bound for Leyte. The day was hot and the sea was a glassy calm on that 24 July afternoon as the *Underhill* led a convoy of ships filled with battle-weary American soldiers of the 96th Division. Sailors on board the destroyer escort had spotted a Japanese airplane in the distance earlier that morning, but the aircraft never got within firing range. The snooper plane was suspected of gathering information on American ship movements and sending that information to Japanese submarines prowling the area.

Suddenly sonar picked up a metallic object in the water, wrote James W. Gannon, the ship's machinist's mate. The captain swung the *Underhill* around to investigate. "As we drew nearer he [the antisubmarine officer] first reported it as moss, and later as it got nearer he reported that it had prongs or horns," Gannon recalled. Closing in, it was identified as a mine floating about twenty-five yards away, directly in the path of the convoy. As the *Underhill* sailors fired machine guns to explode the mine, sonar picked up another contact. But this new contact was no mine—it was moving. "Periscope on the starboard side," a lookout shouted. At least two and possibly as many as seven *kaitens*, accompanied by their "mother" submarine, thought to be *I-53*, were heading on a direct collision course with the convoy of American ships.

"Following the noon meal I was standing on the fantail talking with a group of shipmates when battle stations were called," noted *Underhill* electrician's mate Rodger J. Crum, who had finished watch at noon before taking lunch. Rushing to his battle station in the number one engine room, Crum put on his sound powered phones. Then he heard a command from the captain that always generated an unsettling anxiety on board a ship: Stand by to ram. Unable to see what was going on topside, some sailors simply prayed while others braced themselves and just waited. Placing his back against a stantion in front of the switchboard, Crum held on to the wooden bar that ran the length of the switchboard.

Donald Kruse, the eighteen-year-old Troy, New York, kid who, thirty-one months earlier, had his bags packed and ready to leave for Navy boot camp when the mailman delivered his Army draft notice, was stationed in the engine room along with Crum, who shouted, "Krusey, stand by for ram!" The *Underhill* successfully had depth charged one of the suicide submarines, confirmed by the dark, oily debris that bubbled to the surface. Now it was increasing its speed and preparing to ram the other Japanese submarines before they could collide with the convoy.

It was a surreal period for the sailors belowdecks, when time appeared to stand still. Then it happened—a terrible crash and explosion. The ship went dark. "Next thing I knew I was bouncing around the engine room," Kruse said. "One hit and then about forty seconds later the second hit—one on the starboard side beneath the bridge and the other between the bridge and the stack on the port side. Everything started to break loose." Some believe the *Underhill* hit the larger mother submarine with its bow, and then one of the *kaitens* crashed with its explosive head directly into the port side of the DE. Witnesses feel there were at least two *kaitens* and these were what collided with the *Underhill*. Japanese authorities insist only one *kaiten* was launched from *I-53* that day—the one they say sunk the *Underhill*. Regardless of the type or number of submarines, a huge explosion followed, with orange flames reaching into the clear blue skies as heavy black smoke poured out of the mortally wounded ship.

A dazed and bloody Kruse, suffering head and shoulder injuries, rushed topside, but when he started to walk forward, he was shocked to find half of his ship was gone. The *Underhill* had split in two and the ship had started to sink. Machinist's Mate Crum was still in the engine room, which was filling with steam, smoke, and water. He tried to open the forward port escape hatch but it wouldn't budge. He and the other men were able to climb out through the starboard aft hatch.

"When I walked onto the open deck I was startled to see the bow of a ship in a horizontal position a hundred or so yards away," Crum wrote. "Then I looked forward and realized that it was the bow of our ship." Bodies of dead and dying shipmates were scattered across the deck, many covered with oil and other debris from the wounded ship, some badly burned from the explosion. Steel rubble was strewn about the deck. Joseph H. Timberlake, the ship's engineering officer, was holding on to the handrail of the raised platform near the throttle board when the explosion catapulted him into the air. As he fell to the deck, a second explosion threw him into a mass of twisted pipes and plates, where he held on as the floor plates dropped to the lower level. He lived, along with 116 crew members who were rescued, but 113 men, including forty-eight-year-old Capt. Robert M. Newcomb and 9 of the ship's 14 officers, perished.[17]

Lt. Nathaniel G. Benchley was skipper of *PC-1251*, one of the patrol crafts in the convoy with the *Underhill*, and witnessed the explosion and sinking of the destroyer escort. "On my ship, the *PC-1251*, most of the crew were reading their newly arrived mail, the executive officer and the communications officer were playing cribbage, and the gunnery officer was making peanut-butter fudge," Benchley wrote, adding that he remembered the *Underhill* as a "well run . . . happy ship." Having just arrived from duty in the Atlantic, the *Underhill*, Benchley noted, had run with "much faster company" battling Hitler's U-boats and it was clear to him that the destroyer escort would be running a very efficient screen for the convoy: "The contagion of efficiency spread from the *Underhill* to the other ships, and we felt that we could take on any Japanese who might be so rash as to try to intercept us." That theory was about to be tested.

The sun was extremely hot and the ship railing burned to the touch. Benchley turned over command to the officer on the deck, retiring to the cooler ward room, where he started a game of cribbage with Howard Tampke, a blond gunnery officer who hailed from Texas. A short time later, a signalman entered the ward room and handed Benchley a message. The *Underhill* was offering ships in the convoy five gallons of ice cream each day in an order of rotation. Today was Benchley's turn. "That's pretty damned nice," he said, initialing the message. A happy signalman left with the hope that he would be enjoying some cold ice cream in about a half hour. But before any could be transferred, word came from the *Underhill* that the ice cream would have to wait. The destroyer escort had spotted a floating mine and was trying to sink it. Benchley went topside and peered through his binoculars as the *Underhill* fired at the mine. Then the intercom on the bridge sputtered: "Tell the captain the DE says he's got a sub contact. He's leaving the mine to chase the contact."

"Five will get you seven it's a whale," Tampke told the captain. "Last ship I was on, we got two whales, one certain and one probable." Benchley agreed. "This guy's just out of the Atlantic. He probably thinks every contact he gets is a sub," he said, peering through the glasses at the *Underhill* and the white puffs of smoke as the DE launched its depth charges.

"I strained my eyes looking through the glasses, but the *Underhill* was beginning to shimmer in the horizon heat waves, and for a moment I lost sight of her," Benchley said. "Then I saw a burst of smoke, and thought excitedly that she might have exploded the sub, but the smoke turned into a boil of orange flames and started to rise straight upward; it bubbled and boiled and churned in a curdling of orange and black until it got up to about ten thousand feet, and then the smoke flattened out and mushroomed dirtily into the base of the white cumulus clouds."

"The *Underhill* disappeared from sight," Benchley said, as sailors squinted into the distance in stunned silence. "That dark mushroom of smoke from the *Underhill* hung in the sky until the last pink streaks of afterglow were blotted out by the oncoming night." The *Underhill* had accomplished its mission to protect the convoy of American ships, which safely arrived to the Philippines. The ship and half its crew, however, were entombed at the bottom of the ocean.[18]

Charles Esch, a seventeen-year-old Colorado Springs native who had dropped out of high school in the eleventh grade to join the Navy, was assigned as a radioman on board the USS *Haas* and was on board as the ship headed through the Panama Canal in December 1944 to assist with the invasion of the Philippines. As the *Haas* traversed the locks and entered the Pacific, the young sailor, whose father was in the infantry in World War I and now had a job as a sheet metal worker, was impressed with the calm, mirror-like ocean. "Boy, we're in heaven now," Esch thought, although it would not be long before he realized that those beautiful blue waters were just as dangerous as the waters on the other side of the canal.

Two months after arriving in the Pacific, the *Haas* and five other destroyer escorts were escorting a convoy of troop landing ships in the middle of a rainstorm when one of the ships, a seven-month-old landing ship, LST-577, exploded and sank off the Philippines, the victim of a torpedo fired from a Japanese submarine, which had escaped detection by sonar on any of the escort ships. Although they made at least two runs on the submarine, they were unable to locate it. Five hundred Marines died in the explosion. The destroyer escort, like many others assigned to the Pacific, went on to provide shore bombardment during the invasion, clear free-floating mines from the water, and even assist in a submarine attack near Leyte Gulf, which Esch recalled resulted in an oil slick five miles long.[19]

Kamikazes were one of the more feared and deadly weapons used against American ships in the Pacific. Coming out of the sun without warning, these suicide planes laden with explosives and often a full fuel tank, plunged directly into a ship, exploding on contact. Americans knew that the pilots of these planes had no plans to go home and were intent on one mission only—finding an American ship and flying their plane directly into it.

For a sixteen-year-old kid from Pittsburgh, Pennsylvania, the kamikazes were a nightmare come true. After dropping out of school and lying about his age, John Kunsak Jr., one of twelve children born to immigrant parents, was assigned to the USS *Rall* and was on board the ship off Okinawa when five kamikazes appeared in the bright afternoon skies, heading on a collision course for the little destroyer escort.

"I saw all five planes peel off," said Kunsak, who was firing from his battle station on the 3-inch, .50-caliber gun. "We got three of them. A cruiser in the area shot down the fourth one." But there was still one kamikaze left, "and he was flying directly for my gun." Kunsak said he was about to shoot the kamikaze down when he was ordered to hold fire by his gunnery officer. It appeared that a Marine Corsair fighter was directly behind the Japanese plane attempting to shoot it down. It missed. But the kamikaze did not. "Within fifteen seconds the kamikaze hit right below my gun and dropped a 500-pound bomb that exploded on the other side," Kunsak said. "During that time, I was shot in the leg, the arm, and I had twenty-six pieces of shrapnel in my buttocks. They thought I was dead."

But he wasn't. "I woke up in a pool of blood," Kunsak recalled. Later he was transferred to a hospital ship. The kamikaze, with its 500-pound bomb slung beneath the plane, crashed into the starboard side aft as the bomb tore through the ship and exploded in the air about fifteen feet from the port side.

Ens. Richard Graves remembered the horrific aftermath. Damage to the ship was severe. Blood and bodies were everywhere. One sailor was killed instantly when a piece of shrapnel pierced his heart. A gunner's mate, still at his duty station, had blood streaming down his face, his bones protruding from his left arm as it hung limply at his side. Nineteen-year-old Tom Cooney, who had signed up for the Navy while still attending high school in Springfield, Massachusetts, was on the number two gun and was thrown overboard by the impact. Some sailors were crushed by the plane as it crashed into the DE. Twenty-one sailors died and thirty-eight were injured. But damage control was able to keep the ship afloat and it would live to sail again.[20]

Kamikazes, or bogeys, as they were known among sailors, were especially deadly for those serving picket duty around Okinawa, along the so-called bogey highway. Some ninety-seven destroyers and at least fifty-one destroyer escorts were assigned this dangerous duty to screen for possible submarine attack, vital in support of amphibious operations on Okinawa. On picket duty, sailors would watch, wait, search, and pray—they did a lot of praying along the "bogey highway." Some called this the toughest duty of the war. These ships would bear the brunt of kamikaze attacks, suicide swimmers, suicide boats, torpedoes, submarines, midget submarines, and floating mines. It wasn't duty for the faint of heart.

Robert D. Piper, a native of Naperville, Illinois, served as assistant communications officer on board the USS *O'Flaherty* when the newly commissioned ship was assigned picket duty along the bogey highway. It was dangerous duty, and ships serving in that capacity frequently were badly damaged or sunk. Piper remembered Capt. Paul L. Callan's concern over the assignment and the skipper decided he was going to do something to ensure that his men had enough firepower should the kamikazes show up.

Lt. Norm Givens had a brother who was a Marine colonel on Okinawa, Piper said, and they were able to get a message to the colonel. "We offered him a case of beer for every 50 caliber machine gun," Piper recalled. "We were in Buckner Bay on the east side of Okinawa," he said, when they put Givens and Piper ashore to get the machine guns. After hitchhiking through the island to find the colonel, the two men finally located him in the northern section. They had dinner and then got down to business. "We loaded the ten 50-caliber machines guns and they threw in two .30s," Piper recalled. They then proceeded to a signal tower to send a message to the *O'Flaherty*: "Have guns . . . send beer." The whaleboat showed up with the beer and the exchange was made.

"They mounted them [the machine guns], five on each side, starboard and port, right along the edge of the deck," Piper recalled. "The two .30s were mounted on the bridge." But the new guns would not stay mounted for long. Within a short time the *O'Flaherty* was back with its carrier group and, before too long, came alongside the flagship carrier with the admiral on board. Once he got a look at the machine guns mounted on the little DE, he called over an order to "deep six all unauthorized ordnances" and the sailors were forced to drop the machine guns over the side. The machine guns were gone and so was their beer. "We were all kind of bummed," Piper said.[21]

John P. Cosgrove and his ship, the USS *Gendreau*, spent twenty continuous, anxiety-filled days on picket duty, going to battle stations sixty-seven different times. Growing up in Pittston, Pennsylvania, where his father sold

Model T Fords, young Cosgrove was working in Washington, D.C., when he heard FDR deliver his "Day of Infamy" speech. He enlisted in the Navy immediately. Having worked at the Associated Press, Cosgrove was assigned to the Navy's office of censorship, a disappointment for the Pennsylvania native, who really wanted to be at sea. "I felt like I was masquerading as a sailor," Cosgrove said of the "plush assignment" in the censorship office. Eventually he got his wish and went off to boot camp after having worked in a clerical capacity in Navy for almost two years. Assigned as a yeoman on board the USS *Gendreau*, he stepped on board on St. Patrick's Day and was happily out to sea.

After escorting convoys between Hawaii and the Marshall Islands, the *Gendreau* returned to Oahu as part of the welcoming party for President Roosevelt, who arrived on board the USS *Baltimore* in July 1944 to participate in a military conference with Adm. Chester Nimitz and Gen. Douglas MacArthur. John Cosgrove will never forget that day. Most of the crew of his ship were looking forward to some liberty once they arrived in Pearl Harbor. Then came the startling announcement over the *Gendreau*'s public address system: "This is the captain speaking, and I repeat . . . there will be no liberty until after the Roosevelt visit." Cosgrove recalled thinking, "What in God's name is Mrs. Roosevelt doing out here? Delaying our longed-for liberty, that's what she was doing." He, like many of his shipmates, thought the globe-trotting first lady was making a visit to their neck of the woods.

But they quickly learned that the "Roosevelt" visiting was, in fact, Franklin, not Eleanor. Now the crew had its work cut out for them, cleaning the ship, getting into whites, and scores of others things that the crew must do before an inspection, especially one by the commander in chief. "We were proud of our location," Cosgrove said. "Our little destroyer escort docked directly across from the berth assigned to the USS *Baltimore*, soon to arrive carrying the presidential party." The crew was thrilled with their ring-side view of the president—that is until two water barges came alongside, were secured, and spoiled the DE's view of the president's ship. The *Gendreau*'s skipper requested and was granted a slight change of location so they could have a better view of the *Baltimore*.

FDR surveyed the harbor and spotted the little destroyer escort, according to the story circulated in DE circles for years. The president's sweep became fixed and his eyes quizzical. After a studied silence, he asked, "What is that vessel over there?" An aide told him it was a destroyer escort, to which the president smiled and reportedly replied that it was the first DE he had seen that looked like two water barges—the best camouflage job he had ever seen. "The president did recognize our DE," Cosgrove was convinced—certainly since his son, FDR Jr., was serving as the skipper on board one.[22]

Later in 1945, following several months of routine escort duty (except the day the *Gendreau* collided with the escort carrier USS *Breton* while refueling on heavy seas), the destroyer escort was assigned to the southeast coast of Okinawa protecting amphibious ships that were unloading troops for the assault. That's when the first kamikaze arrived.

"I was asleep in my bunk when the first attack occurred," Cosgrove said. It was Easter eve as the kamikaze came in at bridge height, headed right for the ship. "It was so close you could see the pilot," said Yeoman John A. Virum, a Minneapolis, Minnesota, native who had celebrated his eighteenth birthday just two days earlier. From his battle station on the 20-mm antiaircraft gun, the Japanese pilot looking very young, he remembered: "They were kids just like us." The *Gendreau* and a host of landing ships started firing at the plane, shearing off its wing. It crashed in the water about fifty yards from *Gendreau* on the starboard side. But the kamikazes were not yet finished with the little destroyer escort. More suicide planes would be taking aim at Cosgrove's ship. In fact, the *Gendreau* would have five more kamikaze assaults in the next two months.

As dawn broke on April Fool's Day, *Gendreau* began its shore bombardment of Okinawa in support of American landing forces. Later, it was stationed along the dreaded and deadly picket line. One kamikaze made a strafing run from port to starboard, but his aim "reminded us of a blind man at a turkey shoot," Cosgrove said. The gunners fired but were unable to hit the aircraft, which circled the ship and then made a suicide run right through the gunfire toward the ship. "This time we really filled him with lead, but he kept coming; with a quick change in speed and course we outmaneuvered him, but his wheels barely missed the antenna aft of the stack," Cosgrove said. Virum, who slept all night in the gun tub, said he fired his 20-mm gun at the plane before it exploded in flames and crashed into the ocean twenty yards on their port beam. "We wiped the sweat from our brows and secured from battle stations," Cosgrove said.

But the *Gendreau*'s troubles were not yet over. More suicide bombers soon would have the little ship in their sights. One evening, a little after sunset, a kamikaze showed up. Although guns on the ship were blazing, the plane just kept coming, dodging bullets as it barreled on a collision course with the *Gendreau*. The skipper maneuvered the ship and the gunners kept firing, finally scoring a fatal strike—but not before the kamikaze had released a torpedo that exploded in the water. The plane burst into flames and crashed five hundred yards astern of the ship. The ship was credited with three more kamikaze "kills" while serving picket duty.

The *Gendreau*'s good fortune was about to run out. It was a clear and sunny day as the destroyer escort was escorting landing ships along the western and southern tip of Okinawa. "I was standing on the poop deck waiting for the breakfast chow line," Cosgrove said. "Suddenly I heard a swoosh." One of the Japanese shore batteries opened up on the ship with a direct hit in the number one fireroom, ripping open a ten-foot-square hole in the ship. Three other shells landed astern of the vessel. No one was certain what had happened. Some thought the ship had hit a mine while others thought one of the ship's boilers had exploded.

Battle stations alarms sounded but the circuits of the ship were shorted out so all the sailors heard was a dull hum over the PA. Word was passed frantically over the phones for everyone to go to battle stations—the ship was under attack. Rushing to battle stations, Cosgrove said, he saw steam and a choking, acrid odor poured out of the fireroom, filling the passageways and officers quarters, making breathing difficult. Two sailors, one of whom had been on board only a week, were lying dead covered in the oil and water of the now-flooded fireroom. Two other sailors were seriously wounded.

As the American destroyer pounded the beach with gunfire, the *Gendreau* —dead in the water—drifted dangerously toward shore and the Japanese gunfire. The guns on the destroyer became too hot to continue the shore bombardment, leaving the wounded destroyer escort on its own. No matter, for the *Gendreau* was able to take care of itself. Damage crews shored up the bulkheads and secured the damaged fireroom, getting the ship under way and away from shore. The DE left under its own power for repairs at Kerama Retto, a nearby American-held island southwest of Okinawa used as a staging area for the assault.

Picket duty, or ping line duty, as some sailors called it, consisted of sailing in a figure-eight pattern in the assigned area, keeping a sharp eye out for enemy planes or submarines. Robert D. Young, who had joined the Navy after graduating high school in Thomaston, Maine, was assigned to the USS *Seder-strom*, ordered to take up its place on the ping line off Okinawa in April 1945. "I most certainly would have preferred to continue operations with the carriers, but we had no choice but to do as ordered," Young said, well aware of the danger involved in this assignment. Young said that in making the circle eight, the ships on the picket line would always turn seaward so their sonar would scan away from the land. "If we turned toward land and pinged seaward, our sonar would echo off our own wake," he recalled.

As the sun set on 22 April, ship radar picked up eight bogeys about thirty-five miles away, closing fast on the *Sederstrom*. As the eight twin-engine bombers raced toward the destroyer escort, four split off and headed north and the other four flew in a direct collision course with the ship. Gunners on board the ship opened fire as the four planes, one of which was a kamikaze, as they emerged from the clouds.

Young was stationed in the radio room and could not see the action from his windowless compartment. But he knew the ship was under attack. Gunners fired at the planes as they made a run for the ship. Young is convinced they splashed three of the enemy planes, although the ship is officially credited with one. The planes retreated from the intense gunfire and disappeared from radar until one of them returned, making a suicide run on the ship. As the plane circled stern to port, it headed right for the *Sederstrom*'s bridge. "It was so close that the captain was shooting at it with his pistol," Young said. Gunners fired on it with a barrage of antiaircraft fire until the plane rolled over and crashed into the water, only twenty feet from the ship.

On fire with heavy smoke pouring out, the mortally wounded suicide plane made its final run on the ship and showered the deck with gasoline and pieces of metal as it passed over the DE, crashing into the water. Oren McDermitt, the ship's barber and loader on the 20-mm gun, was discovered to be missing. He had dived overboard to avoid getting hit by the gasoline and metal pieces. Young said McDermitt was probably the "smartest man topside," although he could have been sucked into the ship's screws and chopped to pieces. "When we secured from general quarters," Young recalled, "I went below and noticed McDermitt sitting on a locker, looking like a drowned rat."[23]

Earlier in February, as Americans and Japanese were in a bloody battle to seize control of the island of Iowa Jima, the USS *Silverstein* was on its way to provide replenishment for the fast attack carriers, already strafing the island with gunfire. Irving Mesher was a New York City boy who had learned to play the trumpet while he was in high school. Knowing he soon would be drafted, the twenty year old signed up for the Navy and, because of his musical talent and keen hearing, was assigned as a soundman on board the *Silverstein*. He, like many DE sailors, secretly maintained a diary while at sea.

"Today was a rather big day for the *Silverstein*," Mesher wrote on 16 February 1945 as the Iowa Jima assault was under way. "We were detached all alone from our task unit to investigate a small craft 7 miles away. When we arrived at the craft we sent our motor whale boat and our boarding crew to investigate." Mesher said they found a Japanese wooden troop barge with six emaciated soldiers on board. "The Japs looked like living skeletons," he wrote. The Americans retrieved some Japanese army manuals and other material. They took the prisoners on board the whaleboat and then sunk the barge with gunfire and eight depth charges.

The six Japanese soldiers were conducting interisland transport of soldiers when they ran into a typhoon, according to Radioman William Harney, who also maintained a war diary. The storm wrecked their boat and left them adrift for twenty days living on rice and shrimp. "They were nothing but skin and bones. . . . There wasn't one of them that was taller than my armpit," Harney wrote. Hauled on board the *Silverstein*, the Japanese prisoners were given soup and cigarettes. At first they were blindfolded so they could slowly get used to the sun. "The Japs thought that the blindfolds meant that it was all over for them and got down on their knees to be shot," wrote Harney. "They couldn't get over it when they saw they weren't going to die. All grins and happy. One of them wanted to join the American army."[24]

The public has long identified Iwo Jima with the famous flag-raising by the Marines on Mount Suribachi. But the Marines, some 110,000 of them, needed the Navy to get there, transported to the volcanic island in what was one of the largest amphibious operations in the Pacific. There was plenty of ferocious fighting as the operation proceeded, and nine destroyer escorts played a pivotal role in the historic capture. As the assault continued, the dreaded kamikazes showed up, taking aim at the aircraft carrier, the USS *Saratoga*, and smashing into its flight deck, killing 110 sailors and wounding an additional 180. The escort carrier *Bismarck Sea*, commissioned nine months earlier and having earned battle stars for its service at the Leyte Gulf and Lingayen Gulf landings, was next in the kamikazes' sights.[25]

Edward M. Docalovich, radioman on board the destroyer escort USS *Edmonds*, was on duty as daylight faded on 21 February 1945 off Iowa Jima. "I was the supervisor in the radio room and we were on the sound-powered phones," said the Carbondale, Pennsylvania, native, whose father worked in the coal mines. The evening was calm and the teenager was thinking about the nineteenth birthday he would celebrate the next day. Suddenly the battle station alarm sounded. "CIC called the bridge and told us we had a bogey flying low," he said. The carrier *Saratoga*, four miles away, already had been hit, and the captain thought the planes, rather than being kamikazes, were likely American aircraft looking for a nest. Radar did not detect an IFF, which was an electronic signature identifying the aircraft as friend or foe.

One of Docalovich's shipmates, an African American sailor named Jim, was the captain's cook on board the segregated ship. He rushed to his battle station on board the 40-mm gun once the alarm sounded. Docalovich, with his sound phones on, heard the conversation between Jim and the ship's skipper as the airplane came low and fast out of the early evening sky. "Captain, request permission to open fire, that's a Japanese airplane," Jim said. "I've heard too many of those engines . . . that's a Japanese plane." Docalovich said the captain, still believing it was a friendly aircraft, refused the order to fire. "It flew right over the *Edmonds* . . . it wasn't looking for us," Docalovich said. "It was so low that the guys on the weather deck said the air wash from the plane whipped up their dungarees. . . . That's how low it was."

But it was no American plane, as the *Bismarck Sea* was about to discover. "That suicide plane hit the *Bismarck Sea*," Docalovich said. Actually, two kamikazes crashed into the carrier, igniting the ship's torpedoes when they hit. An explosion followed with flames reaching one hundred feet into the night sky. It capsized and sank within ninety minutes. Docalovich recalled that neither Jim nor anyone on board his ship ever spoke openly of the incident, but he remembered the captain stayed out of sight and alone in his stateroom for more than a week. "It was sad," Docalovich said.

Ellsworth Kendig was the ship's twenty-three-year-old assistant gunnery officer, whose father sold life insurance in Detroit, Michigan. He recalled that the ship's captain was not too well versed in airplane identification, which may have accounted for his belief that it was a friendly aircraft rather than a Japanese suicide plane. But he also said that it is possible that another factor played a role in the skipper's decision not to fire. "The plane was in between us and the destroyer," Kendig said, and if the DE had fired on the plane, the shells might have hit the American destroyer.

The *Edmonds*, along with the USS *Melvin R. Nawman*, which had been damaged but survived Typhoon Cobra, then went about the task of picking up survivors. A number of enlisted men and officers from the *Edmonds* donned life jackets and jumped into the water to rescue sailors struggling in seas strewn with debris and the corpses of American sailors.

"We spent hours that night rescuing survivors," Kendig said. "It's amazing the Japanese were not over there with their submarines. . . . We had our searchlights on trying to pick up guys in the water." Kendig recalled one shipmate, John Brown, the assistant engineering officer, who was a former world-class swimmer at Princeton University. "We tied a rope around his waist and he dove in to rescue men," Kendig said. "We picked up the captain and the doctor, who turned our ward room into an operating room." The ship's dining table became an operating table and the doctor worked all night to save as many men as possible. Many would not live to see dawn.

Some 347 men died in the blast, but more than 375 were rescued. Four more American ships—an escort carrier, two landing ships, and a cargo ship—also were struck by kamikazes that day, making it one of the worst days for the Navy during Iwo Jima.[26]

But the suicide planes, or "divine wind," as they were known in Japan, still had plenty of fight left in them. In fact, the month of May 1945 was a particularly bloody thirty days for U.S. destroyer escorts. Seven were attacked and damaged by kamikazes during that period, all in the Okinawa area. The USS *England* and USS *Oberrender* both were damaged on the same day by kamikazes, which crashed directly into the vessels. The USS *Bright, John C. Butler, O'Neill, William C. Cole*, and *Halloran* all were targeted and attacked by the Japanese divine wind.

Warm and gentle breezes were blowing on Mother's Day 1945, but the day would turn out to be a far cry from the previous Mother's Days Charles R. Cox had celebrated in the small coal-mining town of Shamokin, Pennsylvania. Cox dropped out of Coal Township High School in the eleventh grade to join the Navy, and after six weeks of boot camp at Sampson, he was on board the USS *Bright* and on his way escorting a troop ship to Pearl Harbor. After escorting another convoy to Okinawa, the *Bright* would take up picket duty, keeping a sharp eye out for enemy planes or submarines trying to break through the picket line off Okinawa.

Most of Mother's Day was pretty uneventful for Cox and his shipmates. As the sun began to set and the gentle evening winds picked up, however, radar detected an airplane that then quickly disappeared behind Tonachi Jima, a nearby island. Within three minutes, the CIC reported that there was a friendly airplane in the area, with a strong IFF signature. But that was not the only plane in the sky. A second bogey, with a weak IFF signal, appeared about eight miles away and started flying directly for the *Bright*. The captain sounded the battle station alarm.

Cox rushed to his battle station on the 20-mm gun as the bogey, now identified as a kamikaze, dropped out of the sky and flew about three hundred feet above the water on a direct collision course with the destroyer escort. "As that plane came in, all guns on the port side fired," Cox said. "I only got to fire one magazine and the plane hit us." Cox said that his fellow gunner's mate, Robert F. Thomas, was able to score a direct hit on the plane's engine and left wing.

As Thomas continued to fire, his gun suddenly locked up. He stayed at his battle station even though the plane continued flying directly toward him. At about 750 yards from the ship, the plane burst into flames, its port wing falling into the water. The rest of the plane crashed into the *Bright*'s port depth-charge racks, its 500-pound bomb exploding on impact.

The *Bright*'s rudder jammed hard left and the ship lost steering. The after engine room was completely demolished, both port and starboard depth-charge racks were damaged and inoperative, and smoke-screen generators were blown off. The main deck aft buckled and water poured into the ship, which was now circling aimlessly in the water. Within minutes of the attack, another kamikaze appeared and gunners from the USS *Barr* as well as those still at their battle stations on board the *Bright* fired at the suicide plane, scoring direct hits. The plane crashed into the water. Miraculously, only two sailors were injured on board the *Bright*. Both men—Peter D. Vercolio from Ottawa, Illinois, and Harold E. Crane Jr. of Elizabeth, New Jersey—were rescued from the burning after-steering compartment and survived.[27]

Over the course of the Pacific war, the need arose for light transport ships with a relatively shallow draft with the capacity to move Army and Marine troops to the various Pacific islands. Old World War I four-piper destroyers were transformed into high-speed transport ships. In addition some 103 destroyer escorts also were converted to haul troops and underwater demolition teams—predecessors of the Navy Seals—throughout the Pacific island–hopping campaign.

Another deck was added to the DEs, along with troop berthing and eating areas. A set of large gravity davits or cranes were installed on either side, from which from 36-foot assault landing craft could be launched. In addition to troops, the converted DEs could move supplies, light trucks, and jeeps to where they were needed.

The USS *Blessman* was just such a ship. Originally commissioned in the Hingham Shipyard in September 1943, the destroyer escort provided escort to convoys in the North Atlantic and participated in the Normandy invasion. As action shifted to the Pacific and the need increased to move large numbers of troops into the western theater, the ship was redesignated a high-speed transport ship ten months after it went into service and was on its way through the Panama Canal to Pearl Harbor.

Underwater demolition teams, which played an important role during the Normandy invasion, took on even more vital importance in the Pacific war. Removing obstacles that might impede amphibious landings on the islands as well as providing preinvasion intelligence on gun embankments and layout of the beaches prior to the various island assaults, these highly trained frogmen risked hypothermia, severe cramps, and their very lives gathering reconnaissance for American forces. Wearing swim trunks, masks, and fins, the teams would be sent out in rubber boats to gather intelligence. When encountering coral reefs or other obstacles that prevented passage of their boats, they often would remove their clothes, except for underwear, and swim over the reef in order to get a better view of the area. Many were killed or wounded from shore-side gun batteries.

Edward Hinz was a quartermaster on board the *Blessman*. Born in Chicago, he had decided to enlist in the Navy after receiving his Army draft notice. With six Atlantic convoy crossings and the Normandy invasion under his belt, he stayed on board when his ship was converted to a high-speed transport and headed through the Panama Canal to Pearl Harbor, where it picked up the underwater demolition team and 8,000 half-pound blocks of TNT.

As morning dawned on 17 February 1945, the *Blessman* was heading toward Iowa Jima as shore bombardment commenced. "We had gone in to make a reconnaissance of both sides of Iowa Jima," Hinz said. As they moved near the mainland to drop off the underwater team, Signalman Johnny Yarbrough looked over the rail and asked Hinz, "What kind of fish are those?" Those were no fish. They were Japanese shells plopping in the water from a beach assault. Before long, one would hit its mark, killing Frank W. Sumpter, one of the underwater dive team members, who was struck in the back of his head under his helmet.

With the crew's work complete, the *Blessman* proceeded to rejoin with the other ships heading away from the island. Accelerating to twenty miles per hour to catch up with the fleet, the *Blessman* was cutting through the dark seas, leaving a phosphorescent wake in the moonless night. Then it happened. With the phosphorescent wake helping to guide its aim, a Japanese bomber came out of the sky and dropped a 500-pound bomb right on top of the little ship. "I was in my bunk," Hinz said. "I don't remember hearing the bomb, but all of a sudden everything was silent. We were dead in the water."

Sonarman Sidney Marshall had just returned from the mess hall where he had won ninety dollars in a poker game. Lying on his bunk, Marshall counted his money and said that once they arrived in Pearl Harbor, he would send a money order to his wife so she could buy a new coat. He left the compartment to return to the mess, where he hoped to add another ten dollars to his winnings, so he would have an even one hundred for his wife's coat. He never returned, and later several shipmates reported he had been sitting near the starboard outer bulkhead, where a fifty-foot hole now existed.

"I saw everybody in my compartment run toward the stern, and I got up and put my pants on and got to the foot of the ladder to get up to the main deck," Hinz said. "When I get up to the main deck I saw the flames shooting up and shells going up like skyrockets." He rushed up the ladder to the pilothouse and gathered the top-secret documents so he could throw them overboard if the ship started to sink. When he arrived the pilothouse was an inferno. He tied a rope to his waist, grabbed a gas mask and battery-powered lamp, and rushed into the smoke-filled CIC to retrieve the secret documents and put them in a weighted bag so they would be ready to be tossed overboard if necessary.

The bomb went through the stack and landed in the middle of the mess hall, instantly killing all the cooks and destroying the galley. Power was knocked out to the ship, lights were out, and fires erupted, with flames shooting high into the night sky. "The underwater demolition guys were pushing buckets down with their feet in order to get water into them. We had no power, no pressure, none of the hoses worked, and the fire was going up into the sky," Hinz said, adding that had the bomb hit about fifty feet farther aft, the fifty tons of tetrytol would have exploded, causing even more damage and casualties.

The USS *Gilmore* came alongside and threw its hoses over to help extinguish the flames. But the damage already had been done. "The stench of burned flesh permeated the air," Hinz said, adding that they used foxhole shovels to scrape body parts off the bulkheads. Sailors used dog tags, jewelry, tattoos, and clothing to identify the dead. Forty-two men were killed, including twenty-three underwater demolition sailors, and thirty-nine were injured.

With the flames finally out and the ship badly damaged, sailors surveyed the once-proud vessel, which had served America so well both in the Atlantic and Pacific. Hinz will never forget one of his southern shipmates who, looking over the rubble and dead bodies strewn about the deck, remarked, "Twarn't no crow that shit on us." But the *Blessman* would live to sail another day. After repairs were made in Saipan, the ship returned to the western Pacific, where it served with the occupation forces of Japan.[28]

As the United States continued its successful island-hopping strategy in the Pacific, it still was not enough to convince the Japanese to surrender. It appeared to the nation's new president, Harry Truman, that only a massive assault—an atomic bomb as it turned out—would be able to do that. Enter the heavy cruiser USS *Indianapolis*, once a favorite of President Roosevelt, who took it back from his summer home on Campobello Island, New Brunswick, following his famous 1933 New England cruise on board the schooner *Amberjack II*. FDR also selected the vessel to carry him on his 1936 cruise to South America, where an Inter-American Conference was being held in Buenos Aires, Argentina.

Over the course of the war, the *Indianapolis* participated in most major Pacific battles serving as the flagship for the fifth fleet. But by July 1945 the aging cruiser was no longer the gleaming new warship that had transported FDR in 1933. The fifteen-year-old ship had survived dozens of battles, fighting off Japanese bombers, submarines, and warships and earning ten battles stars. Now it was about to be selected for one of the most important assignments of its long service, an assignment that was destined to be its last: The USS *Indianapolis* would transport a plywood crate packed with uranium-235 and bomb components from the United States to the Pacific island of Tinian, where the atomic bomb would be assembled.

The *Indianapolis* swiftly and efficiently carried out its mission in a record-setting five-thousand-mile dash from San Francisco across the Pacific Ocean, reaching Tinian in only ten days. After dropping off its top-secret cargo, the ship stopped by Guam to discharge men and then headed, without escort, to Leyte. It would never arrive.

A little past midnight on 30 July, the ship exploded after being hit by two torpedoes on its starboard side. More than three hundred sailors were killed by the bomb. Nine hundred of their shipmates were cast into the churning Pacific waters, watching in horror as their ship disappeared beneath the waters. They were now alone in the vast open ocean—alone, that is, except for the sharks, which would arrive at dawn.

Four days went by before anyone noticed that the *Indianapolis* had not arrived at Leyte. Meanwhile, suffering hypothermia, dehydration, and physical and mental exhaustion, the men, many delirious, struggled to survive the shark-infested seas. The nearest land was 350 miles away. Once it was discovered that the vessel was overdue, search parties were dispatched. Making a flank-speed run to the site, several ships, including the destroyer escorts USS *DuFilho* and *Cecil J. Doyle*, were the first to spot the American sailors, many burned from the sun, dehydrated, and hallucinating, with open sores covering their bodies.

Carlos R. Monarez, who had quit school in the eighth grade to join the Navy, was not quite prepared for what he saw once they arrived at the site of the ship sinking. Wreckage from the *Indianapolis*, along with life rafts, jackets, and scores of dead and dying men, were strewn about the area. Monarez recalled that many of the sailors' upper bodies were floating in the water, supported by life rings—but the lower parts of their bodies were gone, chewed up by the sharks. "They were half men," the twenty-year-old Newton, Kansas, native said. Their bodies were burned red from the intense sun. Corpses were floating as far as the eye could see.

Only 321 men of the original crew of 1,196 on board ship when the *Indianapolis* left Guam were rescued. Monarez said his ship was only able to pick up a single survivor. "We spotted one kid who was on top of five life preservers, all by himself," he said. "When we picked him up, he could hardly see, his eyes were burned from the sun." But he was one of the lucky ones who would live to see another day.

Picking up survivors of sunken ships and splashed airplanes, battling sui-cide bombers, and dodging Japanese torpedoes was steady fare for most of the destroyer escorts assigned to the Pacific. Yet there were other, seemingly more mundane duties that, although not as glamorous as sinking submarines and downing enemy airplanes, were every bit as important in the United States' Pacific theater operations. The USS *Wiseman* was a destroyer escort that played one of those behind-the-scenes supporting roles.

"This is Cedric Foster speaking to you transcribed from Manila in the Philippine Islands," began the wartime Boston radio commentator in July 1945. "No matter how trite and bromidic the phrase may sound, necessity still is the mother of inventions." Foster went on, describing how the devas-tated city of Manila obtained its electrical power—not from an onshore power station but from one of the United States' destroyer escorts.

Commissioned in April 1944, the USS *Wiseman* made three convoy mis-sions before it was called back to the Charleston Navy Yard to be fitted with some special new equipment. The seven-month-old vessel was converted to a floating power station, removing its 40-mm guns on the boat deck and install-ing reels of electrical power cables and a large electrical transformer. Although other ships have provided power to shore operations, this is believed to be the first to be specifically converted for that mission. Conversion complete, the *Wiseman* was on its way in January back to the Pacific, where it was destined to make some history providing electrical power in April to Manila, left in ruins by the Japanese.[29]

Sailing into Manila Bay, still under siege, the *Wiseman*'s fire controlman, George R. Dawson, said they observed the hulks of more than one hundred sunken ships, with Japanese soldiers hiding in some of them. "We waited about one week and sneaked into what was left of Pier 1, Manila," Dawson recalled. He said the concrete piers all were in shambles. When they went ashore, Dawson said, they were not prepared for what they found. "We found a lot of dead Japs laying around onshore and in the sunken ships. The stench was terrible, but the Army had not the time to bury them, they were busy fighting the Japs."

"We encountered quite a challenge running our electric cable from our ship to shore," Dawson recalled. "We had to keep guns with us to keep the Japs (from) destroying our cable." He said the island natives and the Army assisted sailors from the DE in laying the cables from ship to shore using kapok floats every ten feet.

"The electricity from this man-of-war reaches dry land by means of enormous cables, a thousand feet long, which are supported in the water by floatation equipment," Cedric Foster told his radio audience. "From early morning to late at night the humming generators make it possible to live in the City of Manila. The electric lights shine in Manila only because of this naval vessel. . . . These elevators run up and down in the bomb-battered buildings and construction continues . . . reconstruction work . . . for the same reason."

In addition to supplying more than 5.8-million kilowatt hours of electricity to the city for more than five months, the destroyer escort also provided clean drinking water to the residents since the Japanese had smashed all of the island's water mains. Using the ship's evaporators, the DE supplied more than 150,000 gallons of fresh drinking water to Army facilities and the harbor area.

Although this was not direct combat duty, it was a definite challenge for the men on board the *Wiseman* to stay safely docked, supplying power and water to the bombed-out city when Japanese soldiers still prowled the area. The Japanese presence threatened not only the laying of the cable but also its continued operation. Dawson said two Japanese disguised as Filipinos were discovered working on the cable, attempting to destroy the Army's stepdown shore transformers. Armed guards were posted to continually patrol the perimeter of the ship.

"We had a pretty tough time laying the cable in the water with floats and lights," Frank Frazitta, the *Wiseman*'s electrician's mate, wrote in the diary he kept while on board ship. "Many times I was in the dirty water helping out. They also have a guard with a gun watching the cable leading to the pole." But sailors on board the DE did have some time for a little entertainment. "We also have been lucky, we get 2 cans of beer every other night before the movies," Frazitta wrote.

Sailors enjoyed movies shown on a makeshift screen set up on the bombed-out dock alongside the ship. "They are first run pictures which you see back home," Cedric Foster told his radio listeners. "They are a powerful link between those who fight the war against Japan out here in the Philippine Islands . . . a powerful link between these men and their loved ones in every state of the union."

"This is Cedric Foster speaking to you transcribed from Manila. I now return you to Boston."[30]

EPILOGUE

Gray Ghost from the Past

The rusty old warship, like a gray ghost from another era, slowly made its way north on New York's Hudson River in October 1997. The USS *Slater*, its engines now silent, once faced down Hitler's U-boats and Japan's dreaded kamikazes, but today it was being towed like a damaged old war relic to a place far from the Atlantic and Pacific, where it had so valiantly served her nation.

But this was not the end of the USS *Slater*. In fact, it was the beginning of a third chapter in the destroyer escort's remarkable life. Built in only ninety days at the height of World War II, it was about to be reborn, not as the fighting warship it once was but as a floating museum—a legacy that forever would remind Americans of the sacrifices made by so few on behalf of so many, as Winston Churchill observed. People from small towns and villages lined the shores of the Hudson River, waving and cheering as they witnessed history in the making. After all, it is not every day an American warship travels through the upper Hudson River.

When the ship arrived in Albany, the city's mayor, Gerald D. Jennings, was on hand to greet it. But he was not alone. Hundreds of veterans, state and local officials, and scores of residents from all around the capital gathered at the Port of Albany to welcome the American warship. With flags flying and uniformed sailors manning the port rail, the ship neared the dock as the band struck up "Anchors Aweigh" and "Semper Paratus." The USS *Slater*, the last World War II destroyer escort still afloat in the United States, had found a new home.

But the ship's trip had not been an easy one. In fact, the voyage to Albany had begun far from New York City, where the *Slater* had been temporarily docked at the Intrepid Sea-Air-Space Museum on the Hudson River at Forty-sixth Street. The long journey began in Greece, where the vessel had been transferred following World War II under terms of President Truman's Mutual Defense and Assistance Program. From 1951 until it was decommissioned in 1991, the *Slater*, renamed the *Aetos* by the Greeks, served with honor and distinction in the Greek navy. Now it faced the scrap heap.

The United States built 563 destroyer escorts in World War II. By the time the Greeks decided to scrap *Slater*, most of the trim but deadly little warships were long gone. But there was hope the *Slater* might survive—at least in the hearts of destroyer escort veterans around the country. The Destroyer Escort Sailors Association, a group of DE veterans assisted by historian Martin Davis, who served as a pharmacist's mate on board the USS *Pettit*, opened negotiations with Greece to see if the DE could be returned to the United States.

Those negotiations proved fruitful. If the DE sailors wanted the rusty old ship, the Greeks said, they could have her, provided they paid to have her towed from the Isle of Crete to the United States. So the aging veterans went right to work and raised $275,000 to pay for a Finnish-built towboat with a Ukranian crew to bring the *Slater* home. They raised the money within a few months, with contributions coming from Navy and Coast Guard veterans who had served on board the "speedy and dangerous" ships, as President Roosevelt called them. The Destroyer Escort Historical Foundation was formed and received title to the ship.

"Operation Homeport USA" was a success, the USS *Slater*, a bit worse for the wear, arriving at the museum in New York City. "Seeing this relic of World War II coming up the Hudson was a dream come true," declared emotional foundation president Sam Saylor, who had served as a gunner's mate on board the USS *Connolly*. Misty-eyed DE veterans, now in the twilight of their lives, watched in awe as the ship took her berth in New York City. Now the real work to restore the vessel would begin.

As restoration was under way, the Intrepid Sea-Air-Space Museum decided it no longer could accommodate the *Slater*, so once again the DE sailors had to look for a new home. This time they looked north—in fact, all the way to New York state's capital city. But would Albany want this rusty old war relic along its waterfront, a waterfront that Jennings, the city's new mayor, was trying to revitalize? Much to their delight, Mayor Jennings, a former high

Lt. Harold Poulson on board the USS *Slater* somewhere in the North Atlantic. Poulson served as executive officer on board the DE. Speaking about his teenage crew, Poulson said, "We gave them a job. They did their job and didn't ask any questions. They were pretty adaptable." *Courtesy the Destroyer Escort Historical Museum*

school history teacher, jumped at the opportunity and agreed to make his city the *Slater*'s permanent new home.

Gazing at the vessel with its peeling paint and silent engines as it was towed to the Port of Albany, Mayor Jennings must have wondered for a moment whether he had made the right decision. But once he saw the excited reaction of the World War II veterans assembled to greet the *Slater*, the mayor knew his decision had been correct. And thousands and thousands of visitors who tour the warship—now fully restored to its original wartime configuration and listed on the National Register of Historic Places—agree.

Teams of volunteers, many World War II veterans who served on board DEs, began the restoration process. Led by acclaimed ship restoration expert Tim Rizzuto, they went to work and transformed the vessel into one of the most visited attractions along Albany's revitalized waterfront. More than 15,000 visitors walk the decks and peer into the compartments of the World War II ship every year, experiencing the thrill of learning just what it was like to live, eat, sleep, and fight on board these tiny warships.

The story of the *Slater*, though, is more than a story about a ship. It is a remarkable tale about the resolve of World War II veterans, a generation of Americans whose determination and courage helped the Allies achieve victory in the greatest conflict this world has ever seen. These same men, determined to leave a permanent monument to their sacrifices, once again defied the odds, saving a ship from the scrap heap, raising enough funds to bring it home, and then transforming it into a living legacy so Americans will never forget.

As Harold Poulson, executive officer of the *Slater*, observed in speaking about his 1945 teenage crew, "We gave them a job. They did their job and didn't ask any questions. They were pretty adaptable." Today, although they may be older and a little grayer, it doesn't sound like these resolute sailors have really changed much over the years.

APPENDIX I

Destroyer Escorts Lost during World War II

The following destroyer escorts were lost or damaged beyond repair. Those damaged but returned to service are not listed. *Source:* Destroyer Escort Sailors Association.

USS *Bates*	Kamikaze attack
USS *Donnell*	U-boat attack
USS *England*	Kamikaze attack
USS *Eversole*	Japanese submarine attack
USS *Fechteler*	U-boat attack
USS *Fiske*	U-boat attack
USS *Frederick C. Davis*	U-boat attack
USS *Holder*	German air attack
USS *Leopold*	U-boat attack
USS *Oberrender*	Kamikaze attack
USS *Rich*	Struck mine
USS *Roche*	Struck mine
USS *Samuel B. Roberts*	Japanese warships attack
USS *Shelton*	Japanese submarine attack
USS *Solar*	Damaged by explosion while unloading ammunition
USS *Underhill*	Japanese suicide submarine attack

APPENDIX II

Shipyards in which Destroyer Escorts were Built

The 563 destroyer escorts in World War II were constructed in seventeen shipyards, both public and private, located throughout the United States. Under FDR's Lend-Lease program, 78 were transferred to England, 6 to the Free French, and 8 to Brazil. *Source:* Destroyer Escort Sailors Association.

Bethlehem Steel Shipyard, Hingham, MA
Boston Navy Yard, Boston, MA
Bethlehem Steel Shipyard, Quincy, MA
Bethlehem Steel Shipyard, San Francisco, CA
Brown Shipbuilding, Houston, TX
Charleston Navy Yard, Charleston, SC
Consolidated Shipyard, Orange, TX
Defoe Shipyard, Bay City, MI
Dravo Shipyard, Pittsburgh, PA
Dravo Shipyard, Wilmington, DE
Federal Shipbuilding, Newark, NJ
Mare Island Navy Yard, Vallejo, CA
Norfolk Navy Yard, Norfolk VA
Philadelphia Navy Yard, Philadelphia PA
Puget Sound Navy Yard, Bremerton, WA
Tampa Shipbuilding, Tampa, FL
Western Pipe and Steel, San Pedro, CA

APPENDIX III

Destroyer Escorts Manned by The United States Coast Guard

O f the 563 destroyer escorts in World War II, 30 were manned by the United States Coast Guard, although they were officially listed as United State Navy ships. The first destroyer escort sunk by enemy action was the Coast Guard–manned USS *Leopold* in March 1944. *Source:* Destroyer Escort Sailors Association.

USS *Poole*

USS *Peterson*

USS *Marchand*

USS *Hurst*

USS *Camp*

USS *Howard D. Crow*

USS *Pettit*

USS *Ricketts*

USS *Sellstrom*

USS *Harveson*

USS *Joyce*

USS *Kirkpatrick*

USS *Leopold*

USS Menges

USS *Mosley*

USS *Newell*

USS *Pride*

USS *Falgout*

USS *Lowe*

USS *Ramsden*

USS *Mills*

USS *Rhodes*

USS *Richey*

USS *Savage*

USS *Vance*

USS *Lansing*

USS *Durant*

USS *Calcaterra*

USS *Chambers*

USS *Merrill*

NOTES

Chapter 1. Like Lambs to the Slaughter

1. Walter L. Roberge Jr., interview with the author, 29 February 2004; James Graham, interview with the author.
2. Terry Thomas, interview with the author; Terry Thomas, *Everybody Has a Story: This Is Mine* (Linden, Mich.: Leader Printing, 2006), 55–56.
3. Lee Kennett, *GI: The American Soldier in World War II* (New York: Charles Scribner's Sons, 1987), 19–20; Lt. T. A. Larson, *History of the U.S. Naval Training Center, Great Lakes, Illinois in World War II* (Washington, D.C.: U.S. Navy Department, 1945), 163–64. Standards for military service were stringent, and the Navy was always more selective than the other armed services in choosing recruits. Critics complained that the Navy tried to skim the best, leaving the remainder to be drafted into the Army. As manpower needs escalated, the Navy became less selective and, eventually, drew its manpower from the Selective Service system, although still maintaining a more selective process. A so-called prosthetic regiment was established in June 1943 at the Great Lakes Training Center in Illinois. Incoming recruits requiring dental prosthesis were segregated in the 31st Regiment, where training was longer to allow for completion of dental work.
4. Samuel I. Rosenman, *Public Papers and Addresses of Franklin D. Roosevelt, 1940* (New York: Macmillan, 1941), 428–31; Kennett, *GI*, 4. In Kennett's excellent account of the American soldier in World War II, the author notes that by the end of the war, the Selective Service had recorded the names of 50 million American males, between the ages of eighteen and sixty-four, feeding 11 million into the armed forces.
5. William Riemer, interview with the author.
6. John "Bo" Keally, interview with the author.
7. Lee Kinnett, *G.I.: The American Soldier in World War II* (New York: Charles Scribner's Sons, 1987), 19.

8. Ibid., 20; "Veterans of the Navy's V-12 Program," U.S. Navy Memorial, http://newsite.navymemorial.org/v12history.php/.

9. Donald Kruse, interview with the author.

10. Ernest J. King, *U.S. Navy at War, 1941–1945* (Washington, D.C.: U.S. Navy Department, 1946), 25; New York State Military Museum Web site, http://www.dmna.state.ny.us/historic/mil-his/.

11. Charles M. Hatcher, "Great Lakes Today: The Expansion of a Training Base in Wartime," *Our Navy*, mid-October 1943, 16–17.

12. Larson, *History of the U.S. Naval Training Center*, 1.

13. Committee of Friends of the Navy, *Gates to Glory: An Illustrated History of the U.S. Naval Training Center* (Zion, Ill.: Committee of Friends of the Navy, 1996), 15.

14. Ibid., 25; Richard Lara, "Great Lakes, the Golden Thirteen, and the Two Ocean War," 3, Commander Navy Installations Command, https://www.cnic.navy.mil/greatlakes/.

15. Committee of Friends of the Navy, *Gates to Glory*, 3; *The Navy in the Heartland: The Great Lakes Story* (Great Lakes, Ill.: Great Lakes Naval Museum Foundation, 1991), 28.

16. Larson, *History of the U.S. Naval Training Center*, 29.

17. Ibid., 33; Martin Davis, *Traditions and Tales of the U.S. Navy* (Missoula, Mont.: Pictorial Histories, 2001), 11. The term "boot" originated during the Spanish-American War when recruits wore canvas leggings called boots. Once their training was complete, they could remove the canvas leggings and be full-fledged apprentice seamen.

18. Robert Holman, interview with the author.

19. Manuel Maroukis, oral history, 19 November 2002, Guggenheim Memorial Library, Monmouth University, West Long Branch, N.J.

20. Leonard Bulwicz, oral history, 12 November 2002, Guggenheim Memorial Library, Monmouth University, West Long Branch, N.J.

21. Larson, *History of the U.S. Naval Training Center*, 33; Lara, "Great Lakes," 3.

22. Larson, *History of the U.S. Naval Training Center*, 35–36.

23. Committee of Friends of the Navy, *Gates to Glory*, 26; Larson, *History of the U.S. Naval Training Center*, 125.

24. Committee of Friends of the Navy, *Gates to Glory*, 27.

25. *Bluejackets' Manual*, 1943 (Annapolis: United States Naval Institute, 1943), 263.

26. Lara, "Great Lakes," 3; Hatcher, "Great Lakes Today," 77.

27. Jarvis Baillargeon, interview with the author.

28. John Acer, oral history, 23 November 2002, Guggenheim Memorial Library, Monmouth University, West Long Branch, N.J.

29. Eleanor Roosevelt, "My Day" newspaper column, January–March 1948, Box 3150, Speeches and Articles File, Eleanor Roosevelt Papers, Franklin D. Roosevelt Library, Hyde Park, N.Y. (hereafter cited as FDRL).

30. Jerry Hammon, interview with the author; "Events of Interest in Shipping World," *New York Times*, 1 August 1943. Jerry Hammon realized his twin ambitions: He rose quickly through the ranks to become an executive officer and later captain of a destroyer escort. After the military, he went back to college and became a physician.
31. Martin Davis, oral history, 14 November 2002, Guggenheim Memorial Library, Monmouth University, West Long Branch, N.J.; Martin Davis, interview with the author.
32. Thomas interview.

Chapter 2. Good Luck . . . and Good Hunting
 1. Geoffrey C. Ward, *Closest Companion* (New York: Houghton Mifflin, 1995), 278–79.
 2. Samuel I. Rosenman, *Public Papers and Addresses of Franklin D. Roosevelt, 1944–1945* (New York: Harper & Brothers, 1950), 70–72; John H. Crider, "President Salutes France's Millions of 'Underground,'" *New York Times*, 13 February 1944; "Roosevelt Salute to France," *New York Times*, 13 February 1944; "President Going on Radio," *New York Times*, 11 February 1944; "Destroyer Escort Is Given to French," *New York Times*, 3 January 1944; "Algiers Plays Up Speech," *New York Times*, 14 February 1944.
 3. Destroyer Escort Sailors Association (hereafter cited as DESA), http://www.desausa.org/.
 4. Lewis M. Andrews Jr., *Tempest, Fire and Foe* (Charleston, S.C.: Narwhal Press, 1999), 1; Robert Greenhalgh Albion and Robert Howe Connery, *Forrestal and the Navy* (New York: Columbia University Press, 1962), 117; Norman Friedman, *U.S. Destroyers: An Illustrated Design History* (Annapolis: Naval Institute Press, 1982), 141.
 5. J. Armand Burgun, interview with the author; Joseph Alexander, correspondence with the author; Jim Larner, correspondence with the author, in the possession of Jim Larner; Jim Larner, "All in a Day," personal war diary, 1944.
 6. Robert Abraham and Lucas Bobbitt, "When Ships Go Down: The Loss of the Leopold," *Sea Classics*, July 2002, 15.
 7. Andrews, *Tempest, Fire and Foe*, 27–31.
 8. Burgun interview.
 9. Abraham and Bobbitt, "When Ships Go Down," 16; Andrews, *Tempest, Fire and Foe*, 27.
10. Andrews, *Tempest, Fire and Foe*, 28–30.
11. Burgun interview.
12. Thomas interview; Thomas, *Everybody Has a Story;* Daniel Farley, interview with the author; Andrews, *Tempest, Fire and Foe*, 43.

13. Edmond J. Anuszczyk, "Task Force 65 Escort Convoy UGS 37," n.p., Destroyer Escort Historical Museum, Albany, N.Y. (hereafter cited as DEHM); Naval History Division, Department of the Navy, *Dictionary of American Naval Fighting Ships*, vol. 3 (Washington, D.C.: U.S. Government Printing Office, 1977) (hereafter cited as *DANFS* 3), 334; biography of the USS *Hissem*, prepared by ship's quartermaster, DEHM; Charles Berry Grunewald, "The USS Holder, My Point of View," 1990, unpublished personal recollection, courtesy Destroyer Escort Historical Museum; Joseph Carinci, correspondence with the author.

14. Clay Blair, *Hitler's U-boat War: The Hunted, 1942–45* (New York: Modern Library, 2000), 522–23; Samuel Eliot Morison, *The Atlantic Battle Won: May 1943–May 1945*, vol. 10 of *History of United States Naval Operations in World War II*, by Samuel Eliot Morison (Edison, N.J.: Castle Books, 2001), 256–57; Naval History Division, Department of the Navy, *Dictionary of American Naval Fighting Ships*, vol. 4 (Washington, D.C.: U.S. Government Printing Office, 1969), 323; Robert McMichael, correspondence with Victor Buck, 19 August 1999, DEHM; New York Navy Yard shipworker, "*Menges-Holder* Kill," 19 June 1945, 4, DEHM. Despite a third of its stern being blown away, the USS *Menges* lived to fight another day. Towed to the New York Navy Yard, it joined the USS *Holder*, which had been torpedoed by a German bomber. In one of the more unusual repair jobs in naval history, the Navy decided that one complete destroyer escort could be salvaged from the two wrecked vessels. It was decided to weld the 94-foot section of the stern of *Holder* onto the forward section of the *Menges*. The Coast Guard crew nicknamed the new ship *Mender*, a tribute to the repair crews at the naval yard. In March 1944 *Menges*, as part of a hunter-killer group, assisted the USS *Lowe* (DE-325) in sinking *U-866* about one hundred miles east of Halifax.

15. Blair, *Hitler's U-boat War: The Hunted*; Naval History Division, Department of the Navy, *Dictionary of American Naval Fighting Ships*, vol. 4.

16. Daniel Sileo, interview with the author; Naval History Division, Department of the Navy, *Dictionary of American Naval Fighting Ships*, vol. 2 (Washington, D.C.: U.S. Government Printing Office, 1977), 288–89; Blair, *Hitler's U-boat War: The Hunted*, 510; Bruce Hampton Franklin, *The Buckley-Class Escorts* (Annapolis: Naval Institute Press, 1999), 102; Andrews, *Tempest, Fire and Foe*, 25–26. Franklin notes that six other DEs—four American and two British— later served as permanent power supply ships: DE-59, DE-634, DE-667, DE-669, and British ships DE-563 and DE-574.

17. Howard R. Bender, correspondence with Victor Buck, 12 April 2002, DEHM; Blair, *Hitler's U-boat War: The Hunted*, 525; Burton Kyle, correspondence with Victor Buck, 17 May 2002, DEHM; Action Report, USS *Fechteler*, 12 May 1944, Office of Naval Records and Library, National Archives and Records Administration, College Park, Md.

18. William Quackenbush, correspondence with Victor Buck, 8 and 10 May 2002, DEHM.
19. "Coffee Mugs Help in U-boat Sinking," *New York Times*, 30 May 1945; E. J. Kahn Jr., "Hand to Hand," *New Yorker*, 8 February 1988, 73; Blair, *Hitler's U-boat War: The Hunted*, 546; Morison, *Atlantic Battle Won*, 284–85. *U-188*, the "milk cow," actually was close enough to witness the gun flashes and beat a hasty retreat, returning to Bordeaux.
20. Kahn, "Hand to Hand," 73.
21. Ibid., 74.
22. Blair, *Hitler's U-boat War: The Hunted*, 548; Kahn, "Hand to Hand," 74; *New York Times*, 30 May 1945. After repairs and a refresher training course at Casco Bay, Maine, in July 1944, the *Buckley* escorted two convoys to North Africa. Later it performed antisubmarine and convoy duty along the eastern coast and in the North Atlantic. In April 1945 the *Buckley* and USS *Reuben James* (DE-153) sunk *U-548*.
23. Joseph Alexander, correspondence with the author; Harold Peterson, correspondence with the author.
24. Robert White, interview with the author; Action Report, USS *Fiske*, 8 August 1944, U.S. Navy, DEHM; White interview; Robert White, correspondence with Victor Buck, 21 December 2001, DEHM; Blair, *Hitler's U-boat War: The Hunted*, 595; Philip Karl Lundeberg, "American Anti-Submarine Operations in the Atlantic, May 1943–May 1945" (Ph.D. diss., Harvard University, 1963), 389.
25. Leo F. Stinson, correspondence to Victor Buck, 27 December 2002, DEHM.
26. Harold Newman, correspondence to Victor Buck, 9 January 2002, DEHM.
27. Capt. John Comly, Action Report, 31 August 1944, excerpt courtesy of DEHM; "Sub Sinks Ship of Phila. Officer," *Philadelphia Inquirer*, 12 August 1944, courtesy of Cdr. E. Andrew Wilde Jr.
28. George Brodie, report of sinking, *DESA News*, July 1982, DEHM; "Destroyer Escort Is Sunk in Atlantic," *New York Times*, 13 August 1944, 19; William Geiermann, correspondence with Victor Buck, 10 January 2002.
29. Morison, *Atlantic Battle Won*, 32–33; Andrews, *Tempest, Fire and Foe*, 4; Franklin, *Buckley-Class Escorts*, 6. Some historians trace the earliest origins of DEs to 1939, when Cdr. Robert B. Carney, USN, recommended their construction based on a design prepared by Capt. E. L. Cochrane of the Bureau of Ships. Interestingly, Knox, Roosevelt's new secretary of the Navy, had been in Theodore Roosevelt's Rough Riders and was the 1936 Republican candidate for vice president, running against FDR's ticket. He was a staunch New Deal critic, calling FDR's programs "a complete flop."
30. Rosenman, *Public Papers and Addresses of Franklin D. Roosevelt*, 1940, 375–90;

Harold G. Bowen, *Ships, Machinery and Mossbacks* (Princeton, N.J.: Princeton University Press, 1954), 59.

31. Morison, *Atlantic Battle Won*, 32–33; "Two Swedish Ships Victims of U-boats," *New York Times*, 4 January 1940, 4; "Britons Laud a German," *New York Times*, 18 February 1940, 29; John Malcolm Brinnin, *The Sway of the Grand Saloon: A Social History of the North Atlantic* (New York: Delacorte Press, 1971), 509–10; "Ship Defies U-boat," *New York Times*, 7 March 1940, 1.

32. Francis L. Loewenheim, ed., *Roosevelt and Churchill: Their Secret Wartime Correspondence* (New York: Saturday Review Press/E. P. Dutton, 1975), 122–26.

33. Robert F. Cross, *Sailor in the White House: The Seafaring Life of FDR* (Annapolis: Naval Institute Press, 2003), 134–35.

34. *Presidential Press Conferences*, 1940 (New York: DaCapo Press, 1972), Press Conf. No. 702, sec. 350–56.

35. Russell D. Buhite and David W. Levy, eds., *FDR's Fireside Chats* (New York: Penguin, 1993), 163–73.

36. Ibid.

37. Loewenheim, *Roosevelt and Churchill*, 131.

38. Frederic C. Lane, *Ships for Victory: A History of Shipbuilding under the U.S. Maritime Commission in World War II* (Baltimore: Johns Hopkins University Press, 2001), 3–10.

39. Winston Churchill, *The Hinge of Fate* (Boston: Houghton Mifflin, 1950), 376.

40. Proceedings of Conference in the White House, 23 June 1942, *Foreign Relations of the United States: The Conferences at Washington, 1941–42 and Casablanca, 1943* (Washington, D.C.: GPO, 1968), copy in FDRL.

41. Thomas Buell, *Master of Sea Power: A Biography of Fleet Admiral Ernest J. King* (Annapolis: Naval Institute Press, 1995), 285–86.

42. Theodore R. Treadwell, *Splinter Fleet: The Wooden Subchasers of World War II* (Annapolis: Naval Institute Press, 2000), 9–15; Donald Scott Carmichael, *FDR: Columnist* (Chicago: Pellegrini & Cudahy, 1947), 61–63.

43. Henry Stimson, *On Active Service in Peace and War*, vol. 2 (New York: Harper and Brothers, 1948), 508–9.

44. Samuel Eliot Morison, *Battle of the Atlantic, 1939–1943* (Edison, N.J.: Castle Books, 2001), 310; "Protection for Convoys," *New York Times*, 7 December 1942.

45. Morison, *Battle of the Atlantic*, 8–10, 25, 318.

46. Ibid., 286–89; Cross, *Sailor in the White House*, 70–71, 74–76.

47. Loewenheim, *Roosevelt and Churchill*, 196, document 110; Morison, *Battle of the Atlantic*, 288.

48. Morison, *Battle of the Atlantic*, 268–76.

49. Arthur D. Camp, "At Sea with the Picket Patrol," *Yachting*, December 1942.

50. Ibid.

51. Morison, *Battle of the Atlantic*, 273–75.
52. Wayne G. Broehl Jr., *Cargill: Trading the World's Grain* (Hanover: University Press of New England, 1992), 593–94.
53. Morison, *Battle of the Atlantic*, 290–91; Knox to FDR, 10 November 1941, FDRL; FDR to Knox, November 11, 1941, Naval Building Folder, FDRL; *Presidential Press Conferences, 1942* (New York: Harper & Brothers, 1950), 190–92.

Chapter 3. Reversing the Tide
1. Richard Warner, interview with the author, 31 January 2004; Richard Warner, correspondence with the author; Richard Warner, oral history, 17 October 1994, East Carolina Manuscript Collection, Joyner Library, East Carolina University, Greenville, N.C. While ice cream machines were not standard issue for DEs, it turns out another DE—the USS *Day*—also was outfitted with one. According to Jim Larner, the fire-control striker on board the *Day*, Capt. Kendall E. Read noticed a large crate on the dock while his ship was in Boston in September 1944. The skipper told the crew to haul the crate, which contained an ice cream machine destined for a cruiser, on board. They cut a hole through the deck above the crew's mess and lowered the machine through it. While some cruiser lost its ice cream machine, the crew on board the USS *Day*, nicknamed "Lucky Day," could not have been more pleased.
2. Robert Sherwood, *Roosevelt and Hopkins* (New York: Harper and Brothers, 1948), 684–85.
3. Herbert A. Werner, *Iron Coffins* (New York: Holt, Rinehart and Winston, 1969), xv–xvi.
4. Axel Niestle, *German U-boat Losses during World War II: Details of Destruction* (Annapolis: Naval Institute Press, 1998), 4.
5. Loewenstein, *Roosevelt and Churchill*, 262–64, 287–92.
6. Alva Johnston, "The Mysterious Mr. Gibbs," *Saturday Evening Post*, 20 January 1945.
7. Ibid.; Walter C. Bachman, *William Francis Gibbs, 1886–1967*, in National Academy of Sciences, *Biographical Memoirs*, vol. 42 (New York: Columbia University Press, 1971), 54–55; history of Gibbs & Cox, Gibbs & Cox, Inc., http://www.gibbscox.com/index.htm/.
8. Frank O. Braynard, *By Their Works Ye Shall Know Them* (Gibbs & Cox, 1968), 9–11.
9. Ibid., 12. In 1916 William Francis described his plan to build the ocean liners to Secretary of the Navy Josephus Daniels. Although it is assumed that Assistant Navy Secretary Franklin Roosevelt attended, this could not be determined because Daniels' diaries for 1914 and 1916, if they ever existed, are missing.

10. Ibid., 19–22.

11. John Maxtone-Graham, *The Only Way to Cross* (New York: Macmillan, 1974), 166–69.

12. John Malcolm Brinnin, *The Sway of the Grand Saloon* (New York: Delacorte Press, 1971), 474.

13. Braynard, *By Their Works*, 35–41; Bachman, *William Francis Gibbs*, 50.

14. Johnston, "Mysterious Mr. Gibbs," 10; Richard Austin Smith, "The Love Affair of William Francis Gibbs," *Fortune*, August 1957, 140.

15. Winthrop Sargeant, "The Best I Know How," *New Yorker*, 6 June 1964, 62–63.

16. Office of War Information, War Production Board, press release WPB-2259, 18 December 1942, Mariners' Museum Library, Christopher Newport University, Newport News, Va.

17. William Francis Gibbs to C. E. Wilson, Vice Chairman, War Production Board, 14 December 1942, William Francis Gibbs Papers, 1910–1969, MS179, Mariners' Museum Library, Christopher Newport University, Newport News, Va.

18. "The Work of Gibbs & Cox," November 1946, 1–50, report prepared by Gibbs and Cox, courtesy Gibbs and Cox; "The Big Ship" *Smithsonian*, Spring/ Summer 1990; Bowen, *Ships, Machinery and Mossbacks*, 61, 124–25.

19. Cochrane to Gibbs & Cox, telegram, 12 June 1943, Mariners' Museum, Newport News, Va.

20. Jerome C. Hunsaker, *Edward Lull Cochrane* (New York: Columbia University Press, 1961), 33–36; Bowen, *Ships, Machinery and Mossbacks*, 69.

21. *Compass Points* (Gibbs and Cox newsletter) 5, no. 6 (June 1947): 5–12; Johnston, "Mysterious Mr. Gibbs," 20.

22. "Events of Interest in Shipping World," *New York Times*, 1 August 1943.

23. Braynard, *By Their Works*, 101; "Events of Interest in the Shipping World," *New York Times*, 1 August 1943.

24. Braynard, *By Their Works*, 101–2; "Warship Is Launched 8-1/2 Days after Start," *New York Times*, 2 September 1943.

25. "Work of Gibbs & Cox," 2–13.

26. Albion and Connery, *Forrestal and the Navy*, 117–19; "Work of Gibbs & Cox"; Robert P. Post, "Setback in Battle of the Atlantic Seen in Rise in Sinkings off US," *New York Times*, 7 February 1942, 3; Ashley Halsey Jr., "Those Not-So-Little Ships—the DEs," Naval Institute *Proceedings* 69, no. 9 (September 1943): 1201–4; "Events of Interest in the Shipping World," *New York Times*, 12 September 1943.

27. "Challenge in Escorts," *Time*, 1 February 1943.

28. C. P. Trussell, "Navy Called Slow in Submarine War," *New York Times*, 22 April 1943.

29. "Knox Hits Reports on Ship Sinkings," *New York Times*, 24 April 1943; Trussell, *New York Times*.
30. "New Craft Ready to Fight U-Boats," *New York Times*, 6 March 1943, 1.
31. "Forrestal Asserts U-boat Toll Indicates End of Menace Is Near," *New York Times*, 30 May 1943, 1; "Promises New Peak in Curbing U-boats," *New York Times*, 7 November 1943.
32. Albion and Connery, *Forrestal and the Navy*, 117–19.

Chapter 4. Away All Boarding Parties
1. Daniel A. Gallery, *U-505* (New York: Paperback Library, 1967), 261–65.
2. Daniel A. Gallery, "We Captured a German Sub," *Saturday Evening Post*, 4 August 1945, 9; Wayne Pickels, interview with the author, 14 April 2007. Philip K. Lundeberg, in his 1953 dissertation "American Anti-Submarine Operations in the Battle of the Atlantic," points out that a submarine capture had been accomplished by both British and German forces earlier in the war, assisted by the cooperation of surrendering crews.
3. Gallery, *U-505*, 10.
4. Ibid.
5. Ibid., 10; Gallery, *U-505*, 263; Lundeberg, "American Anti-Submarine Operations," 351–52.
6. Pickels interview, 14 April 2007.
7. Gallery, "We Captured a German Sub," 11; Lundeberg, "American Anti-Submarine Operations," 352.
8. Pickels interview, 14 April 2007; Gallery, "We Captured a German Sub," 72; Theodore P. Savas, ed., *Hunt and Kill* (New York: Savas Beatie, 2004), 148–49. Lange's exiting before his crew is not viewed as an act of cowardlice. Standard operating procedure for a U-boat is for the skipper to leave first and assist and direct the rest of the crew to safety, according to Savas.
9. Savas, *Hunt and Kill*, 232–33; Gallery, *U-505*, 211.
10. Pickels interview, 14 April 2007.
11. Ibid. Pickels used the Monte Blanc fountain pen until the ink ran dry. He called the company office in New York City to order a replacement refill. They told him they did not have refills for such an old model. Once they found out where he obtained the pen, they offered to send him a free replacement if he would send them the one he retrieved from *U-505*. He declined their offer and instead donated the historic pen to the U-505 exhibit at the Museum of Science and Industry in Chicago.
12. Lundeberg, "American Anti-Submarine Operations," 354; Mark E. Wise and Jak Mallmann Showell, "The Role of Intelligence in the Capture of U-505," in Savas, *Hunt and Kill*, 118–19. Savas included the authors' essay, which stated that more than twelve hundred items were taken from *U-505*, including

eight hundred technical documents and navigation charts, torpedoes, codes, ciphers, manuals, ship logs, receipts, papers, and radio equipment.

13. Lundeberg, "American Anti-Submarine Operations," 353.

14. Gallery, "We Captured a German Sub," 70; Frank P. Denardo, "Capture of the U-505: A First Person Account," DEHM.

15. Gallery, "We Captured a German Sub," 70; Pickels interview, 14 April 2007.

16. Gallery, top secret order, 14 June 1944, DEHM.

17. Joseph Villanella, interview with the author. Villanella wanted to donate the swimming trunks and other memorabilia to the Destroyer Escort Historical Museum, but he says a workman stole the box containing the trunks and other historical items from his attic.

18. Arthur Overacker, interview with the author.

19. Ibid.; Savas, *Hunt and Kill*, 164, 123.

20. Robert Storrick, interview with the author.

21. Ibid.

22. Gallery, *U-505*, 232.

23. Ibid., 234–35; Timothy P. Mulligan, *Lone Wolf* (Westport, Conn.: Praeger, 1993), 196.

24. Villanella interview.

25. Roger Cozens, interview with the author; Mulligan, *Lone Wolf*, 199–201. Werner Henke was imprisoned at Fort Hunter about seventeen miles south of Washington, D.C., where U-boat prisoners were interrogated. On the evening of 15 June 1944 he was shot and killed while trying to escape over the barbed-wire fence.

26. Pickels interview, 14 April 2007.

27. Charlie F. Field, interview with the author; Charles F. Field, correspondence with the author; Charlie F. Field, *Captain's Talker* (N.p.: Longacre Publishing, 1999); Niestle, *German U-boat Losses*, 143–44.

28. Field interview; Blair, *Hitler's U-boat War: The Hunted*, 567–68; Action Report, USS *Thomas*, 6 July 1944.

29. Field, *Captain's Talker*, 19–20; Field interview.

30. Blair, *Hitler's U-boat War: The Hunted*, 502; Field, *Captain's Talker*, 19–20; Niestle, *German U-boat Losses*, 74, 83.

31. Blair, *Hitler's U-boat War: The Hunted*, 535–36; Field, *Captain's Talker*, 31–33.

32. Blair, *Hitler's U-boat War: The Hunted*.

33. David Graybeal, oral history, 18 November 2002, Guggenheim Memorial Library, Monmouth University, West Long Branch, N.J.; Blair, *Hitler's U-boat War: The Hunted*, 541–42.

34. Blair, *Hitler's U-boat War: The Hunted*.

35. Graybeal oral history.

36. Field interview; M. Williams Fuller, *Axis Sally* (Santa Barbara, Calif.: Para-

dise West, 2004). Fuller notes that after the war, American military officials found Mildred Gillars (Axis Sally) living in a cellar of a bombed-out building in Berlin. She was shipped home in 1948 to stand trial for treason. On 10 March 1949 she was found innocent of treason in seven of the eight counts; she was found guilty of treason on count eight, that of portraying an American soldier's mother in a broadcast drama, "Vision of the Invasion." She was sentenced to ten to thirty years in federal prison. A model prisoner at West Virginia's Alderson Federal Prison, she was paroled in 1962. (She served time with her fellow inmate, Iva Ikuko Toguri, known as Tokyo Rose.) After parole, Gillars worked for more than twenty-five years in a Catholic Convent teaching music to kindergarten children. She left at the age of seventy to finish her college education, graduating in 1973 with a degree in speech. She died at eighty-seven in Columbus, Ohio, in 1988.

37. Earl Charles White Sr. to Earl Charles White Jr., 17 March 1945 to 28 September 1945. This remarkable collection of letters was provided courtesy of Penny Ellis Shaw, granddaughter of Earl Charles White Sr. Shaw said her mother remembers that after young Charles returned home from the war in 1945, his whole body would shake whenever the town fire whistle sounded, an obvious reminder of the whistle calling him to battle stations on *Halloran*. Charles Jr. died in 1963. *DANFS* 3:217.

38. Morison, *Battle of the Atlantic*, 231–33; Grover Theis, "Subsea Snake Hunters" *Motor Boating*, April 1943, 21.

39. Edward J. Day, *An Unlikely Sailor* (Parsons, W.Va.: McClain Printing, 1990), 43. Day served on board the USS *PC-597* and then as a junior officer on board the USS *Fowler*, named for a Naval Reservist, Robert Ludlow Fowler III, who was killed during action in the South Pacific in October 1942. Later in life Day would serve as postmaster general of the United States under President John F. Kennedy and was credited with introducing the zip code to America.

40. Theodore Roscoe, *United States Destroyer Operations in World War II* (Annapolis: Naval Institute Press, 1953), 62; *Motor Boating*, 19–20.

41. "Six Day Officers Training Cruise Aboard Destroyer Escorts at SCTC-Miami for Command Group Students," January 1944, Box 306, Franklin D. Roosevelt Jr. Naval Files, FDRL.

42. Ibid.; "Change of Duty Orders," Lt. Franklin D. Roosevelt Jr., 10 April 1944, Box 306, Franklin D. Roosevelt Jr. Naval Files, FDRL.

Chapter 5. The Only Man on the Place

1. Naval History Division, Department of the Navy, *Dictionary of American Naval Fighting Ships*, vol. 6 (Washington, D.C.: U.S. Government Printing Office, 1976) (hereafter cited as *DANFS* 6), 366–68; William Wolf, *German*

Guided Missiles: Henschel HS 293 and Ruhrstahl SD 1400X "Fritz X," Military Monograph 53 (Bennington, Vt.: Merriam Press, 2006).

2. Roger Ford, *Germany's Secret Weapons in World War II* (Osceola, Wisc.: MBI, 2000), 91–93; Samuel Eliot Morison, *Sicily-Salerno-Anzio,* vol. 9 of *History of United States Naval Operations in World War II,* by Samuel Eliot Morison (Edison, N.J.: Castle Books, 2001), 283.

3. Morison, *Sicily-Salerno-Anzio;* Roscoe, *United States Destroyer Operations,* 341.

4. George Gowling, interview with the author; Frank McClatchie, interview with the author.

5. Ibid.

6. Ibid.

7. Ibid.; Riemer interview; *Trim But Deadly* (DESA newsletter) 7, no. 2, DEHM.

8. Gowling interview; Ford, *Germany's Secret Weapons,* 82; Riemer interview; "The Anzio Jam-Boree," *Trim But Deadly* 7 (2): 5, DEHM.

9. Blair, *Hitler's U-boat War: The Hunted,* xi.

10. Elmo Allen, interview with the author; Elmo Allen, correspondence with the author.

11. Allen interview; Robert G. Shanklin, "Enemies Meet After War, Amazing Encounter," unpublished personal recollection, courtesy Elmo Allen.

12. Roscoe, *United States Destroyer Operations,* 504–5; Robert C. Stern, *Battle Beneath the Waves* (Edison, N.J.: Castle Books, 2003), 146–47; Blair, *Hitler's U-boat War: The Hunted,* 531.

13. Roscoe, *United States Destroyer Operations,* 504–5; William T. Y'Blood, *Hunter-Killer* (Annapolis: Naval Institute Press, 1983), 252; Andrews, *Tempest, Fire and Foe,* 88.

14. Ernie Pyle, untitled column, courtesy of Owen Nicholson.

15. Ernie Pyle, "Switching Ships at Sea," 1945, courtesy of Owen Nicholson.

16. Ibid.; Thomas J. Cutler and Deborah W. Cutler, *Dictionary of Naval Terms* (Annapolis: Naval Institute Press, 2005), 34.

17. Owen Nicholson, interview with the author; Owen Nicholson, personal diary, provided to author courtesy of Owen Nicholson.

18. Ernie Pyle, untitled column, courtesy of Owen Nicholson. This column was one of fifteen Pyle mailed from the western Pacific in 1945 that were never published. The live-action copy during the Okinawa campaign took precedent, and consequently, these columns remained in Scripps-Howard files.

19. Ibid.; Ernie Pyle, "Swede the D-E Comedian," courtesy of Owen Nicholson; Nicholson interview. Six days following the death of President Roosevelt, Ernie Pyle was shot and killed by Japanese machine-gun fire near Okinawa. He was mourned by American military men, especially Army men. Hollywood later made a movie about the famous reporter, *Ernie Pyle's Story of G.I. Joe,* starring Burgess Meredith.

Chapter 6. Blood Frozen in My Veins

1. Lundeberg, "American Anti-Submarine Operations," 413, 431–33; Capt. Paul Just, *Vom Seeflieger*, translated, courtesy DEHM.
2. Levi Hancock, interview with the author.
3. Roy Adcock, interview with the author.
4. Ruolff F. Kip, interview with the author. Ensign Kip, along with twelve other survivors, had been recommended for a Purple Heart. Unfortunately, the recommendation never was acted upon. Kip never knew he was on the list until years later, when Lundeberg researched naval records. Lundeberg advised the Navy Department, which scheduled a private ceremony on board the USS *Intrepid* in New York City. The medal was pinned on Kip, who was wearing the same Princeton letter sweater credited with saving his life in 1945. Andrews, *Tempest, Fire and Foe*, 136–37; Roger W. Cozens, "Loss of the Davis DE-136 and Subsequent Sinking of U-546," *DESA News*, July–August 2004, DEHM.
5. Philip K. Lundeberg, interview with the author; Andrews, *Tempest, Fire and Foe*, 136; Peter Karetka, interview with the author.
6. Ibid.
7. Ibid.
8. Ira Wolfert, "The Silent, Invisible War Under the Sea," *Reader's Digest*, November 1945; Lundeberg, "American Anti-Submarine Operations," 434–37; Just, *Vom Seeflieger*.
9. Pellegrino Soriano, oral history, 3 August 2003, Guggenheim Memorial Library, Monmouth University, West Long Branch, N.J.
10. Ibid.; Morison, *Atlantic Battle Won*, 355; Robert Jackson, *Kriegsmarine* (Osceola, Wisc.: MBI, 2001), 53–54; Just, *Vom Seeflieger*.
11. Soriano oral history, 7; Blair, *Hitler's U-boat War: The Hunted*, 687; Just, *Vom Seeflieger*, 192; Pickels interview, 10 November 2007.
12. Warren Kerrigan, interview with the author.
13. Warren S. Kerrigan, *USS Frost: U-Boat Killer* (N.p.: Privately published, 2001), 19; Kerrigan interview; Stan Mosky, correspondence with author; Dennis Carpenter and Joseph Dorinson, *Anyone Here a Sailor* (Great Neck, N.Y.: Brightlights, n.d.), 31–32; Helen E. Grenga, *Movies on the Fantail* (Newnan, Ga.: Yeoman Press, 2001), 90–91; Ensign Herb Golden, USNR, "The Navy Way: A First-Hand Account on How Ships at Sea Exchange and Show Films," *New York Times*, 12 November 1944.
14. "Lt. Eddie Duchin Here in Preparation for Sea Duty," *Quincy Patriot*, 14 September 1943. Following the war, Duchin reformed his band, but he died shortly thereafter, in 1951, from leukemia.
15. Ibid., 29, 36, 37; Kerrigan interview.
16. Kerrigan, *USS Frost*, 58.

17. Kurt Bunzel, "A U-boat Goes to Sea—as the U-boat Dying Had Already Begun," personal recollection, n.d., courtesy of DEHM.

18. Ibid.

19. Ibid.

20. Frank Musumeci, interview with the author; William Creech, interview with the author.

21. Bunzel, "U-boat goes to sea."

22. Kerrigan interview; Holman interview.

23. Blair, *Hitler's U-boat War: The Hunted*, 621–22.

24. Ibid.; Kerrigan, *USS Frost*, 97–98.

25. Roscoe, *United States Destroyer Operations*, 502–4; Naval History Division, Department of the Navy, *Dictionary of American Naval Fighting Ships*, vol. 8 (Washington, D.C.: U.S. Government Printing Office, 1981), 114–16; Cdr. Robert A. Dawes Jr., *The Dragon's Breath: Hurricane at Sea* (Annapolis: Naval Institute Press, 1996); Creech interview; Keally interview.

26. Cross, *Sailor in the White House*, 185.

27. Kerrigan interview; Musumeci interview; Kerrigan, *USS Frost*, 135.

28. Blair, *Hitler's U-boat War: The Hunted*, 686; Y'Blood, *Hunter-Killer*, 260.

29. Morison, *Atlantic Battle Won*, 348–49; Richard Wallace, *DESA News*, July–August 1982; Kerrigan, *USS Frost*, 135–55.

30. Morison, *Atlantic Battle Won;* Morison; Lundeberg, "American Anti-Submarine Operations," 425–26.

31. Halsey, "Those Not-So-Little Ships," 1204; "To Alter Chapel Window: Artist Pictured Virgin Mary with Destroyer Escort in Arms," *New York Times*, 29 March 1944.

32. Halsey, "Those Not-So-Little Ships," 1203.

33. Andrews, *Tempest, Fire and Foe*, 3–4.

34. Graybeal oral history.

35. Davis oral history.

36. John Lampe oral history, 16 November 2002, Guggenheim Memorial Library, Monmouth University, West Long Branch, N.J.

37. Ibid.; Arthur C. Fleischman Sr., interview with the author; Robert N. Bavier Jr., USNR, "North Atlantic Storm," *Yachting*, August 1944.

38. Charles Lovett, oral history, 21 November 2002, Guggenheim Memorial Library, Monmouth University, West Long Branch, N.J.

39. McClatchie interview; Kenneth H. Hannan, interview with the author; Blair, *Hitler's U-boat War: The Hunted*, 690.

40. McClatchie interview.

Chapter 7. Off the Shores of New Jersey

1. Muth interview; Muth correspondence.

2. Blair, *Hitler's U-boat War: The Hunted*, 651–53; Harold Moyers, "The Sinking of the *U-869*," U.S. Coast Guard, http://www.uscg.mil/history/webcutters/U869_Crow_Koiner.asp/.

3. Howard Denson, interview with the author.

4. Muth interview.

5. Ibid.

6. Log Book, USS *Crow*, 1 February 1945–28 February 1945; I. George King, interview with the author.

7. "Sole Survivor," transcript of *Nova* interview with Herbert Guschewski, PBS, June 1999; Robert Kurson, *Shadow Divers* (New York: Random House, 2004), 232.

8. Moyers, "Sinking of the *U-869*."

9. Robert Quigley, interview with the author.

10. Theodore Sieviec, interview with the author.

11. Axel Niestle to author, e-mail, "Re-assessment of German U-boat Losses in World War II: The Loss of U-869," 9 March 2007.

12. Ibid.

13. Quigley interview.

14. Ernest Hughes, interview with the author.

15. Ibid.; John Boy, interview with the author.

16. Hughes interview.

17. Norman C. Taylor, interview with the author.

18. Ibid.; Robert Hoenshel, interview with the author; "54 Men Are Lost," *New York Times*, 19 April 1944.

19. William C. Stanback, interview with the author; Blair, *Hitler's U-boat War: The Hunted*, 560–61.

20. Ibid.

21. Stanback interview.

22. Milton Stein, interview with the author; Milton Stein, correspondence with the author.

23. Stein correspondence.

24. Ibid.

25. *DANFS* 6:93–94.

26. Tom Eddy, personal diary, USS *Bates*, courtesy of DEHM; "Naval Officers Here Tell of Invasion," *World-Telegram*, 2 August 1944; King, *U.S. Navy at War*, 137–40; Samuel Eliot Morison, *The Invasion of France and Germany, 1944–45*, vol. 11 of *History of United States Naval Operations in World War II*, by Samuel Eliot Morison (Edison, N.J.: Castle Books, 2001), 170.

27. "Invasion Service of DEs Described," *New York Times*, 3 August 1944.

28. Edwin B. Black, *The Last Voyage of the USS Rich* (Pembroke, N.C.: WFC Press, 1996), 85.

29. Ibid., 80–81.

30. Ibid., 93–96.

31. Morison, *Invasion of France and Germany, 1944–45*, 173; Ford, *Germany's Secret Weapons*, 131; Sonke Neitzel, "The Deployment of the U-boats," in *The Battle of the Atlantic, 1939-1945*, ed. Stephen Howarth and Derek Law, 276 (Annapolis: Naval Institute Press, 1994).

32. Clay Blair, *Hitler's U-boat War: The Hunters, 1939–1942* (New York: Modern Library, 2000), 121–26.

33. Ibid., 127; Winston Churchill, *The Gathering Storm* (Boston: Houghton Mifflin, 1948), 506.

34. Blair, *Hitler's U-boat War: The Hunters*, 128.

35. James Mitchell, interview with the author.

36. Ibid.; *DANFS* 6:136.

37. "14 Dead in 2 U-boat Sinkings Off East Coast as V-E Neared," *New York Times*, 10 May 1945; "The Last German U-boat to Sink an American Ship in World War II Was Herself Sent to the Bottom," *World War II*, February 1999, 20; Adam Lynch, "Kill and Be Killed? The U-853 Mystery," *Naval History* 22, no. 3 (June 2008): 39–40.

38. William Tobin, interview with the author.

39. "200 Depth Charges Beat a Davey Jones Dirge for Last U-boat Bagged off East Coast," *New York Times*, 15 May 1945; Tobin interview; Roscoe, *United States Destroyer Operations*, 514.

40. Carl Barth, interview with the author; Tobin interview. Franz Krones was sent to Camp Edwards, Massachusetts, and later released back to Germany. Finding his home destroyed and family displaced, he finally located his mother and moved to Otzberg, where he worked on a farm. He married in 1951, and he and his wife have a son, daughter, and four grandchildren. Krones later worked as a civil servant for the German Federal Armed Forces.

41. Lewis Iselin interview, 10 April 1969, 11, Archives of American Art, Smithsonian Institution, Washington, D.C. After the war, Iselin went on to become a prominent sculptor of portraits and other figurative works. Among his best known works were *Face of Our Time*, four faces cast in bronze at Midland's Mutual Life Insurance Company in Columbus, Ohio, and *Memory*, a draped marble figure of a widow created as a World War II memorial for the United States Military Cemetery in Suresnes, France. Barth interview.

42. Tobin interview.

43. Ibid.

Chapter 8. Sailors in the Shadows

1. Rackham Holt, *Mary McLeod Bethune: A Biography* (Garden City, N.Y.: Doubleday, 1964), 190–91.

2. Ibid., 193; Pickels interview, 10 November 2007. Mary McLeon Bethune first met Eleanor and Sara Roosevelt at a luncheon for the National Council of Women of the U.S.A. Eleanor Roosevelt hosted in her New York City home. Bethune was the only black among the thirty-five guests. Sara Roosevelt noticed the apprehensive glances from southern women as Bethune was ushered to the table. Sara quickly took the arm of Bethune and seated her in a place of honor, immediately to the right of Eleanor, which delighted the black servants in the Roosevelt household. Bethune and the Roosevelt women became instant friends.
3. Holt, *Mary McLeod Bethune*, 194–95.
4. Walter White, *A Man Called White* (New York: Viking Press, 1948), 190–91; Jervis Anderson, *A. Philip Randolph: A Biographical Portrait* (New York: Harcourt Brace Jovanovich, 1973), 255.
5. White, *Man Called White*, 191; Eric Purdon, *Black Company: The Story of Subchaser 1264* (Annapolis: Naval Institute Press, 1972), 13.
6. White, *Man Called White*, 191; Samuel I. Rosenman, *Public Papers and Addresses of Franklin D. Roosevelt*, 1941 (New York: Harper & Brothers, 1950), 233–37; Anderson, *A. Philip Randolph*, 241–42; "President Orders an Even Break for Minorities in Defense Jobs," *New York Times*, 26 June 1941.
7. Samuel I. Rosenman, *Public Papers and Addresses of Franklin D. Roosevelt*, 1942 (New York: Harper and Brothers, 1950), 39.
8. Gerald Astor, *The Right to Fight: A History of African Americans in the Military* (Cambridge, Mass.: DaCapo Press, 1998), 143–44; "Ready for Good Will Trip," *New York Times*, 8 November 1934.
9. Astor, *Right to Fight*, 144. Interior Secretary Harold Ickes indicated that FDR was in favor of allowing African Americans to train as pilots. "Air Corps to Form Negro Squadron," *New York Times*, 17 January 1941; "Army Calls Negro Fliers," *New York Times*, 22 March 1941.
10. Astor, *Right to Fight*, 160; Purdon, *Black Company*, 18.
11. Ibid.
12. Carmichael, *FDR*, 103–5.
13. Ibid. FDR is credited with bringing blacks into the government for the first time in history, and gathered informally as the president's "black cabinet." FDR also appointed the first black federal judge and named several blacks to the various federal agencies and departments.
14. Harold Ickes, *The Lowering Clouds: The Secret Diary of Harold L. Ickes* (New York: Simon and Schuster, 1954), 323; David Kennedy, *Freedom from Fear: The American People in Depression and War, 1929–1945* (New York: Oxford University Press, 1999), 765; Dennis Nelson, *The Integration of the Negro into the U.S. Navy* (New York: Farrar, Straus and Young, 1951), 11; Richard E. Miller, *The Messman Chronicles* (Annapolis: Naval Institute Press, 2004), 6.

15. Ickes, *Lowering Clouds*; Kennedy, *Freedom from Fear*, 768–71.

16. B. Joyce Ross, "Mary McLeod Bethune and the National Youth Administration: A Case Study of Power Relationships in the Black Cabinet of Franklin D. Roosevelt," *Journal of Negro History*, January 1975, 1.

17. Benjamin Garrison, interview with the author; Mary Pat Kelley, *Proudly We Served: The Men of the USS Mason* (Annapolis: Naval Institute Press, 1999), 17–18.

18. Graham interview. The Navy later opened a second training facility for blacks at the Hampton Institute in Virginia.

19. Adolph W. Newton, *Better than Good: A Black Sailor's War, 1943–1945* (Annapolis: Naval Institute Press, 1999), 14–17.

20. Ibid.

21. Ibid.

22. Graham interview.

23. Larson, *History of the U.S. Naval Training Center*, 262.

24. Ibid., 263–64; Nelson, *Integration of the Negro*, 28, 31.

25. Nelson, *Integration of the Negro*, 39, 42, 43.

26. Ibid., 45–46.

27. Graham interview; Ward, *Closest Companion*, 175–76.

28. Ward, *Closest Companion*, 176.

29. Thomas Howard, interview with the author. A smaller warship, a sub chaser, the *PC-1264*, also was manned by a mostly black crew and patrolled coastal waters.

30. Garrison interview.

31. Ibid.

32. "New Navy Crew Mostly Negroes," *New York Times*, 21 March 1944.

33. "First Negro-Manned Naval Vessel Is Commissioned," *Norfolk Journal and Guide*, 25 March 1944.

34. Mary Pat Kelly, *Proudly We Served: The Men of the USS Mason* (Annapolis: Naval Institute Press, 1999), 56–57.

35. Ibid., 64.

36. Graham interview.

37. Mansel G. Blackford, ed., *On Board the USS Mason: The World War II Diary of James A. Dunn* (Columbus: Ohio State University Press, 1996), 7.

38. Thomas W. Young, "War Goods Delivered on USS Mason's First Combat Assignment," *Norfolk Journal and Guide*, 1944.

39. Allen interview.

40. Charles Dana Gibson, *Ordeal of Convoy N.Y. 119* (Camden, Maine: Ensign Press, 1992); Capt. Russ V. Bradley, "USS Edgar G. Chase, Convoy NY 119," DEHM.

41. National Weather Service, Eastern Region Headquarters, http://www.erh.noaa.gov/akq/Hur40s.htm/.

42. Bradley, "USS Edgar G. Chase," 3.
43. Gibson, *Ordeal of Convoy N.Y. 119*, xxiii.
44. Bradley, "USS Edgar G. Chase," 3.
45. Ibid.
46. Ibid.; Allen interview.
47. Bradley, "USS Edgar G. Chase," 6–7.
48. Kelly, *Proudly We Served*, 100; Bradley, "USS Edgar G. Chase," 6–7.
49. Kelly, *Proudly We Served*, 115–16.
50. Blackford, *On Board the USS Mason*, 35, 46.
51. Ibid., 47.
52. Garrison interview.
53. Howard interview.
54. In 1995, the sailors on board the USS *Mason* finally received the commendation for which they were recommended in 1944. Thanks to the work of Naval Institute Press author Mary Pat Kelly, the African American sailors still living were honored by President Bill Clinton.
55. Garrison interview; Davis oral history.
56. Cassin Craig, interview with the author.
57. Thomas W. Young, "Writer Says USS *Mason* Showed White and Colored Men Mix Well in New Navy," *Norfolk Journal and Guide*, 30 September 1944.
58. Thomas W. Young, "Irish First to Treat USS *Mason* Crew Like Real Americans," *Norfolk Journal and Guide*, 14 October 1944.
59. Ibid.
60. Kelly, *Proudly We Served*, 92.

Chapter 9. Coming Right at Me

1. Richard Warner, interview with the author, 31 January 2004; Robert J. Cressman, "USS *Ulvert M. Moore* (DE-442)," *Sea Classics* 13, no. 2 (March 1980); *DANFS* 6:598–99. The USS *Stafford* returned to St. Pedro Bay, Leyte, on 16 January and went into dry dock for hull repairs. It continued antisubmarine patrols. It was decommissioned in 1947, after earning two battle stars.
2. Dale Anderson, interview with the author.
3. George Lawson, interview with the author.
4. Richard Warner, interview with the author, 31 January 2004.
5. Christopher Roosevelt, correspondence with the author; "Hewitt Decorates F. D. Roosevelt Jr.," *New York Times*, 17 November 1943.
6. Ted Barnhart, interview with the author; Robert W. Schwier, correspondence with the author; William Bell, interview with the author.
7. Barnhart interview; Warner interview, 31 January 2004; Warner correspondence, 13 January 2004.
8. Ibid.; Daniel Sutelle, interview with the author.

9. Warner interview, 31 January 2004; Warner oral history; Anderson interview; Naval History Division, Department of the Navy, *Dictionary of American Naval Fighting Ships*, vol. 5 (Washington, D.C.: U.S. Government Printing Office, 1979), 154; Samuel Eliot Morison, *The Liberation of the Philippines, 1944–45*, vol. 13 of *History of United States Naval Operations in World War II*, by Samuel Eliot Morison (Edison, N.J.: Castle Books, 2001), 101.

10. Bell interview; William Bell, correspondence with the author. Elliott joined the Army Air Corps in 1940, compiling an outstanding war record. He served as a reconnaissance pilot in the North Atlantic, North Africa, and the Mediterranean, ending the war as a brigadier general. James entered active service in the Marines in November 1940, first serving as a military observer in the Middle East and Far East. After the attack on Pearl Harbor, he chose combat duty and was awarded the Navy Cross and Silver Star.

11. Ibid.; Naval History Division, Department of the Navy, *Dictionary of American Naval Fighting Ships*, vol. 7 (Washington, D.C.: U.S. Government Printing Office, 1981), 392. Although debate remains as to the identity of the Japanese submarine sunk by *Ulvert M. Moore*, many experts believe it was *RO-115*.

12. J. Henry Doscher Jr., *Little Wolf at Leyte* (Austin, Tex.: Eakin Press, 1996), vol. 7; Larner, "All in a Day"; "4 Small U.S. Ships, Lost, Averted a Possible Philippines Disaster," *New York Times*, 15 November 1944.

13. Robert W. Copeland with Jack E. O'Neill, *The Spirit of the Sammy B* (N.p.: USS Samuel B. Roberts Survivors' Association, September 2000), 35–36.

14. Ibid.; Doscher, *Little Wolf at Leyte*, 35.

15. Copeland with O'Neill, *Spirit of the Sammy B*; Doscher, *Little Wolf at Leyte*, 40; Charles W. Touzell, interview with the author; Charles W. Touzell, correspondence with the author; Fred Graziano, interview with the author; Fred Graziano, correspondence with the author; Donald Derwoyed, interview with the author; Vern Kimmell, interview with the author; Howard W. Fortney, interview with the author; Robert L. Johnson to wife, n.d.

16. Doscher, *Little Wolf at Leyte*, 40–41.

17. Ibid., 44; Tom Stevenson, interview with the author; Jack Yusen, interview with the author; Thomas J. Cutler, *The Battle of Leyte Gulf* (New York: Harper Collins, 1994), 232.

18. Stevenson interview.

19. Ibid.

20. Doscher, *Little Wolf at Leyte*, 16, 58; Richard Rohde, interview with the author; James D. Hornfisher, *The Last Stand of the Tin Can Sailors* (New York: Bantam Books, 2004), 36.

21. Rohde interview; Stevenson interview; Yusen interview; Doscher, *Little Wolf at Leyte*, 48.

22. Glenn Huffman, interview with the author; Whitney correspondence, courtesy of DEHM.

23. Copeland with O'Neill, *Spirit of the Sammy B*, 60; David Sears, *The Last Epic Naval Battle* (New York: New American Library, 2005), 215.

24. Copeland with O'Neill, *Spirit of the Sammy B*, 62–63; Rohde interview; Huffman interview; Stevenson interview.

25. Vern Kimmell, interview with the author; Franklyn Jeff Conley, interview with the author.

26. Robert L. Johnson to wife.

27. Tomiji Koyanagi, "With Kurita in the Battle for Leyte Gulf," Naval Institute *Proceedings*, February 1953, 119–34.

28. Conley interview; Howard Fortney, interview with the author.

29. Robert L. Goggins, interview with the author; Robert L. Goggins, personal war diary provided to the author; *DANFS* 6:327; Samuel Eliot Morison, *Leyte, June 1944–January 1945*, vol. 12 of *History of United States Naval Operations in World War II*, by Samuel Eliot Morison (Edison, N.J.: Castle Books, 2001), 301.

30. Morison, *Leyte, June 1944–January 1945*, 301.

31. Albert R. Pincus, interview with the author; Albert R. Pincus, *From Brooklyn to Tokyo Bay: A Sailor's Story of WW II* (Paducah, Ky.: Turner, 2004), 35–41.

Chapter 10. Pink Streaks of Afterglow

1. Roberge interview, 29 February 2004; Walter L. Roberge Jr., *Dog Easy One Eight Six* (N.p.: Privately published, spring 1995), 83; Bob Drury and Tom Clavin, *Halsey's Typhoon* (New York: Atlantic Monthly Press, 2007), 3; Lt. Cdr. Henry L. Plage, oral history, courtesy DEHM; Roscoe, *United States Destroyer Operations*, 448.

2. R. B. Hillyer, *The Greatest Anti-Submarine Action of All Wars* (N.p.: Privately published, n.d.), 98.

3. Roberge interview, 29 February 2004.

4. Plage oral history.

5. Ibid.; Capt. C. Raymond Calhoun, *Typhoon: The Other Enemy* (Annapolis: Naval Institute Press, 1981), 110; William F. Halsey and J. Bryan III, *Admiral Halsey's Story* (New York: McGraw-Hill, 1947), 239.

6. William Fairlee correspondence, courtesy DEHM; Henry Eugene Davis, interview with the author; letter from unnamed sailor on board the USS *Melvin R. Nawman*, courtesy Robert H. Dreher.

7. Hanson W. Baldwin, "The Law of Storms," *Crowsnest*, October 1953.

8. Drury and Clavin, *Halsey's Typhoon*, 218; Calhoun, *Typhoon*, 114. Keelhauling is the ancient punishment of hauling a man from one side of the ship to the other under the bottom by means of ropes passed under the keel. Cutler, *Battle of Leyte Gulf*, 126; Halsey, "Those Not-So-Little Ships," 240.

9. Roscoe, *United States Destroyer Operations*, 450–51; Calhoun, *Typhoon*, 116.

10. Roscoe, *United States Destroyer Operations*, 450–51.

11. Davis interview; war diary, 1 January 1944, kept by commanding officer, USS *Bangust*, National Archives and Records Administration, College Park, Ms.

12. Dale P. Harper, "The Destroyer Escort England Was One of the U.S. Navy's Most Prolific Killers of Japanese Submarines during World War II," *World War II*, n.d., courtesy DEHM; A. B. Feuer, "The Killer Dillers and the Hedgehogs," *Sea Classics*, December 1988; John A. Williamson to Richard E. Warner, 22 January 1993, courtesy Richard E. Warner.

13. Andrews, *Tempest, Fire and Foe*, 164–65; Roscoe, *United States Destroyer Operations*, 410; Robert Currie, interview with the author.

14. Daniel R. Gallagher to Victor Buck, 8 December 2000, DEHM; Stanley G. Skebe to Victor Buck, 19 October 2000, DEHM; Roscoe, *United States Destroyer Operations*, 436–37; Capt. George E. Marix, Action Report, USS *Eversole*, 7 November 1944.

15. Roscoe, *United States Destroyer Operations*, 492; Owen Gault, "Sighted Subs, Sank Six," *Sea Classics*, 73.

16. Richard W. Graves, interview with the author; Richard W. Graves, *Men of Poseidon: Life at Sea aboard the USS* Rall (Nevada City, Calif.: Willow Valley Press, 2000), 70–71; William Shumate, interview with the author.

17. Kruse interview; James W. Gannon correspondence, DEHM; Rodger J. Crum correspondence, DEHM; Edward Pinkowski, "The USS Underhill," *Our Navy*, mid-December 1945, 42–43; Ens. Robert P. Cook, "The Sinking of the USS Underhill," n.d., DEHM.

18. Nathaniel G. Benchley, "Sorry, No Ice Cream," *New Yorker*, 30 May 1953, 1–3. Benchley would go on after the war to author several best-selling books, including *The Off-Islanders*, later made into a motion picture, *The Russians Are Coming, the Russians Are Coming*.

19. Charles Esch, interview with the author.

20. John Kunsak Jr., interview with the author; Graves, *Men of Poseidon*, 140–41; *DANFS* 6:22.

21. Robert D. Piper, interview with the author.

22. John P. Cosgrove, interview with the author; R. B. Paynter and John Cosgrove, *The Gendreau Story* (San Francisco: Destroyer Escort Sailors Assn., n.d.).

23. Cosgrove interview; John Virum, interview with the author; Robert D. Young, interview with the author; Robert D. Young, *From Maine to Bounding Main*, 41–45.

24. Irving Mesher, interview with the author; H. C. Finch, ed., *USS Silverstein: History and Sea Stories* (N.p.: Privately published, 2002), courtesy of Irv Mesher.

25. Roscoe, *United States Destroyer Operations*, 462.

26. Ibid.; Edward M. Docalovich, interview with the author. The USS *Melvin R. Nawman* was damaged the next day when it collided with a tank landing ship.
27. Charles R. Cox, interview with the author.
28. Edward Hinz, interview with the author. Hinz recorded his recollections in a book, *The USS* Blessman *and I* (N.p.: Xlibris, 2007).
29. *DANFS* 3:433–36; Cross, *Sailor in the White House*, 103–5; Doug Stanton, *In Harm's Way* (New York: Henry Holt, 2001), 249 and 165; Carlos R. Monarez, interview with the author.
30. George R. Dawson, personal recollections, courtesy of Frank Frazitta; Frank Frazitta, personal diary provided to the author; Cedric Foster, "As Broadcast over Yankee Network," transcript, July 1945, courtesy of Frank Frazita; *DANFS* 3:438.

BIBLIOGRAPHY

Books

Albion, Robert Greenhalgh. *Makers of Naval Policy, 1798–1947*. Edited by Rowena Reed. Annapolis: Naval Institute Press, 1980.

Albion, Robert Greenhalgh, and Robert Howe Connery. *Forrestal and the Navy*. New York: Columbia University Press, 1962.

Anderson, Jervis. *A. Philip Randolph: A Biographical Portrait*. New York: Harcourt Brace Jovanovich, 1973.

Andrews, Lewis M. *Tempest, Fire and Foe*. Charleston, S.C.: Narwhal Press, 1999.

Astor, Gerald. *The Right to Fight: A History of African Americans in the Military*. Cambridge, Mass.: DaCapo Press, 1998.

Bailey, Thomas A., and Paul B. Ryan. *Hitler vs. Roosevelt: The Undeclared Naval War*. New York: Free Press, 1979.

Baron, Scott. *They Also Served*. Spartanburg, S.C.: MIE, 1998.

Bates, F. W. *Pacific Odyssey: History of the USS Steele during WW II*. Edited by Walbrook D. Swank. Shippensburgh, Pa.: Burd Street Press, 1998.

Beyer, Kenneth M. *Q-Ships versus U-Boats: America's Secret Project*. Annapolis: Naval Institute Press, 1999.

Blackford, Mansel G., ed. *On Board the USS Mason: The World War II Diary of James A. Dunn*. Columbus: Ohio State University Press, 1996.

Blair, Clay. *Hitler's U-boat War: The Hunted, 1942–45*. New York: Modern Library, 2000.

———. *Hitler's U-boat War: The Hunters, 1939–1942*. New York: Modern Library, 2000.

Bluejackets' Manual. Annapolis: Naval Institute Press, 1943.

Boyd, Carl, and Akihiko Yoshida. *The Japanese Submarine Force and World War II*. Annapolis: Naval Institute Press, 2002.

Braynard, Frank O. *By Their Works Ye Shall Know Them*. N.p.: Privately printed by Gibbs & Cox, 1968.

Brinnin, John Malcolm. *The Sway of the Grand Saloon.* New York: Delacorte Press, 1971.

Broehl, Wayne G., Jr. *Cargill: Trading the World's Grain.* Hanover, N.H.: University Press of New England, 1992.

Buell, Thomas. *Master of Sea Power: A Biography of Fleet Admiral Ernest J. King.* Annapolis: Naval Institute Press, 1995.

Buhite, Russell D., and David W. Levy, eds. *FDR's Fireside Chats.* New York: Penguin Books, 1993.

Calhoun, C. Raymond. *The Other Enemy.* Annapolis: Naval Institute Press, 1981.

Carmichael, Donald Scott. *FDR: Columnist.* Chicago: Pellegrini & Cudahy, 1947.

Chester, Alvin P. *A Sailor's Odyssey: At Peace and at War 1935–1945.* Miami: Odysseus Books, 1991.

Churchill, Winston. *The Hinge of Fate.* Boston: Houghton Mifflin, 1950.

Collingwood, Donald. *The Captain Class Frigates in the Second World War: An Operational History of the American-Built Destroyer Escorts Serving under the White Ensign from 1943–46.* Annapolis: Naval Institute Press, 1999.

Cressman, Robert J. *The Official Chronology of the U.S. Navy in World War II.* Annapolis: Naval Institute Press, 2000.

Cross, Robert F. *Sailor in the White House: The Seafaring Life of FDR.* Annapolis: Naval Institute Press, 2003.

Cutler, Deborah W., and Thomas J. Cutler. *Dictionary of Naval Terms.* Annapolis: Naval Institute Press, 2005.

Cutler, Thomas J. *The Battle of Leyte Gulf.* New York: Harper Collins, 1994.

Davis, Martin. *Traditions and Tales of the U.S. Navy.* Missoula, Mont.: Pictorial Histories, 2001.

Dawes, Robert A., Jr. *The Dragon's Breath: Hurricane at Sea.* Annapolis: Naval Institute Press, 1996.

Day, Edward J. *An Unlikely Sailor.* Parsons, W.Va.: McClain, 1990.

Doscher, Henry J., Jr. *Little Wolf at Leyte.* Austin, Tex.: Eakin Press, 1996.

Drury, Bob, and Tom Clavin. *Halsey's Typhoon.* New York: Atlantic Monthly Press, 2007.

Farago, Ladislas. *The Tenth Fleet.* New York: Ivan Obolensky, 1962.

Finch, H. C., ed. *USS Silverstein: History and Sea Stories.* Published by the author, 2002.

Flynn, George O. *Lewis B. Hershey, Mr. Selective Service.* Chapel Hill: University of North Carolina Press, 1985.

Ford, Roger. *Germany's Secret Weapons of World War II.* Osceola, Wisc.: MBI, 2000.

Franklin, Bruce Hampton. *The Buckley-Class Escorts.* Annapolis: Naval Institute Press, 1999.

Friedman, Norman. *U.S. Destroyers: An Illustrated Design History.* Annapolis: Naval Institute Press, 1982.

Gallery, Daniel A. *U-505.* New York: Paperback Library, 1967.

Gannon, Michael. *Operation Drumbeat*. New York: Harper & Row, 1990.

Gibson, Charles Dana. *Ordeal of Convoy N.Y. 119*. Camden, Maine: Ensign Press, 1992.

Graves, Richard W. *Men of Poseidon: Life at Sea Aboard the USS Rall*. Nevada City, Calif.: Willow Valley Press, 2000.

Grenga, Helen E. *Movies on the Faintail*. Newnan, Ga.: Yeoman Press, 2001.

Hague, Arnold. *Destroyers for Great Britain*. Annapolis: Naval Institute Press, 1990.

Halsey, William F., and J. Bryan III. *Admiral Halsey's Story*. New York: McGraw-Hill, 1947.

Hickam, Homer H., Jr. *Torpedo Junction*. Annapolis: Naval Institute Press, 1989.

Hillyer, R. B. *The Greatest Anti-Submarine Action of All Wars*. N.p.: Privately published, n.d.

Holt, Rackham. *Mary McLeod Bethune: A Biography*. Garden City, N.Y.: Doubleday, 1964.

Hornfisher, James D. *The Last Stand of the Tin Can Sailors*. New York: Bantam Books, 2004.

Howarth, Stephen, and Derek Law, eds. *The Battle of the Atlantic, 1939–1945*. Annapolis: Naval Institute Press, 1994.

Hoyt, Edwin P. *U-Boats Offshore: When Hitler Struck America*. Chelsea, Mich.: Scarborough House, 1990.

Ickes, Harold. *The Lowering Clouds: The Secret Diary of Harold L. Ickes*. New York: Simon & Schuster, 1954.

Jackson, Robert. *Kriegsmarine*. Osceola, Wisc.: MBI, 2001.

Kelly, Mary Pat. *Proudly We Served: The Men of the USS Mason*. Annapolis: Naval Institute Press, 1999.

Kemp, Paul. *Convoy! Drama in Arctic Waters*. Edison, N.J.: Castle Books, 2001.

Kennedy, David. *Freedom from Fear: The American People in Depression and War, 1929–1945*. New York: Oxford University Press, 1999.

Kennett, Lee. *GI: The American Soldier in World War II*. New York: Charles Scribner's Sons, 1987.

Kerrigan, Warren S. *USS Frost: U-boat Killer*. N.p.: Privately published, 2001.

King, Ernest J. *U.S. Navy at War, 1941–1945*. Washington, D.C.: U.S. Navy Department, 1946.

Kurson, Robert. *Shadow Divers*. New York: Random House, 2004.

LaMont-Brown, Raymond. *Kamikaze: Japan's Suicide Samurai*. London: Cassell, 2000.

Land, Emory S. *Winning the War with Ships*. New York: Robert M. McBride, 1958.

Lane, Frederic C. *Ships for Victory: A History of Shipbuilding under the U.S. Maritime Commission in World War II*. Baltimore: Johns Hopkins University Press, 2001.

Larson, T. A. *History of the U.S. Naval Training Center, Great Lakes, Ill. in World War II*. Washington, D.C.: U.S. Navy Department, 1945.

Lott, Arnold S. *Brave Ship Brace Men*. Annapolis: Naval Institute Press, 1964.

Marolda, Edward J., ed. *FDR and the U.S. Navy.* London: Macmillan, 1998.

Maxtone-Graham, John. *The Only Way to Cross.* New York: Macmillan, 1974.

Miller, Richard E. *The Messman Chronicles.* Annapolis: Naval Institute Press, 2004.

Morison, Samuel Eliot. *History of United States Naval Operations in World War II.* 15 vols. Reprint ed. Edison, N.J.: Castle Books, 2001.

———. *The Two-Ocean War: A Short History of the United States Navy in the Second World War.* Boston: Little, Brown, 1963.

Mulligan, Timothy P. *Lone Wolf.* Westport, Conn.: Praeger, 1993.

Naval History Division. Department of the Navy. *Dictionary of American Naval Fighting Ships.* Vol. 2. Washington, D.C.: U.S. Government Printing Office, 1977.

———. *Dictionary of American Naval Fighting Ships.* Vol. 3. Washington, D.C.: U.S. Government Printing Office, 1977.

———. *Dictionary of American Naval Fighting Ships.* Vol. 4. Washington, D.C.: U.S. Government Printing Office, 1969.

———. *Dictionary of American Naval Fighting Ships.* Vol. 5. 1970. Reprint. Washington, D.C.: U.S. Government Printing Office, 1979.

———. *Dictionary of American Naval Fighting Ships.* Vol. 6. Washington, D.C.: U.S. Government Printing Office, 1976.

———. *Dictionary of American Naval Fighting Ships.* Vol. 7. Washington, D.C.: U.S. Government Printing Office, 1981.

———. *Dictionary of American Naval Fighting Ships.* Vol. 8. Washington, D.C.: U.S. Government Printing Office, 1981.

Nelson, Dennis. *The Integration of the Negro into the U.S. Navy.* New York: Farrar, Straus and Young, 1951.

Newton, Adolph W. Newton. *Better than Good: A Black Sailor's War, 1943–1945.* Annapolis: Naval Institute Press, 1999.

Niestle, Axel. *German U-boat Losses during World War II: Details of Destruction.* Annapolis: Naval Institute Press, 1998.

Pincus, Albert R. *From Brooklyn to Tokyo Bay: A Sailor's Story of WW II.* Paducah, Ky.: Turner, 2004.

Purdon, Eric. *Black Company: The Story of Subchaser 1264.* Annapolis: Naval Institute Press, 1972.

Rathbone, A. D., IV. *He's in the Sub-Busters Now.* New York: Robert M. McBride, 1943.

Roberge, Walter L., Jr. *Dog Easy One Eight Six.* N.p.: Privately published, spring 1995.

Robertson, Terence. *Escort Commander.* Garden City, N.Y.: Nelson Doubleday, 1979.

Rohwer, Jurgen. *Axis Submarine Successes of World War II.* Annapolis: Naval Institute Press, 1999.

Roscoe, Theodore. *United States Destroyer Operations in World War II.* Annapolis: Naval Institute Press, 1953.

Rosenman, Samuel I. *Public Papers and Addresses of Franklin D. Roosevelt.* Vols. 1–5. 1928–36. New York: Random House, 1938.

————. *Public Papers and Addresses of Franklin D. Roosevelt*. Vols. 6–9. 1937–40. New York: Macmillan, 1941.

————. *Public Papers and Addresses of Franklin D. Roosevelt*. Vols. 10–13. 1941–45. New York: Harper & Brothers, 1950.

Ross, Al. *The Destroyer Escort England*. London: Conway Maritime Press, 1985.

Runyan, Timothy J., and Jan M. Copes, eds. *To Die Gallantly: The Battle of the Atlantic*. Boulder, Colo.: Westview Press, 1994.

Savas, Theodore P., ed. *Hunt and Kill: U-505 and the U-Boat War in the Atlantic*. New York: Savas Beatie, 2004.

Sears, David. *The Last Epic Naval Battle*. New York: New American Library, 2005.

Sherwood, Robert. *Roosevelt and Hopkins*. New York: Harper and Brothers, 1948.

Simpson, B. Mitchell, III. *Admiral Harold R. Stark: Architect of Victory, 1939–1945*. Columbia: University of South Carolina Press, 1989.

Stanton, Doug. *In Harm's Way*. New York: Henry Holt, 2001.

Stern, Robert C. *Battle Beneath the Waves*. Edison, N.J.: Castle Books, 2003.

Stimson, Henry. *On Active Service in Peace and War*. Vol. 2. New York: Harper and Brothers, 1948.

Thomas, Evan. *Sea of Thunder: Four Commanders and the Last Great Naval Campaign, 1941–1945*. New York: Simon & Schuster Paperbacks, 2006.

Thomas, Terry. *Everybody Has a Story: This Is Mine*. Linden, Mich.: Leader Printing, 2006.

Treadwell, Theodore R. *Splinter Fleet: The Wooden Subchasers of World War II*. Annapolis: Naval Institute Press, 2000.

Tuttle, William M., Jr. *Daddy's Gone to War: The Second World War in the Lives of America's Children*. New York: Oxford University Press, 1993.

The U-Boat Commander's Handbook. Gettysburg, Pa.: Thomas Publications, 1989.

Walling, Michael G. *Bloodstained Sea*. Camden, Maine: International Marine, 2004.

Ward, Geoffrey C., ed. *Closest Companion*. New York: Houghton Mifflin, 1995.

Warner, Denis, and Peggy Warner with Cdr. Sadao Seno. *The Sacred Warriors*. New York: Van Nostrand Reinhold, 1982.

Werner, Herbert A. *Iron Coffins*. New York: Holt, Rinehart and Winston, 1969.

White, Walter. *A Man Called White*. New York: Viking Press, 1948.

Williamson, Gordon. *Wolf Pack: The Story of the U-boat in World War II*. University Park, Ill.: Osprey Direct, 2005.

Winton, John. *Ultra at Sea: How Breaking the Nazi Code Affected Allied Naval Strategy during World War II*. New York: William Morrow, 1988.

Y'Blood, William T. *Hunter-Killer*. Annapolis: Naval Institute Press, 1983.

Newspapers and Periodicals

DESA News
Motor Boating
Naval History

Naval Proceedings
New York Times
New Yorker
Norfolk Journal and Guide
Quincy Patriot
Reader's Digest
Saturday Evening Post
Sea Classics
Smithsonian
Time
Trim But Deadly
World-Telegram
Yachting

Personal Communication
INTERVIEWS
All interviews conducted by telephone.
Roy Adcock, USS *Frederick C. Davis*. 5 March 2005.
Elmo Allen, USS *Edgar Chase*. 12 March 2005.
Dale Anderson, USS *Ulvert M. Moore*. 13 March 2004.
Jarvis Baillargeon, USS *Rudderow*. 19 March 2005.
Ted Barnhart, USS *Seiverling*. 15 January 2007.
Carl Barth, USS *Atherton*. 18 October 2008.
William H. Bell, USS *Ulvert M. Moore*. 29 April 2007.
John Boy, USS *Holton*. 11 August 2007.
J. Armand Burgun, USS *Leopold*. 13 October 2007.
Jeff Conley, USS *John C. Butler*. 10 January 2009.
Tom Cooney, USS *Rall*. 30 March 2007.
John P. Cosgrove, USS *Gendreau*. 14 January 2007.
Charles R. Cox, USS *Bright*. 25 January 2009.
Roger Cozens, USS *Flaherty*. 14 April 2007.
Cassin Craig, USS *Mason*. 21 July 2007.
William Creech, USS *Frost*. 31 March 2007.
Robert Currie, USS *Riddle*. 12 March 2005.
Henry Eugene Davis, USS *Bangust*. 31 January 2009.
Martin Davis, USS *Pettit*. 3 February 2007.
Preston Davis, USS *Atherton*. 19 October 2008.
Howard Ken Denson, USS *Howard Crow*. 18 February 2007.
Donald Derwoyed, USS *Raymond*. 19 January 2009.
Edward M. Docalovich, USS *Edwards*. 24 January 2009.
Charles Esch, USS *Haas*. 31 January 2009.

Daniel Farley, USS *Savage*. 11 August 2007.

Charlie Field, USS *Thomas*. 5 September 2004.

Arthur Fleischmann, USS *Gantner*. 25 January 2009.

Howard W. Fortney, USS *Raymond*. 3 February 2009.

Benjamin Garrison, USS *Mason*. 21 July 2007.

Robert L. Goggins, USS *Coolbaugh*. 25 January 2009.

George W. Gowling, USS *Frederick C. Davis*. 26 February 2005.

James Graham, USS *Mason*. 13 April 2007.

Dick Graves, USS *Rall*. 30 March 2007.

Fred Graziano, USS *Dennis*. 19 January 2009.

Jerry Hammon, USS *Otter*. 28 January 2009.

Levi Hancock, USS *Frederick C. Davis*. 5 March 2005.

Kenneth Hannan, USS *Swearer*. 24 and 28 February 2004.

Edward Hinz, USS *Blessman*. 1 February 2009.

Robert Hoenshel, USS *Marchand*. 26 January 2009.

Gordon Hohne, USS *Pillsbury*. 21 April 2007.

Robert Holman, USS *Frost*. 16 March 2007.

Thomas Howard, USS *Mason*. 21 July 2007.

Ernest Glenn Huffman, USS *Samuel B. Roberts*. 2 January 2009.

Ernest Hughes, USS *Holton*. 28 July 2007.

Peter Karetka, USS *Hayter*. 1 February 2009.

John "Bo" Keally, USS *Johnnie Hutchins*. 1 August 2004.

Ellsworth Kendig, USS *Edmonds*. 4 February 2009.

Warren Kerrigan, USS *Frost*. 16 March 2007.

A. G. Kessinger, USS *Raymond*. 19 January 2009.

Vern Kimmell, USS *Raymond*. 2 January 2009.

George King, USS *Howard Crow*. 17 March 2007.

Ruolff F. Kip, USS *Frederick C. Davis*. 27 February 2005.

Donald Kruse, USS *Underhill*. 26 August 2004.

John Kunsak Jr., USS *Rall*. 30 March 2007.

George Lawson, USS *Ulvert M. Moore*. 28 February 2004.

Philip K. Lundeberg, USS *Frederick C. Davis*. 19 February 2005.

Frank McClatchie, USS *Neal A. Scott*. 6 January 2007.

Irving Mesher, USS *Silverstein*. 31 January 2009.

James Mitchell, USS *Roche*. 13 August 2007.

Carlos R. Monarez, USS *Dufilho*. 24 January 2009.

Frank Musumeci, USS *Frost*. 16 March 2007.

Harold Muth, USS *Howard Crow*. 12 March 2005.

Owen Nicholson, USS *Reynolds*. 5 April 2008.

Art Overacker, USS *Jenks*. 27 October 2007.

Wayne Pickels, USS *Pillsbury*. 14 April and 10 November 2007.

Albert Pincus, USS *Chaffee*. 28 July 2007.

Robert D. Piper, USS *O'Flaherty*. 24 January 2009.

Harold Poulson, USS *Slater*. 21 March 2004.

Robert Quigley, USS *Howard Crow*. 5 March 2007.

William Riemer, USS *Frederick C. Davis*. 21 February 2005.

Walter L. Roberge Jr., USS *Swearer*. 29 February and 31 July 2004.

Richard Rohde, USS *Samuel B. Roberts*. 1 January 2009.

William Shumate, USS *Rall*. 1 April 2007.

Theodore Sieviec, USS *Howard Crow*. 7 March 2007.

Daniel Sileo, USS *Donnell*. 29 November 2008.

William C. Stanback, USS *Gandy*. 28 April 2007.

Milton Stein, USS *Brough*. 19 March 2005.

Tom Stevenson, USS *Samuel B. Roberts*. 1 January 2009.

Robert Storrick, USS *Frost*. 31 March 2007.

Daniel Sutelle, USS *Seiverling*. 11 August 2007.

Norman Taylor, USS *Weber*. 28 July 2007.

Terry Thomas, USS *Rhodes*. 27 January 2009.

Bill Tobin, USS *Atherton*. 19 October 2009.

Charles W. Touzell, USS *Dennis*. 9 January 2009.

Phil Trusheim, USS *Pillsbury*. 21 April 2007.

Joseph Villanella, USS *Chatelain*. 24 November 2007.

John Virum, USS *Gendreau*. 27 October 2007.

Richard Warner, USS *Kendall C. Campbell*. 31 January and 21 February 2004.

Robert White, USS *Fiske*. 21 October 2007.

Robert Young, USS *Sederstrom*. 29 January 2009.

Jack Yusen, USS *Samuel B. Roberts*. 2 January 2009.

CORRESPONDENCE

Elmo Allen

John W. Avener

Jarvis Baillargeon

Ted Barnhart

Carl Barth

William Bell

Francis A. Belongie

John B. Boy

Leonard A. Bulwicz

John P. Cosgrove

Charles Cox

Roger W. Cozens

Cassin W. Craig

Robert N. Currie

Robert Daily

H. E. Davis

Martin Davis

Preston Davis

Howard K. Denson

Edward M. Docalovich

James A. Doran

Robert H. Dreher

Charles Esch

Daniel Farley

Charlie K. Field

Arthur Fleischmann

Howard W. Fortney
Frank Frazitta
Paul Gagnon
Nat Gayster
Robert L. Goggins
George Gowling
James W. Graham
Richard Graves
Fred Graziano
Jerry Hammon
Fred Harris
Ray Heller
Norman E. Henderson
Thomas R. Hendrix
Horace Herron
Edward Hinz
Robert Hoenshel
Robert Holman
Ernest L. Hughes
Joseph Irving
William T. Jones
Peter Karetka
John Keally
Ellsworth Kendig Jr.
Warren J. Kerrigan
A.G. Kessinger
Vern Kimmell
Byron C. King
George King
John Krantz
John Kunsak Jr.
James Larner
Harry Leippe
A. E. Lewis
Philip K. Lundeberg
Jack MacMillan
Frank McClatchie
Dominic Mesciano

Irving Mesher
James R. Mitchell
Carlos R. Monarez
Russell T. Morris (courtesy of Susan M. Morris)
Frank Musumeci
Harold Muth
Owen Nicholson
Arthur L. Overacker
Joseph Padorski
Alvin C. Peachman
Wayne Pickels
Albert R. Pincus
R. D. Piper
Gerald E. Rehbein
William Riemer
Walter L. Roberge Jr.
Eli Roffman
Richard Rohde
William Shumate
Bertram Sikowitz
Frank Smith
William K. Smith
Milton A. Stein
Robert W. Storrick
Stanley Suzdak
Norman C. Taylor
Terry Thomas
Charles W. Touzell
Philip Trusheim
Paul J. Velky
Joseph Villanella
John A. Virum
Richard Warner
Donald Watson
Edward H. Watts
Edward L. White
Robert D. Young

INDEX

ABOUT THE AUTHOR

Robert F. Cross, author of the presidential biography *Sailor in the White House: The Seafaring Life of FDR,* is a trustee of the USS *Slater,* the last destroyer escort still afloat in the United States. The museum ship is fully restored to its original World War II configuration and is moored on the Hudson River in Albany, New York. Cross currently serves as commissioner of the port of Albany and is water commissioner for the city of Albany. He previously was an assistant environmental commissioner for New York State.

Cross, a former award-winning newspaper correspondent, has written for the *New York Times, Wall Street Journal, Conservationist, Historic Nantucket, Offshore,* and *Seaport* magazines, among other publications. He has been involved in environmental and historic preservation affairs for many years. Cross, a native of Port Jervis, New York, received his Bachelor of Science degree from the State University of New York at Albany and his Master of Arts degree from the State University College at New Paltz. He lives in Albany, New York, and Nantucket, Massachusetts, with his wife, Sheila, a physician, and Fala, their West Highland White Terrier.